D1598102

Birth of the Multinational

There is nothing new under the sun.
...The Preacher, Eccl. 1:9

Karl Moore and David Lewis

Birth
of the Multinational

2000 Years of Ancient Business History
– From Ashur to Augustus

Copenhagen Business School Press

Birth of the Multinational
© *Copenhagen Business School Press*, 1999
Printed in Denmark 1999
Set in Plantin by AKA-Print, Aarhus
Printed by AKA-Print, Aarhus
Cover designed by Kontrapunkt, Copenhagen
Book designed by Jørn Ekstrøm

ISBN 87-16-13468-0

HD
2756
.M66
1999

Distribution

Scandinavia:
Munksgaard/DBK, Siljangade 2-8, P.O.Box 1731
DK-2300 Copenhagen S, Denmark
phone: + 45 3269 7788, fax: +45 3269 7789

North America:
Copenhagen Business School Press
Books International Inc.
P.O. Box 605
Herndon, VA 20172-0605, USA
phone: + 1 703 661 1500, fax: + 1 703 661 1501
E-mail: intpubmkt@aol.com

Rest of the World:
Marston Book Services, P.O. Box 269
Abingdon, Oxfordshire, OX14 4YN, UK
phone: + 44 (0) 1235 465500, fax: + 44 (0) 1235 465555
E-mail Direct Customers: direct.order@marston.co.uk
E-mail Booksellers: trade.order@marston.co.uk

To Brigitte, Érik and Marie-Evé
for their love, understanding, and support.
KJM

Contents

List of Figures

Foreword

This is one of the most fascinating and intriguing – not to say original – monographs on international business history I have read for many years. The authors are to be congratulated for trespassing into virgin territory yet one which, as they well articulate, has many parallels with the kind of landscape normally explored by international business scholars.

Viewed from the lens of contemporary international business theory, Drs. Moore and Lewis cleverly trace the origin, growth and decline of cross-border transactions engaged in by the dominant global economies and political dynasties from around 2000 BC through to the early Christian era. As they summarize in their final chapter, many of the characteristics associated with the transnationalization of economic activity today, no less applied at the time of the Assyrians, Phoenicians, Greeks and Romans.

The authors, for example, reveal the critical role played by a common language in, and of the social and cultural imperatives for, successful development and colonization. They identify one of the earliest regional integration schemes of the Early Bronze Age. They point to the different motives for trade and foreign direct investment, e.g. to seek out natural resources (in the case of the city states of Mesopotamia in (circa 2600-2500 BC) or to seek out new markets and rationalize a (then) global division of labor, as in the case of the Roman Empire (circa 150 BC onwards). They identify some of the earliest trading companies and merchant colonies established by Phoenician enterprises; and give examples of the non-tariff barriers and extra-territorial jurisdiction implemented by the Phoenician authorities. They emphasize the significant of agglomerative or clustering economies in neighboring Phoenician city states. e.g. in Ugarit, which were ideally placed to develop as *entrepot* ports for Near Eastern trade. They point to the importance of knowledge and product branding as ownership specific advantages of internationally oriented forms throughout the pre-Christian era. They identify various unique forms of corporate governance and of collaborative ventures between state and private companies in Babylonia around 2000 BC, and of the establishment of trading networks among neighboring territories in Asia Minor.

Naturally, of course, there are huge differences between the ancient economies and their modern counterparts; and these are described in some detail by the authors of the book. While many of these are technological, Drs. Moore and Lewis tend to focus on systemic organizational and institutional differences. These vary from, what they describe as, the merchant capitalism of Mesopotamia through mercantile capitalism of the Phoenicians and the free market capitalism of Greece, to the legionary capitalism of Rome. Here again there are interesting parallels with the various shades of twentieth century capitalism. They suggest, for example, that the industrial-feudal mercantile structure of the Phoenician economy foreshadowed that of the industrial samurai of nineteenth century Japan; while the (relatively) free-market economy of ancient Greece had many similarities to that enthusiastically endorsed by Adam Smith and his compatriots in late 18th century Britain. The volume also draws valuable historical lessons from the fact that each economic civilization sewed the seeds of its own creative destruction – albeit these were different from each other.

As Drs. Moore and Lewis point out, much of the commercial history of pre-Christian times remains to be written. But their volume contains a host of fascinating glimpses into the extent, pattern and form of cross-border transactions over 2500 years. They describe, for example, the role of religious temples not only as centers and protectors of trade, but as initiators and enforcers of standards of business conduct, and promoters of innovations. Here the role of trust, forbearance and reciprocity – so important to the success of modern day alliance capitalism – played a critical role in fostering many of the early trading, colonizing and collaborative ventures in the Near East and Southern Mediterranean.

The authors recount in fascinating detail, how the rise of the Tyrian multinational business enterprise empire produced an enormous social and economic revolution in Iberia and other countries where it had substantial investments; and how it helped develop, not only large scale silver and iron mining ventures, but the construction and pottery making industries and the production of luxury items. They also offer an intriguing insight into the origin of modern coinage, which in the 6th century BC began to replace the use of barter and money in the form of ingots or pieces. The first coins apparently appeared in the Greek Kingdom of Lydia, and by the end of the 6th century, most Greek cities were producing their own coinage. The spread of this new form of currency gave Greek traders an enormous competitive advantage over their foreign rivals, and greatly facilitated the emergence of one of the world's first genuine market economies. It also paved the way for the first democratic and civic urban society in Athens, which, by the 5th century BC, had not only become the dominant state in Greece, but the initiator of a new business culture, based on the twin forces of the market and the law. This heralded a new era of international business activity, which, for the first time, was financed by private banking institutions.

Although the Hellenic market economy spread throughout much of the Mediterranean, it failed to take root in the way its successor of the late 18th century did. This was because it was "grafted on" to a social order and institutional framework better suited to the Oriental feudal tradition. Eventually, as the authors describe, more socialist policies, introduced in Ptolemaic Egypt, prevailed. Although Rhodes remained in the Athenian free-market system, eventually the economic dominance of Greece gave way to that of central Italy and Rome. However, this was not as a result of market failure, as we know it today, but of governmental weakness in the political and military arena, and the Hellenistic kingdom's lack of political and social unity, which allowed it to be conquered by Rome.

The contribution of Rome to the understanding of international business activity is another fascinating area explored by the authors.

What were the competitive advantages of Roman firms? Why did they colonize the foreign territories they did? How did they organize their overseas ventures? While most certainly the technical and economic prowess of Roman business was equal, or superior, to that of its Greek counterpart, it was the political administrative structure of the Roman republic erected after 509 BC, and the war-like and familial character of Roman society, which gave its particular strength and fashioned its commerce. In this respect, Roman style capitalism was different from that of its predecessor. Though market-oriented, it was conditional and fashioned less by free trade and more by the territorial conquests of its armies. Drs. Moore and Lewis describe it as legionary capitalism. It was strongly state controlled. It was based on a strongly hierarchical and stratified society. In their overseas ventures, firms were supported by "publican" firms, which essentially were the economic arm of the Roman army and the forerunners of today's state owned corporations.

In their description of the Roman economy between 100 BC and 200 AD, the authors go as far as to assert that, in its time, it was the equivalent of today's global economy. The significance of trade and foreign investment, of an extensive network of commercial links between the countries within the Roman Empire of Pax Romana and the evolvement of a single money economy of Roman Europe and Roman Asia (shades of the European Monetary System); of a considerable amount of intra-firm (including intra-"publican" firm) trade; of the emergence of shopping *emporia* (rather like supermarkets or large department stores of today); of a quite sophisticated international specialization of economic activity (a good example given by the authors is the production of sarcophagi [stone burial caskets]); of the issuing of shares, and the innovation of the new methods of corporate governance, e.g. rudimentary limited liability; and of the origin of the virtual corporation – as witnessed by the small number of employees of, yet an important role played by, some "publican" firms.

More specific competition advantages of Roman business cited by Drs. Moore and Lewis include those of shipbuilding and road building technology, and those arising from the setting up of large scale partnership and financial concerns, which provided the internal markets, without which, in the authors' words, "bulk shipment of goods across very dangerous seas would have been impossible." (p238)

The volume closes by offering a paragraph on the story of Rome's hegemonic decline – which, unlike that of Greece, was more due to internal economic and moral failure, rather than that of technical administrative military deficiencies. Whatever the reasons, it took over a millennium before the living standards of most of the (then) developed world were to once again match that of Imperial Rome at its pinnacle.

I warmly commend this study to a wide range of readers – be they historians, political scientists, sociologists, economists, business strategists or statesmen. There is much for each and all to learn from the painstaking and erudite scholarship of Drs. Moore and Lewis.

John H. Dunning
Rutgers and Reading Universities
May 1999

Acknowledgments

A book like this takes an enormous input from a multitude of people to help bring it to fruition. From the international business research community we would like to give special thanks to Alan Rugman and John Dunning. From the history community we would like to thank the numerous Oxford dons who kindly commented on our various drafts, especially Professor Robin Osborne, and from University College London, Professor Amélie Kuhrt. At Templeton we would like to make special mention of Keith Grint, Michael Gestrin, Leslie Willcocks and Sue Dolson. We would like to thank Karl's secretary Carole Priestley for her help on numerous occasions. Brenda Plonis for her excellence in copy-editing. We very much appreciate our publisher, Lauge Stetting of the Copenhagen Business School Press for his encouragement to write this book and his wisdom along the way. The maps are thanks to Angus Colquhoun and Professor Hawari Mahmoud of British School of Archeology in Jersualem. The pictures from the Ashmolean Museum in Oxford.

Chapter 1

Introduction

Over the last twenty years a plethora of academics, management gurus and executives have proclaimed the dawning of a new economic age, a global knowledge economy.[1] An economy dominated by a mix of transnational giants and fleet of foot small and medium size firms which network their way to success. Proponents of this emerging new economy present this as an entirely new and modern phenomena. But is that the case? In this book we will argue that much of today's economic structures existed in prototype forms several thousand years ago. To make our point we will sketch the history of international business from Assyria around 2000 BC through the Phoenician, Carthage, Greek and into the Roman empires, ending shortly after 1 AD. Along the way we will encounter evidence of the first multinationals, run by Assyrians, from Phoenician times, the first transcontinental firms which took advantage of multiple sources of innovation, one of the key arguments put forward for firms to adopt global strategies in our century.[2] We will see evidence of the rise of the first entrepreneurial culture in Athenian Greece and the vitality of family capitalism in Rome.

What started us on this quest was a statement by Professor John Dunning, probably the leading international business academic. In his recent massive work on MNEs Dunning states that, "…earlier examples of embryonic MNEs can, most surely, be found in the colonizing activities of the Phoenicians and the Romans, and before that, in the more ancient civilizations…However, this sort of history…remains to be written."[3] Considerable literature has recorded the evolution of MNEs in Europe since the early Middle Ages.[4]

There have also been a number of books and articles written on the economic history of the ancient world.[5] However, as Professor Dunning points out, little has been written concerning the earliest recorded MNEs and their far reaching activites.

One of us has contributed to international business theory,[6] the other is a historian.[7] The blending of our disciplines offered a starting place to explore the economies of ancient times with a different set of lens. In our effort to shed light on embryonic MNEs and other forms of international business in ancient civilisations we brought together a modern theory of the MNE and literature on the ancient world. The lens by which we chose to view the ancient world was that of the *Eclectic Paradigm* – one of the leading theories explaining multinationals. We start with ancient Assyria where we find evidence of the first multinationals. Toward the end of the Assyrian empire we present evidence that the city-states of ancient Phoenicia became the greatest sea-faring traders of ancient times and these early Canaanite traders were architects of the first truly intercontinental multinational enterprise, spanning parts of Asia, Africa and Europe. The managed business hierarchy created by the merchants of Ugarit and Tyre, moreover, foreshadowed, in some of its features, the international *keiretsu* networks of contemporary Japan. Next in time comes a free-market revolution in the Aegean from 800-400 BC where we find the Greeks with the first truly entrepreneurial economy. After the Greeks however, never again in antiquity, would the rule of hierarchy and the importance of the state be challenged so effectively. In Carthage and even in Rome, the multinational enterprise would again survive and prosper.

In the closing chapter we will suggest some parallels between these ancient events and our modern economies. The central point we will make will concern the current idea held by some, for example Alan Greenspan,[8] that the Anglo-American model has 'won'. Some suggest that the rest of the world must move toward this model. Our contention will be that when we consider the history of the world economy we find that this view is rather naïve.

Before we turn to the events of thousands of years ago we first turn the readers' attention to two important topics: the basic ideas of a leading theory of the multinational enterprise – the *Eclectic Paradigm* and the nature of evidence from ancient times. For international business scholars the first of these two scene-setting chapters will undoubtedly be a review and for historians the second would prove to be an unnecessary read. However, we would encourage the respective experts to consider the other chapter, which would typically lie outside of their experience. Both are pivotal to understanding our arguments. One of us is a historian, the other an international business researcher. We must confess that we had to rather concentrate on the other's discipline in these next two chapters.

Chapter 2

The *Eclectic Paradigm*

Though there are competing theories[1] seeking to explain why a firm sets up international activities, we will adopt John Dunning's *Eclectic Paradigm* as our lens to understand the ancient economy. Dunning is considered by many to be the doyen of international business studies. His *Eclectic Paradigm* is the result of over forty years of research in the field of international business and is considered among the leading theories in the field of international business studies.

The eclectic theory or paradigm may be handily summarized by the acronym OLI, or *ownership*, *location* and *internalization* advantages. It is the existance and arrangement of these advantages, which either encourage or discourage a firm to undertake foreign activities and become a multinational firm. We will explain each of the three types of advantages in a moment but first we will define a foundational term, the Multinational Enterprise (MNE). The definition of MNE we use is the one accepted by two leading centres of research on the global economy, the Organization for Economic Cooperation and Development (OECD) and the United Nations Center for Transnational Corporations (UNCTC), "an enterprize that engages in foreign direct investment (FDI) and owns or controls value-adding activities in more than one country".[2] We would like to highlight two key parts of this definition which have special relevance for the arguments we make in this volume. The first is, foreign direct investment, which is simply investing resources on a long-term basis, in other countries. Secondly, value-adding activities, or activities which increase the value of an item, for example, refining raw ore into a finished or semi-finished metal, dyeing a piece of cloth with Phonenican purple dye, performing a distribution function, such as a Walmart or Tesco does today, providing service which surrounds a product such as a Xerox service rep fixing an errant machine in Helsinki, or creating a copy of a piece of Corthinan pottery. It is interesting to note that many countries today, including many in the EU, have value added taxes (VAT) which in very practical ways reflect governments seeking to create tax revenues from value-adding activities in the modern world. Having discussed the defintion of an MNE we will now turn to discussing each of the three types of advantages suggested by the *Eclectic Paradigm*. Readers familiar with the paradigm may wish to skip this section.

Ownership advantages or firm-specific advantages (FSAs) are the strategic competencies[3] of a firm or in simpler terms, the capabilities and assets which provide competitive advantage to a firm and allow it to succeed in the marketplace. Some examples of FSAs of a few well known firms may help to explain the idea: Virgin's brand and managerial expertise to bring discipline to a slow moving industry segment; Intel's propriety knowledge of semiconductor manufacture; Benetton's subcontracting relationships combined with its powerful brand; Nokia's ability to combine technologies; and 3M's innovative capabilities. Researchers have suggested a number of potential firm advantages which may serve as strategic competencies, for example: those associated with the size of firm (e.g., economies of scale, product diversification); management of organizational expertise; brands; the ability to acquire and upgrade resources; labour or mature small-scale intensive technologies; product differentiation; marketing economies; and access to domestic markets. Others are the ability to foresee and take advantage of global production and marketing opportunities; capital availability and financial expertise; access to natural resources; and the ability to adjust to structural changes.[4]

As a firm grows it looks for new opportunties to earn additional profits or rents (to use the economists' term) from their FSAs.[5] In most cases a firm first turns to expand in its home country. Over time however, the easy expansion opportunities in the home country are exhausted, and firms often turn to foreign markets for further growth.[6] In today's globally interlinked economy this process of undertaking foreign activities has been hastened by the increase of foreign competition in a firm's home market which often encourages firms to undertake activities outside the home country and to learn more about foreign competitors in order to compete more effectively against them in the important home market.

By entering any national market, a foreign company suffers from disadvantages in comparison to local competitors, at least at their first entry into a country. Being more familiar with the local culture, industry structure, government requirements and other aspects of doing business in a country, domestic competitors enjoy a considerable natural advantage. Existing relationships with customers, suppliers, regulators and other key players provide additional advantages that foreign firms either must match or overcome to be successful. Hence, the firm must have strong FSAs to be successful in entering a foreign market. This helps explain the importance the eclectic paradigm puts on FSAs in a firm's decision to undertake foreign activites and thereby becoming a MNE.

Internalization advantages are the advantages which a firm gains when it seeks to take advantage of its ownership-specific advantages discussed above within its own organisation rather than sell them or the right to use them to other firms. That is, internalise or bring them internally within the hierarchy of the firm rather than exploit them through other means, such as an arm's length relationship in the market, licensing agreements, strategic alliances or any of the relationships shown in Figure 1.

From the viewpoint of economic theory, internalisation advantages are based on the suggestion that firms grow by replacing imperfect (or non-existent) external markets by internal ones.[7] Several intriguing ideas are contained in this definition.

The first is that firms can be the most efficient means of production when imperfect markets exist. The most important imperfect market for firms is the pricing of proprietary information which is generated by a firm but has many of the attributes of a public good. Proprietary information can include, among others, knowledge developed by the firm by R&D (both technical and marketing), managerial experience, new production techniques, production differentiation and market knowledge. A public good is a good for which consumption by one party does not reduce the consumption of others. Knowledge is considered a public good because it can be ap-

Figure 1. Markets to Hierarchies

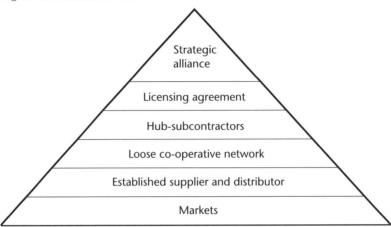

Source: David Faulkner, Oxford University

plied by any person or organization to a specific problem without destroying the ability to apply the knowledge to another use. The market prices public goods considerably below their social value (value to society). The market cannot price a public good, hence an imperfect market from the viewpoint of the firms which may spend many millions to develop a new way of making computer chips but if copied by competitors they lose the potential to make profit and indeed perhaps even recover the costs of their R&D to develop the new process. Thus, in order to profit from investment in knowledge development, the firm "internalises", using its internal market to monitor and control the use of the knowledge in a way the market is unable. In that sense it is easy to see why the firm might internalise a new process because they have greater control over their employees, the process and how it is exploited in the marketplace – to the firm's greatest profit. Alternatively the firm might try to sell the process in the market to its competitors. The difficulty comes in controlling what the competitor does with the process and ensuring that they do not sell it on to other competitors at a low price which would benefit the competition but does not earn the full potential for the creating firm.

Other market imperfections include government regulations, taxes, controls, tariffs, non-existent futures markets, and inequality between buyers' and sellers' knowledge of the value and quality of the product. In the last twenty-five years, through eight rounds of general agreement on tariffs and trade (GATT) agreements and at a regional level the EU and NAFTA agreements, the world has enjoyed a general reduction of certain types of government erected barriers. However, many tariff barriers still exist. All of these distort market prices and act as additional incentives to utilize internal markets. As the reader might note, many of the above are national level imperfections which affect foreign firms more than national firms. Hence, internalisation advantages are relevant for any firm and serve to explain why we see hierarchies rather than pure markets. But as the above examples demonstrate, there exist additional internalisation advantages for MNEs which encourage firms to expand into foreign markets not through foreign agents, joint ventures or other non-hierarchical forms but through their own internal organisation – foreign subsidaries.[8]

Location Advantages or Country Specific Factors concern those advantages which does a firm gains from operating in a particular country. In the last two decades globalising firms in many industries have moved considerable parts of their activities overseas in order to take advantage of location factors.[9] Prominent examples include: taking advantage of low wage rates in South East Asia and Mexico, seeking to crack emerging markets such as China, head offices moving from Sweden and France to the U.K. in order to avoid higher taxes rates in their home countries,[10] locating to increase organisation learning by starting up R&D labs in the Silicon Valley or side-by-side with great universities like Oxford and Cambridge. Here the focus is on what economists call the national factor endowments of a nation.

More formally, potential advantages might include: input costs (such as low labour wages and inexpensive national resources); labour productivity; the size and character of markets; transport costs; and the physical distance from key markets and the home country of the MNE. There are also tariff barriers; the taxation structure; risk factors; attitudes toward FDI; and the structure of national competition within an industry. From a historical viewpoint market-seeking and resource-seeking activities are of special note. A modern day example of market-seeking behaviour would be the many firms setting up ventures in China in the early 90s in order to have an opportunity to market to well over a billion potential consumers. Resource-seeking behaviour in recent times would include oil companies setting up subsidiaries in a large number of countries in order to obtain precious crude petroleum supplies for their downstream retail marketing activities, that is petrol or gas stations.

Having finished this brief introduction[11] of the central ideas of the *Eclectic Paradigm* we will turn to the ancient world with the next chapter, looking at the nature of archeological evidence, using the Assyrian empire as our exemplar. Important terms from this chapter which we will continue to return too through the rest of the book include: *Foreign Direct Investment (FDI), Multinational Enterprise (MNEs), market-* and *resource-seeking, Ownership Advantages, Location Advantages* and *Internalisation Advantages.*

Chapter 3

An Empire Comes To Life

Reconstructing the Story of the Ancient World

Anyone even vaguely familiar with the history of the ancient world will have some knowledge of the Assyrians. To most people, the word "Assyria" conjures up the image of the most warlike people of antiquity, comparable in ferocity to the Romans, the Huns or the Mongolians. Ashur the Conqueror is well-known; Ashur the International Businessman is less known but no less important. Long before their armies marched up and down the Tigris and Euphrates to terrorise the ancient world, groups of talented Assyrian traders peacefully took up residence in foreign countries hundreds of kilometres away from home, being welcomed by the princes of Babylon, Aram and even distant Anatolia as a blessing and not a scourge. As they formed their numerous commercial colonies in foreign lands, these Old Assyrian merchants of the second millennium BC perfected a thousand-year-old system of private enterprise inherited from Sumer and Babylon. Living and trading near the dawn of civilisation, these corporate traders, moreover, were innovative to a startling degree, for the commercial structures they created may rightly be described as one of the first attempts at the "entrepreneurial government" being celebrated in the 1990s. Even more importantly, the businesses operated by the ancient Assyrian colonists constituted the first genuine multinational enterprises in recorded history.

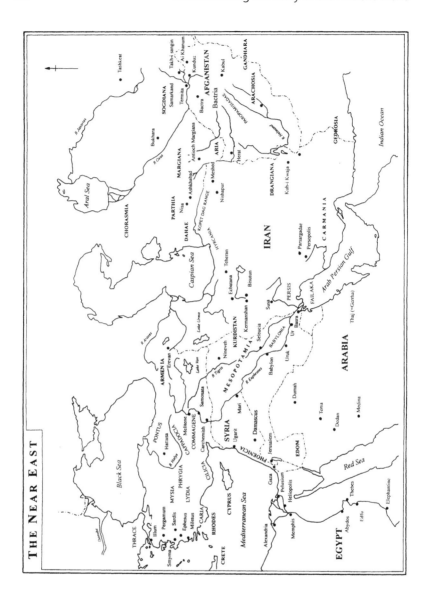

There is, sadly, much truth to the terrifying reputation the Assyrians have left in the history of the world. It was well-earned. Beginning in 1100 BC a long line of aggressive kings with names such as Ashur-Uballit, Tiglath-Pileser, Ashurnasirpal and Shalmaneser reorganised their society on highly authoritarian lines, created an enormous standing army and set forth on a career of conquest which terrified the ancient world for almost four centuries. Most ancient nations, were guilty of war and atrocities. Assyria erected imperialism and conquest into a coherent theology. For generations the powerfully-built warrior-kings of Nineveh and Ashur were to boast, in all sincerity, of the mission entrusted them by their national god, Ashur: to subdue other nations and bring the Four Quarters of the Earth under his domination. The incomparable Assyrian army sought to carry out this mission with the utmost zeal, waging war with iron discipline, lightning speed and a policy of "calculated frightfulness" which foreshadowed the SS of World War II. Waging countless wars upon nations near and far, the kings of Assyria not only recorded but glamorised their acts of mass destruction, reprisal, tortures and deportation in their art and literature for posterity.

Typical of these boasts was that of Tiglath-Pileser I, whose policies of terror were later to be perfected by Ashurnasirpal, Sennacherib and Ashurbanipal:

The corpses of their warriors I hurled down in the destructive battle like the storm god. Their blood I caused to flow in the valleys and on the high places of the mountains. I cut off their heads and outside their cities, like heaps of grain, I piled them up.[1]

Assyria, however, has not been without its defenders, among them being the English Assyriologist H.W.F.Saggs who insisted that the popular image of a barbarian Assyria was unfair and greatly overdone. A more balanced picture of Assyria, he insisted, would reveal a highly creative and extremely progressive race of people open to new ideas in science, technology, administration, philosophy and commerce. Far from being the destroyers of Mesopotamian civilisation, kings like Ashurbanipal were great scholars. As for their atrocities, they were never committed at random but only as reprisal to be meted out in the case of rebellion. According to Saggs, unprovoked acts of sadism among Assyrian soldiers, who usually behaved themselves in a disciplined and correct manner, were the exception rather than the rule. As for their wars, many of them were waged against enemies like the Moschians, Tibareni, Medes, Elamites, Chaldeans and Arameans who could be just as fierce and cruel as the Assyrians themselves, though far less efficient. In their self-appointed role of defending Mesopotamia from less refined nations, the Assyrians, in the eyes of their apologists, ought to be remembered as the preservers, not the destroyers of Near Eastern civilisation.[2]

While perhaps overstating their case, Professor Saggs and other admirers of Assyria were convincing in their insistence that Assyria's often fanatical aggressiveness and cruelty had to be seen in a larger context. Beginning around 1100 BC, Assyria's incessant wars of conquest were the sequel to a national history which stretched back for more than a millennium into the Middle and even Early Bronze Ages. A Semitic-speaking people related to the Babylonians, Arameans and Hebrews, the ancient Assyrians occupied a narrow strip of land along the Tigris in the what is now the oil-rich Mosul-Kirkuk district of Iraq. With few natural resources, no outlet to the sea, a lack of defensible borders and a series of powerful, hostile neighbours, the people of ancient Assyria lived in constant danger of impoverishment as well as foreign domination. Emerging as an independent kingdom around 2000 BC, they entered history not as warriors but as world traders. For most of her existence, Assyria was not a particularly warlike or imperialistic nation. Geography and history were eventually to make it so, but only after more peaceful avenues and options for national survival were closed.

The story of how Assyria created the most innovative and progressive business organisations of their time has only been understandable in the later twentieth century. Prior to recent decades one simply did not know enough about the details of life in the ancient world to understand how commerce and society in the Middle Bronze Age (approximately 2300-1600 BC) worked. Any study of life or business enterprise in such distant times had to be based on some form of evidence. How was it possible for anyone to know anything at all about an empire destroyed 2,500 years ago or enterprises that existed 3,500 years ago? Assyrian commerce, wars, politics, religion and everyday existence would have remained unknown mysteries were it not for the efforts of a century and a half of archaeologists, language experts, and dedicated volunteers labouring to dig out and interpret the multitude of artifacts hidden in the soil of the Near East. It is only through the excavation of buried cities and the decoding of tens of thousands of clay tablets bearing mysterious writing in long-dead languages that any coherent story of the first 2,000 years of mankind's civilisation, let alone a detailed description of its business practices, could be told at all.

Nevertheless, more has been learned about ancient Assyria and its neighbours since 1850 than was known 1,000 or even 2,000 years ago. The Assyrian Empire collapsed in 606 BC, its cities and towns put to the torch by Median and Babylonian invaders anxious to avenge the destruction of their own lands. Unlike the structures of Babylon, which survived as a major centre well into Christian times, the brick buildings of Nineveh, Ashur and other ruined Assyrian centres rapidly succumbed to the rains and then the dust storms of Iraq. Two centuries after Nineveh fell, the Greek warrior Xenophon could barely distinguish the outline of the city's silt-covered walls. As the ages rolled on and the desert sands encroached, the land that had once been Assyria passed into the hands of Babylonians, Achaemenid Persians, Greeks, Romans, Parthians, Sassanid Persians, Arabs, Mongols and Turks. Assyria and its secrets seemed forever beneath hundreds of dome-shaped desert tells, or mounds, dotting the arid Mesopotamian landscape.

The legend of the militaristic, all-conquering empire nevertheless lived on in the pages of the Old Testament and the historians of Greece and Rome who spoke of Ninus, Sardanapulus, Sennacherib and other Assyrian rulers. Forming their own Christian church, descendants of the Assyrian peasantry survived in Iraq itself where they preserved the folk legacy of their ancestors. Even their far more numerous Muslim neighbours were haunted by Ashur's vanished presence, pointing out to all interested foreigners the alleged site of the Nebi Yunus, the sacred mound where the Prophet Jonah preached.[3]

The rediscovery of Assyria in earnest began in the 1600s with the discovery by sojourning Europeans of bricks and stones covered with a beautiful but exotic writing made up of wedge-shaped characters which no one at that time could read. What came to be known as the cuneiform alphabet might have remained indecipherable for a long time had not a key accidentally been found allowing patient scholars to unlock its secrets. At the time of the American Revolution a bold Dane, Carsten Niebuhr, was exploring the ruins of the ancient palace of King Darius at Behistun in Persia when he discovered, carved on a huge rock high above the ground, an account of the Iranian ruler's conquests written in three languages.

Two versions of the account, one in Babylonian and the other in
Elamite, were written in the mysterious wedge script which Niebuhr could not understand. Next to them, however, the same account appeared in Persian, a living tongue which he and many others could then use to discover the meaning of the Mersopotamian
characters. Painstakingly duplicating and later publishing a repro-
duction of the Mesopotamian characters alongside their Persian
equivalents, Niebuhr made it possible to at last understand the
long-silent tongues of Babylon, Elam and, eventually, Sumer, Hatti
and Assyria, for the same script had been in use throughout the ancient Near East. By 1800 fully one-third of the cuneiform characters had been deciphered.[4]

While the first Orientalists strove to understand the ancient Bab-
ylonian-Assyrian script, an Englishman named Claudius James
Rich earned the title of being the first modern scientific archaeologist. Settling and working in the vicinity of Baghdad, Rich was well
aware of the location of the ancient city of Babylon, whose ruins he
began to excavate in the early 1800s. Publishing his findings on Babylon in 1813, Rich then turned his attention to the rediscovery of
Assyria. In the summer of 1820, he journeyed to the north in search
of the sites of Nineveh and Ashur. The former, he suspected, now
lay near the modern city of Mosul beneath the huge, flat 14-metre-
high mound with steep sides called Kuyunjik, which was 12 kilometres long and 40 kilometres in circumference, large enough to hide
a city. Meanwhile, Rich sought and found along the banks of the
Tigris, the site of the city of Ashur, beneath another mound called
Qal'ah Shergat. Stretching along the shore of the ageless river for
three full kilometres, the six-metre-high walls of the ancient capital,
mixed with piles of brick and rubble, were still visible after 2,500
years.[5]

Assyriology might well have remained the pastime of a few eccen-
trics had not the political and intellectual climate of Victorian Britain contributed to a widespread popular interest in the lands associated with the Bible. In the early and mid-nineteenth century all of
English society experienced a strong revival of popular Christianity,
spearheaded by the Methodist and other non-Anglican denomina-
tions. The new British religiosity was, however, soon challenged by
the growing influence not only of Darwin, who questioned the literal truth of Genesis, but of a school of critical scholars, centred in

German universities, who questioned the historical accuracy of both Old and New Testaments. Consequently, many devout Englishmen, Welshmen, Scots and Irish were prepared to fund and publicise excavations in the Near East in the hope of confirming the literal truth of Scripture. The British Foreign Office itself underwrote such expeditions to the sites of Nineveh, Ashur, Babylon and elsewhere as a convenient pretext to establishing a British diplomatic presence in areas vital to protecting her Indian empire and trade, particularly when the French government was already funding the work of the violently anti-British archaeologist Paul-Emile Botta on the site of Kuyunjik.[6]

By the 1840s Botta, Layard and Rawlinson had captured the European public imagination with their astounding discoveries on the sites of Nineveh and Calah (Nimrud). The soil of ancient Assyria slowly divulged its secrets in the form of gigantic statues of winged bulls, magnificent palaces, and terrifying propaganda portraits glamorizing the war-making abilities of Sargon II, Esarhaddon and Ashurbanipal, all of whom now shown to have been real. In the decades that followed, both archaelogy and Assyriology became modern, fully-fledged sciences. By 1849, Rawlinson had succeeded in fully decoding the ancient alphabet.[7] By 1855, he had collected 15,000 tablets from the Royal Library of King Ashurbanipal himself. Transported to the British Museum and elsewhere, these tablets revealed much about the religion, wars, literature, commerce, medicine and daily life of a vanished world. Other scholars, notably the Germans, were to join the British in bringing the long-dead empires to life. By 1900 another 10,000 Assyrian and 69,000 Babylonian tablets had reached the British Museum alone. By 1962 some 250,000 cuneiform tablets, many of them still unpublished, could be found in libraries and museums around the world.[8]

By the First World War the major digs in Mesopotamia were complete and enough information was compiled to make it possible to reconstruct an outline history of Assyria divided into three major periods. An Old Assyrian Kingdom existed sometime in the early second millennium BC between the time of the original Mesopotamian empire of Sargon of Akkad, based in northern Babylonia and the Old Babylonian of the famous lawgiver, Hammurabi. Following this, around 1600-1100 BC a Middle Assyrian Kingdom played an insignificant role alongside more powerful states like Kassite Babylon and the Indo-Aryan kingdom of Mitanni. This long period of humiliation paved the way for the better-documented history of the Neo-Assyrian Empire, in which a revived Assyrian state became the Prussia of the Orient, eventually conquering and plundering a domain which, under Ashurbanipal (668-27 BC) extended from the mountains of Persia to Thebes in Egypt.[9]

Despite a century of sensational discoveries and painstaking research, serious obstacles remained, and to some degree still remain, to a full understanding of Assyrian history and life. Unearthing a vast amount of pots, jewels, artifacts and tablets is ultimately of little value unless one is able to make sense of them and fit them into a larger picture. Assyriologists and other students of the ancient world have faced many problems with their evidence unfamiliar to historians dealing with more recent times who were at least able to accurately date and verify their findings. Historians of the nineteenth and twentieth centuries possessed thousands of documents, newspapers, broadcasts, books, articles, company records and perhaps even the testimony of surviving witnesses. They had no need to question whether the Habsburg Empire ever existed or if there had been one World War or two. Modern historians could scarcely imagine being forced to wonder if the documents of the German Foreign Ministry in 1915 were proof that Kaiser Wilhelm II actually ruled all of Europe or merely expressed his claim and desire to do so. What would it be like not knowing the dates for any kings of England or France prior to 1750? How confident would British historians have been if they were never certain whether the Tudors preceded or followed the Stuarts or whether the rule of the Houses of Orange, Hanover and Windsor signified that Britain had been invaded and conquered first by the Netherlands and then one or more German states?

Fanciful as the above examples appear, they present some idea of the magnitude of difficulties historians of antiquity have still encountered even in the 1990s. It was as difficult for an Assyriologist to try to determine what happened and when it happened as it was for a modern historian to interpret the meaning of far more recent and certain events. While the Orientalist of the 1980s and 1990s was blessed with a multitude of source material, he or she still found that tablets and painted pottery would tell one less than written books and daily newspapers. Without a reliable chronological framework within which they could be interpreted, even thousands of inscriptions and artifacts would be meaningless. The history of ancient Mesopotamia had to be reconstructed piece by piece in much the same manner as a paleontologist rebuilds the skeleton of a dinosaur or a large prehistoric mammal.

Archaeologists had to begin with dates and events of which they were certain, working backwards to establish the dates of earlier events and the reigns of earlier kings. While difficult, this task was not quite impossible, given the existence of a few fragments of ancient historical works by the astronomer Claudius Ptolemæus, the Egyptian priest Manetho and the Babylonian priest Berossus, all of whom lived in the Hellenistic era (330-70 BC). Greek scholars at this time were still able to read and interpret the cuneiform records of ancient Babylon. On the basis of these records Ptolemæus compiled in 265 BC a record of the Babylonian kings beginning with Nabonassar in 747 BC and ending with Alexander the Great in 323 BC. Verified by records of lunar eclipses, the Greek astronomer's Canon is still accepted by historians today as the reliable foundation for all other Mesopotamian dates and chronology. Discovered in 1889, the Babylonian Chronicle not only mentioned the same eclipses as Ptolemæus but synchronised the dates of these eclipses with the reigns of late Assyrian as well as Babylonian kings. Meanwhile, Sir Henry Rawlinson had decoded an Assyrian text, discovered in 1862, the Eponym Chronicle, which outlined the history of Assyria on a year-by-year basis as far back as 911 BC. The scribes of the Neo-Assyrian Empire were discovered to have been efficient record keepers, carefully dating long strings of events according to a year-by-year system in which every year bore the name of an important Assyrian official. An eclipse of the sun taking place on June 15, 763 BC was listed in the Eponym Chronicle under Year 10 of King Ashur-Dan, the year when one Bur-Sagale held the position of eponym. Using this firm date as an anchor, archaelogists had a fairly easy task dating and making sense of the events of Mesopotamian history after 911 BC.[10]

Historical reconstruction for both Assyria and Babylon became much more difficult for those scholars interested in the periods before 911 BC. It is no exaggeration to say that virtually no definite,

verifiable dates exist for Near Eastern history before the first milennium BC. Assyrian eponym lists are either too fragmentary or do
not exist at all before that time. A comprehensive Assyrian King
List was discovered in 1927 which claimed to list all 109 rulers of
Assyria beginning with the founder Tudiya who "dwelt in tents"
and ending with Shalmaneser V, who conquered Samaria and the
northern Kingdom of Israel around 720 BC. Firm and verifiable
dates, however, for any of these earlier kings were impossible to obtain. Babylonian records offered little help, for while they listed
many rulers, some of whom could be synchronised with an Assyrian
contemporary, their lists were never continuous. While one knew
who reigned and in what order within the various second-millennium Babylonian dynasties, no one could determine the exact order
of the dynasties themselves or be certain that their attempts to fit
them into a coherent succession were completely accurate.[11]

The further Assyriologists attempted to penetrate into the past,
the murkier their historical picture became. Much of the Middle Assyrian period remained a "dark age", while the Old Assyrian Kingdom presented mysteries of its own. Aside from a few building inscriptions, the record of tablets from Assyria circa 2000-1600 BC
was basically nonexistent. Following the work of Rawlinson, massive
excavations on the site of Ashur were conducted by the Deutsche
Orientgesellschaft from 1903 to 1913. As before, these large-scale
digs concentrated on the period of the Neo-Assyrian Empire and ignored earlier times. A serious effort to uncover the secrets of second-
millennium Ashur was not made until the interwar period when archaeologist A.E.L. Mallowan and others found evidence of some
houses, a temple dedicated to Ishtar and some building inscriptions
which mentioned Erishum and several of the other rulers from the
Assyrian King List.[12] This meager record of the earliest periods of
Assyrian history is, moreover, likely to remain all that scholars will
have to examine from the Assyrian heartland itself, given the difficulties of excavating beneath the sites of the later Assyrian Empire:

*Very little of the Old Assyrian period remains investigated...due to the
fact that a large section of the Ashur-temple lay under a Turkish police-
post, while elsewhere later monuments and buildings from the great imperial phases of Assyria's history are too important, and simply too
large to make fuller excavation feasible.[13]*

The problem of establishing firm dates for Old Assyria was itself well-nigh insurmountable. The Assyrian King List shows 39 rulers from the nomad Tudiya to the warrior Shamshi-Adad I, but further research suggested that the document was untrustworthy. Comparing the names of the first 17 kings with those of the founders of the First Dynasty of Babylon revealed them to be identical, suggesting later scribes wished to forge an Assyrian pedigree for the Amorite usurper Shamshi-Adad. One could not be certain that many of the Old Assyrian kings had ever reigned unless their names appeared in other inscriptions. Nonetheless, the carvings on the Ashur temple permitted scholars to be certain that the Old Assyrian Kingdom had been ruled by a series of obscure kings in the following order of succession as shown in Figure 2.

Assyriologists tried to place this and other very early dynasties in time by fixing the dates of the First Dynasty of Babylon, whose chief ruler, Hammurabi, vanquished the last Old Assyrian ruler, Shamshi-Adad I. The only clue to these early Babylonian dates, though, was a vague astronomical reference to certain movements of the planet Venus in the reign of one of Hammurabi's successors, Ammisaduga, which might have taken place in either 1977, 1702, 1646-38, 1582 or even 1418 BC. Discarding the "high" date of 1977 as improbable, most scholars since the 1970s have followed the Cambridge Ancient History in accepting the date of 1702 for the Venus observations, generating a "middle" date of 1792-1750

Figure 2. Old Assyrian Kingdom Rulers[14]

Ruler
Puzur-Ashur I.
Shallim-Ahhe.
Ilushuma
Erishum I
Sargon I
Puzur-Ashur II
Naram-Sin
Erishum II
Shamshi-Adad I, followed by Hammurabi and Babylonian rule

for Hammurabi, and the approximate dates for the Old Assyrian realm are shown in Figure 3.

While these "middle" dates have become standard and have been used in this book, a lower chronology based upon the other Venus dates may also be plausible. Jørgen Læssøe lowered Hammurabi's reign by 64 years to 1728-1686 BC, and the dates for Old Assyria from Puzur-Ashur I to Shamshi-Adad I to 1940-1716 BC[16]; Peter James has been more radical, placing Hammurabi's reign at 1627-1584 BC which would lower the Old Assyrian dates by 165 years as shown in Figure 4.

Figure 3. "Middle" Old Assyrian Chronology[15]

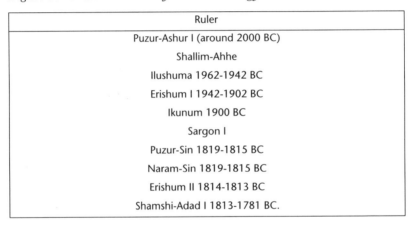

Ruler
Puzur-Ashur I (around 2000 BC)
Shallim-Ahhe
Ilushuma 1962-1942 BC
Erishum I 1942-1902 BC
Ikunum 1900 BC
Sargon I
Puzur-Sin 1819-1815 BC
Naram-Sin 1819-1815 BC
Erishum II 1814-1813 BC
Shamshi-Adad I 1813-1781 BC.

Figure 4. "Super-Low" Old Assyrian Chronology[17]

Ruler
Puzur-Ashur I (around 1835 BC)
Shallim-Ahhe
Ilushuma 1797-1757 BC
Erishum I 1756-1716 BC
Ikunum 1714 BC
Sargon I
Puzur-Ashur II
Naram-Sin 1654-1650 BC
Erishum II 1649-1648 BC
Shamshi-Adad I 1648-1616 BC.

Thus, the Old Assyrian kingdom flourished over a 200-year period as early as 2000-1800 or as late as 1800-1600 depending upon
which dates are most accurate. For the purpose of this book, the
dating is not overly important but we felt that this discussion would
be useful to provide the non historian reader with an brief understanding of some of the issues facing students of these ancient
times.

Establishing a chronology represented only the first of the challenges facing archaeologists who still knew next to nothing about
the particulars of Old Assyrian life in the absence of substantial
documentation from Ashur itself in the early second millennium
BC: "Virtually nothing is known about Ashur and the rest of North
Mesopotamia in the Ur III period, beyond the names of a few local
rulers."[18] An unexpected solution to this dilemma, though, started
to emerge in the 1920s, not in Mesopotamia, but far to the northwest in the heart of the Anatolian Plateau in a place called Kültepe
near the modern Turkish city of Kayseri. By the 1880s the archaeologist A.H.Sayce had convinced himself and others that a series of
sculptures and mysterious hierogyphic writings uncovered in Turkey were the work of the ancient people known to the Assyrians as
Hatti, to the Egyptians as Kheta and to the Hebrews as Hittites (II
Chr. 1:17; II Ki. 8:6-7). Descending upon the Anatolian peninsula
in the decades that followed, German and English archaeologists
rapidly unveiled the history and civilisation of the vanished Hittite
Empire and the other kingdoms of Asia Minor. While many of the
ancient writings discovered there were in the various languages of
Hatti, Palaic, Luwian and the other languages of Anatolia, a few
tablets coming from Kültepe appeared to be written in an unusual
Semitic dialect strongly akin to Assyrian.[19]

Puzzled by these finds, the Czech Hittitologist Bedich Hrozny
began excavations at Kültepe in 1925. Digging in a large 400 x 800
metre terrace on the site of the ancient Anatolian city of Kanesh, he
discovered, within only a week, a huge find of tablets which he took
home to Prague. Hrozny's findings were to electrify Orientalists in
Europe and America when they were published in 1926 and 1927.
The Kültepe-Kanesh documents were clearly of a mercantile nature. They spoke of contracts, partnerships, profits, consignment of
orders and other transactions. Obviously, Hrozny had been digging
in the business district of a prosperous trading city. The language of

the tablets, however, was the same peculiar north Mesopotamian dialect he had seen before, a language which, with a few changes, was almost identical to that on much younger tablets recovered from first-millennium Ashur and Nineveh. Could it be that Kanesh, or at least part of it, had been populated not by Hittites but by ancestral Assyrians? The language and personal names on the Kanesh tablets was unmistakable, as were the references to kings named Erishum and Ikunum.[20]

In-depth excavations in Kanesh by the University of Ankara under the leadership of Turkish archaeologist Tahsin Özgüç began in 1948 and continued throughout the 1950s, 1960s and beyond. The meticulous Turkish investigations confirmed what Hrozny and others before him suspected, that Kültepe-Kanesh had been the site of considerable economic activity and that the ancient city had in fact harboured a large and permanent colony of Old Assyrian subjects who had settled there neither as refugees nor visitors but as permanent residents. The Kanesh tablets, numbering over 10,000 and written in what was now recognised as the language of Old Assyrian, helped to reveal, along with similar Assyrian tablets found at other Turkish sites, notably Böghazkoy and Alaça Hüyük, many of the details of the Old Assyrian world which the native soil of Ashur itself concealed. What Ashur has concealed, Kültepe-Kanesh have, at least in part, revealed.[21]

Özgüç uncovered four successive layers of occupation at Kanesh, each of which was assigned a Roman numeral by his archaeologists. The oldest, Level IV, lay on the bottom of the others and represented the first evidence of organised human occupation on the site. The artifacts found in both Level IV and the Level III indicated that during the third millennium BC. Kanesh and much of Anatolia experienced growing population, increasing commerce, the evolution of a culture which foreshadowed that of the Hittites and brutal rounds of warfare. By comparing the styles of pottery, tools, weapons and the other artifacts found in these bottom levels, Özgüç and his team were able to date Levels IV and III to the Early Bronze Age, which, in Mesopotamia coincided with the Early Dynastic, Akkadian, and Ur III periods, all of which preceded the foundation of an independent Old Assyrian kingdom. Even in this early period, however, the Turkish archaeologists discovered evidence of commercial links between the eastern and central parts of Anatolia and the plains of Syria, northern Mesopotamia and even the Sumerian cities of southern Mesopotamia. Finding affinities in the art and engineering style of bronze spearheads and other Kanesh artifacts with those found on the southern side of the Taurus Mountains that separated Asia Minor from Syria and Mesopotamia, Özgüç and others knew that the region of Kanesh played an important part in world commerce prior to 2000 BC, long before Assyria arrived on the scene.[22]

Level II, however, contained the most important discoveries of all for the business historian as well as the Assyriologist. Here, where Hrozny had uncovered his tablets, Özgüç found a well-planned Anatolian city with a vast business district. Further digging showed Kanesh II was neatly divided into various quarters, divided by streets wide enough for carts. The city centre contained large workshops, foundries, other businesses and even restaurants. Özgüç's team also found over a hundred windowless brick houses, into which both sunlight and fresh air entered via open roofs and doors. In the northern and central parts of Kanesh such homes were occupied by a self-contained community of Assyrians. Within the ruins of their closely-bunched 6-8 room homes the Turks were pleased to discover enormous numbers of business tablets, filed in vases in special rooms. Living in one part of their homes, it was clear that the Assyrian traders maintained their offices in another. The state in which the Old Assyrian tablets of Level II were found, either being baked in the fireplace, or left unopened in their envelopes, together with extensive evidence of fire on the ruins themselves, moreover, indicated that the city and its colony had been suddenly attacked and largely destroyed by an unknown invader. Level IC, just above Level II, showed little evidence of settlement.[23]

In Level IB, however, both the city and the Assyrians returned. Kanesh IB was even bigger and more crowded than Kanesh II, its buildings rising upon the burnt rubble of Level II. The brick houses, meanwhile, gave way to stone. Eventually this city as well was to be destroyed, again by fire. When the final level, Kanesh IA, was reached, all traces of the Assyrians were gone and the culture of the emerging Hittite Empire became dominant.[24]

The discovery of an extensive body of correspondence between the Assyrians of Kanesh and their contacts in Ashur made serious study of the Old Assyrian kingdom and its commerce possible. One could now attempt a more genuine reconstruction of the full history of Assyria as well as obtain a full understanding of the larger picture of trade and commerce in the northern and western half of the ancient Near Eastern world. Nevertheless, the victory of the Assyriologist was even then only partial. Many documents covering the period after 2000 BC remained unpublished well into the 1990s, while many of those that were described little more than narrow transactions such as "Ashur-Nirari acknowledges receipt of x shekels of silver and y amount of textiles." Certain of the Kanesh tablets, though, have shed light on larger issues of law, business ethics, regulated commerce, religion, marriage, international diplomacy, and political power. It is only through a systematic study of the data presented in these latter that a credible overall picture of Old Assyria has finally emerged. As sketchy as this portrait was, it nonetheless remained full and detailed enough to tell the important story of Assyria's vital contribution to the growth of international business.

Having come to understand the nature of archaeological evidence and how it is possible to know about and understand the history and commerce of very ancient times, in the next chapter we will examine the evolution of Bronze Age capitalism and the first world economy in which Assyria was to play a very significant part.

Chapter 4

Reinventing Government 1900 BC

Privatisation and the Birth of Assyrian Multinational Trade

What purpose did the mysterious Assyrian colonies in the heart of Anatolia, hundreds of kilometres from home, play in the economy of the Old Assyrian kingdom and the Near Eastern world? Were they military outposts, trading stations, or perhaps something of more profound importance to historians: an enterprise of an entirely new type? The significance of the Assyrian settlements in Asia Minor could only be understood by examining them in the context of the entire economy of the ancient world of which they were a part. The story of the Assyrian merchant colonies of Anatolia was and is inseparable from the greater story of the birth and rise of international business in the ancient Near East itself.

Human history and civilisation as we view it arose in the valleys of the Tigris and Euphrates Rivers during what is known as the Chalcolithic, or the Copper Age sometime around 4000 BC. Even though rival civilisations began to emerge slightly later along the Nile Valley to the west and the Indus and Hwang Ho Valleys to the east, the culture known as the Sumerian was, from both a political and an economic point of view, destined to become far more dynamic than the others. Arising in the mid-fourth millennium BC, Sumer and its daughter civilisations of Babylon and Assyria led Western civilisation for 3000 years, half of recorded human history. Why did Mesopotamian Iraq come to excel in world politics and trade while richer lands like Egypt, India and China played more peripheral roles? The answer, once again, appeared to rest in the comparative historical geography of these Cradles of Civilisation. All of these ancient societies arose along the banks of major rivers, but Mesopotamia alone occupied a strategic position. More significantly, each of the villages and towns along the Tigris and Euphrates had its own independent land or sea routes to the outside world. Mesopotamian geography was two-dimensional, that of ancient Egypt, India and China was, on the other hand, one-dimensional. The towns of Egypt, for example, were flanked on east and west by a savage African desert broken only by the narrow fertile valley of the Nile. By gaining control of the northern and southern exits of the latter, a long line of Pharaohs beginning with Menes and Khufu were able to suppress all local initiative and autonomy in Egypt and erect a permanent centralised bureaucratic state which monopolised all commerce and became the forerunner of the centrally-directed and semi-communistic empires of modern times: the Sassanid, Mongol, Ottoman, Manchu, Moghul, Aztec, Inca and perhaps even the Czarist and Soviet regimes of Russia.[1]

History took a different course in Sumer, Babylon and Assyria, which were ultimately destined to become the true cradles of private initiative and capitalism, the evidence for which in Mesopotamia is as old as writing itself. The oldest written documents of human civilisation itself, dating from 3200 BC if not earlier, evoke the crude and primitive business transactions of the very ancient communities arising just north of what was then the swampy coastline of the Arabian Gulf. Far more suited as a source of irrigation water than the swift-flowing Tigris, the Euphrates in the fourth millennium BC became the major locus of settlement in Sumer.[2]

Even though at first there was human life along the lower Tigris, both rivers and their adjoining canals constituted an interlocking web of land and water routes that would eventually "tend to strengthen local or regional units and impede the trend towards [Sumerian political] unification" permitting the rise of multiple power centres.[3]

It would be too simple to assume, however, that geography of and by itself led to the rise of capitalism in Mesopotamia; it merely removed a major bureaucratic obstacle by preventing any single municipality or settlement from monopolising access to the outside world. Instead of encouraging a one-state monopoly upon trade and commerce, the terrain of Mesopotamia permitted an environment of competition to develop among various Sumerian towns that would help generate the revolution in technology which, after 3100 BC, would usher in the Bronze Age.

Certain references in the Book of Genesis suggested a distant historical memory of Sumerian times, even among those like Yale's William J. Hallo and William Kelly Simpson who could hardly be described as Biblical fundamentalists. The account of Cain, who was "building a city" is followed by that, six generations later, of Tubal Cain who "forged all kinds of tools out of bronze and iron" along with the culture hero Jubal and the cattleman Jabal.[4] The reference in Genesis 4 to the bronze-worker Tubal-Cain may well be a reference to this time when Sumerian, Anatolian and other smiths, long accustomed to forging primitive copper tools, began around that time to discover that when they mixed their soft red-brown copper ore together with sufficient amounts of tin in a super-hot furnace, they would produce a harder alloy called bronze.[5] The more tin they mixed with red copper, the yellower and harder the new metal, known as bronze became. The invention of bronze alloys in foundries where the fires were heated to between 590 and 790 degrees centigrade made it possible for professional metallurgists to mould soft copper and tin into sturdy plows, building tools, kitchen ware and other items destined to vastly increase human productivity in a manner comparable to that of the Industrial Revolution of modern times. The very map of Mesopotamian civilisation itself was redrawn after 3100 BC. Sumerian farmers could now plow their lands to grow enough food to enable others to enter more specialised occupations and live off the new surplus produced by an increasingly capitalised agriculture. An urban, commercial and money economy was thus made possible through the moulding of bronze ploughs, sickles and the invention of wheeled donkey-carts, all of which made it possible for the Sumerian farmer to send his excess wheat and barley to feed the new sculptors, carpenters, leather-workers, brick-layers, scribes and others now able to earn a living in places like Uruk.[6] The evolution of Sumerian civilisation between 4000 and 2100 BC and its rough parallel to the Genesis account may briefly be summarised in the timetable in Figure 5.

In the Copper Age before 3100 BC, the people of southern Mesopotamia dwelt, as did the rest of humanity in the Near East, in an almost completely rural subsistence economy. Sumerians and others lived in towns along or near their river valleys or wherever sufficient rainfall and moisture permitted them. Only one or two of these towns such as Eridu and Uruk merited the title of city.[7] The Sumerian landscape then changed dramatically between 3100 and 2900 BC as the Bronze Age Urban Revolution began to gain momentum. The Tigris-Euphrates and western Iran quickly acquired dense clusters of concentrated farms and towns and a dozen growing cities like Kish, Ur, Lagash, Umma, Awan, Hamazi and Shuruppak. The same phenomenon would, within several centuries, come as well to other regions: Anatolia, the Indus Valley, northern Mesopotamia and Syria, but not before the Sumerians, crowding into their cities in search of new economic opportunities and military security, had clearly taken the lead in capital formation, technology and urban development.[8]

Even into the 1990s any reconstruction of the history of Mesopotamia between 2900 and 2300 BC remained very imperfect at best. Archives of cuneiform tablets unearthed from Ur (2700-2600 BC), Shuruppak (2600-2500 BC), Girsu near Lagash (2430-2340 BC) and the site of Ebla in Syria (2450-2350) have all illuminated Early Dynastic civilisation, but scholars have, in general, had relatively few documents to work with for the period before 2500 BC.[9] After 2500, the cities of Early Dynastic III began to mushroom in size and what was a mere trickle of written records in 3200 BC and a small rivulet in 2600 of the ancient world became more of a full-fledged stream by 2400, although, as in the case of the later texts from Kanesh, their individual focus was often very narrow. Taken in their totality, though, the cuneiform tablets of 2500-2300 BC have been extensive enough to tell the historian something about Mesopotamia's evolving economy and society as well as its domestic and even international political order.[10]

The Urban Revolution gave birth to forms of politics, diplomacy, war and business which, if different from our own, are, for the first time recognisable. Evolving from pictograms which appeared at the end of the Uruk period (3500-3200 BC), the cuneiform alphabet of 3200-2900 was sufficiently streamlined and detailed enough to provide an eyewitness commentary upon Early Dynastic civilisation.

Humanity's first urban and capitalist civilisation and its development were revealed day-by-day in the tablets of the time as well as
in the silent testimony of the ruins of its royal tombs and impressive
buildings. Decorated with images of ears of corn and stalks of
wheat, the vases of Uruk spoke as much about the nature of its
economy as volumes of tablets.[12]

Figure 5. Archaeological Timetable for Sumer 4000-2100 BC[11]

Chalcolithic: Copper Age: 4000-3100 BC
Ubaid period: 4000-3500 BC: Cain a "wanderer" (Gen.4:10-1).
Uruk period: 3500-3100 BC: Cain "building a city" (Gen.4:17).

Early Bronze I: 3100-2900 BC Protoliterate-Urban Revolution in Sumer: Tubal-Cain
"forged all kinds of tools out of bronze and iron" (Gen.4:22).

Early Bronze II: 2900-2300 BC "when men began to increase in numbers on the
earth" (Gen.6:1):
Early Dynastic I: 2900-2700 BC: "Golden Age": primitive democracy and first god-
kings: "Sons of God" (Gen.6:2).
Early Dynastic II: 2700-2500 BC: "Heroic Age" of Gilgamesh, Aka and international
trade: "Heroes of old, men of renown" (Gen.6:4).
Early Dynastic III: 2500-2300 BC: "Dynastic Age" of wars, larger-scale "national"
states and social distinctions: "the earth was corrupt...and...full of violence"
(Gen.6:22).

Early Bronze III: 2300-2100 BC
Akkadian period: First universal empire and centralised world commerce: "Nim-
rod...the first centers of his kingdom were Babylon, Erech [Uruk], Akkad and Calneh
[Nippur] in Shinar [Sumer]" (Gen.8:10).

In the centre of the developing institutions of these emerging sophisticated urban communities were the temples of their gods and
the palaces of their *lugal*, "big men" or kings. Following the work of
Sumerologist Anton Deimel in 1931, five decades of scholars believed that the city-states of the ancient Near East were "socialist"
theocracies in which the temple exercised supreme political power
and owned all of the land. Private ownership of land was felt to be
nonexistent until it was recognised in the early 1960s that city-states
such as Lagash controlled large tracts of rural territory owned by
family groups.[13] Individual and family property and commercial
markets were an integral part of the Mesopotamian economy from
the beginning, existing alongside and in perfect harmony with the

public enterprises of the palace and temple. The average Sumerian
peasant was more than capable of supporting himself and his family
from his irrigated plot on which he usually grew vegetables and
wheat while raising chickens. Documents from Lagash prove that
most of these plots were privately owned, even by the poor, and that
real estate was a thriving business even in Early Dynastic times.[14] If
the urban Mesopotamian economy rejected communism, it was by
no means a *laissez-faire* system either. Tablets from both Sumer and
Ebla picture a very patrician and paternalistic form of mixed economy which gave entrepreneurs certain freedoms within a mercantilist framework of strongly regulated commerce, much of which was
still state-run:

> *All sectors of production, from agriculture to industry, stand subject to*
> *an iron-handed administration which…not only controls and registers*
> *every phase of the work, but also plans and promotes it.*[15]

The history of the ancient Near East between 3000 and 2000 BC
was one of expanding trade and commerce, growing social inequality and the rise and fall of a centralised bureaucratic government
many of whose functions were later assumed by new commercial
organisations in the Assyro-Babylonian private sector. During the
pre-urban Uruk period and even in the early part of the Urban Revolution, Sumerian temple clergy dispensed relief to the indigent and
deemed everyone a mere servant created for the pleasure of the
storm-god Enlil, Enki and other powerful dieties and able to face
them on an equal basis.[16] Political power, it would seem, rested in
more worldly hands from the beginning. In a society dominated in
the beginning by tribal and kinship ties, various chieftains must
have embarked upon temple construction and other projects in the
hope of enhancing their personal prestige and upstaging their rivals.
The effect of this was to further stimulate the economy and advance
the Urban Revolution. Urban settlement steadily increased in density and size from the late Uruk period on so that by 2500 the vast
majority of Mesopotamians lived in cities some of which, like Shuruppak, the reputed site of Ut-Napishtim, the Sumerian Noah,
grew in area from 40 hectares in 3000 BC to between 70 and 100
hectares by 2300. Many Sumerian cities now contained, within
their walls, some 15-30,000 people.[17]

As the various cities of the Mesopotamian flood-plain began to perfect the arts of weapon-making and political organisation, they began to train and equip humankind's first armies designed to enforce the ambition of their rulers and deter the ambition of neighbouring rulers. What may well have been tribal democracies led by chieftains in the Uruk period eventually became monarchies as the various *lugal* arrogated to themselves hereditary and even semi-divine powers. Ethnic loyalties gave way to the political ones embodied in the massive palaces springing up in Mesopotamia, Syria and Anatolia after 2500 BC. No longer just servants of the gods, the kings of ancient Iraq became, in the eyes of those they defended, first supermen and then semi-divine "sons of God" themselves.[18]

By 2600-2500 BC the city-states of Mesopotamia and its periphery were beginning to evolve from city-states into what can only be described as rudimentary nation-states, controlling large tracts of rural territory beyond their urban cores. Remaining competitive and sovereign, the smaller states became vassals of more powerful domains. The archives of Ebla illuminate the growth of a vast commercial empire to the west of Mesopotamia, rich in wheat, barley, cattle, silver, gold and textiles which exercised control over much of Syria, northern Mesopotamia and even part of Anatolia. Ebla, however, was soon vanquished as great power by Kish, which earned the position of "first among equals" and the right to arbitrate disputes among the other Sumerian city-states. The title "King of Kish" would eventually be bestowed by the priests of Nippur upon whichever Mesopotamian ruler became the most powerful and influential at that time. Around 2500 BC Kish itself was challenged, not only by Uruk and Ebla, but by Lagash, whose warlike ruler, Eannatum claimed the title of "King of Kish" due to his rulership over Umma, Uruk, Ur, Elam and even distant Mari. The Early Dynastic period seems to have ended in a savage series of wars between those states ruled by Lagash and those, led by Kish and Akshak, who resisted that rule.[19]

This power struggle accelerated the development of international business and long-distance trade. "Men of renown" like Mesilim of Kish, Gilgamesh of Uruk or Eannatum of Lagash and their armies were dependent upon endless supplies of copper and bronze for their donkey-drawn chariots, battle-axes, swords, spears, daggers, rectangular shields and arrows. Blessed with abundant agricultural production, the cities of Sumer were nevertheless situated a long distance from the large deposits of precious stones, copper and tin they now needed to manufacture the goods, tools and weapons their new level of civilisation demanded. Unable to find these resources within Mesopotamia, Kish, Ur, Uruk and their neighbours had to obtain them from the outside in return for their surplus food and the textiles produced by their weavers. In the terms of the modern international business research we see evidence of resource-seeking behaviour and the theory of competitive advantage in action. The needs of urban life, consequently, made every major city in Bronze Age Mesopotamia a vital part of a growing web of international commerce between Iraq and the outside world: [20]

> *At least as important as these local resources is the lack of other important raw materials, which all had to be imported. South Mesopotamia has no source of metals, no trees that produce suitable timber for larger constructions and only insignificant amounts of stone. The focus of much documented commercial and imperial activity is the acquisition of these items.* [21]

With Mesopotamia at its hub, a genuine international economy was in full operation in Early Dynastic times, if not before. Goods floated up and down the Tigris and Euphrates and their tributaries in reed boats and then overland by donkey between the various cities of Sumer bound for ultimate destinations as far west as Troy and as far east as India and even Central Asia. Here we find not only evidence of resource-seeking as suggested previously but also market-seeking activities. The existence of this extensive network of commerce was proven not only by the presence of distant styles and artifacts in Sumer and Ebla themselves, but by references in Sumerian and later Babylonian literature. The epic of *Enmerkar and the Land of Aratta* spoke of a long-distance trade in which King Enmerkar of Uruk bartered his city's abundant grain for the minerals of the distant eastern land of Aratta. Huge deposits of copper, tin and precious stones like lapis lazuli have been found, together with evidence of mining, in central Iran, Uzbekhistan and Afghanistan.[22] The knowledge that Indus Valley smiths had begun to smelt copper and tin into bronze at the same time as their counterparts in Sumer, around 3100 BC, also lent support to the probability that both

Sumerians and Indians derived their tin from this common Aratta source: "Afghan deposits are among the best candidates for the source of Mesopotamian tin."[23] If the evidence in *Enmerkar* was correct, Sumerian merchants were packing their foodstuffs and cloth wares in leather bags on the sides and backs of their donkeys and venturing across the Iranian plateau to exchange the former for the tin and precious stones of Afghanistan and India some 3,000 years before the Christian era.

Similar long-distance trade developed between Mesopotamia, Syria and other kingdoms to the west. In addition to Afghanistan, another source of precious metals existed in the Anatolian Peninsula in what is now the modern nation of Turkey. As much as in Sumer, Early Bronze times in Anatolia were "full of violence"[24] with the region's territory becoming the battleground for a number of warring city-state kingdoms, isolated from one another by mountains and valleys but just as dependent upon international trade as their Mesopotamian equivalents. Lacking adequate food supplies given their barren soil, the kingdoms of Asia Minor could only obtain food and textiles in return for the extensive reserves of silver and tin which lay in south central Anatolia in the Konya Plain.[25]

While Anatolians could theoretically obtain their imports from Sumer, it was easier and more profitable for them to look closer to home in the territories of the Levant and northern Mesopotamia which, sometime between 2600 and 2300 BC, formed part of the vast commercial empire of Ebla. Contemporary with either the rulers of Early Dynastic II or Early Dynastic III in Sumer, the prosperous and relatively liberal Eblaites exercised dominion over some seventeen kingdoms, including Kanesh, all of Syria and even large portions of Palestine and northern Mesopotamia. Still the seat of a minor kingdom, Ashur along with its first king, Tudija, also appeared in the Eblaite records.[26] It was under the domain of Ebla that both Ashur and Kanesh first appeared as historical locations and destinations of trade. Weapons in northern Mesopotamia and Syria were identical to Sumerian types; lapis lazuli from the east was unearthed at Mari; stone sculptures in Ashur were identical to those further south.[27]

It would appear that the Eblaites and their short-lived but very extensive commercial empire were forerunners of the Old Assyrian kingdom in organising the northern portion of the Near Eastern trading system. Ebla, however, possessed advantages Ashur would never enjoy. The Aleppo region, richly blessed with some of the most fertile soil in the Near East, produced enough wheat, barley, wine and olives to feed 18 million souls! Ebla abounded in livestock, the royal herds alone boasting, without exaggeration, 80,000 cattle and 80,000 sheep. Ebla was no less successful in the realm of industry, its textile mills being equal if not superior to those of Sumer. The kingdom also possessed enormous reserves of silver and gold, which even then began to be used as a medium of exchange. Through bilateral trade agreements with its neighbours, Ebla provided the first documented legal framework for international commerce. Trading as far south as Sinai, as far west as Cyprus and as far north as Kanesh, the Eblaite dynasty linked these regions with the new cities of Mari and Ashur through a fixed system of prices based on silver and gold and a series of treaties creating an early Common Market and a body of international law by which trade routes were safeguarded and the flow of merchants and goods guaranteed.[28]

In spite of its vast domain, the economic *imperium* of Ebla lasted no more than seven decades. Peaceful, affluent and even liberal by ancient standards, Ebla was eventually dethroned by her more authoritarian and bellicose Sumerian rivals. The climax of the Early Bronze Age came around or after 2300 BC when the entire Tigris-Euphrates basin was, for the first time, to be politically united, first under Lugalzagesi of Uruk and then by a usurper who wasn't even a Sumerian at all, but a Semite who called himself Sharrukenu, or Sargon, "the legitimate king". Conquering and ruling a domain that stretched from the Mediterranean to the Arabian Gulf from his new city of Akkad, Sargon the Great organised history's first true imperial state and the model for all supranational empires to come. Permitting his subjects local self-rule, Sargon nevertheless embodied a radical departure from the old Sumerian pattern, introducing garrisons, forts, a true central government and a claim to renown, divinity and world rule that outraged the priests of Nippur.

Important as the kings of Akkad were in battle and conquest, they need also to be remembered for their role in the vast expansion of international trade they subsidised and encouraged. Both the later literature of Sumer and a growing record of royal inscriptions and public and private business transactions show that the unified Akkadian realm rapidly became the hub of a constant flow of goods, money, knowledge and resources moving in all directions. Mesopotamian commerce was now carried on by sea as well as by land, as state-subsidised vessels from Lagash, Larsa, Umma and Ur carried Sumerian wheat and textiles to points along the Arabian Gulf and even the Indian Ocean while bringing back copper, tin and precious stones in far greater quantities than donkeys could ever dream of carrying. The god Enki in the myth of Enki and Ninhursag is said to bless the land of Dilmun (modern Bahrein) as the destination of the wares of eight different countries, including Magan (Oman), Meluhha (India), Elam and, of course, Sumer.[29]

May the land Meluhha [bring(?)] to you tempting, precious carnelian, messhagan-wood, fine "sea" (?)-wood, and large boats...

May the land Magan [bring(?)] to you mighty copper, the strength of ... diorite, u-stone, and shuman-stone...

May the wide sea bring (?) you its abundance;
The city-its dwellings are good dwellings,
Dilmun-its dwellings are good dwellings...[30]

A more philosophical explanation of how the world operated was contained in *Enki and the World Order*, which again alluded to seaborne trade, conducted by *Dilmun*-boats, *Magan*-boats and *magilum*-boats sailing back and forth between India, the Horn of Arabia and the river-ports of Sumer. In a revealing passage, the god Enki includes the Gulf trade as part of the global order over which he presides:

The l[ands] of Magan and Dilmun
Looked up at me, En[ki], Moored the Dilmun-boat to the ground(?),
Loaded the Magan-boat sky high;
The magilum -boat of Meluhha
Transports gold and silver,
brings them to Nippur for Enlil, the [king] of all the lands.[31]

Sargon's traders journeyed west as well as east, absorbing the commercial sphere of Ebla as well as that of Sumer. The Enki myths allude not only to the importation of copper, exotic goods and gold from the east, but to developing trade between Sumer and king-doms like Ebla to the west. Enriched by a growing import-export business, the cities of Mesopotamia were themselves joined by an extensive river-borne commerce following the route of the god Enki as his boat journeyed along the Tigris and Euphrates from Ur in the south to Ashur in the north.[32]

The tablets of the Akkadian period gave little mention of Kanesh or Anatolia. The evidence, nevertheless remains strong that Sargon and his heirs obtained much of their silver and tin from the miners of Burushattum (Purushkanda), a place which a much later epic sit-uated at the northernmost terminus of Sargon's domain, where lay the Cedar Forest and the Silver Mountains. A small monument, found in southern Iraq in 1953, portrayed Akkadian soldiers lead-ing captives whose hair styles, short daggers and two-handled drinking vessels were unmistakably Anatolian, strongly implying that the legends of a Sargonic army fighting to protect the rights of Mesopotamian traders in Anatolia were something more than myth.[33] Other evidence began to accumulate in the 1960s of trading posts in north Iraq, Syria, on the Upper Euphrates and even in Anatolia, in which Sumerians and Akkadians founded settlements among the resident population. Similar posts appeared to have been founded by Elamites along the donkey-routes to Aratta in the east. In both cases the primitive cuneiform script of the tablets implied the posts belonged to common networks.[34]

Even though Sargon was unlikely to have occupied Anatolia, in-stead preferring to influence it by controlling the Taurus passes, there is little reason now to doubt that his actions ensured Kanesh remained a chief mineral supplier to the burgeoning industries of Mesopotamia. Asia Minor with its state-of-the-art foundries was now an integral part of a network of world commerce stretching from the Hellespont to the Hindu Kush. With Ebla no longer a fac-tor, Sargonic Mesopotamia became the breadbasket and industrial workshop of the Oriental world, trading its finished goods for the raw materials of the periphery needed to produce more goods. The international money economy pioneered in Ebla was continued in Akkad in the form of a uniform exchange standard in which all goods, loans and commodities were now priced and quoted in terms of silver. Not yet minted in coins, silver was nonetheless ex-

changed in the form of ingots and even rings worn by parties to the
various transactions. Where silver was not available, grain and even
cattle, pigs or donkeys took the place of a universal currency.[35]

Who carried out this extensive and evolving trade and how was it
organised? Was it a state enterprise left in the hands of the temples
and royal palaces, or did it eventually become the work of self-sup-
porting private individuals seeking profit on their own? Was the
emerging merchant, known as a *dam-gàr* in Sumerian and a *tamkâru* in Akkad and later, Assyria, a mere public employee, or did he
begin to trade on his own behalf, being motivated by profit as well
as patriotism? Defining the role and place of merchants in Bronze
Age society is confusing in a society like our own, accustomed to
debating the merits of individualism versus collectivism and state
control versus privatisation. The Mesopotamian trader, however,
was neither a paid civil servant nor a totally independent entrepreneur in the sense these terms are understood today. When he first
emerged on the Mesopotamian social scene before and around
3000 BC, the larger Sumerian *dam-gàr* generally operated in the
employ of his city's temple or the palace of his chieftain or *lugal*.
The archives of Akkadian Mesopotamia paint a portrait of a new
thriving class of enterprising capitalists profiting from both state
contracts and private deals. While private property and commerce
became increasingly abundant within the various cities, a close
reading of the tens of thousands of cuneiform tablets unearthed
from Umma, Lagash, Ebla and Ur all confirm that in the Early Dynastic and even the Akkadian eras, all trade to places outside the
Mesopotamian realm rested in the hands of crown and temple merchants, for only public institutions funded by taxes and tithes had
the capital and the organisation to finance long journeys by boat or
donkey caravan to Kanesh, Meluhha or Aratta:

> There is in short no evidence in the available records that the Sargonic
> *dam-gàr* played any significant role in the acquisition of products for-
> eign to Mesopotamia, or was anyone other than a businessman who
> sought profits for clients, including the state, in Mesopotamian markets
> with mostly Mesopotamian goods.[36]

Under the new economy, however, the *dam-gàr* was much more
able to accumulate more and more of his own capital and to assume

the role of creditor, moneylender and independent agent. From the Akkadian period on, the cuneiform records suggest that while many merchants still continued to take advantage of state-sponsored opportunities, reflected in the bureaucratic language of temple and palace transactions, a growing number of traders now acted on their own. The business records of the latter are much more personal and informal and show subjects of the Sargonic Empire engaged in a wide variety of profit-making activities. Many of these merchants, now engaging in business on their own behalf through buying, selling and speculation were able to become independently wealthy even though many of their transactions still involved the government: Ur-Sara of Umma, for example, raised state livestock; his contemporary Ginunu traded in grain and silver; Sunitum in barley and other foodstuffs. Women such as Ana-é dealt in real estate, metals and grain. Nonetheless, dam-gàr do not appear in the list of state households in Akkadian times. They were government customers and agents, not public employees.[37]

Beneficial as it had been to the rising merchant class, the collapse of the Akkadian superstate sometime after 2300 would eventually fragment the international economy into the Sumerian-dominated eastern and Semitic-dominated western spheres of trade that existed in pre-Sargonid times. Within a century or two, the eastward trade of the Gulf was revived under a succession of mini-empires led by Ur, Isin- Larsa and, ultimately, the Babylon of Hammurabi, all of whom sought to adapt the Sargonic model to suit their own interests and times. The Middle Bronze Age commercial records of the neo-Sumerian kingdom of Ur, more extensive and detailed than any preceding save those of Ebla, enabled the historian to construct the most detailed picture yet of Near Eastern business practices. The picture emerging from these records was astonishing, for while the Early Bronze patterns of trade persisted, they now, in the Middle Bronze Age, manifested themselves in revolutionary new ways. The functions of government and business themselves begin to change. The textiles and food of Mesopotamia still flowed east; the copper, tin and luxuries of India, Afghanistan and the Gulf still flowed west. As in Ebla, the evolving price-structure of these exchanges, perhaps more significant than in Akkadian times, indicated the increasing role of money in an economy in which barter still played a significant role. Much of the produce shipped eastward such as fish, textiles, barley and wheat was classified by the palace of Ur-Nammu, Shulgi and their heirs reigning in Ur as exchangeable goods and was assigned a fixed value in terms of silver. In contrast to the fixed prices of these exchangeable goods, which both in Ur and in the subsequent Assyrian and Babylonian realms would be used in place of silver, the prices of many other items such as copper, tin, lumber, spices, wines and cattle fluctuated greatly according to their markets.

The merchants conducting it, however, were now more and more operating on their own as international trade began to pass into the hands of self-employed rather than crown merchants. This privatising trend would accelerate in the Old Babylonian period which superseded the Sumerian between 1800 and 1600 BC. As an illustration, the *Dilmun*-boats which traversed the Gulf in the days of Ur-Nammu (2100 BC) weighed some 90,000 litres. Three centuries later, the vessels of Hammurabi's time rarely weighed more than 12,000 litres. The use of smaller boats suggested that voyages to the east now had to pay for themselves in the absence of royal subsidies or temple tithes:

> *It is noteworthy that, whereas the rulers of pre-Sargonic Lagas and of Akkad talk of direct trade with Meluhha, Magan and Tilmun, in Ur III times the Mesopotamian ships reach only to Magan, and in Old Babylonian times no further than Tilmun. This may reflect conditions in the Gulf...but it may also have to do with a shift within Mesopotamia from publicly supported ventures to private enterprise, which would probably imply less capital investment.*[38]

As the rule of the Ur dynasty gave way to the less powerful kingdoms of Isin and Larsa around 2000 BC, the new kings possessed neither the capital nor the personnel to renew state-sponsored international commerce on a large scale. Given that Sumer and its heir, Babylon, needed to trade or die, it is not surprising that something akin to the 1990s trend to privatisation took place, with the merchant community itself stepping forward to fill the vacuum vacated by the public sector on its own initiative.[39] Supervision of international trade devolved upon a new commercial institution, known as the *kârum*, a term best translated as "harbour". The *kârum* had its origin in the communities of traders living alongside

the docks of large Sumerian port cities like Ur, Umma and Lagash
connected with Gulf commerce. Out of necessity, these informal associations of *dam-gàr* gradually formed themselves into guild-like
associations which were granted a semi-official status by a local *lugal* or king. By the time of Hammurabi, the Babylonian *kâru* were
recognised organisations headed by a chief merchant *orwakil tamkâru*, who was granted administrative authority from the crown to
conduct and even regulate commerce. *Kâru* in various cities were
then empowered to exercise the commercial and even legal and administrative duties the public sector could no longer afford to sustain. Meanwhile, both donkey caravans and *Dilmun*-boats continued to carry the copper, tin, wheat and textiles that had journeyed
in and out of Mesopotamia for generations.[40]

The rise of a capitalist economy, international trade and the dev-
olution of state power and enterprise to the realm of the private
kâru in Babylonia were paralleled in the northern regions once
dominated by Ebla. The neo-Sumerian realm of Ur controlled the
city of Ashur; its successors in Isin and Larsa were too weak to do
so. Around 2000 BC Puzur-Ashur fortified the wall of Ashur and
Assyria entered history as a commercial power in its own right and
heir to the northern economic sphere including Kanesh, Mari and
Ebla. Situated in northern Iraq in the vicinity of Mosul, the core
Assyrian homeland was no bigger than the combined English counties of Norfolk and Suffolk or the state of Connecticut. Bordered by
a flat plain on the west open to both grain-growing and Amorite invasions and partially encircled on the east and north by the mountain ranges of Kurdistan, Armenia and Persia, the lands of the upper Tigris and Euphrates remain to this day vastly different in climate, soil and geography from the sites of Sumer and Babylon lying
to the south of Baghdad. Assyria was a land of small farms and few
major cities. In contrast to the palm trees, swamps and irrigated
deltas of Babylonia, the plains occupied by the settlements of
Ashur, Nineveh and Erbil were temperate in climate, rolling and
green as they shaded off to the hills in the east and the Aramean
wheat-fields of Gozan in the west.[41]

Unlike Ebla or Babylonia, Assyria was not naturally a rich country. Even though her pastures were suited to sheep-raising, the narrow triangle of territory bounded by Ashur, Nineveh and Erbil was
hemmed in by both the mountains and rival kingdoms of Hurrians,

Amorites and others so that her soil "yielded hardly enough agricultural products to support its population".[42] Consequently, Assyria,
much like modern Germany or Japan was compelled to trade or die:
"the Assyrians looked beyond the narrow borders of their own land
in order to supplant their own resources by trading with other countries."[43] Like modern day Germany and Japan, Assyria was very
much in the resource-seeking mode.

Even though evidence of human occupation in northern Mesopotamia dates back long before the time of Sargon, it is only after
2000 BC that the Assyrians enter the pageant of Mesopotamian history as an isolated outpost of Sumerian and Akkadian civilisation.
With the collapse of the Third Dynasty of Ur the civilisation of
Sumer and Akkad gave way to that of Babylon in the south and Assyria in the north. Led by Puzur-Ashur who rebuilt the walls of
Ashur and established the city's independence, the first Assyrian
kingdom inherited the language of Akkad and much of the religion
and social structure of the Sumerians in a manner similar to which
the medieval Holy Roman Empire absorbed the culture and tradition of Classical Rome.[44] Unlike the kings of the south who now
claimed to exercise an absolute authority descended from heaven,
however, Old Assyrian rulers such as Ilushuma (1962-1942) and
Erishum (1941-1902) considered the national god Ashur, ancestor
of all true Assyrians, as the true king of Assyria and themselves
merely his *waklum* or overseer. The evidence of the Anatolian tablets, moreover, indicates that this Assyrian monarchy, far from being a despotism, actually ruled in accord with an oligarchical council of elders.[45]

As heir to the northern and western half of the trading networks
erected by Sargon of Akkad, kings such as Ilushuma and Erishum
followed in the footsteps of those southern rulers who were rein-
venting and privatising the functions of government and state-run
trade by devolving them to private enterprise. Erishum's adaption
of the Sumerian-Babylonian *kârum* system would leave the initiative
for large-scale domestic and international commerce almost entirely
in the hands of the private sector, perfecting "in modern terms...the
first experiment of free enterprise on a large scale".[46] The Old Assyrian public sector continued to exist, especially within the city of
Ashur itself, but the main financing for Assyrian international trade
was now to be borne by private associations willing to accept the

risks and reap the profits of the long-distance ventures and transactions undertaken by the *kârum* and its merchants.[47]

No longer an appendage of the richer kingdoms to the south, the newly independent realm of Assyria faced certain economic strangulation unless it organised its own web of international commerce. Still dependent upon imports for food, textiles, copper and tin, Ashur would have to seek both markets and resources beyond its borders. Far weaker than Akkad at its zenith, Ashur lacked the means in its early years to wage a Sargon-style war of conquest. In the absence of a war of conquest they could ill afford to wage, the princes and merchants of Old Assyria evolved a novel solution to their economic dilemma based upon the institution of the *kârum,* which in their hands became a means of revolutionising international commerce.[48] Instead of relying upon roving traders or costly wars, the merchants of Ashur cultivated the favour of foreign princes, obtaining the legal right to settle as permanent residents in an organised body on the princes' territory, where they could directly supervise economic activity which was in the interest of the host country, Assyria and the merchants themselves. In place of obtaining tin from distant Aratta, Assyrian merchants gained access to a much closer source of the metal on their own doorstep by establishing a *kârum* at Nuzi in the vicinity of the tin mines of Kurdistan along the Lower Zab, a tributary of the Tigris. A second *kârum* was founded in the Akkadian city of Sippar in order to ensure that the precious trade in clothing and foodstuffs remained as much as possible in Assyrian hands.[49]

The vast bulk of the new Assyrian merchant colonies, however, arose far to the northwest of the Ashur-Nineveh-Erbil triangle where the abundant forests and mines of Syria and Anatolia had once attracted the traders of Ebla and later of Akkad. Rather than import the bulk of its copper and tin across the Iranian Plateau or all the way from Magan via the Gulf and a politically unstable Sumer, an independent Assyria turned to sources more familiar to its own, more northerly economic sphere: the rich mines of Burushattum near the Taurus Mountains in Cilicia. Consquently, in the decades following 1950 BC hundreds of Assyrian merchants formed themselves into self-governing *kârum* and established a score of commercial settlements along the caravan routes which led across the mountains of Syria and Cilicia and deep inside the plateau of

Anatolia, over a thousand kilometers from Ashur itself[50] exhibiting resource-seeking activities.

The rise and fall of the Assyrian trading colonies in Asia Minor coincide with the rise and fall of the Old Assyrian domain itself. A comparison of the archaeological record of Anatolia with what is known of the history of Mesopotamia during the Middle Bronze Age (2100-1600 BC) reveals that the Assyrian presence in Kanesh began within a few decades of the collapse of the neo-Sumerian kingdom of Ur and the attainment of Assyrian statehood around the year 2000 BC. The final extinction of the Assyrian presence in Anatolia, moreover, took place not long before or after Ashur itself was subjugated by the Babylonian kingdom of Hammurabi. The chronology of Kanesh and that of Mesopotamia may be synchronised as follows:

By the time of Erishum (1960 BC) a network of Assyrian *kârum* and lesser trading posts occupied formed a trail of settlement stretching from the western doorstep of Assyria to the mouth of the Halys on the southern shore of the Black Sea. The *kâru* at Zalpa and Nihrija occupied the bend of the Euphrates in the vicinity of Haran. Those at Ursu (on the site of Ebla), Hahhum, Hurama and Durhumit followed the Euphrates upstream to where it met the upper reaches of the Halys. On the Anatolian side of the Taurus lay the most westerly *kâru* of Purushaddum and Wahsusana in the vicinity of Lake Tuz and the silver mines of the Taurus – 200 kilometres to the north. *Kârum* Hattusas lay in the future capital of the Hittite empire. Between them lay half a dozen lesser trading stations.

The largest and most important Assyrian outpost, however, was *Kârum* Kanesh, situated on the Halys in the very heart and crossroads of the river and land routes of Asia Minor.[53] In essence, Erishum and his heirs revived and likely expanded a network of trading posts that had existed in Sargonid and even Sumerian times. Contrary to what earlier historians thought, the Assyrian colonisation of Asia Minor was purely commercial. Not one shred of evidence has supported the notion of an Old Assyrian Empire marching its troops deep into Anatolia and forcing its will upon the native princes of that region. No record of any Assyrian military presence or of tribute being paid from Anatolian princes to Ashur was ever found by either Hrozny or the archaeologists of Ankara

University in the strata of Kanesh I or II. On the contrary, the
Kanesh tablets showed that the native princes were fully sovereign
and even levied taxes upon the Assyrian *kâru*. Prior to the reign of
Shamshi-Adad I, who did manage to briefly establish an Assyrian
military presence over Syria and northern Mesopotamia, any imperialism undertaken by the kings of Ashur was along purely economic lines, in the form of bilateral trade and international marketing arrangements similar to those undertaken by the merchant-
kings of Ebla some 500-600 years before:

> *Nothing was of greater concern to Assyria than opening up the rich*
> *treasure-bearing regions of Anatolia as a market for her own exports,*
> *and as a permanent area of commercial exploitation. We recognise this*
> *very clearly as market seeking behaviour. We strongly believe that the*
> *Old Assyrians accomplished what no other Mesopotamian power had*
> *succeeded in doing previously – systematically knitting together a vast*
> *trading 'empire' in a foreign area without recourse to war.*[54]

Dwelling in their own communities with the consent of the native
princes as resident aliens, the Assyrian merchants of Kanesh II
adopted many of the material aspects of the Anatolian civilisation
around them. A house in the Assyrian quarter of Kanesh was built
according to the same architectural model as an Anatolian house
several blocks away. In more social matters the Assyrians tended to
keep more to themselves, a fortunate development for any Assyriologist hoping to use the Kanesh records to learn more about the vanished culture of second-millennium Ashur itself. The Assyrians of
Kanesh and other *kâru* continued to address one another in their
own Mesopotamian language, sacrifice to Ashur and Ishtar and to
consider themselves subject to Assyrian law. Relations with their
neighbours were no doubt correct and cordial, even though the evidence of the Kanesh archives suggested that the sons of Ashur
looked upon themselves as somewhat culturally and intellectually
superior to their new neighbours.[55] Assyrians took up residence in
Kanesh neither to escape tyranny at home or to establish a new
identity for themselves. Their motives were more likely a mixture of
the desire for material gain and loyalty to the greater interests of
both their firm and the kingdom of Ashur, which needed their trade
to survive.[56]

Figure 6. Composite Timetable for Mesopotamia and Anatolia: 4000-2100 BC[51]

Chalcolithic: Copper Age: 4000-3100 BC:

Ubaid period: 4000-3500 BC.

Uruk period: 3500-3100 BC.

Kanesh IV: first evidence of occupation.

Early Bronze II: 2900-2300 BC:

Early Dynastic I: 2900-2700 BC.

Early Dynastic II: 2700-2500 BC.

Kanesh III: wars, palaces, Mesopotamian contacts but no Assyrian presence.

Early Dynastic III: 2500-2300 BC: Foundation of Ashur.

Ebla-Anatolia trade.

Early Bronze III: 2300-2100 BC:

Akkadian period: Ashur subject to Sargon, Akkadian traders in Anatolia.

Gutian period: Mesopotamia subject to barbarian invaders.

Middle Bronze: 2100-1600: Pre-Assyrian Levels IV, III of *kârum* site occupied:[52]

Neo-Sumerian kingdom of Ur: 2100-2000: Ashur subject to Sumer.

Old Assyrian period: 2000-1781 BC: Dynasties of Isin and Larsa reign in Sumer.

Puzur-Ashur I (around 2000 BC).

Shallim-Ahhe.

Ilushuma 1962-1942 BC.

Kanesh II: extensive Assyrian occupation on Level II of *kârum* site.

Erishum I 1942-1902 BC.

Ikunum 1900 BC.

Sargon I. Old Babylonian period begins with

Sumuabum: 1894-1881BC.

Puzur-Ashur II.

Destruction of *kârum* after 62-80 years occupation.

Kanesh IC: no *kârum* occupation on Level IC of *kârum* site.

Naram-Sin 1819-1815 BC.

Erishum II 1814-1813 BC.

Kanesh IB: stone buildings, return of Assyrians to Level IB of *kârum* site. References to King Anittas of "Nesha" (Kanesh?).

Shamshi-Adad I 1813-1781 BC. Hammurabi reigns in Babylon: 1792-1750 BC.

Second destruction of *kârum* Kanesh ends all traces of

Assyrian presence.

Kanesh IA: Hittite buildings, *kârum* site deserted on Level IA.

Old Babylonian period continues after Hammurabi defeats

Assyria:1781-1595 BC.

The benefits to Assyria itself from this trade were no doubt substantial, for the existence of the *Kâru* guaranteed her survival. The overall picture of the Assyrian economy during the five generations in which her foreign colonies were in existence was that of "commerce without an extensive productive branch".[57] Having few productive industries or natural resources and barely able to feed themselves, the estimated 10,000 inhabitants of the city of Ashur were no match as producers for the weavers, farmers and cattlemen of Sumer- Babylonia as their vanished predecessors and neighbours in Ebla had been. The former would therefore strive to fill the post-Akkadian vacuum in the economic sphere of northern Mesopotamia by becoming highly efficient and competent middlemen controlling the trade between the productive Gulf-oriented Babylonian economy, itself with its eastern links and the extractive metal-based economy of the Anatolian Plateau with its western links.[58]

From the evidence provided in the Kültepe tablets and elsewhere, it would appear that Erishum and his successors presided over and regulated a new Ebla-like network of trade, organised by the leading *kâru* of Assyria which received goods by boat and caravan from the Sumerian-Babylonian trading sphere to the south and shipped them on to other Assyrian *kâru* and *wâbartum* (trading posts) in Syria and Asia Minor. This trade was in private hands but nevertheless strictly controlled. Unable themselves to compete with the numerous textile workshops of Ur, Larsa, Isin and Babylon, Assyrian merchants established a *kârum* at Sippar, through which they purchased vast quantities of fabric and clothing for resale to thousands of Anatolian buyers. Even though Babylonian, Sumerian, Akkadian and Elamite traders might enter Assyria to sell their wares, no alien *kâru* or foreign merchants were permitted on Assyrian soil where they would be permitted to disturb the latter's tightly-knit web of trade from within.[59]

The vital trade binding Ashur and her Syrian-Anatolian colonies lay in the hands of the same donkey caravans that nurtured Mesopotamian commerce for a thousand years. Given a bank loan to cover their expenses, the caravan drivers loaded their animals with sealed packages of textiles and other southern goods and bills of lading written on clay in Old Assyrian cuneiform, the seals to be broken when the caravan reached Kanesh. The journey itself was not without its hazards. Donkey caravans generally numbered less than twenty, and in most cases groups of no more than two or three animals could be found undertaking the thousand kilometre journey which usually took two months. While losses were few and plenty of Assyrian settlements dotted the way, traders remained in constant peril from bad weather, wild animals, brigands and the loss of donkeys. Taxes had to be paid to Assyria, Kanesh and whatever Amorite or Anatolian principality the caravan traversed. Finally, the caravan reached Kanesh where its goods were either unpackaged or sent on to the other posts of Asia Minor under Kanesh's jurisdiction. Most of the donkeys themselves were also sold. In return, the drivers and agents of the *kârum* brought back copper and silver from the mines of Burushattum. The profit margins, 100% on Assyrian tin and even more on Babylonian textiles and garments, made up for all the hazards, overhead and taxation encountered on the northward journey. Returning to Ashur with their ingots of copper and silver, the mobile agents of the *kârum* repaid their loans, pocketed their profits and traded half their silver for fresh shipments of tin and textiles for the next caravan.[60]

Entering the arena of world trade and politics at a time when state-sponsored enterprise was being replaced by capitalist initiative and royal authority devolved to private authorities like the *kârum*, the rulers and merchants of the Old Assyrian kingdom "fashioned a highly organized commercial enterprise, an international import-export business in the fullest sense".[61] Subject to Assyrian law and connected to *kâru* located hundreds of kilometres to the south and east in Assyria proper, the hundreds of Assyrian traders settled in Anatolia were, like their counterparts in northern Babylonia, Kurdistan, Syria and Anatolia neither wandering peddlers nor military conquerors. Instead, they were members of the most advanced and complex system of international commerce yet to evolve in Bronze Age Near Eastern history. The trading system of Old Assyria itself was the end-product of a long process of urban growth and economic specialisation perfected over fifteen centuries in Mesopotamia. The invention of bronze permitted a tribal system of barter and subsistence farming to be replaced by a money economy and an urban system of managed trade and state-directed capitalism which complemented and eventually assumed many of the functions of the state itself. By the time of the Old Assyrian kingdom, business institutions had become professional, international and a serious force in Near Eastern politics and society.

To add a human face to this chapter we will finish the chapter with a portrait of the well-documented life and business dealings of the Assyrian merchant families of Pusu-ken.

Pusu-ken, Son of Suejja

This section focuses on the activities of one businessperson, Pusu-ken of Ashur, and his family.[62] He appears to have lived around the time of King Ikunum of Assyria, somewhere between approximately 1900 and 1875 BC by the Middle Chronology.[63] Evidence suggests his was the first generation to move from Ashur to take up permanent residence in Kanesh. In a parallel with modern day life, records suggest that Pusu-ken's wife, Lamassi, spent her married life living in the capital while her spouse spent all his time in a foreign country. The growing importance of their foreign activities is suggested by a change in the living arrangements of several of their four sons, Suejja II, Ashur-muttabbil, Buzazu and Iku-pasha, who either brought their wives with them from Ashur or married a local from an important family.

The importance of the family's business activities in society are evidenced by the considerable correspondence between Pusu-ken and King Sargon I. By having important family members move to a "foreign" location one sees early efforts to internalize international business activities within the hierarchy of the firm.[64] Additional evidence is presented by Veenhof [65] who suggests that Ashur's textile production was largely performed by women of the merchant houses, many of whom had husbands who worked in Anatolia. In this context the family may be seen as an early business network. Within this family historians have found evidence of occasional strained relationships. For example, the sons and daughter of Pusu-ken brought a dispute over his will before the city-assembly of Ashur.[66] A relevant ancient Arabic saying is *Tahababu wa-tahasabu*, "love each other, but make accounts with each other."[67]

Pusu-ken appears to have been a sedentary merchant who traveled little, while having a large staff of employees or subordinates in Anatolia. This hierarchy managed the day-to-day affairs of the firm, as was the case with other firms, sending employees and other agents to cities throughout the Anatolian region for extended periods, again demonstrating one of Dunning's four main types of foreign production, market-seeking behaviour.

As was typical of firms in this age, non-Assyrian natives of the area, from Pusu-ken's view foreigners, were usually limited to inferior and peripheral jobs.[68] In contrast, Assyrians residing in Anatolia were allowed the same rights and status as if they had resided in Assyria proper,[69] in a manner similar to many of today's expatriates. Evidence is found in the cuneiform tablets of the era of business-people of varied origins, including Syrian and Eblaite, suggesting the possibility of a multi-cultural workforce.

Financing of the enterprise was most likely provided by a partnership based on a *naruqqum,* essentially a capital fund invested by several investors for a merchant active in foreign trade. The *naruqqum* was similar to a long-term partnership entered into by a group of people and provided a considerable amount of capital for the firm operated by the merchant. The single contract which has to date been unearthed is that of Amur-Ishtar who himself invested four *minas* of gold in the "sack" or partnership and 14 others who invested an additional 26 *minas* of gold. The agreement stipulated he would conduct business with these 30 minas for a period of 12 years, and also included provisions for the distribution of profits and a penalty for early withdrawal of funds from the investment pool.[70] This suggests an early type of stock market complete with shareholders, shareholders rights, a long term perspective and obligations and a "professional manager". In this case the manager, Amur-Ishtar received one-third of the profits, a handsome reward, even by today's standards.

In common with today's business people, Pusu-ken had to deal with governmental involvement in his business activities. The Ashur city assembly imposed strict controls on the import of textiles from Anatolia to Ashur. Documentary evidence shows that Pusu-ken was fined for trying to circumvent the protectionist policies of the government.[71]

In this chapter using the tools of modern theory, we examined the workings of the Assyrian *kârum* in detail, we saw that constituted history's first recorded multinational enterprises, complete with head offices, branch-plants, corporate hierarchy, extraterritorial business law, foreign direct investment and value-added activity.

Chapter 5

The First Industrial Samurai

The Myth of the Dark Age and the Coming of the Phoenician Corporate State: 1100-850 BC

Arising in a narrow strip of coastal land in what is now Lebanon and Syria, the Phoenicians burst forth around the year 1000 to become the most formidable seafarers and traders of the ancient Near East. Voyaging across the Mediterranean and even into the Indian and Atlantic oceans, the sturdy longboats and galleons of Ugarit, Sidon, Byblos and Tyre foreshadowed the ocean-going ships used more than 2000 years later by Erikson, Magellan, Columbus and Drake to rediscover and colonise a new world and try and monopolise the trade of the old. The impressive achievement of Phoenicians and Carthaginians in navigating, exploring and even colonising the isles and coastlines of the world, however, becomes even more impressive when one recognises that their voyages resulted in the creation of a vast and well-organised network of trade and investment which spanned three continents. Borrowing much from the Mesopotamian models of managed enterprise, the merchants of Tyre would expand them to create the first multinational trading hierarchy of intercontinental proportions.

The rise and remarkable success of Phoenician business can best be understood in its historical context. Beginning well before 2000 BC, a network of international trade had arisen in Mesopotamia which stretched from Egypt and Greece in the west to India in the east, with the cities of the Tigris and Euphrates in Sumer at its core. As recounted earlier in this book, within this network, the first documented example of large-scale foreign direct investment appeared in the fasci-

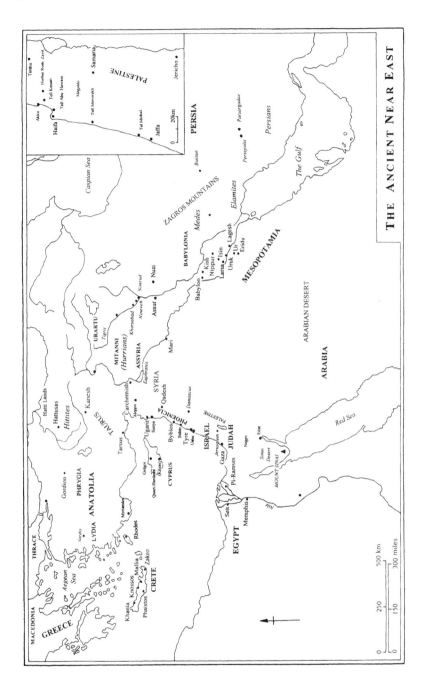

THE ANCIENT NEAR EAST

nating organisation of Assyrian *tamkâru* who, operating crown-sup-
ported private family firms in the Old Assyrian capital of Ashur, set
up a branch-plant offices at Kanesh in the heart of what is now
Turkish Anatolia.

The colonies of Kanesh vanished from the historical record at the
same time as the first Assyrian kingdom was overthrown by the rapid rise of the new Amorite dynasty of Babylon led by their famous
lawgiver Hammurabi. Quickly overrunning Sumer, the Babylonian
armies soon absorbed Assyria as well. Enough records have survived from the Old Babylonian kingdom, mostly clay tablets from
the ruins of Sippar, to show that the business and trading practices
of Hammurabi and his successors closely resembled those of the
Sumerians who preceded both them and the early Assyrians. Babylonian *tamkâru* continued to control the caravan routes across Iran
to Afghanistan and to sail the Arabian Gulf to Dilmun, Arabia, east
Africa and the Indus valley.

Babylonian trade remained a mixed enterprise, with the crown
and private merchants each contributing 50% of the capital. Relations between king and nobility, including *tamkâru*, remained on a
feudal basis in which nobles and merchants received land grants in
return for military and other forms of homage not unlike those familiar in medieval times. Profits from royal herds and lands con-
tracted out to *tamkâru* were subject to crown royalties. As in Sumer
and Assyria, crown and temple sought to control prices, facing the
same difficulties that prices and incomes policies have encountered
in more recent times, that of black markets and little relation to true
market value.[1]

Following the death of Hammurabi, who reigned from 1792-
1750 according to the accepted Middle Chronology and 1627-
1584 according to the revised chronology of Peter James,[2] the Babylonian empire began to shrink, with parts of Sumer becoming
temporarily independent and Assyria becoming subject to the new
kingdom of Mitanni. For the remainder of the millennium Babylon
itself passed under the rule of a foreign dynasty. Emerging from
western Iran, the Cossaei, Kahshu, or Kassites ruled southern
Mesopotamia for some four hundred years, replacing the old Sumerian city-states with a unified Babylonian nation-state which, under various rulers, was to last until the Persian conquest of 538
BC. Her history illuminated from the tablets of Nippur and a few

references from the Egyptian diplomatic archives of El Amarna, Kassite Babylonia likewise followed in the pattern of trade and economy charted by Gligamesh, Sargon, Ur-Nammu and Hammurabi. Babylonia, as it was now called, remained a large important state and the trading partner of the new Egyptian kingdom of the Eighteenth Dynasty, conventionally dated 1550-1300, but 1300-1050 on the revised scale.[3]

The reunification of Babylonia under kings like Kurigalzu I and Burnaburiash II, who adopted the Babylonian language and considered themselves good Babylonians, brought the return of both the Gulf trade and renewed prosperity to southern Iraq. There is even evidence of foreign direct investment, uncovered by a Danish archaeological team, in the form of a royal *kârum*, administered directly from Babylon, operating from a Kassite fortress planted on Bahrein in the heart of the Gulf, seeking to control the ancient maritime trade routes of Sargon. The impressive island fortress of Dur-Kurigalzu, planted near Baghdad, moreover, sought to control the mountain passes to the east, which now provided horses, now far more important to trade and power than donkeys. By the end of the second millennium, the horse-drawn chariot had become the decisive weapon in war, the Late Bronze and early Iron Age equivalent of the tank or even the airplane. Consequently, the nation which had access to the regions of Iran where such horses could be raised and found would possess an important advantage, making it necessary for any Near Eastern power to control the mountain passes bounding the land of the Two Rivers on the east.

If horses and the wealth of the east flowed from Babylonia to Egypt, the copper of Cyprus, the ivory of Africa and the gold of Egypt flowed into Babylonia from the west. The period of the Eighteenth Dynasty in Egypt and the Kassite kingdom of Babylonia, the so-called Amarna Period, was one of relative stability in world history. The similarities between the Near East in the late second millennium and Europe in the century and a half before the Industrial Revolution were quite remarkable. Several major powers, Egypt, Babylonia, Hatti, Mitanni maintained a balance of power which was to be challenged by several new ones, Assyria and Elam in Mesopotamia, the Moschi and Tiberani in Asia Minor and the Aramean, Canaanite and Hebrew city states and tribal kingdoms of the Levant. Clear rules governed international trade during the

Amarna period. The major courts treated one another as equals
and all corresponded in Akkadian, the language of diplomacy. In
Egypt and Babylon, court theologians and thinkers explored issues
relating to the meaning of life, codifying epics of the gods and ad-
dressing problems of suffering and injustice. The old Mesopotamian models of mercantilist business endured. *Tamkâru*, both royal
and private, continued to play a political as well as a commercial
role. Private and public enterprise not only coexisted but were so
interwoven as to be virtually indistinguishable.

The El Amarna world of mixed enterprise and great-power equilibrium was quite conducive to the healthy growth of international
trade and of new trading powers among the numerous small city-
states of the Syro-Palestinian region who now parcelled out the territory once occupied over a thousand years before by the commercial colossus of Ebla. This region, ideally suited by climate, geography, location and tradition to provide commercial advantages to anyone willing to seize them, merely needed the right circumstances
and market conditions for a new Levantine trading power to
emerge. First controlled by the Arameans, then passing to the
Egyptian warrior-kings Thutmose II and Amenhotep II, the Canaanite principalities of the coast eventually came under the rule of
the multi-ethnic Hittite Empire of Suppiluliumas I and his successors. Ruling over the various kingdoms among whom the Old Assyrian *tamkâru* once traded and dwelt, the cosmopolitan multilin-
gual Hittite domain bordered on Mycenaen Greece, Troy, Assyria,
Aram and the Egyptian vassal states of the Levant. In addition, the
kings of Hatti now controlled the silver mines once sought by Sargon and the merchants of Ashur. Militaristic but tolerant, the kings
of Hatti permitted their subject peoples a fair amount of autonomy
and identity. In return for tribute and military obligations, however,
their new Canaanite vassals obtained access to the resources and
markets of Anatolia.

The rise of an aggressive new centre of international business in
the region where the Hittite, Egyptian and Mesopotamian spheres
of trade and influence intersected might well have remained unwit-
nessed and undocumented. In 1928, however, a team of French archaeologists digging at the site of Ras Shamra uncovered the site of
the thriving city of Canaanite Ugarit. Rows of two-story houses,
business quarters, temples dedicated to Baal and Dagon and, most

importantly, the ruins of a huge royal palace over one hectare in area. The palace of Ras Shamra soon yielded its most valuable secret, a treasure of clay tablets written in cuneiform script and a Canaanite language akin to Akkadian, Eblaite and Hebrew. The Ras Shamra texts and other tablets unearthed at the site of Ugarit shed light on all aspects of Canaanite life at the end of the Bronze Age in the late second millennium.[4] The tablets from Ugarit represent the only substantial body of first-hand source material available to scholars interested in the life and commerce of the ancient Canaanites. Nevertheless, they are sufficient to paint a picture of an emerging Phoenician business culture not unlike that previously encountered in Sumer, Assyria and Babylonia.

Ugarit's geographical position offered her merchants a tremendous location or country-specific advantage. Situated at the hub of the western axis of international trade among the three greatest powers of the day, Egypt, Babylonia and Hatti, the northern Canaanite principalities were in a position to control or access both seaborne and overland commerce moving from north to south or east to west. Goods moving from Babylon to Thebes either had to pass through Phoenician ports or move on roads that passed close to Phoenician territory. The same applied to trade between Anatolia and Egypt. With most of the good farmland in the Syrian-Palestinian region occupied by the Arameans and the Israelites, the city-states of what was to be later known as Phoenicia seemed naturally suited for export, manufacture and trade. Having a dense and increasingly urbanised population, excellent harbours, an ample supply of lumber and a highly-skilled and educated population, the cities of the Levant were ideally suited to develop a trade-based maritime economy not unlike Britain or Japan. The dense urbanisation of Ugarit and other Phoenician city-states, combined with the scarcity of grazing land for donkeys and horses, made the latter too expensive to breed in a forested region where shipbuilding was far more cost-effective and promised far more trade advantages, an example of the theory of comparative advantage in action. Other nations could grow food and make war. Let Phoenicia sell them the metals and even the tools, growing rich and powerful in the process: "with its face to the sea, Ugarit developed several industries and crafts which were of purely maritime character, such as purple dye manufacture, and shipbuilding."[5]

The merchants of Ugarit and her neighbours quickly seized the opportunity to become the key middlemen in the evolving Near Eastern trading system. Vast trading fleets built from the forests of Lebanon sailed between Egypt, Cyprus, Canaan and the Cilician coast of the Hittite empire. Grain grown in Egypt or Babylonia was traded to the Cypriots and Hittites in return for their precious copper and other metals which were processed in Phoenician workshops or shipped by caravan and Euphratean reed boat to Babylon, Sippar, Ashur, and points east. Kassite horses were sold to Egypt; Egyptian ivory to Mesopotamia, Elam and Hatti. Imported into Ugarit's harbours from the mines of Cilicia and Cyprus, copper and precious metals were distributed to guilds of merchants and traders by the harbour master. Both profits and royalties paid to the crown were then re-invested in the construction of even more seagoing vessels, organised into fleets which grew along with the volume of international trade now passing through the harbours and along the roads under Phoenician control. Within the cities and towns of Ugarit and the other Phoenician city-states guilds of highly-skilled craftsmen, most of them now self-employed, beat and smelted the raw copper and tin, plus the gold and ivory of Egypt into finished products which could be shipped by caravan to Mesopotamia via Carchemish or even Hatti or Egypt. Royal factories also sprang up along the Mediterranean shore, home of the murex shellfish, from which the famous and much-coveted Phoenician purple dye was made. A highly specialised Phoenician garment industry exported over a thousand different items to Thebes, Troy, Rhodes, Hattusas, Babylon and every bazaar of the ancient world Canaan's traders were able to reach.[6] These small companies had a specialised knowledge which would lead them to enjoy high profits for a considerable period of history.

Most historians believe that Ugarit and her trade empire flourished between 1400 and 1200 BC, after which the merchant city was destroyed. The period from 1200 to 900 BC appears as a prolonged Dark Age in the archaeological record. Not only in the Levant, but in Anatolia, Greece and Babylonia the historian is confronted with three centuries of stark silence, after which the cultures of the Iron Age emerge:

The remarkable fact about the situation at this time is that it is quite a long time (not until the tenth century) before there is evidence of real

recovery. A 'dark age' seems to descend, and when the historical pic-
ture clears again a change in the overall political pattern has taken
place: there are several new states (e.g. Israel, the Philistine Pentapolis)
dominated by peoples scarcely attested in the Levant.[7]

The Dark Age is generally believed to have been caused by a massive invasion of Anatolia and the Levant by legions of invaders from
the Aegean known as the Sea Peoples. The Lukka, Peleset, Shrdu,
Shkelesh, Tjekker and others, identified with Lydians, Philistines,
Sardinians, Sicilians and others are held to have annihilated the
Hittite state, destroyed Ugarit, colonised the Levant and invaded
Egypt, drawing down the veil on Bronze Age civilisation. Phoenician activity ceases for two or three hundred years after the destruction of Ugarit, resuming around 1050-1000 with the trading voyages of Byblos, Sidon and Tyre.

A few historians in the 1990s, however, now question the accepted picture of barbarian invasion and Near Eastern Dark Age. The
portrait of the Sea Peoples as invaders rests on very slim evidence,
the only mention of them being two Egyptian inscriptions, the first
by Merneptah and the second by Rameses III. The reliefs of the alleged invaders show not horsemen in chariots but families migrat-
ing in oxcarts. The portraits of the Philistines and other soldiers on
these reliefs are identical to those of mercenaries who served not
only in the Egyptian army, but also in the pay of their Libyan rivals.
Admittedly coming from the Aegean, the Sea Peoples were, according to Amélie Kuhrt, mercenaries and refugees, not conquerors.
The Philistines came to Gaza as settlers, not invaders. Hatti may
have been destroyed by other peoples. As for Ugarit, her collapse
came about either through the raids of pirates or even an earth-
quake.[8] Led by Peter James and David M. Rohl, a group of British
historians has gone even further, arguing quite persuasively that the
Near Eastern Dark Age never existed. Examining the royal tombs
and monuments of the later dynasties of ancient Egypt, both James
and Rohl argued that the dates assigned to the reigns of every Pharaoh who reigned prior to approximately 650 BC were too high. Giv-
en that Egyptian chronology remains the basis for the chronology of
the entire Near East, the effect of revising the dates of the former
would be to shorten the entire history of the ancient world by two to
three centuries. Still contested by the majority of scholars, the new

dating systems advocated by James and Rohl had enormous implications. The beginning of the Iron Age was redated from 1200 to 1000-900. More significantly, the lack of documentation during the Near Eastern Dark Age could now be very simply explained: the Dark Age never existed at all. If a gap of two or three centuries supposedly existed in the history of the ancient world, why, asked James, Rohl and others, were the cultures of Anatolia, Babylonia, the Aegean, Canaan and elsewhere in 900 BC so strikingly identical to those of 1200 BC?

A new super-low chronology would place the history of Phoenicia in an entirely new focus and context. Documented by the El Amarna diplomatic archives, the Late Bronze period of the Hittite empire, Kassite Babylonia, the resurgent, militaristic Middle Assyria of Ashur-uballit, Tukulti-Ninurta I and Tiglath-Pileser I, and New Kingdom Eighteenth and Nineteenth Dynasty Pharaohs like Amenhotep III and Akhenaten would now be redated from 1550-1300 to 1200-950. The early Canaanite city-states of Ugarit and Hazor would become immediate precursors of the Iron Age kingdoms of Byblos, Tyre and Sidon, if not outright partners and contemporaries. The El Amarna letters themselves showed this to be the case. A letter (El Amarna 89) of Rib-Hadda, Prince of Byblos, to Akhenaten implied both Ugarit and Tyre were flourishing together around 1100-1050 BC: "See, there is no mayor's residence that can compare with that of Tyre. It is like the residence at Ugarit. Extraordinarily large are the riches there."[9] Another El Amarna letter from the same time (EA 147) came from Prince Abimilki of Tyre himself, lamenting the inability of Amenhotep III or Akhenaten to come to his aid in the Philistine wars of the time of Jephthah, Samuel and Saul: "But behold, I am guarding Tyre, the great city, for the King, my lord, until the mighty power of the king come unto me, to give water for me to drink, and wood to warm me." The same letter also mentioned the existence of a royal line in Sidon, represented by Prince Zimreda.[10] On the eve of Ugarit's demise an Egyptian satirical text of the Nineteenth Dynasty, now dated to the time of Israel's united monarchy (1050-950), confirmed that Phoenicia was already the home of several flourishing city-states, namely Byblos, Sidon, Sarepta and "Tyre the port" to which water was "taken...by the boats, and it is richer in fish than the sands".[11] The Hittite text known as *Evocatio* mentioned "the country of Sidon", "the country of Tyre", and "the country of Ugarit" in a list of the states of the Levant and Mesopotamia.[12] The artifacts of the Levant itself silently bore witness to the above texts, testifying in support of a shortened history in which the well-developed craft, metalworking, textile and shipping industries of Byblos, Sidon and Tyre were the pupils and partners of those in Ugarit to the north. Did a flourishing commercial civilisation suddenly reappear from nowhere in southern Lebanon 200-300 years after the destruction of its forerunner in Syria 250 kilometers to the north? How, then, for example, did one explain the remarkable resemblance of Phoenician terra-cotta masks of 900 BC to Ugaritic ones of 1200 BC? The tomb of Ahiram of Byblos, often dated to around 1200 BC was so full of later Hittite and Assyrian objects as to persuade even W.F. Albright to consider a much later date. The astonishing resemblance between the artifacts and material culture at the beginning and the end of the supposed Dark Age, baffling many historians wedded to the traditional schemes of dating, cries, hints at a much simpler explanation:

> *In both metal working and ivory carving, numerous parallels (both in technique and iconography) may be drawn between the Bronze Age material from that site [Ras Shamra] and Phoenician work of the early first millennium BC Such striking parallels have led to the conclusion that the origins of much in Iron Age Phoenician art may be sought in the Late Bronze Age craft traditions of the Syro-Palestinian region.*[13]

A shortened, reworked history of the Near East, Canaan included, would be of immense significance to the business historian. The Mesopotamian-Anatolian models of directed enterprise are no longer separated from their Iron Age heirs by a 300-year gap but are now much closer in time to the economies of Solomon's Israel and Hiram's Tyre. The Old Assyrian enterprises of Anatolia would have flourished not in 1900-1830 but 1700-1630 BC and, according to Rohl's scheme, possibly even 1600-1530. Hammurabi's *tamkâru* would have flourished in the 1600s or even 1500s and their Kassite successors would be manning the forts of the Gulf and the Zagros passes in the closing centuries of the second millennium. More importantly, their Ugaritic trading partners would appear late enough in time to serve as models and examples for the great southern Phoenician cities who rose to power around the year 1000 BC The implications of the new dating are clear when illustrated in chart form.

If, as the above chart indicates, the Bronze Age society of Ugarit and her sister cities in Hittite-dominated northern Phoenicia existed just before and during the time of the Egyptian-dominated Bronze and Iron Age societies of Byblos, Sidon and Tyre, then a more thorough reconstruction of the business structure and practices of the later Phoenician cities becomes much more credible. As literate and advanced as the Canaanites were, the more southerly cities wrote not on clay but on papyrus, ensuring that virtually all of the records of Tyre and her neighbours did not survive. The magnificent Phoenician history of the Beirut priest Sanchoniathon, totally destroyed, has survived only in a few fragments translated into Greek by Philo of Byblos which were quoted by later writers. A few references to Phoenicians survived in the Old Testament, Egyptian and Assyrian annals, Homer, and later classical writers like Diodorus of Sicily and Strabo. The rest of the story of Tyre and Sidon depended on the archaeologists of the Levant, whose task was much harder than that of Layard, Rawlinson or even archaeologists of Israel like Kathleen Kenyon and Yohanan Aharoni. Unlike the dead cities of Babylon, Ashur and Nineveh, Sidon, Tyre and Beirut were not ruins or tells but thriving Lebanese cities.

Artifacts were buried beneath apartments and office towers, not desert mounds. Most of the archaeological evidence for Phoenician settlement, moreover, came from her colonies, and not from the homeland itself, until the 1960s and 1970s, when a few sites in sparsely populated areas of Galilee and Lebanon enabled historians to attempt a reconstruction of Phoenician history based upon pottery and other artifacts also present in Tyrian settlements abroad.[14]

Given the shortage of texts from first-millennium sites, the Ras Shamra-Ugarit tablets still provided the only usable body of Canaanite business documents. With the traditional dating of 1400-1200 for Ugarit, it was easy to discount these texts as describing a model for trading practices in Tyre and Byblos after 1000 BC. If, however, the Dark Age and the higher chronology that assumed it are rejected according to the new datings suggested above, then the business records of Ugarit become an invaluable source in reconstructing the form and practice of the golden age of Phoenician business between 1000 and 600 BC.

Figure 7. Egypt, Phoenicia and Canaan According to Revised Chronology

LB I: 1450?- 1150
Dynasty XVIII: 1300-1050 BC
Egyptian suzerainity over Canaan

LB IIA: 1150-1050
Dynasty XVIII in Egypt
Middle Assyrian Kingdom under Tiglath-Pileser I, then Assyrian eclipse.
Hittite overlordship of Ugarit under Suppiluliumas I.
Ugarit ruled by Ammishtamru I, Niqmaddu II after 1100 BC
Tyre under Abdimilki.

LB IIB: 1050-950 BC
Dynasty XIX rules in Egypt
David and Solomon in Israel
Mursilis is Hittite king.
Ugaritic trade with Aegean.
Niqmepa and other rulers in Ugarit.
Zakar-Baal in Byblos visited by Wen-Amon.
Tyre under Ahiram I (Hiram) 980-47 BC, partnership with Solomon.

Ir IA 950-900 BC
Dynasty XX in Egypt: 950-825 BC
Revival of Aram.
Destruction of Ugarit around 930 BC
Tyre-Israel partnership
Tyre under various kings from Balmazzer: 946-30 BC to
Pilles: 879 BC

Ir IB: 900-800 BC
Dynasty XXI in Egypt: 850-750 BC?
Ashurnasirpal II and Shalmaneser III begin Assyrian westward expansion.
Reign of Itobaal in Tyre: 878-47 BC
Alliance between Itobaal and Ahab.
Tyrian colonies in Israel, Cyprus, Syria, Anatolia.
Jehu leads anti-Baal revolution in Israel.
Carthage founded 814 BC
Balmazzer III and Mattin rule in Tyre (846-32 BC).

Ir IIA: 800-750 BC
Dynasties XXII-XXV rule in Egypt: 825-660 BC
Temporary Assyrian eclipse Israelite revival under Jeroboam II.
Tyrian expansion into Mediterranean
Foundation Motya, Sulcis, Malta
Pumayyaton (Pygmalion) reigns in Tyre: 831-785 BC

Ir IIB: 750-700 BC
Assyria invades Levant under Tiglath-Pileser III, Sargon II, Sennacherib.
Israel conquered and deported.
Tyre under Mitinna and Elulaeus vassal of Assyria.

Ir IIC: 700-450 BC
Neo-Assyrian, Neo-Babylonian, Persian empires dominate Near East.
Tyrian colonies in Cyprus, Spain, Sicily, Sardinia flourish.
Tyrian commercial power weakens after 600 BC with defeat by Nebuchadnezzar II.
Tyre becomes Persian vassal after 538 BC
Tyrian fleet vanquished by Greeks at Salamis 479 BC
Carthage assumes leadership of Tyrian Mediterranean colonies.

Around 1100-1000, according to the revised dates, the other cities of Phoenicia would have been partners along with Ugarit in seeking to expand their roles in the Babylon-Hatti-Egypt triangle of commerce and trade. Political vassals of the Hittites in the north, the princes in the south remained under Egyptian tutelage before the waning of Egyptian power in the time of Amenhotep III and Akhenaten described in the Amarna letters. Becoming independent of Egyptian tutelage, Byblos, Sidon and Tyre began to share in the profitable trade enjoyed by Ugarit. As the Levant entered the Iron Age, its southern shores were settled by the Philistines near Gaza and the Sikala, likely Egyptian Sicilian mercenaries, near Dor. The coast of Galilee near Acre was occupied by the Shardanu, likely Sardinians and the remainder of Palestine by the Israelites beginning to unite under Samuel and Saul. Once occupying much of Israel, Jordan, Lebanon and Syria, Canaanites now survived as a dominant and sovereign population in a 400-500 kilometer long and 20 kilometer wide strip between Achzib and Ugarit on the Lebanese-Syrian coast. The rest was now populated or dominated by Arameans in the north and Israelites in the south. Hemmed in by a barrier of mountains 15,000 miles high and unable to feed a population now mushrooming with the onset of the Iron Age, city-states like Tyre were encouraged to not only follow the example of Ugarit but to go even farther along the route of industry and trade.

The Ugarit texts describe an economic system of managed trade which would continue into the period of Phoenician overseas expansion under the kings of Byblos and Tyre. This system of managed trade can be even better understood by comparing it with the guided marketplace of modern Japan. Comparing the hierarchical structure of Phoenician business to that of contemporary Japan is an interesting and useful exercise. However, one must be careful not to draw the parallel too closely, given the profound differences between the modern Japanese state with its large professional public sector and a more purely feudal ancient society. Many of the functions then performed by *mkrm* (Phoenician merchant princes) and *tamkâru* are now done by salaried civil servants. Japanese businessmen today are not in the direct employ of the Emperor Akihito. Nevertheless, several parallels between the sea-trader society of Phoenicia and today's Japan do exist and can be useful for a historian trying to explain the workings of a 3,000-year-old trading system:

1. Boundaries between public and private personnel and sectors were quite fluid.
2. Warrior aristocrats, soldiers and sailors were also merchants, participating in overseas commerce.
3. Major merchants and business organisations formed relatively permanent subcontracting relationships of honour-bound loyalty directly derived from a culture of landed feudalism.
4. Crown, aristocracy, navy and business formed an interlocked system of managed commerce. Private profit and market considerations were viewed in terms of the overall geopolitical military and strategic considerations of the nation or city-state as a whole.

In Japan, the Emperor and his royal servants were unabashedly accepted as the promoters and partners of a private business culture whose enterprises remain organised in a highly corporatist and feudal pattern highly suggestive of ancient and medieval societies:

> *The state machinery of samurai administrators built a web of enterprises and institutions tied to the 'political merchants',who joined forces with the government while letting the state take many of the social risks. Social ideologies on nationalism and a type of Manifest Destiny provided a form of social glue with the masses, even though the bureaucracy operated on the feudal principles of 'Kanson Minpi' – revere the official, despise the common man.*[15]

Rejecting the free-market model of shareholder capitalism preached by Friedrich von Hayek and Milton Freedman and the statist model of Marxist and Fabian socialism, present-day Japanese business is organised on a non-ideological model of directed capitalism. With its long tradition of Samurai militarism and a Shinto religion based upon the worship of multiple spirits or *kami*, Japanese culture, while absorbing much from Chinese sources, preserved a 3,000-year-old world-view in isolation from Greek, Roman, French and Anglo-American ideas of liberal individualism and egalitarian state socialism. Surviving on a long string of islands at the very eastern rim of human civilisation, the Japanese preserved much of their ancient world view and samurai society well into the industrial age. When the Emperor Meiji began the modernisation of Japan in

1868, he merely imposed current capitalist technology upon a foundation little changed from Babylonian and Assyrian times. In a nation composed of samurai, peasants, artisans and merchants, the old roles of feudal prince and corporate administrator quickly merged. Capitalist competition and profit-seeking emerged in the context of a tightly-controlled honour-bound system. The sons of ancient samurai, with centuries of military loyalties behind them, donned business suits and carried their codes of combat and service into the market sphere. In a nation where major manufacturers and bankers offered incense to the Sun-Goddess at Shinto shrines beneath Mount Fujiyama, ideological debates over whether Adam Smith or Karl Marx had the most rational economic system had and still have little meaning. Given "the absence of a strong anti-business ideology among government officials or anti-government sentiment among business leaders", Japanese rulers and businessmen instead reflected "a considerable degree of non-ideological or pragmatic adjustment to circumstances".[16]

In Japan, government and big business co-habit rather than co-exist; they are partners, not adversaries. Remaining almost totally in private hands, trade and production in Japan is nonetheless strongly directed by the crown in the form of the famous Ministry of International Trade and Industry (MITI). Strongly nationalist in its orientation, MITI serves to co-ordinate the individual business strategies of major Japanese firms, providing them with information on market conditions and global competitors, setting collective and individual market strategies, and often even subsidising their exports while historically erecting non-tariff barriers against foreign companies. While MITI's Industrial Policy Bureau handles the strategic aspects of collective and individual business planning in terms of setting goals and enduring the most efficient direction of resources, other branches such as the Business Behaviour Division regulate labour and ethical questions while the Price Policy Division handles banking and financial questions.[17]

Over 99% of Japanese business, though, remains in the hands of some 800,000 small firms of less than 300 people who employ seven out of every ten Japanese workers. In the United States, relations between companies of this size and larger firms is one of market exchange, where both parties deal with one another on a contract-by-contract basis. In Japan, however, the structure is much more hon-

our-bound. Large firms form long-term agreements with small
companies who pledge to act as their customers and suppliers. The
arrangement extends into the realm of finance as well, for major
Japanese firms will seek out a bank, public or private to serve as its
exclusive partner or *keiretsu*. In this arrangement, the large firms directly follow the plans set forth by MITI, subcontracting much of
the work of production, marketing and sales to their smaller partners. This system of *shinchintaisha*, dividing the labour among
firms, seems ultimately to derive from the ancient feudal tie of lord
and vassal, every large Japanese firm having its share of smaller
companies who are devoted to dealing with the former exclusively
as a medieval count would pledge sole loyalty to his duke.[18]

With the large firms linked to the state through personal ties and
influence and the smaller firms assuring stable supplies to their exclusive partners, the Japanese system outwardly presents the facade
of a monolithic "Japan, Inc." while inwardly being an arena of competing feudal loyalties. All partners in the Japanese economy,
though, are committed to gaining victory for Japan in a worldwide
competition for markets and resources which both Japanese government and business figures regard as a form of warfare conducted by
capital, resources and exports in place of bombers, carriers and
submarines. One of the principal weapons in the Japanese arsenal
has been the *Sogo Shosha*, or trading firm. Fully half of Japanese
overseas trade is in the hands of import-export companies like Mitsui, Mitsubishi, and Sumitomo, all of which are huge multinationals. Operating in league with the government and joining domestic
Japanese firms with partners in the United States and elsewhere,
these trading firms were essential to Japan's emergence as a world
commercial power. Companies like Sumitomo assumed the risks of
selling Japanese textiles, components, cars and computers produced by other companies abroad, helping MITI to co-ordinate international marketing. *Sogo Shosha* devoted and still devote a fair
portion of their budgets to intelligence-gathering on foreign companies, governments and prices, especially in the areas of new technology, goods and markets which is then shared with Japanese agencies
and firms at home. From the beginning Mitsui, Mitsubishi and other *Sogo Shosha* obtained direct government support, their representatives serving as Imperial trade consuls who often doubled as commercial spies. Now subsidised as well by their *keiretsu*, the vast trad-

ing firms helped absorb the exchange and market risks of the coordinated export campaigns to capture global markets in textiles in the 1950s, autos in the 1960s, electronics in the 1970s and high-tech goods in the 1980s.[19]

The Phoenician structure, adapting the Mesopotamian *tamkâru* system to a maritime industrial economy, anticipated certain aspects of the Japanese model, albeit in a more primitive form. As in all ancient eastern societies, the bounds between public and private enterprise were very fluid. The Phoenician equivalent of the *tamkârum*, or merchant prince was known as a *mkrm*. *Mkrm* in Ugarit and elsewhere could be either private or crown traders, and often both. Phoenicia was, like Japan, an industrial-feudal society. Trading abroad on behalf of the Prince (King) of Ugarit, the *mkrm* was awarded a rich landed estate, which often became hereditary.[20] The merchant Abdihaqab, for example, gained houses and fields which he could pass on to his sons forever in return for his service as a *tamkârum*.[21] Some *mkrm* were fully in the employ of the king or even the queen, being fully dependent royal personnel in service of the palace. In the reign of the Ugaritic King Niqmepa the cuneiform tablets recorded the story of Sinaranu, who, like Abdihaqab, received title, horses and fields from the crown on condition he served as a *bns mlk* or royal merchant. As a crown real estate agent, Sinaranu earned far more capital in the form of silver and land than any other merchant in Ugarit. Nonetheless, Sinaranu also had his own shipping fleet, which worked the markets of Crete and the Aegean under Niqmepa's royal protection.[22] Under a special franchise, any cargo imported from Sinaranu's shipping firm would go directly to the king and not to the royal inspector or harbour-master as in the case of more self-employed merchants. Much of Sinaranu's activity was thus to devoted wholly to his ruler. Another function of royal *mkrm* was that of taxman. Having to provide Niqmepa with a certain share of taxes, which the king had to pass on to his own Hittite overlord, Sinaranu delegated many of his company duties to his own vassals.[23]

Neither royal nor private *mkrm* in Phoenicia were lone entrepreneurs, but traded as members of mercantile guilds, every member of which was responsible for any royal personal or financial property. Overseas commerce in Ugarit, Byblos, Sidon and Tyre was dominated by an assembly of private and royal merchant princes which instantly calls to mind a modern Japanese Diet usually dominated by either members or clients of the country's major firms. Another feature of Phoenician commercial life quickly recognisable to modern observers of Japan would be the contract of comradeship or *tapputu*, an early form of international business partnership. A guild or a group of individual Ugaritic merchants would enter into a trading partnership with their counterparts in a nearby Canaanite principality like Usnatu, Byblos or even Tyre. Merchants in several principalities then pooled their assets to trade in Egypt, Greece, Mesopotamia or Anatolia. In one such arrangement, four merchants from the village of Apsuna combined their resources, including 1,000 shekels of silver, which they would trade in Egypt for gold they could resell to their Hittite and Mesopotamian customers at a much higher price. Activities like this on a much larger scale appear in the royal archives of Ugarit, not only supervised by the crown, but often with the crown being a direct participant. In the modern world this policy has seen its fulfillment in the long-term partnerships between Japanese trading and manufacturing firms and other Asian and even American ones.[24]

Much as in the days of Meiji Japan, which provided state "subsidies for Japanese shipping firms [and] assistance for maritime insurance companies".[25] the kings of Ugarit and other Phoenician city-states supported, oversaw and even organised their individual and collective overseas ventures. An expedition sponsored by the ruler of Byblos included some 540 shekels of silver, 50 of which were carried in the king's own personal ship.[26] Joint royal and private ventures such as these saw the crown investing in various trading and shipping companies known as *hubur*. Were such companies the distant ancestors of Sumitomo?[27]

Harbour masters like Ugarit's Abiramu and his superior, the *sakinu*, or vizier played a role in the Phoenician business system not unlike the directors of MITI. If Phoenicia was a system of managed trade, these individuals and the civil servants in their employ were the ones responsible for managing. Some industries, like lumber and shipping, were, in fact, under strict state control.[28] The Ugaritic crown and the Sinaranus and Abdihaqabs in its employ commanded the fleets trading with Cyprus, Egypt and Cilicia. Obtaining grain from the mainland, these fleets shipped it to Cyprus. Given what Linder describes as the "special position of Ugarit as sup-

plier and agent for this essential commodity" the royal grain enterprise benefited from the organisational and internalisation advantages of being "monopolized by the king and shipped by his fleet".[29]
Copper, so vital for Phoenicia's craft and manufacturing industries,
was imported from Cyprus through another monopoly of royal
mkrm who then distributed the copper to others in the harbours of
Ugarit. It is likely that copper, shipped in large quantities in the royal and private fleets of Ugarit, served to stimulate the growth of the
Canaanite merchant fleet. Not only copper but oil was likely a royal
monopoly, supervised by the harbour master. Did merchants like
Sinaranu provide their monarchs and viziers with intelligence data
on market conditions? As for foreign merchants, known as *ubru* in
the Canaanite tongue, their activities were strictly regulated by the
harbour master. Aramean, Hittite, Egyptian and Mesopotamian
courts and business organisations sent resident foreign merchants
into Phoenician territory, where they were still subject to their own
authorities. The regulations imposed by the harbour master, however, presented them with a primitive version of what would today
be described in Japan as non-tariff barriers. *Ubru* could not leave
the foreign business quarter district of the host country, enter the
residence of native traders, and conduct business in a Phoenician
city without strict supervision from the Canaanite harbourmaster.[30]

Phoenician, like Japanese, commerce was organised in a hierarchical structure, in which each firm, small or great, occupied its
own special place in the market. In addition to the *tapputu*-partner-
ships pursued by the big Phoenician merchants, a pyramidal form
of *shinchintaisha* relationships also existed in the Levantine cities.
Unlike the modern Japanese system, however, the private sector
took a direct role in collecting taxes and running local government.
Merchant princes like Sinaranu and Abdihaqab, themselves bound
by feudal oath to the crown, were themselves the overlords and clients of many other lesser merchants, known as *bidaluma*, who were
subject to the larger magnates in a perfect forerunner of the European feudal and the Japanese samurai system.[31] Local merchants in
every town collected royal taxes, skimming off a profit and sending
the rest to national merchants like Sinaranu who presented them to
the king. The private *bidaluma*, bound by oath and contract to their
respective *bns mlk* or other ranking merchant princes, thus occupied
a role very similar to today's small Japanese firms, bound by long-

term allegiances to larger clients.[32] Each of the bidaluma no doubt played an important role in the local municipalities assigned to them. Some of the more higher-ranking ones, or at least prominent *mkrm* like Amtarunu, were even assigned whole towns to rebuild and resettle, notarising deeds on the part of the crown, and playing an active part in public affairs.[33]

Similarities even existed between the modern Japanese samurai trader and the Phoenician *mkrm* in the military sphere. In Meiji Japan, warrior nobles became directors and agents of trading and manufacturing corporations. In Ugarit, as well as throughout the ancient Near East, *mkrm* and *tamkâru* often played roles of a military as well as of a commercial nature. The ties between business, army and navy in Phoenicia were very strong. Trade, especially overseas, was a high-risk venture. Canaanite merchants faced not only storms but pirates and foreign, largely Greek, competition. These dangers helped further a massive buildup of Phoenician seapower. Vast Phoenician fleets were needed to discourage the Aegean pirates and keep the sea lanes open for Canaanite trade. Convoys of round galleons and elongated Viking-style warships sometimes numbered a hundred ships or more, all manned by professional sailors and artisans. Some of their captains became a new naval aristocracy, in which titles, fiefs and capital were bestowed upon them in the manner of domestic nobility. These vast armadas were set up along feudal military lines. Admirals became princes and traders as well as sailors.[34] As a result, the boundaries between trade and warfare in this, the most mercantilist society of the ancient Near East would become quite fluid. If the motto of modern Japan was *Fukoku kyohei*, "rich country, strong army", that of Ugarit, Byblos and Tyre would have been "rich country, strong navy". Would not the dependence of the cities of Phoenicia on foreign trade and the new menace of piracy help encourage the belief that commerce, trade and investment in fact represented the art of war by other means? The capture of markets became as valuable as the ability to make weapons and win battles, and was in fact directly related to it. From this, it was only a short step to the potential organisation of Phoenician commerce along military lines. "The reason" according to archaeologist A.F. Rainey "for this association between business agents and the military is not hard to find. Mercantile enterprise...was a dangerous adventure".[35] *Tamkâru* were often

murdered on their trading ventures, causing trade, war and diplomacy to become inextricably linked. A whole body of treaty law
came into existence to supervise the activities of international merchants. *Tamkâru* were often obliged to serve in various diplomatic
corps. The El Amarna archives spoke of Babylonian merchants as
part of a state mission to Egypt. according to A.F. Rainey, "Commercial, diplomatic and military activity went hand in hand."[36]

The highly mercantilist commercial model of Ugarit was no
doubt produced in Byblos and Tyre which first enter history around
1100-1000 BC as the former's trading partners. The scanty records
of Byblos testify to the managed nature of trade, crown control of
vital industry, and shipping crews manned with royal traders having
extraterritorial guarantees in foreign ports. A letter from the king of
Tyre to the king of Ugarit[37] describes a *tapputu*-partnership of royal
merchants trading in Egypt: "your ship, which you sent to Egypt – it
is (till now) in Tyre."[38] The journey of the Egyptian royal trader
Wen-Amon to Byblos also shows that hierarchical state and feudal
enterprise prevailed throughout Phoenicia. The ruling prince of Byblos, Zakar-Baal, describes shipping in both Byblos and Sidon as
state-sponsored:

> *Perhaps there are not twenty ships in my harbour that trade [hubur]*
> *with Ne-su-Ba-neb-Ded? As regards this Sidon…the other [place]*
> *through which you passed, are there not fifty more ships in it, that trade*
> *with Werket El, and are dependent on his house?[39]*

Wen-Amon asked the Byblite ruler to sell him timber as his father
and grandfather had done. Zakar-Baal, more than willing to do it,
naturally demanded something in return: "In truth, when my people fulfilled this charge, the Pharaoh …sent six ships loaded with
Egyptian merchandize and unloaded them in my storehouses." No
longer a vassal of Egypt and her god, Amon, Zakar-Baal arrogantly
made it clear the Byblite timber industry was under his royal jurisdiction: "If I shout to Lebanon, the heavens open and the logs lie at
rest [on] the seashore!"[40] Three hundred lumberjacks under royal
supervision then felled the trees Wen-Amon desired, but a fleet of
eleven pirate ships rapidly descended upon the Phoenician port.
Summoning his assembly, Zakar-Baal plans to betray the Egyptian
to them, but the later, escaping in a ship manned by a royal crew,

seeks refuge with a Cypriot princess, warning her that if she allowed them to be killed "shall not their lord find ten of your crews, which he will kill?"[41]

By the time the Wen-Amon papyrus was put to pen (1075 BC traditional date, 930 BC revised date), the Phoenician kings "had established very profitable shipping companies" or *hubur* which dominated Levantine commerce.[42] These companies were to be perfected by the greatest Phoenician traders, colonisers and investors of all: the merchants of Tyre. Organised on the Ugaritic pattern of crown, vizier, harbourmaster, royal and royally sponsored *tamkâru* and lesser *bidaluma*, Tyre no doubt continued the traditions of vassaldom, government supervised fleets, merchant guilds and military/diplomatic traders. Beginning around 1000 BC with King Ahiram I, the famous Hiram of the Old Testament, a superbly organised Tyrian business establishment would begin to exploit their enviable geographical, political and business advantages to create the most formidable trading and investing power antiquity had ever seen. Dominating the whole of southern Phoenicia, Tyre's merchant-princes would forge a new kind of empire, based not upon armies and plunder but upon navies, trade and the foreign direct investment one finds in modern multinational enterprises. Situated just off the Levantine shore, the city was even more suited by nature than Ugarit for a future imperial role. Tyre's harbour, surrounded by reefs and hewn out of rock, protected her multitudes of ships from storms and enemy vessels.[43]

The ascendancy of Tyre was aided by a political revolution in the ancient world. The later Amarna archives describe a power shift in which Egypt, Hatti and Mitanni lost their grip over the Levant and northern Mesopotamia and Aram, Assyria and the united monarchy of Israel and Judah under Saul emerged. By 1000 BC political and economic power was shifting to a Syro-Palestinian region no longer dominated by the kingdom of David and Solomon which reigned from the Red Sea to the Euphrates. As Zakar-Baal had boasted, the cities of southern Phoenicia were no longer vassals of the Pharaohs. Breaking the power of both Philistines and Arameans, David's armies ensured not only Tyrian independence, but a favourable climate for her merchants to launch the greatest commercial expansion in ancient history. This expansion was to take place in several stages best summarised in chart form.

Figure 8. Stages of Tyrian Commerical Expansion 1000-600 BC[44]

Tyrian Commerical Expansion
1000-900 BC: Direct investment in and partnership with Israel to exploit Red Sea routes.
1. Hiram: 980-47
2. Balmazzer I: 946-30
3. Abd-Astart :929-21
4. Astart: 920-01
900-800 BC: Investment in Israel, Syria and Anatolia to exploit Assyrian trade.
5. Dalay-Astart: 900-889
6. Astarom: 888-80
7. Pilles: 879
8. Itobal: 878-847
9. Balmazzer III: 846-1
10. Mattin: 840-32
800-600 BC Direct investment in central and western Mediterranean as Assyrian agent.
11. Pumayyaton: 831-785

The expansion of Tyre largely began with Ahiram I, (Hiram) whose strategy was based upon the goal, according to Spanish archaeologist Maria Eugenia Aubet, of "controlling the trade-routes of the Asian continent".[45] A cornerstone of Hiram's strategy for national expansion was to embark upon the policy of *tapputu* on an unprecedented scale in the form of a grand economic partnership between Tyre and the united kingdom of Solomonic Israel. Phoenician building technology and luxury goods were exported to Israel in return for wheat, copper and silver.[46] Hiram gained a food supply for his urbanised kingdom; Solomon gained valuable luxury goods and technology in mining, smelting, shipbuilding and construction. Given that Israel controlled the overland trade routes through her own territory and, for the time being, parts of Syria and Jordan, the grand *tapputu*-alliance with Solomon gave Tyre easy access to the caravan routes joining the Euphrates, the Levant and Arabia.[47]

The presence in Solomon's Israel of Hiram's *bns mlk* (royal merchants) was an early example of direct Tyrian investment on foreign soil. What is significant about this trade is that the Biblical record confirms the ongoing existence of the hierarchical *tamkâru* system in Solomonic and even later times. I Kings leaves no doubt that crown merchants remained the central agencies of that investment. Solomon's own words, moreover, allude to royal business partnership, "my servants shall be with thy servants; and unto thee will I give hire for thy servants according to all that thou shalt appoint," as well as the technological advantages enjoyed by the Tyrian merchants and their employees: "for thou knowest that there is not among us any that can skill to hew timber like unto the Sidonians." Hiram's own commands in supplying the lumber for Solomon's temple hint at his influence, if not his control and ownership, over the growing Tyrian shipping industry:

> my servant shall bring them down from Lebanon unto the sea: and I
> will convey them by sea in floats unto the place that thou shalt appoint
> me, and will cause them to be discharged there…giving food my house-
> hold.[48]

Politically independent of one another, Israel and Tyre merged their trading companies in a multinational partnership which extended into the Red Sea and even the Indian Ocean in a joint naval enterprise "aimed at opening up a new market, the Orient".[49]

Constructed at Ezion-Geber, the modern Eilat, the fleets of Hiram and Solomon imported gold, silver, ivory and precious stones from Arabia, Somalia and even India, reaping vast profits from which the royalties enabled Solomon to construct his many palatial buildings in Jerusalem, Megiddo and elsewhere. Hiram and his top magnates also put their growing profits to use, investing them in the expansion of the island's huge shipyards, palaces, markets and religious shrines.[50]

It is likely the Phoenicians displayed more enthusiasm for the partnership and reinvesting in capital goods like warehouses, ships and wharves than the Israelites did. Far less urbanised and far more tribal than the cosmopolitan Canaanites, the Hebrews of Palestine were a nomadic and agrarian society of small towns that left few artifacts prior to the urban revolution of the Iron Age, redated by Peter James to Solomon's time. Prior to this commercial revolution, likely inspired by the direct investment of Tyrian iron-working technology, "trade was not an important branch of their economy" and is not significantly mentioned until the time of Solomon. Israelites themselves seemed to regard trade as primarily a Canaanite activity, the term "Canaanite" being used as a pejorative synonym for merchant itself. Tyre's business outlook was akin to that of a modern Londoner, Torontonian or New Yorker; Israel's was traditionally more like Ireland, Scotland, Saskatchewan or the American South. Iron tools, weapons, and city life were reserved to the Canaanites of Hazor and the Philistines of Gaza until Hiram and Solomon launched Palestine on a new urban and commercial revolution. If the revised chronology is sound, the investment of Hiram's iron and shipping technology in Israel and the expanded trade it brought was the cause of the sudden appearance of scores of substantial towns in the countryside occupied by the Israelite tribes. Israel's commercial revolution was directly linked to the rise of Tyre and Solomon's involvement in the latter's international trade. Under both David and Solomon a united Israel controlled the "King's Way", a north-south road east of the Jordan over which passed camel caravans bringing gold and other produce from Arabia and even Africa to Damascus and on to Assyria and Babylon. Roads from Ezion-Geber (Elat) crossed the Negev into Israel. Solomon erected forts in the Negev, Damascus and other locations to regulate and profit from this trade, monopolised by the Arabs, whose camels could traverse desert highways far more easily than Mesopotamian donkeys could.[51]

A political and economic partnership between Israel and Tyre was mutually advantageous to both. Israel provided wheat and olive oil, but no doubt Tyrian craftsmen provided her with iron tools to help her harvest more. The territories occupied by Ephraim, Manasseh, Zebulun, Asher and Issachar could now begin to compete with Egypt as the bread-basket of the ancient world in a manner not unlike today's American Great Plains or Canadian Prairies. If even the Assyrians, who finally conquered Israel in the eighth century BC, continued to depend upon the wheat of the conquered, it is only logical to see that densely populated Phoenicia would have been even more dependent upon Israelite wheat long before.[52] For her part, Tyre became "a co-participant in Solomon's trade enterprises with other countries", her naval merchant-princes being invaluable to Solomon's Red Sea-Indian Ocean ventures "primarily because of their shipbuilding and sailing skill".[53]

Political developments in the late tenth and early ninth centuries BC inaugurated the second stage of Tyrian trade expansion and for-

eign investment. The division of Solomon's kingdom into the separate realms of Israel and Judah and the resurgence of Aramean and
Moabite power helped to disrupt the trade routes joining Tyre to
the Red Sea, Indian Ocean and Arabian Gulf. Under Itobaal I
(891-59 BC), the Ethbaal of I Ki. 16:31, Tyre's axis of commercial
expansion and investment was directed increasingly towards Asia.
Tyre herself now absorbed Sidon, creating a single Canaanite state
in southern Lebanon. Itobaal now referred himself as "King of the
Sidonians" and not merely king of Tyre.[54] The new pan-Phoenician
state founded by Itobaal would endure until the Assyrian invasion
and offer new organisational advantages in the realm of trade. The
new enlarged Tyrian realm sought new sources of raw materials and
"a gradual control of the market through an ever more active and
simultaneous presence on three fronts: Israel, Syria and the east
coast of Cyprus."[55] Israel's staple economy continued to play a major part in Itobaal's trading strategy. The northern Hebrew kingdom of Samaria was to be integrated into the Tyrian business hierarchy as had the kingdoms of Sidon, Byblos and Arvad. Itobaal
hoped to cement the partnership begun by his precursor, Hiram
through a dynastic marriage between his daughter Jezebel and Israel's new king, Ahab, son of the chariot general, Omri.[56]

Under the revised chronology, the period known as Iron IB now
coincides with age of Itobaal and Ahab.[57] While the archaeological
record from Phoenicia itself remains scanty, several sites in Palestine, redated to this period, now show evidence of expanded Tyrian
direct investment on Israelite soil. Hazor and Megiddo have yielded
strong evidence of Tyrian architecture and therefore the presence of
Itobaal's guilds of craftsmen. Nowhere is this more evident than in
the capital of the Omrides, Samaria, where Israel's court historians
reported the presence of a *kârum*-settlement of Tyrian merchants in
the city centre. Phoenician ivory and luxuries became status goods,
defining the life-styles of Samaria's political and commercial elites
and, a century later, provoking the populist indignation of the Ju-
dean prophet Amos, who denounced the social inequalities perpetrated by massive Phoenician investment.[58] Such inequalities, resulting from the growth of new enterprises and the concentration of
wealth in the hands of those able to profit from the new iron-working technologies would recur among other Tyrian clients. Perhaps
the most renowned of Tyrian exports, Phoenician ivory artifacts

were likely sculptured by guilds of workmen in Tyrian colonies on foreign soil, from there to adorn Israelite mansions, Greek temples, Assyrian palaces and princely royal tombs in the Mediterranean.[59] Smaller Phoenician commercial settlements were set up in Galilee and Carmel during the ninth century, their presence betrayed by large stacks of jugs manufactured by the potters of Tyre or by resident potters copying the Tyrian style. At sites in the territories of Asher, Zebulun, Issachar and northern Manasseh including Hurbat Rosh Zayit, Achzib, Akko, Tell Keisan, Tell Abu Hawam, Shikmona, Tell Mevorakh, and Tel Michal, the material culture of the period was "distinctly Phoenician".[60] Mostly situated near the seashore or in the midst of grain fields, these settlements appear to have been the residences of a network of Tyrian *mkrm*, charged with the duty of purchasing and organising shipments of Israelite grain by land and sea to the north and distributing the goods made in Itobaal's workshops along with the copper of Cyprus. The settlements along the coast of Asher and northern Manasseh in Israel reinforced his merchants' control of Palestine's maritime trade routes. In these Phoenician business colonies, and especially the settlements along the coast, vessels from Cyprus, known to the specialist as White Painted I Ware, were buried alongside the pots and vases from Tyre. At the same time as Cypriot pottery appears in Israel, Tyrian pottery appears in Palestine and Cyprus. The presence of the Cypriot pottery has been taken by archaeologists as confirming not only that extensive trade went on between Cyprus, Phoenicia and Israel, but that that trade was managed and monopolised within the hierarchical framework of Itobaal's tightly organised network of public enterprise, subsidiaries and partnerships. The planting posts in Cyprus, begun by Ugaritic *mkrm*, were now continued by the *mkrm* of Tyre. A web of commercial settlement and direct investment now extended from Tyre to the Lebanese coast, across to the shore of Cyprus and south to Ahab's Galilee and Samaria. The trail of jugs not only traced the spread of Tyre, Inc. but seemed to give silent testimony to the internalisation advantages its business organisations possessed, showing "the internal movement of goods between the Phoenicians in Dor and those in Cyprus, where intensive Phoenician settlements should have begun".[61]

Breaking out from its Phoenician redoubt during the period of Hiram and Solomon the culture of Sidon and Tyre spread over the

forests, fields and cities of southern Lebanon and northern Israel
during the early ninth century BC time of Itobaal and Ahab. Inspired by a worldly strategy of geopolitics and monopolistic economics, the attempt to create a Levantine economic bloc and perhaps a Tyrian superstate did not go unresisted in the two Israelite
kingdoms. Even if trade was not the sole function of the temple, religion and commerce were inextricably wed in the magical societies
of the ancient East. Gods, priests and shrines played an indispensable part in the hierarchical culture of business in every society beginning from Sumer on. Gods and goddesses were personified as
merchants. Sumer's Enlil, for example, was worshipped as Merchant of the Wide World. Artisans and *tamkâru* had their patron
gods to whom they believed they owed the knowledge of technology
and business itself. The Egyptian smith praised Ptah; the Greek,
Vulcan. The Canaanites was no exception, the Ras Shamra texts
praise Hayyin as the patron of all Canaanite metalworkers: "Hayyin
would go up to the bellows...To melt silver, to beat out gold. He'd
melt silver by the thousands [of shekels], Gold he'd melt by the
myriads."[62] This craftsman-god, also known as Kothar, was even
more involved in the market, building palaces for Baal from the ce-
dars of Lebanon and trading across the Levant and the Aegean:

> *There now, be off on thy way...to Kaphtor, the throne that he sits on,*
> *Hikpat the land of his portion. From a thousand fields, ten thousand*
> *acres, at Kotha[r']s feet bow and fall down, prostrate thee and do him*
> *honor. And say unto Kothar-wa-Khasis, Repeat unto Hayyin of the*
> *Handicrafts: Message of Pui[ssant Baal, Word of the Powerful Hero].*[63]

Fear of Enki, Ashur, Marduk and others was also believed to guarantee honest business practices. The notions that gods bestowed
the blessings of commerce on men and supervised its affairs served
to underpin both the mixed economy and the feudal forms of business organisation found in Ashur, Babylon and Phoenicia. Studying
a variety of Near Eastern commercial organisations, Morris Silver
recently insisted that the religious restrictions and standards of behaviour set upon merchants not only "lowered their costs of cohesion (joint action)" but "facilitated monopolistic business practices
(i.e., restricting production to raise prices and profits".[64] Every
guild celebrated the rituals of its patron god or goddess. The origin

of modern patent laws, enshuring that certain firms would posses and retain organisational advantages in a highly mercantilist world had its origin in the control of economically valuable information by priests who considered it sacred to the gods who possessed it:

> *the magical/holy component associated with new technologies served (like modern patent laws) to reserve them and their economic gains for the innovator and, thereby, encouraged profit-seeking individuals to invest in intellectual capital and consequently to benefit society at large.* [65]

As in the rest of the ancient East, temples in Phoenicia became centres and protectors of trade. Business dealings were conducted under the watchful eyes of the various *baalim,* whose shrines could be found in ports and other major cities, along trade routes and at the border of Phoenician territory, Mt. Carmel being a perfect example. Contracts were drawn, oaths sworn and deals transacted in the presence of their statues and images. The potential wrath of deities against merchants guilty of fraud or wilful breach of contract served to legitimise the public regulation of prices and markets. Priests standardised weights and measures and acted as notaries. Temples served as banks and warehouses storehouses attracting private depositors of silver and other goods. What Canaanite, after all, would want to default on a loan to the priests of Baal-Melqart, the storm god, who might withhold both financial prosperity and rain?[66]

The role of the temple in Itobaal's strategy of international commerce and production itself and that of his heirs cannot be underestimated. Tyrian metal-working shops in Cyprus "communicated directly with a nearby temple" whose walls were covered with graffiti of ships.[67] Not only in Cyprus, but in Ugarit, Byblos and on the shores of the Red Sea, Phoenician temples incorporated anchors into the temple walls. Well-organised under their hierarchy and tax-exempt, temples enjoyed a competitive advantage over private firms allowing them to increase their share of asset ownership and income. Public institutions, temples nevertheless needed and utilised the capital of the *mkrm* and other private entrepreneurs. When a guild of Itobaal's merchants took up residence in a nearby country, they would erect a temple which would give heavenly sanction and earthly direction to their international investments and partnerships. If Cypriots, Arameans, Hebrews and others could accept and incorporate the worship of Baal and other Phoenician gods and goddesses alongside their own, it would provide new organisational and internalisation advantages for the Tyrian trading network. In a magic-oriented society like Tyre, a religious amalgamation with her trading partners represented "a positive incentive for individuals or communities to reduce transaction costs by investing in the creation of common gods".[68] Persuading foreign partners to acknowledge Tyrian gods or goddesses engendered a mutual trust through which *tapputu* and other close business arrangements could be cemented. If the technical secrets of shipbuilding, bronze and iron technology and the knowledge of markets belonged to gods like Kothar and Melqart, to be strictly guarded by their priests, the transfer of those secrets and the goods they produced went hand-in-hand with the spread and adoption of Tyrian religion. References to Phoenician gods in the places where the *mkrm* settled would therefore "signify the impact of a new technology".[69]

The chief religious cult of Tyre, that of Baal-Melqart ("King of the City"), seems to have been unknown before the city rose to commercial power and established its enlarged kingdom on the Lebanese mainland. Byblos had worshipped a whole assembly of gods, some outranking others, who ruled in the affairs of men by consent and consensus. Moving with the times, Melqart was a far more kingly Baal, ruler over many lesser *baalim* who dwelt in mountains, forests, springs, and other cultic locations and were represented forces of nature. As Tyre under Hiram, who likely created the cult and Itobaal, who promoted it abroad, became more powerful, so did the international reputation of Melqart, a Viking-like figure with a horned hat and a battle axe. Melqart pictured the ideal Tyrian king. Founder of Tyre, he was not only the god of rain and storm but of prosperity. Inventor of the dye industry, Melqart was also its patron. As Tyrian seapower grew, Melqart would soon acquire the title of Patron of Westerly Navigation. Temples in his name would soon be erected in not only Samaria, but Syria, Cyprus, Malta, Carthage, Sicily, Malta and most importantly, Spain.[70]

The more international temples expanded, the more they took on the structure characteristic of modern multinational corporations. Egyptian, Sumerian, Assyro-Babylonian, Hittite and Greek as well as Canaanite cults often had "branch temples in several cities".[71]

Local sanctuaries were always in communication with main centres and the financial connections of one temple to another were quite strong, with large amounts of capital and goods being transferred among them. The temple hierarchy of Tyre, exported along with Phoenician dyes, lumber and tools was to become the prime example of this mode. In Phoenicia at the dawn of the Iron Age, a multinational religion in which the gods themselves were traders provided, along with the crown, important advantages of internalisation in dealing with an ever-widening circle of foreign business relationships and markets:

> In explaining financial connections among cults or administrative controls of one cult by another or the sharing of temples or the merger of cults or temple complexes, the economist would of course be inclined to stress explanations in terms of efficient organization or the exercise by mother cults of quality controls over franchiser cults or economies of scale or scope. Standard explanations stress battles over supremacy and cultic imperialism or mere 'friendly connections' between sites worshipping the same deity. [72]

Itobaal's traders expanded north and east as well as south and west. Following the footsteps of the Eblaites, Sargonids and the *tamkâru* of Old Assyria, Tyrian traders and priests opened branch temples and colonies on the Gulf of Alexandra, in the region of Cilicia once traversed by Pusu-ken's donkey caravans. The Tyrian settlement of Myrandrios controlled access to both Anatolia and the Euphrates, along the banks of which Assyrian records of the ninth century B. C. mention the likely presence of yet another Tyrian commercial agency. Not only the ever-present Phoenician jugs, but Phoenician inscriptions in the heart of the Aramaic-Hittite territory affirm direct investment in the strategic territories of southern Turkey and northern Syria before and after 850 BC A monument in Aleppo by the famous King Ben-Hadad of Aram himself, dedicated to Melqart implies not only the presence of a temple of the latter nearby, but of the introduction of both Tyrian political influence and technology. A similar monument has been uncovered in Carchemish, along with strong Tyrian influences in both craftsmanship and architecture:

*Thanks to a network of factorships and trading posts in place in the
Gulf of Alexandretta and the coastal region of Cyprus, Tyre was able to
secure a monopoly of the trade in metals and slaves in Cilicia, the Taurus Mountains and the Euphrates and, at the same time, to control the
sea routes to Cyprus and Crete.[73]*

Itobaal's economic achievement in erecting a vast multinational
business organisation was only partially successful in Israel due to
the unique nature of the latter's social and religious traditions. The
duel between Elijah and the priests of Melqart which took place on
Mount Carmel, on the border between Tyrian and Israelite territory had economic and cultural as well as spiritual implications. The
Biblical account of the religious contest strongly implied that the
450 priests of Melqart and the 400 priests of the local shrines
"which eat at Jezebel's table" were state-supported.[74] The interlocking nature between crown merchants and crown priests could be
further confirmed. Elijah's remarks to these priests, taunting them
that perhaps the unresponding Melqart was "in a journey", hinted
strongly that the Israelite prophet knew the Baal-myths well, particularly those that exalted Melqart as the Prince of Traders.[75]

    While the Elijah-story suggests that most of Israel's elites and
population now worshipped Melqart alongside the God of Abraham, the arrangement was to unravel around 840 BC with the rise
of the House of Jehu. Himself another chariot general and an Israelite nationalist who preferred the domestic state-sponsored cult of
Jeroboam to the imported cult of Melqart, Jehu in his famous
slaughter of the Melqart hierarchy nevertheless demonstrated the
principle ultimate royal jurisdiction over the Melqart hierarchy.[76]
While Phoenician investment in Israel and lesser forms of Baalism
would survive until the fall of Samaria in 722 BC, the merchant-ad-
venturers of Tyre were obviously to be more comfortable dealing
with more polytheistic clients.

Chapter 6

Melqart, CEO

The First Intercontinental Investment Empire:
850-600 BC

The third and climactic phase of Tyre's trade expansion was ultimately inspired by the frightening resurgence of the very nation that
itself had pioneered in multinational enterprise and foreign direct
investment. Following the defeat of its last king, Ishme-Dagan, by
the armies of Hammurabi, the Old Assyrian kingdom passed first
under the dominion of Babylon and then of the Indo-Aryan kingdom of Mitanni. Though the records of Assyria were to be silent for
several centuries, the institutions, native dynasty and cult of Ashur
survived despite a period of foreign domination. The archives of the
El Amarna period, however, show a new, independent Assyrian
kingdom had regained her independence under kings such as
Ashur-uballit I (1365-1330), Tukulti-Ninurta I (1244-1208) and
Tiglath-Pileser I (1114-1076, all dates according to the traditional
chronology). Challenging Babylonian commercial control of the
Mesopotamian world, the new Middle Assyrian kingdom fright-
ened the Kassite kings. One of the Amarna letters (EA 9) records
Burnaburiash II of Babylonia asking his traditional Egyptian ally to
throttle the vigorous new trading competition emerging on the Upper Euphrates:

*Now, as far as my Assyrian vassals are concerned, I certainly did not
send them to you. Why did they come on their own authority to your*

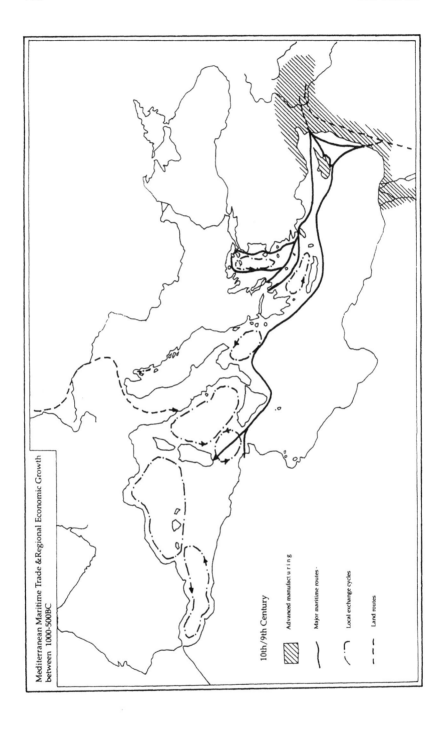

Mediterranean Maritime Trade &Regional Economic Growth
between 1000-500BC

10th/9th Century

▨ Advanced manufacturing

〈 Major maritime routes

〈 Local exchange cycles

- - Land routes

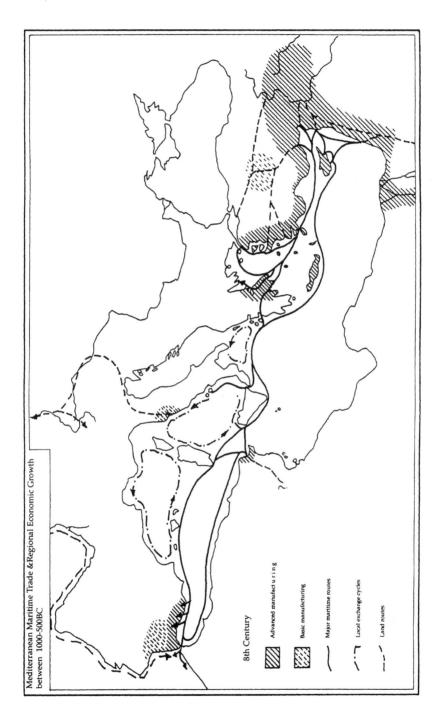

Mediterranean Maritime Trade &Regional Economic Growth
between 1000-500BC

8th Century

Advanced manufacturing

Basic manufacturing

Major maritime routes

Local exchange cycles

Land routes

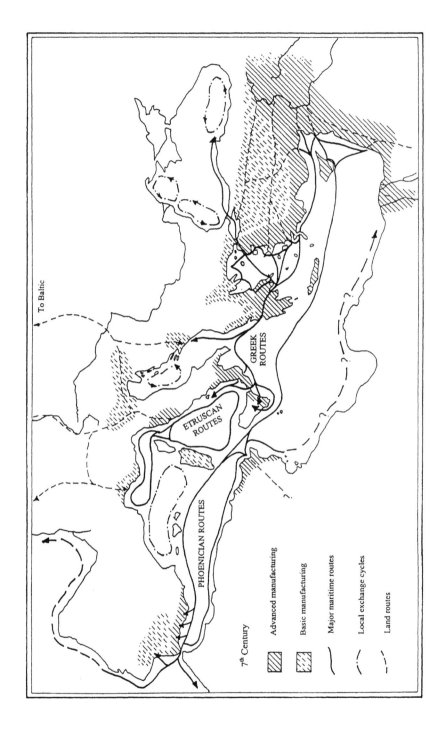

7ᵗʰ Century

Advanced manufacturing

Basic manufacturing

Major maritime routes

Local exchange cycles

Land routes

To Baltic

GREEK ROUTES

ETRUSCAN ROUTES

PHOENICIAN ROUTES

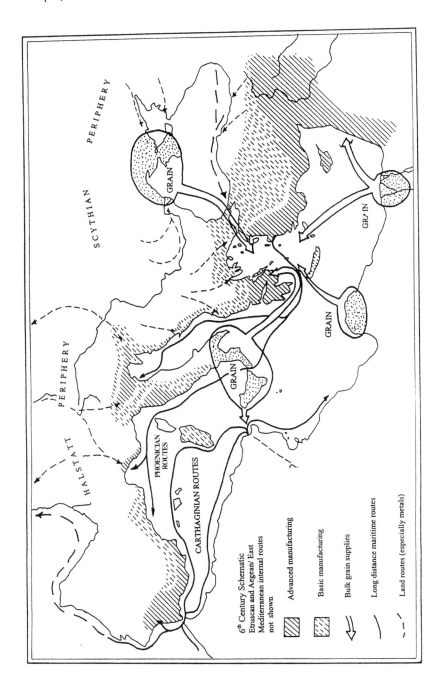

6th Century Schematic
Etruscan and Aegean/East
Mediterranean internal routes
not shown

Advanced manufacturing

Basic manufacturing

Bulk grain supplies

Long distance maritime routes

Land routes (especially metals)

country? If you love me, they will not conduct any business. Send them away to me empty-handed.[1]

The Middle Assyrian kings faced the same economic circumstances as their Old Assyrian ancestors centuries before. Still landlocked and resource-poor as they had been before their long period of vassaldom, the Middle Assyrian kings needed once again to open their trading outlets to the east and west. Middle Assyria and its Neo-Assyrian successor represented a very different society from that which once sponsored the merchant colonies of Kanesh centuries before. The far more aggressive methods used by Ashur-uballit and his heirs to secure and defend their resources and markets would begin to earn Assyria her reputation as one of the most warlike nations in history. Marching into the foothills of Iran and subjugating Babylonia, Tukulti-Ninurta I tried to seize Babylonia's locational advantages for himself, uniting Mesopotamia under his rule until his assassination. Tightening its control over the northern half of Iraq, Assyria rebuilt itself on a foundation of militaristic absolutism not unlike that of the Hohenzollerns in seventeenth- and eighteenth-century Brandenburg-Prussia. Ancient Assyria, like modern Prussia, was less a state with an army than an army with a state. Assyrian nobles became a restricted hereditary caste from which an incomparable general staff and a professional corps of royal officials were drawn. Ruling through them, the king was supreme judge over a population subject to taxation and conscription.[2]

Assyria's mounting power suffered occasional reverses. In eclipse during the time of David and Solomon, it emerged more ferocious than ever under Ashurnasirpal II (883-59) and Shalmaneser III (859-24, traditional and revised dates the same). Under these two kings Assyria fully embraced the ideology and the policy of military terrorism that would make her the scourge of the ancient world. Blocked by the kingdoms of Urartu, Aram and Israel, her ancient trade routes to the west could only be opened by the ruthless application of military force. Marching westward, the armies of Assyria, spearheaded by shock troops of cavalry and chariot armed with iron weapons stormed into the cities of Syria and Lebanon. Special marine battalions floated across river barriers on goatskin packs; battering rams and catapults ancestral to their Roman counterparts tore down the walls of Aramean cities; mounds of human skulls were stacked outside their ruins. Only the combined resistance of a coalition led by Ahab of Israel and Ben-hadad of Damascus at the Battle of Qarqar in 853 BC in which several lesser Phoenician states participated delayed the Assyrian conquest of the Levant and Palestine for a century.

Lying in the path of the seemingly invincible Assyrian armies, neither Tyre nor Sidon actively resisted them, preferring to deter them through a policy of economic appeasement. Silver, gold, and purple cloth flowed from Tyre's commercial ventures to the new Assyrian capitals of Nineveh and Halah.[3] Royal Assyrian annals catalogued the growing redirection of Phoenician trade to Assyria. Ashur-nasirpal II received tribute from Tyre, Sidon and Byblos in the form of "gold, silver, tin, copper, copper containers, linen garments with multicolored trimmings...ebony, boxwood, [and] ivory from walrus tusk".[4] Shalmaneser III, despite his inability to conquer the region, still so overawed the coastal cities that he was able to collect tribute "on ships from the inhabitants of Tyre and Sidon".[5]

Assyria once again fell into a "Weimar period" of weakness and even civil war during the reigns of Shalmaneser IV (782-73), Ashurdan III (772-55) and Ashur-Nirari V (754-45), coinciding with an Israelite resurgence under Jeroboam II in Samaria and Uzziah in Jerusalem. In 745 BC, however, a usurping general, possibly a Babylonian named Pulu, seized the Ninevite throne, assumed the title Tiglath-Pileser (III) and began to turned the kingdom into a Neo-Assyrian Empire lasting for a century and a half and ultimately conquered virtually the entire Near East from Egypt to western Iran. The entire Syro-Palestinian region held immense economic and strategic importance for Tiglath-Pileser and those kings who would follow him, who needed access to timber, wheatlands and seaports. Delayed for a century, the Assyrian storm finally burst upon Aram and the northern kingdom of Israel in 733 and 732 BC in the form of thousands of chariots and tens of thousands of soldiers overwhelming both of those kingdoms. Thousands of Israelites and Arameans were exiled from homelands which now became Assyrian provinces. Tiglath-Pileser died in 726, but his immediate heirs, Shalmaneser V (726-22 BC), Sargon II (721-705 BC) completed the conquest of northern Israel. Tyre and Sidon, however, preserved their precarious independence for a number of years. Dominant on land, Assyria's kings and generals had as little enthusiasm for invading Tyre as Napoleon had for invading England following the destruction of his navy by Lord Nelson at Trafalgar in 1805.[6]

Instead of challenging Tyre's vast armada in a costly naval war, the rulers of the Assyrian Empire found it much more profitable to preserve the city's nominal independence and commercial empire. Just as Hitler sought to preserve Swedish and Swiss independence and the rulers of Beijing the independence of Hong Kong prior to 1997, so did Tiglath-Pileser III and his heirs. The merchant-princes of Tyre, Inc. were still free to pursue strategies of maximum profit and commercial expansion, providing the net result enhanced the war economy of the Neo-Assyrian Empire. Assyrian inspectors were stationed in the harbour districts of Tyre and Sidon with full powers to regulate Phoenician trade and redirect it for the benefit of Assyria.[7]

Under Assyrian overlordship the final stage of Tyre's own strategy of overseas colonisation and investment reached full maturity. In a world where Assyrian swords controlled the Near Eastern markets, food, and water supply, the princes and merchants of Tyre would have to adapt their investment and trading strategy accordingly. This adaptation, begun with the payments of tribute in the days of Ashurnasirpal II, would increase steadily along with Assyrian power. At first supplying Assyria with luxury goods and textiles, Tyrian trading firms quickly faced Assyrian demand for the copper of Kition and other precious metals to equip her state-of-the-art weaponry. Assyrian need for massive amounts of silver to finance her armies was insatiable once Tiglath-Pileser III and his successors decided to pursue the course of conquest and empire. From the Assyrian point of view, only Tyre had the means of access to potential resources beyond the Great Sea and the ability to provide them for Nineveh's vast new empire. So long as they did not trade with Egypt, Tyre and Sidon were far more useful to Assyria as a supplier and financier than as a conquered possession. From the Phoenician point of view, such a role not only guaranteed survival but promised profit on a scale large enough to justify risking unprecedented expansion of the scale of trade and investment.[8]

Only Tyre's skilled shippers, guild organisations temple hierarchy and information capital in the form of knowledge of maritime conditions, metal deposits, smelting and markets enabled her to possess the threefold advantages of location, organisation and internalisation advantages cited by John Dunning to justify her firms' resorting to transnational investment on a grand scale in the eighth and seventh centuries BC. With their home offices headquartered on an island strategically placed at the junction of three continents, Tyrian companies were also placed at the locus of the trade routes of the Neo-Assyrian Empire and the Mediterranean. Command of the sea enabled Phoenician firms to set up posts and offices easily accessible not only to farmlands and mines in host countries, but also to the head offices in Tyre itself. The princes of Tyre and the priests of Melqart presided over a well-oiled multinational trading machine offering the advantages of internalisation in the form of royal and temple support, contractual partnerships, feudal loyalties and family connections.[9] The large-scale intercontinental seaborne trade now undertaken by Tyre's merchants could be profitable only for a "solid and solvent organization" of shippers with a huge fleet of vessels, underwritten by temple and palace, capable of transporting precious ores and finished goods in bulk sufficient to absorb any potential losses while reaping substantial gains:

> *The expansion to the west and the founding of the colonies in southern Spain could only be undertaken by Tyre when she was sure of attaining her objectives: guaranteed silver ore and plentiful food resources, and the certainty of real economic rewards.*[10]

In the ninth and most of the eighth centuries BC, Tyre's shippers at first supplied the Assyrian market from Itobaal's old offices in Carchemish and Cilicia, but as Assyria herself overran those regions and required even more metals and goods, the merchants of Tyre would have to draw upon new sources of ore from regions far to the west. Under Itobaal's successors, Balmazzer III (846-41 BC) and Mattin (840-32 BC), the island city increased her production of goods and began to expand along a new east-west trading axis. With her traditional Israelite partner in civil turmoil under the rule of the anti-Baalist House of Jehu and her supplies of metal from Anatolia either threatened or now inadequate, Tyre herself now suffered food shortages and a need for fresh sources of metals for her workshops. The court, priests, sailors and merchants responded with an aggressive policy of colonisation and investment in far distant stra-

tegic locations on the islands and coastlines of the Mediterranean
hundreds of kilometres from home.[11]

The launching of Tyre's new westward ventures was aided by the
long history of Phoenician colonisation and investment in Cyprus,
which greatly expanded in the reign of Itobaal's successors. The
core of Phoenician settlement and activity remained the site of Kition, founded for the purpose of controlling the island's copper
mines. By 740 BC Kition was flourishing when Tiglath-Pileser's
armies first entered Phoenicia. Rich archaeological finds, including
a temple of Astarte, have been unearthed on the site of Kition. Itself ruled by a servant of the Prince of Tyre, Kition became the
model for Carthage and other western colonies to come. Settlements at Golgoi, Idalim, Tamassos, Marion, and Capethos on Cyprus followed that of Kition. Evidence of metal-working in each of
them suggests the intriguing possibility that these later settlements
were filled with guilds of craftsmen engaging in processing copper
goods not only from the Cypriot mines but eventually from the later Tyrian settlements to be established in the central and western
Mediterranean. Guilds of metalworkers were first mentioned in the
Ugaritic texts as royal dependents. Led by an elder, guild members
did royal military homage like many other merchants in Phoenician society. Obtaining their metals from the prince's stores, they at
first produced for the crown alone. The guilds were hereditary,
their members often receiving royal fiefs in the same manner as
other Phoenician traders. The tradition of an inherited practice
persisted into Tyrian and even Carthaginian times, where one
found the inscriptions of gold-, silver-, copper- and ironsmiths in
Cyprus, southern Phoenicia and Carthage. By this time many of
the guilds were composed of smiths who no longer were royal dependents, but were now self-employed. Nevertheless, feudal loyalties, partnerships and supervision and finance of these Cypro-
Phoenician enterprises by the temple-priests of Kition suggests
Phoenician craftsmen spread abroad still participated in an internalised, managed trade in the form a of Japanese-style form of
shinchintaisha (subcontracting). Under this arrangement, trading
companies in Kition, directed by harbourmaster and temple,
would have permanent and perhaps even hereditary partnerships
with guilds of metalcasters who would turn the copper they were
supplied into finished goods.[12]

The Kition office, functioning as a subsidiary office might today, also managed and supervised Tyre's Aegean subsidiary operations or at least subcontracted shipments of copper and finished goods to private Phoenician traders sailing there. Ugaritic merchants formerly voyaged to Rhodes, Thasos, Kytherias, Melos, Thera and, most importantly, Crete, where Sinaranu held a monopoly of trade. There was, though, little or no evidence of Tyrian direct investment in these regions. What is today known of the "Sidonian" Aegean trader emerges in the writings of Homer and the portrait, given the bard's dislike of money-making pursuits, is less than praiseworthy. The Iliad and the Odyssey described "Sidonians" as very skilled sailors, smiths and weavers, but also as greedy emporos, or private traders peddling garments, cloth, and finished goods like silver cups and bowls, instead of the aristocratic *tamkâru* they knew from Hatti or even Ugarit.[13] Written later, the Odyssey, however, refers to year-long voyages of "Sidonians" sailing to the ends of the earth, all the while manipulating the trade of the Aegean on terms not too favorable to Greeks. The evidence of Homer and the sparseness of Phoenician finds in the Aegean suggests that the region was more peripheral to the Tyrian commercial empire and was worked by independent traders and subcontractors from Cyprus and points west rather than being a major recipient of Phoenician direct investment, which was directed further to the south and west.[14] Other Tyrian settlements, again of traders rather than resident merchant-princes, also sprang up in the Nile Delta, their presence betrayed by red-burnished pottery. Only in less-powerful or less-developed countries, however, would the merchants of Tyre attempt the major projects of resource exploitation, value-added production and foreign direct investment that could be described as "multinational".[15]

Kition would become even more important as a distribution centre for the more distant investment colonies founded on the shores of the central and western Mediterranean in the decades before and after 800 BC These distant settlements played the key role in the commercial strategy of the Tyrian princes beginning with Pumayyaton, the famous Pygmalion, who reigned from 831-785 BC The archaeological record of these settlements is more extensive than that found in Tyre itself. The most famous of these colonies was founded near Tunis in 814 BC by Elissa, great-granddaughter of Itobaal, grand-niece of Jezebel and sister of Pygmalion.[16] Bearing the same

name given to Kition, Kart- or Qart- Hardasht, or ("New City") or
Carthage, as it came to be called by classical writers, along with her
sister African colonies of Hadrumeto and Utica represented,
throughout the eighth and seventh centuries BC, the North African
subsidiary of the Tyrian commercial network. The main purpose of
the African colonies, situated to control what would eventually become the ancient world's granary, was clearly food production.
With supplies from his unstable Israelite granary becoming more
uncertain, Pumayyaton's merchants sought to guarantee themselves
and their growing island population an overseas food supply relatively secure from marching Aramean and Mesopotamian armies.[17]

Ruins of smaller Tyrian settlements were also found in the northwest of Sicily, on the European side of the Tunisian narrows, at Motya, Panormus and Solunto. Large numbers of the same Tyrian jugs
found in ninth- and eighth-century BC Cyprus, Syria and Palestine
appeared not only in the Phoenician colonies in Tunisia but on Sicily, Sardinia, Malta, Gozo, Lampedusa and Pantellaria. The massive pottery finds suggested the simultaneous foundation of a whole
web of central colonies intended to control the shipping routes in
both the central and western Mediterranean in what was a matter of
the utmost national security. Overseas colonies, each supervised by
a naval and temple hierarchy subject to head offices in Kition and/
or Tyre itself, became the final weapon in a battle for economic survival with powerful military implications. If such an explanation
seems far-fetched, the activities of the British East India Company
and Royal Navy occupying the very same territories in more recent
times based itself on the same reasoning.[18] Tyrian business, organised along Japanese-style feudal-military lines by soldier- and sailor-
merchants, considered settling the islands between Calabria and
Tunis "a response to certain basically strategic imperatives".[19] Motya, built on a secure island harbour off the northwestern coast of
Sicily resembled the port of Tyre itself. Founded around its Melqart
temple, the site remained sparsely populated until about 650 BC,
when "large industrial complexes and ware houses" suggesting "the
early appearance of specialized industries-iron and purple" emerged.[20]

Sardinia was more thickly settled by the Tyrians than Sicily. Tyrian activity confined itself to the small harbour-island of Sulcis, located off the southwestern shore, during most of the eighth century

BC Following the pattern established elsewhere, the temple and the marketplace were the first institutions to be erected not only in Sulcis but in her daughter colonies, with civil functions being assumed by the shrine of Melqart. A Phoenician inscription deciphered from Nora not only dated the first settlement of merchants to the reign of Pumayyaton, but illuminated the key role of the army in winning Tyre her trading rights on a hostile island. The inscription records the victory of Milkaton, son of Shebna, general of King Pummay who fought with the Sardinians, drove them out and established peace for himself and his army with the defeated natives.[21] From about 700 BC on, a wave of Tyrian settlement dominated by soldiers, sailors and merchants spread over the southern half of the island, erecting a fortified belt around Sulcis anchored by strongpoints at Salcis, Nora, Cagliari, Bythia, Carloforte and Thairos.[22] The systematic creation of a half-dozen seaports and merchant colonies, in close proximity to one another on the southern coast except for Thairos of the southern coast indicated that the Tyrian subsidiary in Sulcis and those directing it far to the east were pursuing a "genuine territorial strategy...of controlling the hinterland".[23]

The excavations on Sardinia indicated an organised pyramidal relationship among the Tyrian colonies. Founded as a way-station and naval base to guard the routes to the west and east, Sulcis eventually became the site of yet another subsidiary of Tyre, Inc, supervising the extraction of Sardinia's extensive silver and lead deposits. The presence of many military personnel in these colonies further suggested royal accountability of the merchants Sardinia through Sulcis to those either of Kition or directly to the vizier and harbourmaster of Tyre itself. The presence of a single temple of Melqart and burial ground in Sulcis indicated that the city's merchant-princes maintained overlordship over the newer settlements until 400 BC, when a second burial ground, erected in Mt. Sinai, indicated the interior's independence. Given the need of massive capital investment and direction to sustain all of these settlements and their activities, the existence of a royally-directed but market-oriented multinational business organisation is highly plausible:

In this case, the founding of the colony led to a need to bring the coast and the coastal valleys swiftly under its sway, that is, to establish economic and territorial autonomy in relation to the interior and to guarantee peaceful exploitation of the agricultural land and metal deposits. [24]

Impressive though they were, Tyre's subsidiaries in the central Mediterranean owed their eventual rapid growth to an even greater thrust of investment directed to the farthest end of the Mediterranean itself. The settlement pattern established in Cyprus, Sardinia and Sicily repeated itself on a grander scale in the southwestern corner of the Iberian peninsula. Through their commercial network, Tyre's merchants had long known that the land of Tarshish possessed what Diodorus of Sicily described as "the most abundant and most known sources of silver" capable of returning great revenues to anyone with the will, organisation and capital willing to exploit them. [25] Classical references to Phoenicians being in the West from the time of a Trojan War, conventionally dated before 1100 BC are often dismissed by modern historians, who can find no evidence of Canaanite activity there before approximately 770 BC Peter James' new lower chronology lowers the date of the Trojan War so that a Phoenician explorer would reach Spain in the days of Hiram and Solomon. [26] The story of these exploratory voyages was recorded by Strabo the geographer, who wrote that a temple oracle inspired Tyrian sea-merchants to send a voyage to the Pillars of Hercules (Gibraltar), which turned back when a sacrificial omen was not favourable to their colonisation. The same fate befell a second voyage landing near what is now Cape Trafalgar. The third voyage, reaching a narrow island in the mouth of the Guadalquivir was more successful, founding a temple of Melqart, there known as Herakles on the site of Gades, now modern Cadiz. [27] The link between temple and commerce Strabo hinted that the priests of Melqart had market knowledge, including knowledge of the silver deposits further up the Guadalquivir conveyed by earlier Phoenician voyagers who learned about them from native Spaniards, Sardinians or Greeks. Did the temple and court discourage the earlier colonisation efforts because market conditions were not favourable until the time of Assyrian expansion?

Gades was the centrepiece of a coordinated strategy of foreign colonisation and investment. If Diodorus is credible, the Tyrian colonies in the central and western Mediterranean all grew and prospered as a result of the success of the investment in Spain. Trading their luxury goods for Spanish silver, the merchants of Tyre transported the silver in bulk shipments to the east. The profit margins were so huge as to be able to finance further colonisation and investment in the central Mediterranean:

And the result was that the Phoenicians, as in the course of many years they prospered greatly, thanks to commerce of this kind, sent forth many colonies, some to Sicily and its neighbouring islands, and others to Libya, Sardinia, and Iberia.[28]

Strabo and Diodorus implied Tyre's new western and central Mediterranean operations remained in the hands of a well-organised hierarchy on the Ugaritic model. The temple of Melqart in Gades played a key part, according to leading Ibero-Phoenician scholar Maria Eugenia Aubet, in supervising the entire venture corresponding to that of the Phoenician branch-temples in Sulcis and Moyta: "the first Tyrian colonies in the west...started...as sanctuaries administered by a priestly group directly linked to the interests of Tyre" to be very plausible.[29] The massive Gades shrine was, at the same time, itself subject to the Melqart temple in Tyre, from which it derived its architecture, decorative patterns, twin columns, three sacrificial altars and eternal flame. A huge administrative building housed a powerful Melqart priesthood destined to remain in the hands of a handful of aristocratic families.[30] As representatives of a deity worshipped as the supernatural King of Tyre, the Melqart-priests of Gades exercised an immeasurable control over Ibero-Phoenician business. The temple became the commercial as well as religious bond between Gades and Tyre as both guarantor of honest exchange and source of finance capital:

In distant places where he [Melqart] possessed a temple, his function was a very concrete one: to ensure the tutelage of the temple of Tyre and the monarchy over the commercial enterprise, thus converting the colony into an extension of Tyre; and also to guarantee the right of asylum and hospitality which, in distant lands, was equivalent to endorsing contracts and commercial exchanges.[31]

Once again the focal point of the Canaanite diaspora, this time on a grand scale, the Gades temple used fear of Melqart to regulate both society and marketplace. Keeping a register of all transactions, the priests had supreme authority in business matters, enforcing honest deals and consistent exchange rates, weights and measures. As in Tyre, Moyta and Sulcis, the temple itself played its part in a precise political and economic strategy. Phoenician shippers and traders burnt sacrifices to Melqart as protector on their long voyages from Gades to Tyre. Soon after the foundation of their new island temple, the worshippers of Melqart journeyed up the Guadalquivir relying upon the renown of their supreme Baal to help persuade the natives to join in a permanent multinational business arrangement. As in the east, the Phoenicians hoped that the Iberians, in becoming trading partners, would assimilate not only Tyrian technology but Tyrian religion as well, admitting Melqart and Astarte to their native pantheons.[32]

The merchants of Gades and their mentors in Tyre hoped that the prestige of the horned *Baal* would enable them to reach the 100 kilometres-long band of silver and copper lodes stretching across southwestern Spain and southern Portugal which lay in Iberian hands. Long before the first Phoenicians ever reached their shores, the fabled mines of Tarshish were being worked on a small scale by native Spaniards still using crude flint implements unchanged from those of the Stone Age. The heart of the silver deposits lay in the region of Huelva, halfway between the Guadalquivir and the Portuguese border, where over sixty mines operated in the Phoenician times. The greatest finds of all lay on the shores of the Rio Tinto ("Dyed River"), so named from its reddish colour acquired from the vast amounts of iron salts along its banks. Less than a kilometre to the west of the Rio Tinto lay the Cerro Salomón (Solomon's Hill), an Iberian settlement on the southern edge of an enormous silver lode some 800 metres long. Located some 750 metres west of the Rio Tinto, Solomon's Hill was itself some 300 metres south of the former site of a massive slag of silver 1,500 metres long, 500 metres wide and 6 metres thick. The slag accumulated at Rio Tinto was approximately 6 million metric tons.[33]

Excavations begun on the Cerro Salomón in 1962 by the Spanish archaeologists Antonio Blanco-Freijeiro and J.M. Luzón uncovered evidence of the ancient miners of Tarshish before and during the Phoenician era. Engineers as well as archaeologists, Blanco-Freijeiro and Rothenberg dug deeper on the sites of the Rio Tinto mines in 1974, 1975, 1979 and 1980. Working on the summit of Solomon's Hill itself, they soon excavated the miners' homes and workshops. Flimsy and rectangular with slate foundations and earthen floors, the shops themselves contained traces of traditional Iberian metalworking, stone mortars and pestles and bellows. Further down the slopes Blanco-Freijeiro and Rothenberg found larger concentrations of workshops where most of the silver was mixed with lead in furnaces carved into the workshop floor. The houses uncovered were full of Tyrian pottery, together with small amounts of silver slag showing that the mined ore was smelted in Iberian workshops and homes instead of large factories. A succession of strata containing Phoenician and other pottery levels from the nearby sites of Quebrantahuesos and Corta del Lago, correlated with other strata in the Near East, revealed the growth of metal production at Rio Tinto between 800 and 200 BC The lowest Late Bronze Age sites showed spotty silver production; the early Iron Age levels contained the familiar Phoenician jugs bearing olive oil and wine, together with evidence of systematic pit-mining and vastly increased production of silver. The tell-tale Phoenician presented strong evidence that the miners of Rio Tinto and other Iberian sites now had a new and much greater market for their production.[34]

All of the sites uncovered by Blanco-Freijeiro and his associates suggested the silver of Rio Tinto and other Huelvan sites was still extracted by the Iberians themselves and not the Phoenicians. Men of Tarshish continued to mine and smelt the precious metal by the same methods they used during the Bronze Age, only now on a much larger scale. Virtually all the mining technology used by the Iberians in the Iron Age was their own for they had little from the Phoenicians in an area in which they were professionals.[35]

Nevertheless, some technological borrowings were inevitable. The silver was now systematically worked from pits dug into the Corta del Lago and then smelted in bowl-shaped furnaces in the workshops of Solomon's Hill, applying a technique known in the Levant since the time of Hiram.[36] Working in their traditional fashion, the miners of Rio Tinto now did so on a much grander scale with new iron tools and a few new techniques bestowed upon them by the priests of Melqart and the guildmasters who worshipped at his temple: "So we are dealing with an advanced technology and a well-organized mining enterprise. It is not by chance that all this activity in Rio Tinto began at the same time as the first traces of a Phoenician presence appear in the region."[37]

Even if the massive expansion of silver production in the Huelva region did not result in the main from the exportation of Tyrian metalworking technology, the coming of the Canaanites certainly transformed the Iberian economy. The connection between the founding of Gades and the Iron Age revolution in Tartessos was indirect but profound. Now being systematically mined with new imported iron tools in huge quantities from the pits and galleries of Corta del Lago, bulk shipments of silver ore headed southward to meet an insatiable Phoenician demand. Extracted in the form of crude ore and processed into silver ingots, the silver of Tarshish was then floated down the Rio Tinto to the Iberian settlement of Huelva, now a centre of both metal-processing and trade between Tyrian and native merchants. Surrounded by silver mines itself, Huelva also was the site of furnaces for processing the ore of Solomon's Hill. A second route took raw silver from the mines of Aznalcóllar near Seville overland through Tejada La Vieja to the processing centre at San Bartolomé de Almonte, where it was processed into ingots before arriving at Gades.[38]

Neither the waterborne Rio Tinto route nor the overland Aznalcóllar-Tajada-San Bartolomé-Gades route represented a distinct commercial system in competition with the other. Instead, they represented two distinct ways of shipping silver within the framework of a highly efficient Iberian-Phoenician consortium. Silver ore sent south along the Aznalcóllar route was processed at the intermediate locations, some of which used fairly advanced metal-working techniques to add value to the raw ore, turning it into ingots, alloys or even finished goods before it arrived at the temple of Melqart in Gades. The new Iron Age production demanded both technical specialisation and professional direction of a large-scale operation in which ore was often processed in different places from where it was extracted. Such an operation was impossible without the creation of a complex organization, capable of coordinating simultaneously a series of mining centres (Cerro Salomón, Tejeda), metallurgical centres (San Bartholomé, Huelva) and embarkation points.[39] Increased demand for the silver which would eventually pay for Tyre's navies and Nineveh's armies necessitated more Iberian miners to fill that demand and an organisation of Iberian and Ibero-

Phoenician merchants and traders to feed, organise, house and supply them, as well as boatmen and teamsters to ship the ore and ingots to Tyre's harbour warehouses and workshops. As a result, a
well-organised Iberian corporate structure rapidly arose to control
and internalise the growing trade in silver and luxury goods.[40]

From Huelva and Gades, silver and silver goods were shipped in
Tyrian galleys to the settlements of Sulcis, Moyta or Kition and
eventually to Tyre itself, from whence other merchants would take it
by caravan and riverboat to the cities of the Assyrian empire. The
survival and prosperity of such a costly and extensive enterprise with
branches in these remote locations can only be explained in terms of
the enormous profitability and volume of the Gades silver trade and
the existence of a multinational organisation capable of internalising
that trade to the point where the operation could be self-sustaining,
with inexpensive operation profits reaped in the process:

What is more, the traffic in silver ore that we have just described
implies, in addition to considerable economic investment, a high
degree of coordination between the mine and the wharf, such as the
existence of an authority to centralise and coordinate those services.
Given that the chief beneficiary was Tyre, we are bound to think, as
the classical sources from Diodorus[41] insinuate, that Gades was acting under orders from Tyre by way of powerful commercial agents
installed in the west.[42]

The colonies of the well-organised Tyrian merchants were very
different from those of their more free-wheeling Greek contemporaries. The Phoenicians bought raw materials, processed them,
turned them into finished goods (value-added production), distributed the goods and maintained permanent trading and manufacturing operations in distant countries (foreign direct investment) all
within the framework of a vast consortium formed by the partnership of crown, temple, navy, private companies, private subcontractors and the miners of Tarshish:

*The structure of the Phoenician settlements was linked with the home-
land mercantile 'companies', in a family based organisation, which
might have been operating in towns like Ugarit or Tyre. Some of these
'companies' possessed large numbers of ships…[which] would provide
the capital for their trading activity…as sponsoring and protective private institutions. It was indeed a private enterprise, owned by traders,*

who organised their workforce, ships and voyages. The traders seem to have had a high status and an equally high political rank, based on a kinship organisation...This aspect is further emphasised by the Old Testament references to the Phoenician 'household' and Moscati also mentions the textile industry developed at Carthage, which apparently was based on 'family lines' too...[43]

The above evidence of current specialists on Iberian prehistory like Maria Eugenia Aubet and T. Júdice Gamito leads to the conclusion that the business establishments of Tyre's overseas colonies definitely functioned as branch-plants and foreign subsidiaries in a multinational setting. British archaeologist Richard Harrison has been even more explicit in supporting this suggestion, describing both the family-based structure and the internalisation advantages which Tyre, Inc. possessed:

The pattern of Phoenician trade was linked to specialist production centres, connecting different areas and political systems which otherwise would not have been drawn together, and establishing a rate of exchange much to their own advantage. They could do this fairly easily since they had a monopoly on both the specialized manufactures that everyone desired, and the marine transport, so they could stimulate demand where they chose to do so. A virgin market was the ideal since it could be scoured hard for huge profits; this accounts for their interest in Spain, especially in the silver mines behind Huelva in the Rio Tinto, and near Cástulo in the Sierra Morena. The Phoenicians were able to locate new metal sources, and unlock the wealth from them, unhindered, for a century and a half. The traders worked through a system of Phoenician family firms, who had representatives in their home town in the eastern Mediterranean as well as in their new markets and factories; they owned their own ships, too, and were prepared to take risks which their overlords could not well calculate, or were unwilling to do, and so profited greatly.[44]

Gades, thriving to this day as the Spanish port of Cadiz, became the core of Ibero-Phoenician shipping despite its remote location on the storm-swept Atlantic. Even in Roman times, after seven centuries of existence, the city remained the home of those "who fit out the most and largest merchant-vessels" for both the Mediterranean and

Atlantic. Many of these vessels were likely constructed at Gades itself or Ibiza near Gibraltar with wood from nearby pine forests. It is
possible to know what these magnificent ships of Tarshish looked
like from Assyrian inscriptions and an actual example from a
Carthaginian vessel found off the coast of Sicily in 1971. The larger
ships were round, with big square sails and had ample room for pas-
sengers and crew, being approximately 25 metres long. Warships also had square sails, up to 60 oars and battering rams. Smaller ships
were used by fishermen and had horses' heads on the prow. The
Phoenician settlers of Gades later spread to the opposite mainland,
setting up fine pastures and mixing with the Iberian inhabitants.
Smaller posts near Huelva in the mouths of the Rio Tinto and Odiel
devoted themselves largely to the distribution of the wares of Gades
and the silver mined on Solomon's Hill.[45]

The Guadalquivir settlements, with their firm trade links to upstream Iberian mine were soon followed by a strip of Phoenician
settlements in the Málaga region on the Mediterranean shore of
Andalusia. The new settlements east of Gibraltar fit the classic Tyrian pattern, being founded on a series of harbour settlements on peninsulas and islands. Evidence from these sites shows they were occupied between 750 to 500 BC coinciding with the final phase of
Tyrian commercial expansion.[46] Little was known about them until
the early 1960s when the Laurita tombs of Almuñecar, filled with
Phoenician grave goods, were opened. Beginning in 1964, half a
dozen settlements were excavated by the German archaelogists
H.G. Niemeyer and Hermanfried Schubart. By the late 1970s the
site of Mainake/Toscanos yielded abundant traces of direct investment and productive activities by Phoenician colonists. Archaeologists here uncovered a massive 11x15 metre stone warehouse built
between 670 and 650 BC alongside ruins of a fortified citadel and
stone houses dating from 750-700 BC. Slag deposits and other
finds confirmed Toscanos had its own copper and iron processing
industries, as well as a dye industry based upon murex breeding.
Toscanos practiced metallurgy, smithing, pottery, husbandry and
mollusk fishing as well as importing wares from Greece and the
Near East and metal from Tartessos brought along the overland
routes from Upper Andalusia.[47]

The colonies in the Málaga region became self-sufficient on the
basis of farming, cattle-raising, and the production of purple-dyed

garments dyed and Red Slip pottery with technology brought from Tyre itself. The famous Red Slip ceramics have been unearthed all over southern Spain, most strongly in the areas of Phoenician settlement, where they were produced locally in the Phoenician settlements rather than being directly imported from Levantine factories.[48] Even more important was the presence of metal-working industries in the Phoenician colonies. The evidence of metal-working in these colonies, witnessed by the discovery of slag deposits and clay pipes in Toscanos, indicates that the resident Phoenicians turned some of the metal they received from the Iberians into finished articles which they sold back to the latter. The miners of the Sierra Morena and the Iberians in general provided a fine market for Phoenician ceramics, artwork, handicrafts, jewels, ivory, caskets, combs, statues, altars, and amulets, produced either in Phoenicia itself, on Cyprus or within the local colonies.[49] Not easily accessible from Gades or the Huelva region, the Málaga colonies were nonetheless involved in much trade with the Spanish interior, and possibly North Africa and the British Isles. The warehouse at Toscanos was far larger than necessary if it was designed to satisfy the needs of local subsistence alone. More likely, it served as a terminal for silver shipped by their Iberian partners from the mines of the Sierra Morena, accessible to the Ibero-Phoenicians by road from their most easterly settlements of Abdera and Sexi.[50] The grave-finds of Morro de Mezquitilla, immediately to the east of Toscanos, provided striking confirmation, moreover, that all this trading and manufacturing activity was directed by a local Ibero-Phoenician management with family ties to the Phoenician homeland. The richer tombs belonged to leading members of the colony, leading British archaeologist Richard Harrison to surmise they were "probably from important trading families who headed the firms that were based in Tyre and Sidon".[51] The seventh-century graves of Phoenician Spain, their styles copied by Iberians eager to embrace their values along with their gods, "show that an aristocracy was installed in the Phoenician settlements of the West".[52]

During the eighth century BC the Iberian-Phoenician partnership became established along the lines of the partnership model first perfected by Phoenician companies in Egypt, Israel and elsewhere. Not only the Iberian mining industry but the Iberian trading network was integrated into Tyre's vast commercial imperium.

During the final phase of the Bronze Age, Iberians began to import tin from the British Isles, France and northwest Spain, a trade which continued even after the founding of Gades. The Iberian Atlantic trade now merged with the Mediterranean axis of the Ibero-Phoenicians. The trading sphere of the Ibero-Phoenician colonies now not only embraced much of western Europe, but even began to include parts of West Africa. Pottery finds linked the Tyrian colonies of Spain with the coasts of Algeria and Morocco, where further Tyrian branch-settlements on Rahgoun Island, Lixus and the Isle of Mogador had been planted to control the gold trade of Guinea and other points in Sub-Saharan Africa.[53] While Iberia swiftly became the jewel in Tyre's imperial crown, the Phoenician branch-plant colonies founded there were closely integrated with their sister colonies in the central Mediterranean. A Canaanite tomb discovered at Ghajn Ouajjed in Malta contained a horde of Spanish silver, showing that the island served as a way-station between Gades/Toscanos and Phoenician posts to the east.[54] Sulcis in Sardinia and Moyta in Sicily also served as "ports of call on the routes of Phoenician ships coming into the western Mediterranean in order to transport metal to sell in the marketplaces of the Near East".[55] The key entry-point between Spain and Tyre, however, was Cyprus. Artifacts from Egypt and Mesopotamia found in Phoenician Spain in the reign of Pumayyaton and later reached the west via Phoenician-controlled ports, most likely Kition. There is a very strong probability as well that the Red Slip Ware first exported to then produced in Spain had its origin in the web of Tyrian enterprises on Cyprus:

Spain communicated with Phoenicia both directly and through Cyprus's mediation, probably on this island originated the red ceramics technique. A number of parallels are found between the objects of Hispano-Phoenician and Cypriote arts. Some original Cypriote objects were discovered in Spain.[56]

Kition also directed Ibero-Phoenician exports to the Aegean, although direct trade between Spain and Greece also existed. Greek vessels and Cypriot artifacts were found in both Malta and in Iberian and Ibero-Phoenician tombs before 700 BC[57] The regular contacts between Cyprus and the western operations and key role of Kition in the latter was noted as well by the most famous of all Hebrew prophets. Warning of Tyre's doom, Isaiah, then a royal prince in the court of King Hezekiah of Judah in Jerusalem, painted a picture of the city's future destruction and its impact on the overseas empire. Galleons plying eastward from the Iberian mines and factories reaching Cyprus would there learn of Phoenicia's demise and the consequent economic ruin of both Iberia and Kition: "Howl, ye ships of Tarshish: for it [Tyre] is laid waste, so that there is...no entering in: from the land of Chittim it is revealed to them."[58]

The links between the new Tyrian commercial empire and the Neo-Assyrian Empire, established during the ninth century BC and intensified with the Assyrian invasion of the Levant after 745 BC, grew even stronger in the seventh century BC During the reigns of Tiglath-Pileser III, Shalmaneser V and Sargon II the kings of Tyre continued a policy of political neutrality and economic collaborate with their new overlords, relying upon their mineral and capital resources as the guarantee of their sovereignty in much the same manner as Switzerland and Sweden in the Second World War. The situation changed after 705 BC when Luli (Elulaeus) of Tyre attempted to revolt against the dreaded Sennacherib (705-681 BC). The revolt was unsuccessful, with the cities of the mainland being pressured by the Assyrians to lend their seapower to a five-year siege of the island. Luli was deposed and replaced by the more tractable Itobaal II.[59]

Assyrian influence over Phoenicia reached its apex in the reign of the powerful Esarhaddon (680-69), who invaded Egypt, and Ashurbanipal (668-27). Rebelling in the aftermath of the civil war which broke out in the wake of Sennacherib's assassination, both Abdi-Mikulti of Sidon and Baal (Ba'alu) of Tyre quickly faced the wrath of Esarhaddon. Sidon was overrun, Abdi-Mikulti beheaded and massive deportations of population affected on the Phoenician mainland. Tyre and her trade survived, but under harsh new terms. All of mainland Phoenicia was now divided into the three Assyrian provinces of Simya, Sidon and Ushu. The terms of the Baal-Esarhaddon treaty confirmed the position of the Assyrian governor in Tyre itself and listed the Levantine ports thru which Baal's merchants were permitted to trade.[60] The text of the treaty, preserved in the record of Assyrian royal correspondence, reveals more than any other document the managed nature of trade in the Phoenician world:

These are the ports of trade and the trade roads which Esarhaddon king of Assyria [granted] to his servant, Baal: (to wit): toward Akko, Dor, in the entire district of the Philistines, and in all the cities within Assyrian territory, on the seacoast, and in Byblos, (across) the Lebanon, all the cities in the mountains, all the cities...which Esarhaddon gave [to] Baal [...] [to] the people of Tyre, ...in their ships or all those who cross over, in the towns of [Baal], his towns, his manors, his wharves, which [...] to [...] as many as did lie in the outlying regions, as in the past [...] they...nobody should harm their ships, Inland, in his district, in his manors...[61]

The treaty was ratified in the presence of the priests of various Baalim, who would punish any violations on the part of the Tyrian monarch by raising an evil wind against Baal's ships undoing their moorings and sinking them in the sea.[62]

Efforts to channel all of Tyre's trade with Asia trade through a limited number of Assyrian-held harbours were no doubt unpopular on the island. Nevertheless, the power of Phoenician commerce partially seduced even the might of Assyria. Even as Assyrian armies flooded into the Levant and Assyrian provinces replaced many of the region's sovereign states, kings from Tiglath-Pileser III to Ashurbanipal left much of their westward import-export trade in the hands of the Canaanites who managed it best. Assyrian annals tell, for example, of the Sidonian Hanunu (Hanno) chief supplier of the empire's dyed fabrics. Despite the overbearing nature of Assyrian imperialism, the purely business aspects of Assyro-Phoenician trade continued to be managed by the eastern network of Tyrian *mkrm* stationed in Cilicia, Aleppo, Carchemish and even Nineveh and Babylon themselves. Metals mined in Spain and goods processed throughout Tyre's new Mediterranean empire were shipped from Gades and even Africa to Assyria, never leaving the hands of the Phoenician merchant companies who procured them or those of their relatives, partners or subsidiaries.[63]

Dominating the sea to the west, the traders of Tyre maintained a powerful and respected presence in Ashur, Halah and Nineveh itself even at the height of Assyrian power, as investors or even as deportees. Among the discoveries of M.A. Lèvy and Rawlinson as early as the 1850s were a series of tablets from the mound of Kuyunjik written in both the Assyrian and Phoenician tongues. These tablets mention Oubasti, likely exiled by Sennacherib in his youth, but now exercising a powerful role as a chief porter in Nineveh in the reign of Esarhaddon.[64]

In its role of nourishing Assyria, the trading network created by Tyre's merchants in the western and central Mediterranean perfected the old pattern of Levantine-Mesopotamian commerce stretching back to Bronze Age Sumer and Ebla. In the Ugaritic/Kassite period Babylonian merchant partnerships joined with Phoenician to finance the large-scale trade between the two regions as well as longer-distance trade with Egypt and Hatti. Huge quantities of metals, textiles, foodstuffs and processed goods still plied up and down the Euphrates, with bulk shipments from Egypt and Canaan being paid for in silver and textiles by consortia of Babylonian merchants. As in earlier times, the Babylonian temple continued to provide the *tamkâru* with capital, direction and banking and storage facilities. The chief Phoenician product demanded by the Kassite merchants was the purple dye and the garments made from it, still shipped by donkey caravan from the factories of the coast. Commerce in the east remained organised in the traditional hierarchical and partnership patterns which the Canaanites had exported to the west. Kassite, Babylonian and Assyrian *tamkâru* and their employees formed price-fixing partnerships to purchase Phoenician goods and distribute them to their subcontractors.[65]

By the tenth century BC Babylonia was largely reduced to a vassal of the Neo-Assyrian Empire. The kings and merchants of Nineveh now sought to manipulate the Euphratean trading, transportation and distribution system, still operated by private *tamkâru*, for their own national ends. According to A.L. Oppenheim, from the tenth century BC on "the West was the major source of the iron used by the Assyrian war machine."[66] Aram-Damascus and Upper Syria became the source of this supply, providing some 14,000 kilograms alone to the armies of Adad-Nirari III (810-783) BC. From the Tyrians, however, the Assyrians at first primarily wanted the decorated garments of purple. The technique of producing the brightly-coloured Phoenician garments was yet another example of a Canaanite monopoly of a product and technique for which there existed high demand in a Nineveh and Babylon accustomed to drabber wool and linen clothing.[67] The Tyrian *kârum* at Carchemish was the most likely distribution point for silver and other products internalised within the Phoenician network.

The rise of the Tyrian multinational business empire produced an enormous social and economic revolution in Iberia and other countries where it had substantial investments. The impact upon the natives was not unlike that of foreign investment in developing countries today. Public works built on the Phoenician model quickly emerged in the Iberian settlements along the Guadalquivir, Guadalete, Guadajoz and other river valleys. Mud huts gave way to stone houses, fortified defences arose around Iberian cities and a thriving pottery industry arose, manufacturing jugs based upon Tyrian models. Bulk shipments of Spanish silver, copper and beef were traded for Phoenician ivory, pottery, wine, garments and tools of iron. Many of the finished Phoenician goods were likely value-added items produced locally from bronze, gold, glass and ivory in the shops of Gades and eventually Toscanos.[68] The forging of a vast business partnership with Tyre after approximately 775 BC would bring to Spain the same Iron Age revolution undergone by Israel and Phoenicia herself some 150 to 200 years previously. Originally a relatively poor Bronze Age society devoted to grazing and local mining with crude stone tools, the land of Tarshish now entered the capitalist era with a venegeance. The record of Iberian villages' cemeteries in the Huelva region in the Phoenician period painted a fascinating portrait of a pattern all too familiar to contemporary sociologists. The coming of Melqart and his disciples inspired not only large-scale silver mining and iron working, but writing, building construction, pottery-making, and luxury items. Cemeteries at La Joya in Huelva, Setefilla (Seville) and Trayamar told a story of the death of a traditional tribal Spanish society and the emergence of a new urban elite of upwardly mobile aggressive entrepreneurs eager not only to acquire the chariots, ivory carvings and other status goods imported from Gades and Tyre but to flaunt them.[69] Where Iberian graves had once been identical, those of the *nouveau riche* after 650 BC became highly individual, vulgar and ostentatious, documenting the accumulation of wealth in the hands of native leaders.[70]

The graves of Carmona showed not only a healthy market for Phoenician luxuries, but the supplying of those luxuries by means of Ibero-Phoenician subsidiaries. Renowned for their skill in finishing ivory work on African tusks in the east, Tyrian craftsmen/importers set up what Richard Harrison termed "a provincial Phoenician workshop" shop in Spain after 700 BC, producing ivory goods right within Carmona itself.[71] Not only value-added branch-plant production but transfer of technology took place in the areas of luxury-good production. Iberian jewelry from the early Iron Age tombs is radically different in style from that of the previous period, with the gold-working techniques of the new Spanish craftsmen becoming as adept as their Phoenician tutors. The gold jewels and treasure from the El Carambolo cemetery near Seville suggested, again, resident Phoenician craftsmen at work, while the elaborate necklace "may well have come from Gadir itself".[72] The clearest example of technology transfer, however, took place in the explosive growth of the Iberian pottery industry, which instead of a household skill, became a mass-production trade after 650 BC. All over southern Spain workshops arose turning out large quantities of the popular grey and red Tyrian stylishly jugs decorated with bands of red, black and maroon paint.[73]

Based upon the evidence presented above, a reconstruction of the growth and triumph of Tyre's business network would recognise a new, multinational dimension to Phoenician trade in which the westward course of investment and expansion represented only one part of a vast commercial empire reaching even into the very palaces and armouries of the Neo-Assyrian Empire.[74] By the time Esarhaddon marched into Egypt in 673 BC the kings of Tyre had forged an economic investment empire stretching, if one included trading partners, from Spain, the British Isles and West Africa to Babylonia and the Arabian Gulf. A detailed description of this empire, written half a century after its peak, has survived in the writings of the Jewish priest Ezekiel, himself an exile in Nebuchadnezzar's Babylon after 604 BC. No great admirer of Tyre's imperial pretensions, its commerce or especially its religion, Ezekiel compared the arrogant trading city, seen as a bastion of greed fused with idolatry in the eyes of a devout Hebrew monotheist, to one of her own trading vessels.[75] Written about 588 BC, the portrait of Tyre in Ezekiel 26 and 27 provided a detailed description of the city's enormous trading network. "Situated at the entry of the sea...a merchant for many isles," Tyre was described as a ship made of fir, cedar and oak from Lebanon, Syria and Israelite Bashan. The ship-nation was decorated with linen from Egypt and ivory and purple from Cyprus and the central Mediterranean. Ezekiel then alluded to the multinational crews manning her cosmopolitan navy, with Sidonians and men of Arvad working the oars and the elders of Byblos specialising in ship construction, with the *mkrm* of Tyre serving as the chief officers, helmsmen and pilots. The army, meanwhile was equally cosmopolitan, being manned by mercenaries from as far away as Persia, Lydia, and North Africa. Ezekiel assigned the partnership with Spain a special role in Tyrian prosperity:

Tarshish was thy merchant by reason of the multitude of all kind of riches: with silver, iron, tin, and lead, they traded in thy fairs...The ships of Tarshish did sing of thee in thy market: and thou wast replenished, and made very glorious in the midst of the seas...When thy wares went forth out of the seas, thou filledst many people; thou didst enrich the kings of the earth with the multitude of thy riches and of thy merchandise.[76]

Ezekiel's description of Tyre's Iberian trade confirms the cosmopolitan picture of that operation set forth before 750 BC in the story of Jonah. A Galilean of the tribe of Zebulun and a fierce anti-Assyrian nationalist, Jonah "found a ship going to Tarshish" and "paid the fare thereof".[77] When an eastern Mediterranean storm threatened the ship, "the mariners were afraid and cried every man unto his god, and cast forth the wares that were in the ship, to lighten it of them."[78] Both Jonah and Ezekiel indicated frequent and regular voyages between eastern Tyrian settlements and Iberia. Ships carried heavy bulk wares and multinational crews worshipping a number of dieties.

Moving from west to east, Ezekiel addressed Greeks, Anatolians, Arameans, Israelites, Arabians, East Africans and finally Assyrians as Tyrian customers, the text describing the imports Tyre obtained and processed to build her fortunes: timber from the Levant, linen from Egypt and North Africa, copper from the Aegean and Anatolia, wheat and iron from Israel and Aram, ivory from East Africa, and rich apparel from Mesopotamia. A close reading of Ezekiel 26-28 also implied that much of Tyre's trading and investment was now in private hands. The Hebrew word for "merchants" most often used in those chapters was derived from *rokel* "broker, merchant, or trader". The Tyrian *sahar rokelim*, most often mentioned by Ezekiel were private *tamkâru*, in contrast to the *sohare yammelek* or *sohare yadek* of II Chr.1:16 or Ezek. 27:21, who were royal *tamkâru*. Nevertheless, even the major *rokelim* were deeply involved with royal and temple agents.[79]

Establishing trade through a system of partnership and investment with Israel in the tenth and ninth centuries, the merchants of Tyre expanded their operations to Cyprus and the Neo-Hittite states of Syria. By the 800s the rising power of the Neo-Assyrian kingdom and unrest in the Syro-Palestinian region, led Tyre's kings and priests in the reign of Pumayyaton to support expeditions of trade and colonisation which established a Phoenician presence in Malta, Sicily, Sardinia, Carthage and eventually Spain shortly before or after 800 BC. Founding the settlement of Gades under the auspices of priests of Melqart, Tyrian traders bartered their garments and other luxuries for the silver of Rio Tinto. Inspired by this growing demand, Spanish miners obtained iron Phoenician tools and began to create a sophisticated business organisation which, as its production grew, entered into a multinational partnership with its Canaanite client. Shipped down the Rio Tinto or overland to Gades, vast amounts of Spanish silver were transported in galleons along the North African shore to Malta, Cyprus and Tyre, from which silver ingots and goods journeyed overland to the ancient routes of the Euphrates. Sailing from the harbours of Tyre, Sidon, Kition or Acco huge Phoenician galleys, often manned by multinational crews sailed westward, hugging the southern coast of Anatolia, the Dodecanese, the Peloponnesus, the Sicilian and Sardinian coasts, finally arriving at Toscanos or Gades in Spain. Burning animal sacrifices in gratitude to Melqart, they distributed their luxury goods to resident Tyrian merchants who likely belonged to the same family as the shipper or the original producer of the pottery or dye back in Phoenicia.

The great Tyrian empire flourished all during the days of its new Neo-Assyrian patron. By the end of the long and violent reign of Ashurbanipal, who died in 622, the overextended, depopulated Assyrian giant began to stagger and, within twenty years, collapsed under the pressure of the Medes and a resurgent Babylonia under Nebuchadnezzar II. Tyre itself would be humbled by the famous Chaldean king, after which the vast commercial empire began to

splinter and fragment. Mesopotamia would never again be the centre of world trade or the major source of foreign direct investment.
Though Tyre's domain was dissolving, the island city had shifted
the heart of world trade to the Mediterranean, where it would remain for a millennium and a half.

Chapter 7

Free-Market Revolution in the Aegean: 825-336 BC

The managed business cultures of the Near East dominated trade during the second and much of the first millennium BC. The internalised "top-down" model of business management by god-kings, merchant princes, and temple priests paved the way for the first multinational enterprises to flourish in Kanesh, Dilmun, Ugarit, and Tyre. An alternative business model, based upon small, independent enterprises however, so took on shape in the Aegean. Working in a much freer and less urbanised world, the traders of Greece forged history's first free-market economy, bypassing the strictures of the *Eclectic Paradigm*. Greek entrepreneurs traded around the Mediterranean on their own, without the help of large corporate hierarchies or internalised operations. This first truly entrepreneurial business culture was totally dominated by independent traders. It reached its full maturity in Athens of the fifth century BC, with its flourishing overseas trade, private banks, and relatively free capital markets. Here, despite its largely agrarian nature, was an economic system distantly related to the Anglo-American consumer and shareholder capitalism of our own day.

In the beginning, the peoples of the Aegean operated with a regimented palace economy not unlike that found in the Near East. The Minoans of Crete were anything but entrepreneurial. If anything, they were, like the Egyptians, more socialist than capitalist. The palace authorities in Knossos told producers how much to produce and even decided what everyone would live on in what was clearly not a market economy. Foreign trade with Egypt, Cyprus, and Syria in foodstuffs, olive oil, wine, and bronze goods was also the realm of the state, no doubt "operated as a monopoly through the palace system…with little role for independent merchants and traders".[1] Minoan civilisation vanished from history in the mid-to-late second millennium BC, to be replaced by the unmistakably Greek Mycenaean. The Mycenaeans were discovered around 1900 by the famous Heinrich Schliemann who began digging near Corinth in the hopes of uncovering the home of the warriors of the *Iliad*. The people he found were genuinely Hellenic, made weapons of bronze, and even engaged in trade with Egypt, the Levant, and the rest of the Near East. The first recognisable Greek finds, called Middle Helladic, dated from the time of Old Assyria and Babylonia and were accompanied by a primitive form of Greek written in a hieroglyphic script known as Linear B. The full development of this first culture came in the Late Helladic at the end of the Bronze Age at the same time Sinaranu made his voyages from Ugarit to Crete. Mycenaean Greece was made up of a number of tribal kingdoms each based around a palace-oriented economy. In spite of the latter, the rural, localised world of Mycenaean Greece would provide the foundation upon which independent agriculture could prosper and a system of independent enterprise could emerge. The tribal kings had little capital, there were no cities by Oriental standards, and no centralised power in temple or state. The mountainous Greek countryside, absence of roads, and isolation of population in many peninsulas and hundreds of tiny islands guaranteed that religion, economy, and politics would be localised to a degree unknown in the Near East.[2] Late Helladic tribal kings and nobles fought one another in chariots wearing heavy bronze armour and wielding bronze swords produced by local craftsmen.[3] The shipbuilding and seafaring skills of the Bronze Age were sufficient to permit Mycenaean traders to sail to Egypt, Anatolia, and Syria as much as they permitted Ugaritic, Hattian and Egyptian traders to reach Aegean shores, placing the markets of the Aegean and the Near East in closer contact than ever before. At a very early date, Mycenaean Greeks were trading as far as Sardinia and Spain. Their pottery has been found in the Bay of Naples, and at a number of sites in southeastern Sicily and on the heel of the Italian boot. In this early stage of trade, it appears that Minoan control of the eastern Mediterranean diverted mainland traders to more westerly locations. Following the apparent defeat of the Minoans by the Greeks, the full flowering of the mainland palace civilisation in the Late Helladic period coincided with evidence of Mycenaean artifacts in Crete, the Dodecanese, Egypt, Cyprus, Anatolia, and the Levant.[4]

The Helladic Bronze Age in Greece seems to have ended in a wave of destruction in which a resurgence of piracy may well have played an important part.[5]

Very little is known of the succeeding period, which most historians consider to be a 300 year Dark Age (1200-900 BC) similar to the one they believe occurred in Babylonia, Phoenicia, and Anatolia. As in the cases of Phoenicia and Mesopotamia, Peter James and his revisionist colleagues have questioned the existence of this Dark Age, seeing no break between the Helladic/Mycenean Bronze Age and the Homeric Iron Age which begins after 900 BC.[6] Strong evidence of both destruction and depopulation in Greece, however, suggest some kind of break took place.[7] Almost all Late Helladic sites at the end of the Bronze Age are abandoned; town life virtually collapses save in a few areas like Euboea and Achaia. Evidence for population declines sharply and then rebounds. Because Greek dates are linked to Near Eastern ones by pottery and other artifacts, the lower Phoenician, Mesopotamian and Egyptian dating scheme convincingly presented by James and others suggests a lower Hellenic scheme as well, as do the continuities in Greek culture on both sides of the divide. A collapsed Mycenaean likely did take place, but Greece revived within a few generations. Greek pottery, very distinctive in terms of the times and places it came from, when cross-referenced with Egyptian and other artifacts as well as authors like Herodotus and Thucydides, has allowed archaeologists to reconstruct the Hellenic past. Phases in Greek history are therefore named, dated, and described according to the artistic styles found on vases and pots.[8] It should therefore be possible to create a rough skeleton outline for Hellenic history according to the new, lower dates (see figure 8).

The development of the Aegean market economy parallels that of the coming of the Aegean Iron Age. If the lowered chronology is even partly correct, the inauguration of both would be separated

Lowered Hellenic Chronology[9]

Early Bronze (3100-2200 BC)

Late Bronze I: (1300 +-1150)
Late Helladic I-II

Late Bronze II: (1050-925):
Trojan War, Mycenaean Trade
Late Helladic IIIA
Late Helladic III B-C
Devastations in east Mediterranean

"Dark Age": (925-800 BC?)
Submycenaean

Beginnings of Greek Iron Age after 800 BC

"Geometric" Period (775-675 BC)
Protogeometric Pottery
Geometric Pottery
Euboeans trade in Syria, Italy: Greek market revolution begins.
Corinthians colonise Syracuse, southern Italy
Milesians colonise Black Sea
Lelantine War
Homer and Hesiod

"Archaic" Period (675-600 BC)
Formation of Poleis
Rule of oligarchies
Flourishing of Miletus and Corinth

**Age of Tyrants and Monetary revolution
(600-500 BC)**
Phocaean expansion in west
Thales and intellectual revolution in Miletus
Social issues become important
Solon, Peisistratus reforms in Athens
Persian conquest of Ionia

"Classical" Period (500-400 B.C)
Persian Wars
Delian League and Athenian Empire
Peak of Greek population and Athenian prosperity
Herodotus and Thucydides
Peloponnesian War

---

from the Mycenaean era by generations, not centuries. Even though
the traditions behind them go well back into the Bronze Age, the
epics of Homer, written in the late eighth and/or early seventh centuries BC which glamorised Mycenaean life, take on new significance if that life is much closer in time to the writing of *The Iliad*
and *The Odyssey*. The Homeric epics can now provide invaluable
commentary on both the Bronze Age and the birth of the first market economy. Far from collecting myths, Homer was in fact lamenting the age of heroes he saw passing before his eyes to be replaced
by a repulsive new world of petty traders whom the poet and his lis-
teners saw as coarse hustlers, crass swindlers, and craven opportunists.[10] The age *The Odyssey* idealised was one Homer's grandparents
could remember in its fullness. Eighth century Greece was a land of
self-sufficient communities. Families worked their own farms, were
freer than their Oriental counterparts, and could any *basileus* (tribal
king) who sought to rule too harshly. Riches were measured in livestock and land, with manufactured goods owned by the lord or roving tradesmen.[11] In the *Odyssey*, Telemachus told the suitors occupying his home that "it would be far better for you to eat away my
treasures and eat my cattle."[12] Telemachus himself then retreated to
his father's high-roofed storeroom, filled with gold, bronze, garments, olive oil, and wine.[13] As acting patriarch, Telemachus advised Penelope to attend to her domestic "the loom and the distaff,
and see to it that your handmaidens ply their work also" while the
men attended to discussion.[14] Homer's contempt for merchants
masked his genuine knowledge of their practices, which were even
at that early date clearly entrepreneurial.[15] The goddess Athena dis-
guised herself as a merchant, promising to hire the warrior-hero
Odysseus the best ship and the best volunteers, for there were plenty of both in Ithaca.[16] Odysseus, incarnation of all Homer found vir-
tuous in the old Greece, later journeyed to Phaiakia. Once believing
it to be based upon either Smyrna, Miletus, or Phocaea, historians
have become more cautious about identifying this mythical Ionian
city with any single real-life settlement. The portrait of this fictional
emporia (port) showed, though, that the eighth-century Greeks of
Asia Minor were already beginning to make commerce their calling.
Their ruler, Nausithos or Nausikaa, told Odysseus that "the Phaiakians have no concern with the bow or the quiver" which are the
weapons of Asiatics, "but it is all masts and the oar of ships and the

balanced vessels themselves, in which they delight in crossing over the gray sea...."[17] These Ionians were "expert beyond all others for driving a fast ship on the open sea".[18] Homer's dislike of what he, through the eyes of Odysseus, sees is quite evident. The warrior himself is later accused of being nothing but a rootless, greedy trader unworthy of home, tribe, or honour:

No stranger, for I do not see that you are like one versed in contests, such as now are practiced much among people, but rather to one who plies his ways in his many-locked vessel, master over mariners who are also men of business, a man who, careful of his cargo and grasping for profits, goes carefully on his way. You do not resemble an athlete...[19]

Too dishonourable for a noble Hellene, trade and commerce were best left to Phoenicians, who, through Greek eyes, epitomised crookedness itself. Late in the epic the wandering Odysseus encountered an unscrupulous Canaanite who offers him a business proposition trading in Libya. His real intent, however, was to sell the hero into slavery: "there came a Phoenician man, well skilled in beguilements, a gnawer at others' goods, and many were the hurts he inflicted on men, and by his wits talked me over..."[20] Athena herself suggested that the changes in society she, Odysseus and Homer see will not, in the long run, be for the better: "few are the children who turn out to be the equals of their fathers, and the greater number are worse; few are better than their father is."[21]

Behind Homer's lament lay, ultimately, the coming of the commercial and the Iron Age. Production on a large scale of both swords and plowshares of iron would help redefine the economic laws and rules of the ancient world. Everyone would soon want iron swords that could slash through bronze ones and which were cheap enough to equip mass armies. Iron plows could break tough soil in regions where water was relatively scarce and irrigation impractical. Once iron-working spread outside the Near East, the new technology had the potential to feed, equip, and arm whole new centres of population and power anywhere iron ore could be found:

The economic consequences of ...iron tools...affected practically every sphere of human life. They were sufficient to undermine the very foundations of Ancient Oriental civilization, especially as iron ore occurs practically everywhere on our globe in sufficient quantities for early Iron Age production and made the caravan and naval trade of the Bronze Age with the much rarer copper and tin obsolete.[22]

The linkage between iron and European urbanisation must be drawn cautiously, for Crete, Mycenae and Villanovan Italy flourished before the coming of the iron plow. Iron tools and weapons, however, certainly aided the growth of both agriculture and urban life in the Etruscan, Latin, Celtic, Indian, East Asian, African, and other regions with less fertile soils than the Nile, Indus Valley, Yellow River, or the Tigris and Euphrates.[23] Iron helped guarantee the future shift of world power the Euphrates to the Mediterranean, and helped encourage more entreprenurial forms of business exchange, as it "upheld continuously refined principles of individualism in all spheres of human life", in spite of the persistence of hierarchical societies in Assyria and Tyre.[24] According to the late Fritz Heichelheim, the "planning economy of the Ancient Orient and...tribal collectivism of earlier times were...reactionary from the time...of the new age onwards", being replaced by a new age "in which free individualism and its creations had a fundamentally decisive role to play for millennia."[25]

The cultures of the Mediterranean were in fact the first to create a true iron-working economy. Iron had been used for ornaments for centuries, but the Iron Age began when iron tools first appeared alongside those of bronze and, in a later stage, largely replaced them. Bronze goods would continue to flourish in the Iron Age, now produced by iron tools.[26] The Iron Age began in Cyprus, spreading from there to Greece, Phoenicia, and Anatolia. The mercantile activities of Tyre would encourage its spread to Spain and North Africa. In the rest of Europe, even if the invention of iron tools may have been a native development, their adoption and spread was undoubtedly encouraged by contact with those more proficient in the iron-working arts.[27] The copper of Cyprus long contained large amounts of iron ore. The disruptions at the end of the Bronze Age, whatever they may have been, seem to have inspired "a phase of fairly intensive experimentation with working iron" leading to "a full Iron Age...no later than...1050 BC" according to the traditional dating.[28] The lowered dates suggested above, would, however, place the beginning of the Cypriot Iron Age

around 1050 instead of 1200 BC and the full Cypriot Iron Age in
Hiram's and Itobaal's time around 900 BC, at the very end of the
Greek Dark Age.[29] Cypriot smiths began by making iron knives,
then graduated to other implements, providing what Professor Anthony Snodgrass considered the vital breakthrough for the Iron Age
for both Europe and Asia: "The extensive overseas contacts of Cyprus...explain the diffusion of this discovery both eastward and
westward."[30] From Cyprus, the Iron Age spread to the Aegean,
where "developments...follow those in Cyprus with a fidelity which
argues a close dependence on Cypriot technological secrets and
perhaps even a reliance on importing Cypriot artifacts ready-
made."[31] The Iron Age in Greece began with the production of
knives around 900 BC, followed by that of Cypriot-inspired iron
daggers and swords. Iron-working concentrated in Athens, on the
eastern shore of the Greek peninsula, in the Aegean, and on the island of Euboea at the site of Lefkandi can be dated by the presence
of Protogeometric pottery, marked by semicircle designs found in
Cyprus. Cypriot pottery of this time suddenly pictures warriors and
hunters inspired by pottery from mainland Greece. These artistic
exchanges hinted at technology transfers.[32] The shortage of tin
needed to make bronze in Greece encouraged the rapid growth of a
strong iron-working tradition. After 900 BC the entire Greek world
fully entered the Iron Age: iron products were fully in use and had
spread all across the Hellenic peninsula.[33] Greeks, no longer dependent upon Cyprus iron-working expertise, were ready to embark upon their own search for new iron sources. [34]

The large island of Euboea, just off the eastern Greek shore, was
now destined to play a key role in the Aegean commercial revolution. The secure Euboean harbours of Chalcis, Lefkandi, and Eretria were strategically situated at the western edge of the Aegean island chain. Maintaining urban life and even prosperity during the
Dark Age, Chalcis and Lefkandi formed a link between the old
economy of Mycenae and the new economy of Homer's time.[35] Tyrian and Cypriot traders voyaged across the Aegean, docking at the
Euboean ports, bringing knowledge of iron-working, the phonetic
alphabet, and, most importantly, continued knowledge of old
Bronze Age trade routes to both east and west. The foundation of
the new settlement of Eretria around 825 BC indicated prosperity in
Euboea had not only endured but was growing.[36] Gold and ivory

from Cyprus and Phoenicia began to appear in substantial quantities in the graves of Lefkandi in the ninth century BC, as well as in Athens.[37] Greeks, and particularly Euboeans, could not help but be inspired to fit out their own trading ventures along their old Mycenaean trade routes once they "came into early…contact with the much older and much wider Cypro-Levantine network of pan-Mediterranean commerce and communications."[38] A few enterprising Hellenes soon began selling their pottery and drinking-vessels to the Levantine market.[39] The trail of these entrepreneurs, or at least of their goods, was uncovered by Sir Leonard Woolley excavating on the Syrian shore in the 1930s. The presence of Euboean and other Greek pottery near the site of Al Mina at the mouth of the Orontes hints, but does not prove that Euboeans traded there. The pottery finds at Al Mina dated to the ninth century BC were Phoenician, but those dated to the eighth contained shards of Greek pottery much of which could be traced to Euboea. Later finds from this century showed growing amounts of Rhodian, Corinthian, and other pottery. After 700 BC the Euboean pottery disappears in favour of its Greek rivals.[40] The interpretation of the Al Mina finds has played a key role in a heated debate as to how much of a role the Euboeans and other Greeks played in the seaborne commerce of the early Iron Age. It has been traditionally thought that the Euboeans almost single-handedly controlled the trade of the eighth century BC between Greece and the Syrian shore and were also the primary agents in a westward movement of Greek traders to Italy. Al Mina in the east and Pithekoussai, on the island of Ischia in the Bay of Naples in the west, represent Euboean settlements and trading posts. Professor John Papadopoulos of the Getty Institute, on the other hand, sees little evidence Euboeans even traded in the east, insisting that their goods were brought there in Tyrian vessels. Most of the pottery at Al Mina was not even Euboean, but Phoenician, Attic, Samian, Rhodian, Corinthian, Chian, and Milesian.[41] Most of what the Greeks sent east was in the form of open drinking cups called *skyphoi*, while other types of vessels came from Cyprus and the Levant, indicating "a very specific and co-ordinated market strategy that does not clearly point to the Greeks as the instigators."[42]

Euboeans were clearly present in Pithekoussai, but enough Tyrian and other pottery has been found there to suggest that Tyrians, Euboeans, and others lived together in "a large, prosperous and

multinational community".[43] Euboeans, in collaboration with Corinthians and others, may merely have joined an existing stream of
trans-Mediterranean commerce instead of actively seeking the markets on their own.[44]

Robin Osborne and David Ridgway give credit to the role of others pointed out in the Papadopolous interpretation, but find the evidence for an essential Euboean role too strong to dismiss outright.
Euboea's position in the ninth and eighth centuries BC – as the region of mainland Greece with the most prosperity and sailing experience –could not be denied. It is plausible that flourishing centres
like Lefkandi then formed the core of a loose trading federation
covering most of Thessaly and the Aegean islands. The decline of
Lefkandi around the time Eretria, Al Mina, and Pithekoussai all
emerged even suggests that much of Lefkandi's population could
have colonised Pithekoussai, given the latter's ability to support a
large population of metal-workers.[45] Excavations at Pithekoussai of
Euboean and other artifacts similar to those of Al Mina and
Lefkandi, along with iron slag, bellows and mouthpieces, show that
iron from Elba was smelted there, and that Euboeans played an important role in the process.[46] From Pithekoussai, Euboean shippers,
smiths, and craftsmen crossed to the mainland, where they provided the market demand that stimulated the Etruscan Iron Age. To
David Ridgway, the sudden appearance together in the eighth century BC of Euboean vases and Etruscan iron-work appeared as
strong evidence of "Euboean interest in the metals of Etruria".[47]
Mined on Elba by Etruscans and processed on Ischia by Euboeans,
Italian iron ore inspired the "market, or at least resource-seeking
behaviour on the part of the Euboeans" which resulted in their
westward expansion.[48] There was no coincidence between the
spread of the Iron Age from Greece to Italy, the settlement of Pithekoussai, and the subsequent foundation of Greek agricultural colonies further to the south in Italy:

> *The establishment of a permanent Euboean 'home base' abroad – with
> all that such an operation inevitably required in the way of investment
> of men and resources – would surely not have been contemplated with-
> out a preliminary period of elementary market research; and it surely
> would never have undertaken at all unless the cause had been seen to
> take effect, with the mechanics of supply and demand arranged.[49]*

The pottery and iron artifacts of Syria, Cyprus, and Etruria revealed the existence of an eighth century BC international Levant-
Aegean-Tyrrhenian trading network. A collection of Egyptian amulets found in the in a trail from North Syria to Greece to their greatest concentration in Pithekoussai graves of Pithekoussai allowed archaeologists to date the development of the network and confirm
the importance of the Euboean role in it. One amulet mentioned
Pharaoh Bocchoris, reigning around 720 BC, establishing a date for
the Geometric and Protocorinthian pottery of the Euboean network.[50] The Greek traders of this network operated as *private individuals and enterprises operating on a small scale,* not organised firms.
Neither Homer's descriptions of early Hellenic traders nor modern
archaelogy shows any evidence of an internalised business hierarchy
on the Phoenician model among the Greeks overseas. The merchants of *The Odyssey,* like Menelaus, operated independently, buying on a contractual basis, bringing their profits back to Greece
along with iron ore and prestige goods.[51] Menelaus was portrayed as
owning a number of ships employed in his trading voyages across
the eastern Mediterranean:

*Much did I suffer and wandered much before bringing all this home in
my ships when I came back in the eighth year. I wandered to Cyprus
and Phoenicia, to the Egyptians, I reached the Aithiopians, Eremboi,
Sidonians and Libya where the rams grow their horns quickly.*[52]

Greek commerce was becoming fixed in its historic pattern, being
"informal [and] entrepreneurial in a world which provided security
neither of contracts nor possession, and bringing an erratic and un-
predictable return".[53] Iron-working and Euboean trade began to
drive the Aegean market revolution: "It is perhaps not extravagant"
says Professor James Redfield, "to think that the trade route fueled
the whole Greek economic takeoff in the mid-eighth century BC."[54]
Homer was not describing a Greece without traders, but was lamenting the fact that the traders he despised were beginning to re-
make the very map of Greece herself. Iron ingots flowed into
Greece from Italy, where smiths turned then into hoes and plows.
Soon the peasants of Boeotia, Euboea, Attica, and the Peloponnesus were able to grow more wheat. The land was now able to support more people, and the population of the Greek world began to

rise slowly in the eighth century BC New communities began to dot the shores of the Attic peninsula: Eleusis, Palaia, Kokkina, Anaphlystos, Myrrhinous, and Marathon all sprung up near a coastline more and more free from the dangers of piracy. Writing in the fifth century BC, Thucydides hinted at this remaking of the Greek landscape:

> *the cities which were founded in more recent times, when navigation had at length become safer, and were consequently beginning to have surplus resources, were built right on the seashore, and the isthmuses were occupied and walled off with a view to commerce and to the protection of the several peoples against their neighbours.*[55]

Other new towns grew up near Corinth, and no doubt in Ionia, beginning with an outside wall, then houses, local shrines, and the apportionment of farmland. The archaeology of Greece in the eighth century BC shows a surge of building activity and a growing density of sites, particularly around Athens, in northwest Crete, and on the Peloponnesus.[56] A comparison of the graves of children and adults, though, suggests that the rise in population was a gradual one, and not an explosion as previously thought. What the graves do suggest, according to Professor Osborne, is "slow and steady population growth, continuously from the tenth century BC on, not a sudden explosion in the eighth century."[57] The rise in population was nonetheless linked to expanding horizons brought about by increased security, more food production and greater ease in attaining foreign markets and resources.[58]

The grand age of Hellenic colonisation began a generation after the Euboeans came to Pithekoussai. The major colonising towns: Corinth, Megara, Chalcis, Eretria, Phocaea, and Miletus were mostly crowded coastal communities short on fresh farmland. Recent studies have discarded the notion that Hellenic colonisation was a state enterprise in favour of a market-oriented and individualistic interpretation. People went to Italy, Sicily, Libya, and the Black Sea because they as individuals wanted to, their departure being, according to Robin Osborne, less "a measure of state power" than "a measure of the limits to the control rulers could exert".[59] Greek settlement certainly required organisation and cooperation, but they were informal, motivated by concerns of self-interest like "rest-

lessness and ambition among individual Greeks...pushed by poverty, unpopularity, crime or scandal...to get land, a foothold in foreign mineral resources, or just a new life free of irksome relatives".[60]
Few Greek cities were worthy of the name. Athens was as yet insignificant, Sparta only beginning to be so. Corinth, Lefkandi, Chalcis, and Eretria were the sole could be counted as major towns on
the western shore of the Aegean; the towns of Ionia: Miletus, Smyrna, Phocaea, held out more promise. In the eight, seventh, and even
the sixth centuries BC the Hellenic centre of gravity rested on the
western shore of Anatolia.[61] The overseas agrarian colonies in Sicily, Italy, and around the Black Sea exported wheat to metropolitan
Greece, allowing it to support a larger, more urban, and more specialised population. Farmers in Peloponnesus, Attica, and Ionia
turned from growing grain to cash crops like wine, oranges, and olives. Peasants became rural entrepreneurs owing homage to no one
but themselves, their creditors, and the market.[62]

The change from bronze to iron swords was the beginning of a
change in both the tactics and the strategy of warfare which would
also have profound political and economic implications for Greece.
Large standing armies replete with generals, chariots, cavalry, bow-
men and battering rams were an Oriental, not a Hellenic phenomenon. Even in the eighth century Greeks largely fought on foot in
massed ranks. Vases from the seventh century show the Greek foot-
soldier, or hoplite, armed with a shield held by a strap in the left
hand. This shield forced the hoplites to mass together even more
closely. Cavalry could no longer penetrate the hoplite ranks.[63] Because the shield afforded ample protection, hoplites were free to
dispense with expensive body armour. The key to victory in war became the mobilisation of numbers. Because every individual in the
local community now mattered, warfare in many parts of the Greek
world became democratised, the "focus of battle was now as much
on the weak as on the strong".[64] The hoplite revolution in warfare,
together with the division of Greece into scores of tiny city-states,
would help guarantee the existence of independent farming and independent enterprise. Despite its Mycenaean warrior heritage,
Greece between 700 and 500 BC was less militaristic than Assyria,
Babylon, or Persia. In many ways the independent, agrarian Greeks
reflected the ideals later espoused in Jeffersonian America. The yeoman farmer, with his household and slaves, was master of his own

plot and largely exempt from taxation. He provided for most of his own needs, although he often had to engage in trade to do so. He fought in a citizen army. When his little community went to war, the farmer donned his bronze helmet, put on his thick bronze breast-plate and picked up his iron spear or sword. All of these weapons were his own and most every Greek farmer could afford them, as they cost only about three months' wages. Many farmers even had spares, and handed them down from generation to generation. When the time for war came, the farmer became a hoplite, march-ing in a solid phalanx with his neighbours against the phalanx of a rival city state. Hoplite war was mild in comparison with the wars of the Egyptians, Hebrews, and Assyrians. Battles lasted for an after-noon, and few hoplites were killed due to the thickness of their ar-mour. The Greeks of this age practiced limited government and en-gaged in limited warfare. The two were mutually interdependent, and the various city-states desired to make them so. Wars were fought over farmland, not religion or ideology. A greater contrast between early Greek hoplite warfare and that of the Assyrians could not be imagined. There were no chariots, slingers, battering-rams or war fleets in the average Greek arsenal, only heavily-armoured and lightly-armed citizen-soldiers who would fight for a day and then disperse to their farms. In this heavily agrarian and politically fragmented world there was little need for new military technolo-gies or arms races. The weapons of a hoplite in 700 BC were all but identical to those in 500 BC. Wars themselves were not only brief but rare before the Persian conflict.[65]

One of the few major wars which took place during the Archaic period seems to have greatly weakened the prosperity of the Euboean cities and helped shift commercial leadership first to Cor-inth and later to Athens. Little is known about the Lelantine War that took place sometime in the late eighth and early seventh centu-ries BC In the past, historians like Aubrey Gwynn likened this con-flict to modern European colonial wars and even drew up an elabo-rate table of the alliances fighting on both sides. More recent schol-arship is much more cautious in trying to outline the history and particulars of a conflict about which so little is really known. What can be determined is that Lefkandi, Chalcis, and Eretria entered in-to a period of economic decline after this time and commercial leadership in Greece passed to passed to Corinth.[66] Corinth, meanwhile, rapidly took the lead in western trade and many forms of technological innovation. The poet Pindar praised prosperous Corinth as a community upon which the Muses bestowed the gift of inventiveness, the dwelling of *eunomia* (good government) and a secure foundation of wealth.[67] With her colonies in Corcyra, Sicily, Acarnania, Aetolia, Epirus and allies in Ambracia, Leucas, Epidamnus, Apollonia and Potidaea providing markets the Dorian *polis* soon grew rich in revenues. Many of these revenues came from the tolls her officials collected from the tramway over which smaller trading vessels crossed her strategic isthmus. Her trade flourishing due to her key market position and new agrarian empire, Corinth became a key site in the innovative entrepreneurial revolution. The *trireme* warship, eventually adopted by Carthage and Rome as well as other Greeks, was invented here. Responsible for vastly reducing the threat of piracy, the *trireme* was itself to have a multiplier effect on the expansion of Mediterranean trade.[68]

The growth of agricultural prosperity, the coming of iron tools and weapons, and the transformation of warfare was reflected in the strengthening of the city-state as the basic unit of Greek life in the late eighth and early seventh centuries BC. This form of organisation, known as the *polis*, soon overshadowed, but never completely eliminated, the old ethic units. The *polis* was the first community in history organised on a *civic* instead of a tribal or feudal basis. A society in which contracts were increasingly important now began to organise itself on the basis of a contract. Most *poleis* were substantially smaller than modern English counties. The centre of the *polis* was a fortified town built around a main market square called the *agora*. Much of the territory, though, was made up of agrarian villages. The most important aspect of the *polis* was that it was subject to the coded rule of law. Personal loyalty to a *basileus* was replaced by a concept in which most of the inhabitants who were born in a community were considered citizens who enjoyed full equality before the law.[69] The new *polis* was very different from the Near Eastern city-state. Its cohesiveness was based upon a firm sense of community. New theories of citizenship, first expressed by Archilocus, hoped that the *polis* would embody justice for all its citizens and restrain the excesses of market and rural oligarchies. Here was a political entity founded on abstract laws in place of divinely sanctioned men. Aristotle himself would later observe "the law-abiding *po-*

lis...outranks senseless Nineveh".[70] With the evolution of the *poleis*, the political landscape of Greece became the most fragmented in history. There were perhaps 1,300 of these units, each one totally independent and still largely self-sufficient, on the Greek mainland, with another 200 organised in the Aegean. The average size of the larger ones was a few hundred square kilometres, the average population perhaps 5,000. Within them protection and rights were granted to traders and entrepreneurial craftsmen, whether citizens or, more often, the resident aliens known as *metics*. The new citizen-republics were well suited to the new market economy. Even here, market economics and limited government marched hand-in-hand as they would in modern Britain and America. Much as England in the 1700s was much freer than the states across the channel, so were individual Greeks far more free to pursue their commercial interests than Tyrians, Assyrians, Chaldeans, or Persians. The intrusion of the Greek state on its citizens was far less than that of the above states on their own subjects. Consequently, "room for any private enterprise which may be undertaken correspondingly the greater".[71] The governments of the *poleis* were small in size and narrow in scope. Nevertheless even the *polis* was charged with setting limits to what the market could and could not be allowed to do. Property was still primarily conceived of in terms of land ownership, not commercial wealth, though the bounds between the two were becoming ever more fluid.[72]

The seventh century also witnessed the rise of a new form of rulership, that of the tyranny. Down through the centuries, the word "tyrant" has become a synonym for oppressive one-man rule. The negative image of the Greek tyrannies largely, however, derived from the fourth-century BC portraits of Aristotle and others who read into the past their own recent experiences. Historians have seen the tyrants of the seventh century BC as reformers, capitalists, opportunists, depending upon which city-state they discussed.[73] A tyranny may best be defined as a regime in which one man held authority over a *polis*. While some tyrants seized power by force, other tyrannies which were in fact hereditary: the Cypselids at Corinth, the Orthagorids at Sicyon, the Peisistratids at Athens. How then, did tyranny differ from traditional kingship? The most likely difference was that the power of the tyrants rested on other factors than mere tradition, factors which included commercial wealth and hoplite power. Apparently viewing tyranny through the lens of rulers like Dionysius of Syracuse, Aristotle despised the tyrants as demagogues who rose to power by slandering aristocrats. Aristotle also linked the rise of tyrannies to the rise of hoplite warfare, arguing that "as the states grew and the wearers of heavy armor had become stronger, more persons came to have a part in the government."[74] Aware that new forms of warfare had increased their standing in society, the masses of Greek farmers no longer deferred to hereditary monarchs or landed aristocrats. The early seventh-century BC tyrant Pheidon of Argos best fit the Aristotelian model. He was himself likely a leader of hoplites, and may well have defeated the forces of Sparta in the battle of Hysiae around 669 BC[75] Pheidon may also have unified the Argos region. Cleisthenes of Sikyon may also have been a strong military leader.[76] Did their power, as well as that of other tyrants, rest upon the hoplite phalanx? Some historians remain skeptical, but the temptation to assume so in at least some cases is strong. Were the tyrants, as P. N. Ure used to claim, early capitalists? According to this interpretation, tyrannies came into power across first the Aegean and then the mainland as coined money spread through the Aegean in the seventh century BC. Ure's theory, tantalising as it was, has now had to be discarded because coinage in Greece was found to date from the *sixth*, not the seventh century. There was, nonetheless, according to Thucydides, a connection between the rise of capitalism and the rise of tyranny:

> *As the power of Hellas grew, and the acquisition of wealth became more an object, the revenues of the states increasing, tyrannies were by their means established almost everywhere, the old form of government being hereditary monarchy with definite prerogatives, and Hellas began to fit out fleets and apply herself more closely to the sea.*[77]

Tyrants came to power at a time when Greek literature, some of it to be cited below, reflected a growing concern with the interaction of wealth and power. Tyrants all over the Greek world in the seventh century BC were putting up buildings. Theagenes of Megara built a fountain house; Cypselos built a gigantic golden statue; Cleisthenes held an enormously lavish wedding for his daughter. Growing commercial wealth made it possible for one man to hold power in a new form of government whose legitimacy did not rest upon tradition.

Most early tyrants like Cypselus or Peisistratus were not low-borne demagogues as Aristotle claimed, but rather aristocrats out of favour with the dominant oligarchies. The mother of Cypselus was a Bacchiad; Peisistratos opposed two other ruling families. In spite of being aristocrats, these early tyrants were able to muster hoplite armies and generate popular support.[78] While much of his theorising about the nature of tyranny is no longer accepted, the work of P.N. Ure was still useful in showing how some of the early tyrants adapted to the new market revolution. As it slowly accelerated, the market revolution produced not only social discontent a means through which renegade aristocrats could manipulate the politics rich and poor for their own ends. Volunteer armies of hoplites could be won over by political promises or paid to place and keep a tyrant in power. Tyrants became men of business as well as nobility, glimpsing the possibilities flowing from the growing mercantile economy.[79] Theagenes of Megara suceeded in monopolising trade in his city; the tyrants of Miletus controlled the Thracian mines; Polycrates of Samos, son of the shipper Aiakes, traded in metal and wool and controlled the island's shipping, harbour, and waterworks. Cypselus of Corinth was linked to the city's thriving pottery industry, and Peisistratus of Athens allied himself with freemen working the silver mines of Laurion. In most cases the power of the tyrants depended to same degree on their control of money, labour, and trade in their respective *poleis*. Their money-making abilities, in addition to their prowess as soldiers and orators helped motivate some of their countrymen to underwrite their political dreams.[80]

The tyrannies and their business concerns reflected an Aegean world in which the old values of ancient custom were now having to coexist with and adapt to the emerging opportunities for commercial success and the new values these opportunities bred. The seventh-century writer Hesiod recorded that potter was angry with potter, craftsman with craftsman, beggar with beggar, and minstrel with minstrel. Though it did not employ many and was on a very small scale, the pottery industry of Corinth and later, Attica, may well symbolise the very birth of consumer capitalism in a society still largely agrarian. These craftsmen, according to historian Oswyn Murray were "peculiarly open to economic pressures and incentives".[81] Discovered in Pithekoussai, the inscription on a cup imported from Rhodes witnessed the birth of commercial advertising in Homeric times: "Nestor had a most drinkworthy cup, but whoever drinks of mine will straightaway be smitten with desire of fair-crowned Aphrodite."[82] By the sixth century BC Attic craftsmen were advertising their own brand-names on the pots and vases they created. One vase said "Sophilos painted", another boasted "Exekias painted and made me" and one vase of Euthymides bragged that it was of high quality "as never (were those of) Euphronios".[83] The pottery industry in particular shows strong evidence that by the sixth century BC, potters in Corinth and elsewhere in Greece were producing pots targeted to specific markets stretching from Spain to the Black Sea. Market competition became a way of life, for once Corinthian potters produced an attractive brand of vessel which "both guaranteed a contents and marketed an image". Other Greek potters, even if only targeting a local market, were "challenged to produce even more persuasive packaging and even more attractive images".[84]

Modern archaeologists have been able to trace different pots back to their respective makers and workshops by comparing the very individualistic decorations each potter used. As early as the seventh century BC the potters of Euboea began to label their work, and the practice spread to Athens and Corinth in the following century. Sophilos was the first Athenian potter to thus identify his own work. Around the top of his vases Sophilos sometimes paraded the gods of Athens.[85] His signature, as well as that of other potters, indicated "both a pride in the product and a desire to attract future orders", their scale and elaboration "seem to justify the artist's self-promotion".[86] Other Athenian potters went after a mass market, producing vessels of a lesser artistic quality to be exported abroad, especially to the Etruscans and no doubt also the Romans. An example of this was the so-called Tyrrhenian pottery, whose mythological scenes heavily emphasised horrific moments of sex and violence, such as the decapitation of Troilos from *The Iliad*.[87]

In an increasingly profit-oriented society in which one sees the first stirrings of consumerism and free-market competition, the gaps between the new rich and the new poor began to emerge and widen. Not all citizens of the *polis* prospered. Many in Corinth and Athens faced debt slavery or deportation as market forces began to change the social fabric. The Athenian Solon (approximately 640-561 BC), himself one of the most successful of the new entrepreneurs, warned that these changes were not for the better. Proud of the fact that as civil ruler he had rescued many Athenian citizens from slavery and transportation due to debt, one of history's first reform politicians maintained that neither Athena nor even Zeus willed to destroy Athens. That would be the work of Athenians themselves. The cause would be simple: unrestrained commercial avarice:

> But the citizens themselves in their wilderness are bent on destruction of their great city, and money is the compulsive cause. The leaders of the people are evil-minded. The next stage will be great suffering, recompense for their violent acts, for they do not know enough to restrain their greed and apportion orderly shares for all as if at a decorous feast.[88]

Some of the businessman-tyrants and the businessman-politicians who superseded them thus became social reformers. Condemning the greed of his own class like many a modern patrician reformer has done, Solon chided the gentry for "sparing the property neither of the public nor of the gods". Debt slavery and the civil strife it engendered would destroy Athens unless steps were taken to eliminate it. Confronting for the first time the inequalities generated by a largely uncontrolled market society, Solon warned the new landowners and entrepreneurs that greed resulted "when great prosperity suddenly befalls those people who do not have an orderly mind".[89]

By the end of the seventh century BC the market, the *polis*, the hoplite phalanx, and tyranny were well-established in the Aegean. Developments in the sixth century BC were to further transform the Hellenic world in directions conducive to the growth and spread of market capitalism. The growing power of the *polis* was counterbalanced by a pan-Hellenic sentiment which reflected itself in the increased patronage of popular shrines like Delphi and of the Olympic Games. Coined money made its appearance in Asia Minor and spread westward to the Greek mainland, paving the way for the rise of private banking in Classical times. Farmers and immigrant aliens would flock to Athens creating an urban, cosmopolitan society. An intellectual revolution among the urban elite would weaken the power of religious tradition among the upper crust of Greek society. Finally, the challenge of Persia would weld much of Greece together under Athenian hegemony. Greek cities competed with one another in one sphere and and at the same time collaborated in another. Like the modern nations of Europe the Greek *poleis* asserted their differences while also asserting the differences which separated Greek from non-Greek. Political and cultural issues in the sixth century BC became less parochial and more pan-Hellenic, and the same was possibly true in the realm of commerce. The regional pottery styles of the seventh century BC began to give way to a dominant Athenian style during the sixth, with even Corinthian potters succumbing around 550 BC.[90]

The use of coinage, invented in the Anatolian kingdom of Lydia, was to eventually spread across the Mediterranean world due to the trading ventures of the Greeks settled in Asia Minor. It was here that Homer's fictional Phaiakians were located, and from here that the Milesians ringed the Black Sea with their agricultural colonies and trading posts. East Ionian entrepreneurs also traded with Mesopotamia along the traditional overland route joining the Euphrates with Anatolia. Milesian, Smyrnean, and other Ionian traders served as middlemen between Asia and Europe on this overland route. Lydia itself became the source of precious metals for these eastern Greek cities. Iron tools made it possible to extract Lydian gold, as well as a new alloy of gold and silver known as *electrum*. Soon the sixth-century Lydian ruler Croesus began minting electrum coins, which spread throughout Lydia and then into Ionian Greece.[91] Pre-sixth century economies rested on barter and the use of money in the form of ingots or pieces, which Sumerians, Assyrians, Babylonians, Phoenicians, and early Greeks traded for metals, food, textiles, tools, and wares. Tyrians carried bullion in leather bags stamped with silver and the city seal; Mycenaeans and Euboeans traded ingots of copper, iron, lead, gold, and silver that were roughly the same size. Iron tools now made it possible make it possible to stamp and engrave the name of a ruler or a city on metal bars, which was only one step removed from coins with a uniform weight and metal content guaranteed by an issuing government which could weigh them with improved Iron Age scales. After Lydia the first coins circulated in Miletus, Smyrna, and Ephesus, then coinage spread across the Aegean to Aegina, Corinth, and finally Athens.[92]

By the end of the sixth century BC, most Greek cities produced their own coinage, including those in Italy and Sicily. The motivations for the spread of coined money appear to have been political as well as economic. The gold-silver electrum mixture of the Lydian coins depended upon the Lydian government's authority to enforce the respective weight of both metals in the currency. In essence, the money was only valid for local exchange. By issuing such coins, a *polis* could ensure that money circulated within the local economy. The same was true to a lesser degree with the purely silver coins minted by the Greek *poleis* to the west. The new coins in effect represented declarations of economic sovereignty. Unlike the electrum coins, though, the various silver coins of Hellas were more convertible. When one of them, such as the Athenian *drachma*, would be backed by commercial political and military power, it would eventually herald the advent of a more liquid, cash-based economy.[93]

The spread of coined money not only in the cities but also in the countryside of Greece further commercialised *polis* society. Soon even haggling between goatherds and olive-growers in a thousand tiny towns would involve the silver coins of Athens, upon which was stamped the figure of an owl. Barter, a staple of business for over 2000 years, certainly did not disappear from Hellenic life, but pure monetary exchanges more and more permeated society. Coins simplified business dealings and trade and ensured the ultimate triumph of the market in Greece and across the Mediterranean. The law of supply and demand, so essential to market success, could now operate on a much broader scale, favouring the spread in Greece of independent enterprise in place of internalised organisations. Commercial risks could be more easily handled by contractual financial arrangements made in coin than by barter:

> *It is not as yet possible to establish clearly whether the Hellenic spiritual refinement of Mediterranean economy with the help of the coin can be connected, in the final instance, with unwritten economic laws which may have become effective with the transition of mankind to an Iron Age. The approximate similarity of the almost contemporary development in China to that in Asia Minor and the Greek motherland makes such an immanent mechanism appear likely.[94]*

It is no surprise that the spread of coined money and liquid capital reinforced the development of the civic *polis,* and vice versa:

The striking of coin money and the use of capital for interest are eco-nomically unthinkable without a suitable background for profitable capital transactions which the early Greek polis organizations had to create both by laws and by attracting enterprising settlers, if its founders wanted to succeed and endure.[95]

The relationship between market and temple was more complex in Greece than in the Orient. Greek life lacked the powerful, central-ised temple hierarchies of Uruk, Ashur, or Tyre. The priests and se-ers of Hephaestus, Artemis, Aphrodite, Poseidon, Apollo, Hera and even Zeus himself had less control over the market than those of En-lil, Enki, Ashur, Marduk, and Melkart. Greek oracles and shrines were nevertheless connected with commerce, often being posted in economically important and strategic places along boundaries and trade routes in much the same way as Phoenician ones. The temple of Apollo at Delos was connected with the trade of the Cyclades and Asia Minor. Aphrodite shrines served as *emporia* for Greek-Phoeni-cian trade and a shrine of Hera served a similar function in regard to the Etruscans. Within Greece itself the temple of Demeter guarded the narrow pass to the north near Thermopylae, and the shrine of Hera was strategically located in Argos. Sanctuaries of Zeus at Ol-ympia and Dodona were also well-placed to serve travelers.[96] A cen-tral oracle did exist at Delphi, but most Greeks worshipped in small independent *polis* shrines. Religion in the Greek world would have a more entrepreneurial cast than in the Orient. Some would profit from religious activities, although it would be going too far to say that Greek religion itself would follow the dictates of the market. Af-ter 600 BC one finds travelling evangelists for various Greek deities, many of whom are self-appointed and in competition with other shrine prophets. Professor Morris Silver recognised that in Greece, "entrepreneurs also played a central role in cultic innovation."[97]

Plato himself would eventually denounce the proliferation of pri-vate cults in Greece and the ownership of many of these cults by private families. The Eteoboutadai family of Athens operated the shrines of Poseidon and Athena on the Acropolis. The shrine of Zeus was owned by the Praxiergidai and the famous Eleusinian Mysteries were operated by the Eumolpidai and Kerykes. Religious entrepreneurs founded sanctuaries, hired priests, and charged reve-nues, theology itself being somewhat influenced by the market revolution. Euripides and other playwrights, moreover, were not slow to accuse these "religious entrepreneurs" of less than sincere devotion to their gods and goddesses. The ruler Pentheus of Thebes in Euripides' *Bacchae* accused the prophet Teiresias of hoping to make a financial killing in the handsome fees he was charging for divining the will of his new deities.[98]

It would be a mistake to overstate the extent of religious skepticism in either Archaic or Classical Greece, as it would have been to do so in Enlightenment France. Most Greek farmers and traders, the overwhelming majority of the population, continued to believe in, fear, and pray to Zeus and other deities. The sixth-century BC in Greece nevertheless witnessed the flourishing of a small intellectual elite which, for the first time, questioned the supernatural world-views that underpinned so much of Phoenician and Mesopotamian business culture. The rise of the market economy may well have been a factor in this new skeptical attitude on the part of a few towards traditional Hellenic religion. The poet Xenophanes suggested that free markets engendered free minds as well:

> *Our gods have flat noses and black skins say the Ethiopians.*
> *The Thracians say our gods have red hair and hazel eyes.*
> *There is one God-supreme among gods and men–*
> *who is like mortals in neither body nor mind.*
> *They acquired useless luxuries out of Lydia*
> *while still free from her odious tyranny;*
> *paraded to the market place in sea purple robes,*
> *often in bright swarms of a thousand.*
> *They were proud and pleased in their elaborate hairdos*
> *and hid body odor with rare perfumes*
> *The gods did not enrich man*
> *with a knowledge of all things*
> *from the beginning of life.*
> *Yet man seeks, and in time*
> *invents what might be better.* [99]

Even as early as Homer's time, at least a few well-to-do Greeks had begun to question the old moral order along with the old economy. Telemachus symbolised those who, in the eighth century, had already abandoned the faith of their parents:

I believe no messages any more, even should there be one, nor pay attention to any prophecy, those times my mother calls some diviïer into the house² and asks him questions.[100]

Such skepticism must have been more widespread among the elites by the sixth century BC. Traders were exposed to the belief systems of a score of different cultures: Thracians, Scythians, Persians, Medes, Jews, Egyptians, Chaldeans, Phoenicians, Moschians, Lydians, Etruscans, Libyans and others. Seeing that every nation had a different theology, it was difficult for at least some hard-headed merchants to still assert that his gods were superior to those of his customers. Traders such as Thales of Miletus pondered such questions while buying and selling goods from all over the known world. As he toiled to monopolise the market in olive oil in Miletus, Thales began to study both navigation and the movements of the sun, moon, and stars. Unlike the Tyrians, who saw the heavenly bodies and natural phenomena as manifestations of gods, goddesses, and spirits, Thales soon concluded that eclipses and winds, far from being divine omens of Baal and Apollo, operated according to predictable, rational laws. The consequences of Thales' discoveries, and those of other Milesians like Anaximander who accepted them, would slowly weaken the controlling influence religion in the Hellenic marketplace. If some in educated circles no longer believed Zeus would directly intervene in the weather, how then could they view them as able to intervene in other aspects of a society governed by impersonal natural laws? Throughout the sixth century BC, vast new temples were erected to various Greek deities, but the gods and goddesses to whom they were dedicated were now, in spirit, much more confined to their columned stone temples. Their influence upon what went on in the harbour or the *agora* would be less profound. The will of Melkart in the Tyrian marketplace remained inviolable; Apollo and Zeus in Corinth, Miletus, and Athens were more likely not to interfere in the private goings-on of everyday life. A growing free market in ideas was slowly encouraged by a free market in economics: "Once the theology was taken out of causal thinking, it became plain that ideas were, quite simply competing with one another on their own merits."[101]

Some who questioned the sway of Olympus in human affairs would also be led to question both the sway of oligarchs and tyrants beneath Olympus as well as the results of unrestrained avarice under the rule of both. The result was the emergence, especially in Athens, of the social reformer and, ultimately, the democrat. In the meantime, the entire Hellenic world would be challenged by the effort of the Persian Xerxes to extend the old hierarchical model of society from Asia to Europe. In the mid-sixth century BC the armies of Cyrus incorporated Asia Minor, including Ionia, into a vast Persian realm which eventually stretched from the Aegean to India. In spite of its relative religious and political tolerance, the heavy-handed taxation of Achaemenid Persia was not welcomed by the entrepreneurial Greeks of Ionia, who staged an unsuccessful revolt at the end of the century. Persian intervention paved the way for the democratisation of Athens and a major war in which most Greeks united under Athenian leadership to challenge the military and commercial power of the entire Near East. The Persian suppression of the Ionian revolt deprived Athens of important markets, resulting in a political revolution in which the democrat Cleisthenes dethroned the ruling oligarchs and replaced them with a system in which every free man had the right to vote.[102]

The Persian Wars represented not only a struggle between a rising democracy and a Near eastern despotism, but a conflict between two different styles of economic management. Persian business organisation inherited the temple and princely hierarchies of the Levant and Mesopotamia; the Greek city states nourished the new traditions of independent enterprise. Persia managed trade according to the rules of Dunning's *Eclectic Paradigm* while Greece threw them away. Aligned firmly on the Persian side were the merchant-princes of Tyre and Sidon, who feared that the upstart Hellenes threatened their Mediterranean markets. The mariners of Tyre joined forces with the armies and fleets of Cyrus, Darius, Xerxes when they plundered Phocaea and Miletus and invaded the Aegean and mainland Greece itself. Persia's westward thrust ensured that "one of the largest Ionian shipping centres collapsed to the advantage of Phoenician traders" so that the eastern Mediterranean "once again became a Phoenician lake".[103] Redirecting their trade to the vast internal market of Persia, the shipbuilders of Tyre were only too happy to lend their fleet to Xerxes, King of Kings, in his all-out effort to crush the upstart Hellenes and restore Tyre's original trading sphere. The powerful trading organisations of

Phoenicia still functioned in the sixth century BC, but their scope and focus would be redirected from the Mediterranean to the east.[104] In 480 BC Xerxes, supported by a combined Persian-Tyrian fleet, marched a vast army through Thrace, overrunning most of Greece, pillaging Athens, and wiping out the Spartan defenders of Thermopylae. Greece was saved by her new democratic assembly in league with her shipbuilding entrepreneurs. Inspired by the orator Themistocles, the Athenian Assembly had had the foresight to use silver from the mines of Laurion to finance the construction of a large new fleet, whose *trireme* warships (three rowers on each oar) were constructed by private contractors. Luring the Persian-Phoenician fleets into a narrow channel the new Athenian navy routed them at Salamis in 479 BC. Cut off from his supplies, Xerxes abandoned his invasion of Greece. Europe would remain free of Persian domination and instead would embrace the Hellenic and later the Roman models of market enterprise. Tyre and Sidon were finished as world economic powers, being forced to content themselves with a reduced role within a decaying Persian system. Democracy and the market revolution provided Athens and her Hellenic allies the flexibility and the tools to rapidly create a navy equipped with the latest warships. Professor Robert Sallares found a more long-term cause for the triumph of Greece: population growth linked to the market revolution. Not only were the Athenian *triremes* superior to their mostly Phoenician rivals, but the Greek hoplites may even have outnumbered the supposedly huge Persian army on land. Persia had a dense population relative to Babylon and the other Asia regions it absorbed. Her population in comparison with European Greece may have been another matter.[105] The size of the Persian army itself may have been greatly exaggerated by Herodotus. It is thus possible that while an Assyrian army might have been able to conquer the sparsely-populated Greece of the eighth century BC, the armies of Xerxes may have found the Greece of the fifth century BC too demographically strong to absorb:

> *The manpower concentration in a small are, facilitating easy mobilisation of a large force, together with the fact that in Greek poleis the degree of participation of the adult male population in the army and navy could approach 100 per cent in principle, while the degree of participation of the subject peoples in the Persian armed forces was very low*

for the most part, provide the real, sociological explanation...of how it was that the Greeks, in fact only a part of them, were able to resist the Persian onslaught successfully. It is possible to go still further and argue that the attack from the Orient failed because it happened to come at at time when Greece was overflowing with manpower.[106]

Salamis inaugurated the Classical era and the golden age of Athenian commerce and democracy. Greece was now dominated by an Athenian-led alliance known as the Delian League. Athens and the larger states built the *triremes* while the smaller *poleis* provided cash. Eventually, only Athens with its Peiraeus dockyards, workers, and large number of job-seekers was willing to provide the warships, dominating the alliance in the manner in which the United States came to dominate NATO. Military dependence upon Athenian hoplites and *triremes* for their own defence compelled many Aegean states to accept Athenian taxation and regulation of their trade. The League quickly transformed itself into an informal Athenian imperialism. While deterring Persian expansion for half a century, Athens drew what today would be the equivalent of perhaps £125 million in tribute from her allies. This first "Cold War" economy brought unprecedented prosperity to many, if not most Athenians. Given that all classes of the city's 30-40,000 male citizens could vote for the Assembly, both rich and poor had an ongoing stake in maintaining the fleet and seeing to it that the rest of the League financed it. Shipbuilders profited from the manufacture of *triremes*, merchants from selling shipbuilders timber and pitch from the Black Sea, bankers from financing their voyages with exorbitant loans, smiths from making and exporting large quantities of hoplite arms. Masons profited from building fortifications linking Athens and the Peiraeus. Labourers of the poorer classes enlisted in the navy to row the *triremes* about the Aegean and ensured those they elected to the Assembly appropriated the *drachmas* to maintain the fleet and the alliance paying for it in being.[107]

Athens in the mid-fifth century BC reached the height of power and prosperity. The first free-market metropolis in history gave birth to the first democratic and civic urban culture. Within the circle of private homes and small farmhouses clustered in the surrounding villages of Attica, the beginnings of urban Europe were already evident in the rows of open-air Greek houses crowded along the narrow, twisting boulevards beneath the Acropolis. Everywhere were the signs of a confident people. No symbol of that confidence was greater than the vast Parthenon and the other splendid buildings constructed by Pericles on the Acropolis towering over the growing, prospering city.[108] These extravagant structures, costing approximately £600 million in current terms, became the symbols of Athenian pride and glory during the Periclean age. The decor of the massive Parthenon, dedicated to Athena, proclaimed the message that the gods and goddesses of Olympus, or at least Athena, were on the side of Athens, even though the average educated Athenian worshipped them only at his or her convenience. The statues adorning the temple spoke volumes about a society that was more devoted to Athenians than to Athena. For centuries the peoples of the Orient and the Greeks themselves depicted the human form in stiff, idealised poses, of which the sculptures of Egypt were by far the best example. Now, the Classical sculptures of nude male athletes and warriors and women in fine robes with bent arms and muscular torsos adorning the buildings of Pericles pictured humanity on its own terms, in life and in movement, as it really was and not how the gods wished it to be.[109]

Imperial Athens in the first half of the fifth century BC clearly felt a sense of superiority not only over Persian and Phoenician, but no doubt over most Hellenes as well. The economic and intellectual centre of gravity in the Greek world itself had shifted from Miletus and Ionia to Attica. If most Greek culture of 700-500 BC had come from Asia Minor, the culture of Athens fully dominated the post-500 BC era. This culture represented the Hellenic free-market model in its most advanced form. Interestingly, little of the literature of the fifth century BC concerned itself with trade, business, or economics. With commerce flourishing, issues of injustice were seen as having been solved long ago. In addition to the empire, the state-run silver mines of Laurion provided the underpinnings of Athenian wealth. As in Mid-Victorian Britain or America in the 1950s, issues of poverty and the maldistribution of income were largely ignored in a time of evident prosperity. There would be little distress in Attica until the outbreak of war in the 430s BC. Much like the Whig historians Trevelyan and Macaulay in nineteenth-century Britain and the consensus historians in 1950s America, both of which Classical Athens so nicely foreshadows, Herodotus eloquently wrote of the triumph of Hellenic civilisation over Persian tyranny. Beyond this, the fifth century BC in Athens was a time of confident money-making, not philosophising. Foreign traders in ancient Ashur, Ugarit, Tyre, and Carthage were heavily discriminated against in those cities. Overseas commerce had to remain in native hands. Most Hellenic poleis, notably Sparta, enacted similar restrictions. In democratic Athens, however, immigrants were not only welcomed but permitted and even encouraged to transact business. As the metics, as they were called, were not allowed to be citizens or own landed property, most of them entered into the trade and business occupations disdained by many native-born Athenians. All important company managers and most tradesmen were either immigrants from other poleis or outright non-Hellenes. After the Persian War thousands of metics settled in Athens and especially the Peiraeus, where they eventually distinguished themselves in commerce and, eventually, in the arts. One cannot discuss the economy of Athens without making some reference to the role of slavery, which was more tolerable in Athens than elsewhere. Few Athenian slaves were Hellenes. Most belonged to individual owners. The lot of those unfortunate enough to toil in the Laurion mines was, however, much harsher. Much of the labour in small Athenian factories was composed of slaves who worked alongside freemen and earned the same wages. In theory property, Athenian slaves eventually won certain rights from the Assembly, which forbade them to be beaten, killed, or subjected to prolonged abuse. Athenian slaves could even sue to be given a new master. Some eventually could even earn their freedom.[110]

The Athenian business world was unlike any business culture that had previously existed in history. Both the market and the rule of law played a major role in organising society. Traders sailed into the narrow entrance harbour of the Peiraeus to be met by customs officials who inspected their wares and levied a 2% toll. Harbour agents then charged the merchant for using dock facilities. Avoiding the naval harbours where the triremes of the League were docked, private vessels then landed at the business wharves of the emporion. The longest pier was for those ships bringing in grain. The naukleros next had to deal with the middlemen and the local grain inspectors. Nearby, in the same business district were the shops of an emerging consumer society where one could buy pottery, fish, naval stores, textiles and ivory from Africa, furniture from Asia, or meat from Sicily. Throughout the summer the bazaar was the scene of hundreds of deals among the small traders and moneychangers who formed the backbone of the Athenian economy. With the coming of the autumn rains ships were beached and merchants closed up shop until spring. For almost two centuries Athens seemed like the centre of the world to those who lived there. Boasting one of the best harbours, most stable currencies, and freest society in antiquity, Athens offered a sure market for any trader able to reach her shores. Above all, the trade in grain remained paramount. According to the traditional view about 800 voyages from the Pontus each summer were needed to feed 200,000 to 300,000 Athenians, and most of this came from the voyages of small independent traders. More recent scholarship by ecologist Robert Sallares, however, suggests that the slave population of Athens must have been a lot smaller than previously estimated. If this is true, Athens was probably less dependent in peacetime upon the wheat of the Pontus for mere subsistence. Nevertheless, imported cereals and fish still brought great demand. There was no organised fleet on the Tyrian model plying northward from Athens through the Hellespont. Hellenic traders mostly sailed alone, after writing out their individual contracts with shipowners, bankers, and middlemen. Borrowing his drachmas from a banker at the enormous interest rates of around 20-30% for five months, each trader used the loan to charter a ship if he personally did not own one. If he did, his vessel became his collateral, otherwise, he would have to pledge his cargo. The Athenian economy was infinitely more risk-oriented than the Tyrian had been: there was no internalised private-public structure to absorb any losses. The trader might lose his life, the shipowner his vessel, the banker his loan. Once the ships actually sailed, they faced other challenges. Those on the Pontus route had to fight the northerly Etesian winds all the way to Scythia, but had an easy ride home. Those going to Egypt had an easy ride south but had to fight their way back to Athens; those heading west to Sicily had a tail wind on one side of the Peloponnesus and a head wind on the other. Even if he arrived home safely, the naukleros was by no means assured of profit. Grain prices in Greece were not fixed, and, if deflation ensued, a merchant could finish with a loss after repaying the banker and shipowner. Even though the growing trade and financial sector of the

Athenian economy anticipated the future model of Anglo-Saxon capitalism, its role must not be exaggerated. Greece in the fifth century BC was by no means a modern urban society. Though agriculture and industry were becoming market-based and specialised, the independent farmer and tradesman remained supreme. A list of trades at the end of the fifth century BC included agricultural labourer, gardener, oil and walnut peddlers, donkey and mule drivers, potters, builders, carpenters, cooks, bakers, and porters. Rooted in these small enterprises, Hellenic industrial life had less in common with the factory system of modern times than with the re-emerging custom-made production of the post-industrial era. Athenian capitalism knew no factories on the scale of even the Dickens era:

> the largest known are shield factories like those of Pasion or Cephalus, which employed about a hundred slaves. The mines of Laurion were the only exception, and even here the maximum number of slaves working a pit was usually under a hundred. With neither mechanisation, concentration, nor the organisation of work into specialised highly repetitive tasks, few Greek workers felt alienated enough to form unions in the modern sense. Athenian capitalism remained individualistic to its core. Most businesses employed but two or three people. While the Assembly and its inspectors kept a close watch on collecting customs duties and preventing fraud, the fifth-century Athenian state maintained a laissez-faire attitude as far as wages and working conditions were concerned. Prior to the Peloponnesian War, neither politicians nor a work force which could not even conceive of unions seem to have believed that the market itself and personal relationships based on virtue and intelligent self-interest would enable the system to operate.[111]

Private banking was to become a very important aspect of the Athenian economy, by financing the seaborne trade through which Athens and the major city-states now had to feed themselves. Most historians have, until the 1990s tended to stress the "primitive" nature of the Athenian economy. Bankers, in this view, were little more than petty lenders and most loans were given on an interest-free basis. It is true that few bank deposits have been found in inventories of Greek estates. Recent scholarship, though, very much discounts the idea that Athenians buried their money at home. A huge invisible economy based on capital dealings in which avoidance of taxation and creditors and profit-seeking through investment in banking enterprises came into being. Athenian business law recognised disclosed property, which was subject to often punitive taxation, and undisclosed property, which was easier to conceal. In fourth-century Athens, the decline in income from the silver mines and the loss of empire created an intolerable tax burden upon the richest citizens. These citizens, moreover, were obligated to finance the navy, the arts, and other civic projects. The burden of these various taxes helped stimulate the growth of the invisible banking economy. The notion that Athenian merchants and others were gleeful taxpayers motivated by good citizenship must now be revised to reveal an overtaxed business establishment entrusting its liquid assets to private banks where it might be hidden from the tax collector. Bankers made loans in secrecy and were able to publicly shield the identity of their depositors, many of whom, like Demosthenes' father, invested in maritime loans and privately reaped the benefits.[112]

The Athenian bank operated in a society which did not recognise the corporation as a legal person. The Greek tradition of independent enterprise, moreover, frowned upon Athenian citizens performing servile work for another. Slaves and dependent family members, however, became natural employees for Greek bankers, and often inherited the business on the death of the proprietor. Free employees, on the other hand, might eventually set up their own rival businesses in the minimally regulated Greek economy. When Pasion leased his bank to his former slave Phormion, he insisted on an agreement forbidding him from engaging in competition with Pasion. On his deathbed, moreover, he insisted Phormion marry his widow to guarantee that both the bank and his other businesses remained in his household. Slaves handled money, received and gave out deposits, and evaluated security for loans.[113] All Athenian banks and business were considered personal enterprises with no legal existence apart from their owner. Examples were the bed-making shop of Demosthenes' father or the shield factory of the banker Pasion. Money on deposit with a Classical Greek bank was said to be on deposit with the banker. Bankers like Pasion tended to mingle their deposits with their own personal funds, in which case a bank failure would ruin everyone. Greek banks were often managed out of the owners' home, as were many other enterprises. Little equipment was needed, perhaps a table, a scale, an abacus, and papyrus rolls. Unlike his shield shop, Pasion's bank had little value apart from the considerable money that passed through it.[114]

Banking in Athens as a result became highly personal, as bankers formed networks of friends with whom they dealt. Pasion became not only lender but personal confidant to the son of Sopaios. The overseas trader Timosthenes was not only a customer of Pasion but a close friend and business partner of Pasion's own slave, Phormion. The general Timotheos borrowed cloaks, bedding and other items from Pasion's bank to entertain visiting dignitaries.[115]

The life of the Athenian slave-banker Pasion in the late fifth century BC illustrates more than any other the entrepreneurial nature of the Classical Greek economy. Purchased by two Athenian bankers, Antisthenes and Archistratus, the barbarian Pasion began work carrying the heavy bags of owl-faced Athenian *drachma* coins for his masters. In a story not unlike that of the Biblical Joseph, the honest and diligent slave was soon operating a money changing table in the Peiraeus. A superb accountant, Pasion could quickly spot crooked dealers and poor credit risks. He became indispensable to Antisthenes and Archistratus who not only granted Pasion his freedom but eventually, when they retired, turned over to him the ownership of the bank.

Banking in Athens was the province of businessmen, not priests, and Pasion was undoubtedly the best and most reputable of them all. Not only traders but soldiers and politicians became his customers. He performed all the functions expected of the new class of professional Hellenic bankers: storing coins and valuables, transferring funds to banks in Athens or even in other cities. To spare a client the risk of carrying bags of money through stormy, perilous waters, Pasion could write bank drafts which a *naukleros* could cash in Olbia, Sinope, Cyrene, or maybe even Syracuse. As Pasion's Peiraean bank accumulated more and more capital from interest and shipping loans, he became a major investor in the Athenian economy. He formed a shipping company and a munitions factory to arm Athenian hoplites. Not only did he give the army a free gift of a thousand shields but he financed a fleet of five *triremes* for the Athenian navy. The Assembly rewarded its model businessman with the high reward of citizenship. Now an Athenian citizen, Pasion could not only own landed property, but his banking conglomerate could now invest in real estate. In his old age, the former slave found no qualified heir among his children, so he turned the enterprise over to Phormio, his manager and himself a former slave. By marrying Pasion's widow, Phormio ensured that the honest, reputable firms of Pasion remained in family hands.[116]

The story of Pasion and Phormio showed Athens to be a much more fluid, cash-based society than had ever existed before. In Tyre, wealth, status, and citizenship had to be inherited; in Athens even a barbarian slave might possibly become a powerful business manager. Bloodlines, military prowess, temple connections, or feudal loyalties meant little in the merit-based republican Athens. Made up of free entrepreneurs instead of a state-supported network of interlocking hierarchies, the Athenian economy was operated on the liquid flow of cash. Impersonal dealings made in coin and bank notes transferred money from traders to bankers to other traders to moneylenders and other traders. Commodity prices, no longer fixed as they were in Babylonia, fluctuated daily on the Athenian and other price exchanges, bringing into existence a class of speculators. While personal trust and honour in business dealings did not disappear, they certainly carried far less weight than the legal weight of a contract and the credit rating of a client in a market- and cash-based system:

Athens of the fourth century BC was just the time and place where a Horatio Alger career like that of Pasion and Phormio could happen. Commerce was more vital to the city's existence than it ever had been before. In the fifth century Pericles, a soldier and statesman, had led Athens in his office as a member of the board of generals; one hundred years later her destinies were guided by men like Eubulus and Lycurgus, financial experts serving her in the office of chancellor of the exchequer. A web of trade routes criss-crossed the waters between Marseilles and Kertsch, and bankers and shippers and shipowners cooperated in sending over them every conceivable sort of product, especially the basic commodities of the ancient world: wine, oil, and grain. Traders in Byzantium on the Bosporus cocked a wary eye on the crop in Sicily eight hundred miles away; rumors of a bad harvest in Egypt sent prices soaring on the exchanges of half a dozen Greek cities. At the center of this hectic commercial activity stood Athens with its seaport town, the Peiraeus.[117]

The Athenian Empire and commercial transformation of the fifth and fourth centuries BC coincided with the adoption of a mercantile ethic by many Greek farmers as well as urban dwellers. Food now did not have to be grown at home, and more money could now be made by trafficking in pottery, metals, or by mercenary service abroad than by growing grain, wine, and olives in Attica. The urbanised economy of Classical Athens made possible the growth of classes whose wealth was based on commerce and not pure agriculture.[118] The *polis* endured, but its conservative political institutions which still excluded foreigners, freedmen, and slaves, could no longer adapt to commercial realities.[119] These realities, so apparent in the day-to-day interactions of people in the Athenian *agora*, were exposed by the fourth-century orator Demosthenes.[120] Demosthenes described sale and purchase with that of the language of politics and war: the purchaser defeated the seller whenever he bought something, and the seller who refused to take a bribe was likewise a winner over the purchaser.[121] Demosthenes' metaphors could only work on the assumption that "in commercial exchange there were winners and losers, just as in battles and bribery."[122] The Hellenic market economy was a product of a society of independent farmers. Yeoman agriculture encouraged both the formation of the *polis* and the freedom of the independent trader. This egalitarian system, however, had to adapt itself to the market economy it had spawned. By the fifth and fourth centuries BC the new commercial society of Athens still preached the old hoplite ethic of egalitarian landowners, while its reality was that of a city filled with immigrants and slaves none of which enjoyed the rights of formal citizenship. Wealth was now accessible in other forms than household agriculture, through banking, trading, mining, and manufacturing. The old ideals of equality and self-sufficiency were still preached, but they no longer corresponded to the way many and perhaps most Athenians lived. Athens met this dilemma by moving towards democracy, accommodating the landless, building a large navy, and turning to the sea rather than subsistence for a livelihood, all of which betrayed the old ideals of landed self-sufficiency.[123] Every person, every drachma, brought into Athens in some sense eroded the exclusive hoplite/citizen/landowner trinity. That centuries-old entity could cope with the slow economic growth and static military conditions of the seventh and sixth centuries far more successfully

Flagon of polychrome ware-tablets

In what is now Turkey archaeologists found the first multinational business records. Business deals between Assyrian subsidiaries and their Anatolian customers were recorded on the hundreds of clay tablets found in the excavated offices of Kanesh. This cup is a sample of the one of history's earliest files of business records. Tablets recording business deals and invoices were stored in them.

Tablets recording a grain sale – probably from the Assyrian trading colony at Kultepe Cappadocian

Here is a sample of an early Assyrian invoice from the trading colony at Kanesh. It records a business deal in which grain was sold.

Akkadian: Four tablets recording contracts 2400-2200 B.C.

The Assyrian multinationals evolved after centuries of Mesopotamian trading experience. The invention of writing itself is connected with the keeping of business records by the Sumerians and their Akkadian successors. These four tablets, written in Akkadian, from the time of the Sargonid Empire in the late second millennium BC are among humanity's earliest commercial contracts.

Kultepe pottery sherds *contemporary with Assyrian settlement*

Animal forms and heads

Pictures from the Ashmolean Museum, University of Oxford

Cappadocian cylinder seals
1900-1750 BC

Business historians are able to reconstruct what they know of ancient enterprise through over a century of discoveries by archaeologists. Pottery fragments, tablets, and cylinder seals like these found at the time and place of the Assyrian multinational enterprise in Kanesh help us to both date and understand the settlements. The cylinder seals were like today's rubber stamps used to notarise and certify business documents.

Letter from Tirirsama to Niqmepa.
Seal of Tirirsama 14th century B.C.

Early Phoenician business records in the north were written on clay, like their Mesopotamian counterparts, and often involved princes and the Crown as much as civil records did. The tablets of Ras Shamra and Ugarit, since their discovery in and near the ruins of the royal palace of Ugarit, are a major source for understanding Phoenician, Israelite, and Syrian business practices. They show a model of managed feudal enterprise in some ways like that of modern Japan.
Here is a sample Ugaritic document written to Prince Niqmepa from one Tirisama, who may have been a trader, a prince, or both.

Glass vessel restored from fragments 14th century BC.
Ivory toilet box in form of duck from level IV room b of Niqmepa palace Tell Atshana 1939.550-551 LateBronze Age

Merchant princes of Ugarit, like Sinaranu, traded goods such as these glass vessels and toilet box across the Aegean. In doing so, they would begin to draw the Greek world into the network of Mediterranean trade.

Pictures from the Ashmolean Museum, University of Oxford

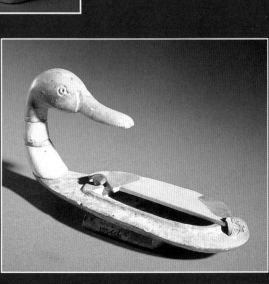

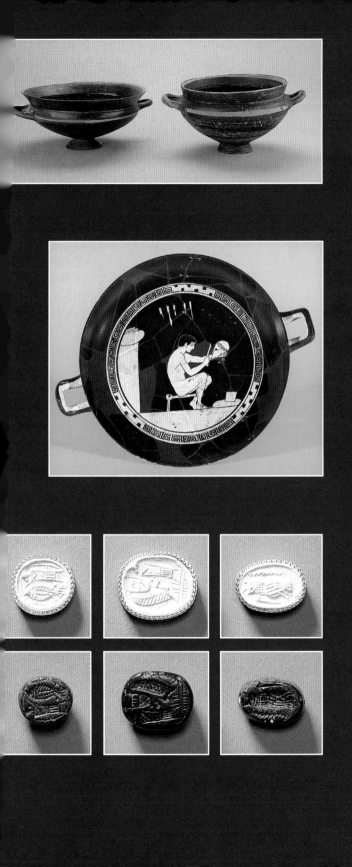

Cups from Al Mina East Greek 7th century B.C.

These Greek cups represent the beginning of the Hellenic entrepreneurial revolution. They are perhaps the first Greek goods to be traded abroad as the merchants of Euboea responded to the stimulus of Phoenician trade. The cups were likely made in Euboea and brought to Syria by either Tyrian middlemen or the first Euboean traders.

Athenian red-figure pottery cup found at Oriveto, Italy
Helmet-maker attributed to "the Antiphon Painter"

An Athenian red-figure cup exported to Oriveto, Italy. Pottery such as this has enabled archaeologists to trace the development of Greek commerce. Cups often bore the manufacturer's personal trademark. The beautiful art and decorations on Greek pottery show the evolution of individual enterprise and the hoplite citizen-warfare which allowed it to flourish.
Athenian art on cups shows the weapons and tactics of the Greek citizen armies and the entrepeneurial nature of Greek business.

The Lyre-Player Group

Trails of artifacts often illustrate ancient trade routes.
These seals show a man playing a lyre, or primitive harp. They come from Syria in the 8th century B.C. and have been found in a trail scattered from Syria to the Aegean to Etruscan Italy. This trail shows the routes followed by Phoenician and later Hellenic traders.

Pictures from the Ashmolean Museum, University of Oxford

Model of Pliny the Younger's Villa on the Laurentine Shore SW of Rome

Villas dotted the shores of Roman Italy in the Late Republic. Many Roman businesses operated from villas such as this where agriculture and industries related to clay could be supervised by the same owners and managers. They were virtually self-contained units but also became centres of trade for Rome's family-based enterprise. Small workshops involved in the making of goods often adjoined villas as precursors of the medieval manor.

Model made by Clifford Pember

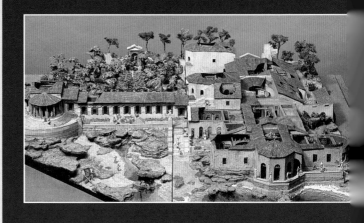

Rectangular stamp of IAN VARUS working for DOMITIA LVCILLA

Roman contractors and managers in the stone, brick, and clay industries in the Late Republic began to identify their manufactured work with stamps such as this. These stamps, which here show the employee or contractor Ian Varus working for Domitia Lucilla, who was likely his manager, allowed Roman consumers and judges to bring legal action against Roman contractors under a growing body of business law. On these stamps, contractors like Varus had to identify the managers of their businesses.

Large Roman Amphorae from shipwreck off Sardinia made 1st century BC or AD

These huge Roman jugs, classified by the archaeologist Dressel were filled with wine exported from the villas of Roman Italy to the shores of France.
Literally hundreds of these jugs have been found on sunken ships off the French Riviera or buried in places like Toulouse, showing the massive Roman investment in selling wine to the Gaulish market at the end of the Republic. Later jugs indicate that during the Empire, Gaulish merchants would begin to steal the Italian market in wine.

than the expansion and monetization of the fifth-century economy. The silver mines of Laurion, the rise of small factories, the growth of fleet and empire all drew slaves and *metics* to Athens in vast numbers. Capital could now be found outside agriculture in large amounts, especially from mining and banking. A new Athenian establishment arose including not only hoplite farmers but rich aliens, freed slaves, and new naturalised citizens. By the fifth century there may have been as many as 40,000 resident aliens and 150,000 slaves in Athens. Out of an adult population of perhaps 250,000, maybe 20,000 were hoplites liable for military service. Many of the old farmers flocked to the city as well, seeing the benefits the new capitalist democracy had to offer. They soon paid commercial taxes and accepted salaries to trade across the Aegean and Mediterranean. Even those farmers who stayed at home were to profit by selling cash crops in an inflationary economy not unlike that of the 1970s. The result was political tension between old hoplites and new Athenians. Farmers fought wage earners as they did in the American 1890s when the former supported William Jennings Bryan and the latter William McKinley. The new money economy was fluid and volatile, the rich getting richer, the poor poorer and the agrarian middle shrinking. The democratisation of the Athenian *polis*, however, did serve to diminish this antagonism.[124]

The Athenian ascendancy lasted but a few decades. It was to be ended by the outbreak of the Peloponnesian War of 431-404 BC which pitted Athens and its allies against the states of the Peloponnesus led by the conservative oligarchy of a Sparta whose values in many ways were still untouched by the democratic and capitalist revolution of Athens. The main causes of the war were geopolitical rather than economic, even though a few historians over the years have tried to prove otherwise. In the 1940s G.B. Grundy insisted that Athens and Sparta went to war over the issue of who would control the trade routes to the west. The alliance between Athens and Corcyra, on the island of Corfu off the Albanian shore, supposedly threatened Corinth, Sparta, and other Peloponnesian states with economic strangulation. When Athens blockaded Megara and Potidaea in 431 BC, denying them grain, the Corinthians, fearing Athens could do the same to them and pressured Sparta to go to war.[125] Most historians still insist that the main cause was the fear of Sparta and her allies of unrestrained Athenian naval power, but market concerns cannot be dismissed. Control of the sea routes to Sicily was strategically very important, and Sparta's rulers knew that the loss of commercial Corinth and its vital navy would destroy the Spartan-led Peloponnesian League and lead to the unchecked rule of Athens. [126]

War began when Sparta sent an ultimatum to Athens which the Athenian Assembly rejected. Corinth was far more hostile in spirit than Sparta was, pressuring the latter to declare war, continue the war, aiding Syracuse against Athens during the war, and demanding the destruction of Athens after the war.[127] Corinthian hostility to Athens is reflected in the archaeological record. Corinthian pottery imports from Attica began to decline around 450 BC, and decreased sharply with the outbreak of the war around 431 BC The imports, though, never ceased during the war. There were a great deal of Attic imports in the mid-fifth century BC which were later replaced by Corinthian imitations. Attic pottery also continued to appear in other cities that were at war with Athens, indicating that "the actual state of war did not seriously disrupt such trade nor was an official or popular embargo on the import and export of pottery encouraged."[128]

The warring states permitted continued trading of non-essential items. It would seem, in fact, that "military or political interference in all trade during the Peloponnesian War appears to have been of sporadic and limited effect."[129] Some evidence does suggest that Athens tried to interfere with the shipment of Sicilian grain to the Peloponnesus and that Sparta tried to do likewise, but that such attempts at economic warfare were ineffective. Athenians moved into the Hellespont to secure the grain of the Black Sea, but they could not prevent the rebelling Mytileneans from importing it. Athens attempted a naval blockade of the Aegean island, but lacked the bases and resources to make it effective. In all of this commercial contracts between citizens of the warring states were still recognised. Strategic economic factors did play a role in the war's conduct. Athens sought to guarantee the importation of timber from Macedonia. Privileges were granted to traders such as Lykon and Phanosthenes to ensure the supply of grain and oars. Neither merchant was forbidden trade with hostile states.[130] The realities of the market were strong enough in Classical Greece as to modify even the realities of war. To ban exports to one's enemy might hurt one's own commerce as well as the foes:

Prohibiting export to the enemy...might diminish the revenues of an enemy state collected through import, export, harbor, or transit taxes, but such moves could also have a reciprocal effect on local tax collection and eliminate overseas markets for local merchants; besides, such a prohibition would be difficult to enforce.[131]

Imports could be more easily controlled, but even this would diminish revenues collected through import tariffs and deprive residents of goods. Merchants were usually left alone during the war, for many were looked upon as mercenaries and foreigners with little to offer in terms of military intelligence and political influence. Regular interference in trade, outside of that in strategic materials, was simply seen as counterproductive. Traders were usually seen as part of an international business class "who followed markets with little regard to their citizenship or residency".[132]

Athenian strategy resembled that of Britain in 1914 and 1939. With a vast fleet of 300 warships, 6,000 talents of silver in their treasury, and the support of most *poleis* in the Aegean, the Athenians, led by Pericles, were supremely confident of victory. Sparta, supported by most of the Peloponnessus, sent its professional army northward to ravage the farmland of Attica. The Athenians retreated behind their fortifications rather than try to meet the Spartans in open battle, their strategy being to attack Sparta from the while supplying themselves from the Laurion mines and Black Sea grain. The Athenian strategy misfired: the people of Attica crowded into Athens, where they strained housing and sanitation. Heavy rains and a heat wave led to crop failure and several years of a pestilence that decimated the population, and especially the army and navy. At least 10,000 Athenians died, including 4,000 hoplites and Pericles himself.[133] The war attained a savage dimension. Sparta invaded northern Greece and temporarily cut the Athenians off from their supplies of gold, silver, and timber. Factions of pro-Athenian democrats and pro-Corinthian oligarchs slaughtered one another and radical demagogues like Cleon appeared in Athens. Athenian hoplites slaughtered the men of Melos, selling the women and children into slavery.[134] Athens lost the war when the young demagogue and inept strategist Alcibiades persuaded the Assembly to invade Sicily in 413 BC. Capturing Syracuse would deprive the Peloponnesians of their market, fleet, and granary and grant Athens strategic control over the entire Mediterranean. The Athenian army and navy were surrounded and crushed in Syracuse harbour. Sparta occupied Attica and captured 20,000 fugitive slaves from the Laurion mines, Chios revolted from the Delian League and Persia entered the war on the Spartan side. Athens surrendered in 404 BC after enduring a Spartan blockade financed by Persia and Tyre. Athens, however, was spared destruction given the Spartan fear of her ally Corinth who now resumed its place as the foremost Greek commercial city.[135]

Greece, and especially Athens, emerged from the Peloponnesian War psychologically wounded in a manner not unlike Britain after the First World War or the United States after Vietnam. One of the long-term casualties of the conflict was the ideology of commercial and military power based on trade and commerce was propounded by the fifth-century BC Athenian establishment. This ideology bore a resemblance to that propounded by Alexander Hamilton and the American Federalists of the late 1700s as well as the American System propounded by Whigs like Henry Clay and Abraham Lincoln in the 1800s. Accepting the free-market system, the "Hamiltonian" thinking of the Athenian establishment stressed a strong trading and business sector as the underpinning of human growth and progress. Trade and commercial exchange were not *publicly* valued money-making activities in their own right but as a means to human, and especially Athenian, progress. In the Periclean ideology, seaborne trade and commerce were the means by which humankind could emancipate itself from dependence upon climate, nature, and perhaps even the gods and goddesses of Olympus themselves. Traders still had little social prestige in an Athens where the hoplite farmer was still praised as the mythical model citizen. Thucydides, Pericles and others still praised the trade of imperial Athens for its fruits in man-made prosperity. Thucydides praised sea trade not because it boosted the Athenian economy but because without it, the Greeks had been at the mercy of the elements and their enemies:

Without commerce, without freedom of communication either by land or by sea, cultivating no more of their territory than the exigencies of life required, destitute of capital, never planting their land (for they could not tell when an invader might not come and take it all away, and when he did come they had no walls to stop him), thinking that the necessities of daily sustenance could be supplied at one place as well as another, they cared little for shifting their habitation, and consequently neither built large cities nor attained to any other form of greatness.[136]

Thucydides insisted nomads and the early Greeks were poor because they had no cities or serious trade. Piracy, on the other hand, was the first form of maritime exchange and the beginning of organisation based on strength alone instead of hierarchy. Thucydides saw maritime exchange and power as interdependent. In his speculative reconstruction of history hereditary monarchy was the original form of government, but as Greece became more powerful and money became more evident, tyrannies were established, revenues increased, shipbuilding flourished and ambition turned overseas. Tyrannies used revenues to stabilise dominion at home, while the later Athenians used it to extend external power.[137] Thucydides saw maritime trade as a means of survival controlled by humans themselves, according to Sitta von Reden "a mode of wealth creation based on the strength of the human mind...the surplus which was gained on the basis of intelligent thought."[138] Deeds could be controlled by human thoughts and speech. In the wartime Funeral Speech of Pericles quoted by Thucydides, the prosperity of Athens was likened to the prosperity of a Greek household, being based on wise business management and not agriculture. The roots of Athenian power for Pericles lay not so much social and economic facts as in a superior relationship between man and nature. The farmer might have to submit to rules of soil and season, the Athenian banker, trader, and shipper less so. Athens as a result was a self-sufficient democratic power:

And if our remote ancestors deserve praise, much more do our own fathers, who added to their inheritance the empire which we now possess, and spared no pains to be able to leave their acquisitions to us of the prsent generation. Lastly, there are few parts of our own dominions that have not been augmented by those of us here, who are still more or less in the vigour of life; while the mother country has been furnished by us with everything that can enable her to depend on her own resources whether for war or for peace.[139]

The war, however, engendered a disillusionment with the official ideology among the intellectual elite, some of whom saw the Athenian defeat as a punishment by Zeus and fate for the brazen pride in human achievement described above. One of these critics was the playwright Aristophanes, whose wartime satires ridiculed the politics of Cleon and others. If Pericles and Thucydides represented a pro-commerce "Hamiltonian" ideology, the plays of Aristophanes symbolised a more "Jeffersonian" longing for a return to the simplicity of the household farm and the rural life. In *The Frogs*, (written 405 BC), Aristophanes lamented the commercialisation of his Athens by comparing the value of his fellow citizens to that of their coinage:

I have often noticed that there are good and honest citizens in Athens, who are as old gold to new money. The ancient coins are excellent in point of standard; they are assuredly the best of all moneys; they alone are well-struck and give a pure ring; everywhere they obtain currency, both in Greece and in strange lands; yet we make no use of them and prefer those bad copper pieces quite recently issued and so wretchedly struck. Exactly in the same way do we deal with our citizens. If we know them to be well-born, sober, brave, honest, adepts in the exercises of the gymnasium and in the liberal arts, they are the butts of our contumely and we have a use only for the petty rubbish, consisting of strangers, slaves, and low-born folk not worth a whit more, mushrooms of yesterday, whom formerly Athens would not have even wanted as scapegoats.[140]

Aristophanes' plays ridiculed the Periclean ideology behind Athenian commercialism and empire. They mocked the lofty language of the Funeral Oration and Thucydides as a mask for the reality of bribery and petty greed. In *The Knights* (written 424 BC, in the eighth year of the Peloponnesian War) Aristophanes likened Athenian politicians to crooked hustlers. He uses one Demosthenes (not the fourth century Demosthenes) as his mouthpiece, quoting him to the effect that "the oracle announces clearly that a dealer in oakum must first govern the city." After this, the city will be governed by a sheep-dealer who is to "reign until a greater scoundrel than he arises; then he perishes and in his place the leather-seller appears, the Paphlagonian robber, the bawler, who roars like a torrent."[141]

The ideal ruler of Athens will at last appear in the form of a sausage-seller, whose political future Demosthenes proceeds to paint:

You shall be master of them all, governor of the market, of the harbours, of the Pnyx; you shall trample the Senate under foot, be able to cashier the generals, load them with fetters, throw them into gaol, and you will play the debauchee in the Prytaneum.[142]

Demosthenes admonishes the skeptical sausage-vendor "you do not yet see all the glory awaiting you. Stand on your basket and look at all the islands that surround Athens."[143] He tells him to look at the storehouses and the shipping and the trading opportunities to east and west. When the sausage-vendor asks how he can become such a great man, Demosthenes tells him "you will be great because you are a sad rascal without shame, no better than a common market rogue."[144] The vendor protests how can he be capable of governing the people? Demosthenes' answer indicates Athenian democracy, corrupted by the market, has become a series of personal deals for self-preservation:

Nothing simpler. Continue your trade. Mix and knead together all the state business as you do for your sausages. To win the people, always cook them some savoury that pleases them. Besides, you possess all the attributes of a demagogue; a screeching, horrible voice, a perverse, cross-grained nature and the language of the market-place. In you all is united which is needful for governing.[145]

The Acharnians (written in 426 BC, in the sixth year of the Peloponnesian War) pictures all of Athens as a market viewed through the eyes of his protagonist Dicaepolis, or Just City. Dicaepolis loathes the noisy markets of Athens where everyone shouts and praises the commodities that are for sale: coal, oil, and vinegar. Dicaepolis wishes to be back home where he never would even hear the words "for sale". Like Plato and Aristotle, Aristophanes praises rural self-sufficiency in opposition to not only market exchange but also the political exchange that has been corrupted by a commercial democracy. Dicaepolis founds an alternative city based on a market economy...with different rules. This ideal market is attached to private households in the countryside. Politicians are elected privately, barter replaces money, taxes are paid in kind, and items are purchased for the common good.[146] Unlike Pericles who saw an Athens able to receive goods from all over the world and in which the city was more important than the local household, Aristophanes saw justice in a rural household based on home production and family life, the sanctity of marriage, and the cycle of farming festivals:

> *Here is a man truly happy. See how everything succeeds to his wish. Peacefully seated in his market, he will earn his living; woe to Ctesias, and all other informers who dare to enter there! You will not be cheated as to the value of wares, you will not again see Prepis wiping his foul rump, nor will Cleonymus jostle you; you will take your walks, clothed in a fine tunic, without meeting Hyperbolus and his unceasing quibblings, without being accosted on the public place by any importunate fellow, neither by Cratinus, shaven in the fashion of the debauchees, nor by this musician, who plagues us with his silly improvisations, Artemo, with his arm-pits stinking foul as a goat, like his father before him.[147]*

Man needed to be content with what the gods had ordained: marriage, sacrifice and agriculture rather than trading, industry, and a vanquished empire. To think that one could defy the natural agrarian order given to humanity by the gods through an economy based on human will and self-assertion was unnatural and perhaps blasphemous in the eyes of the agrarian traditionalists.[148]

Market commerce and prosperity would survive in fourth-century BC Athens in spite of the damage done by the war to civic pride, public morality, and faith in Athena's protection. The loss of empire, markets and tribute would place a strain on the Athenian tax and welfare systems and the liberal spirit of democracy and reform. The literature of the fourth century BC showed an almost fatalistic acceptance of the fading of the *polis* and the old agrarian ideals it represented. Greece itself was looked upon as a decaying farm, the owners of which are growing weak and old and unable to weeds from growing or the barn from falling into disrepair. The miltarisation of Athens and the rise of the immigrant population were seen as symptoms of this aging.[149] The antidemocratic, antimarket seeds planted by Aristophanes continued to germinate, being watered by both both Plato and Aristotle. Democrats, tyrants, and merchants were now ridiculed, kings and aristocrats remembered with nostalgia. Viewing the growing disparity between rich and poor, Plato called for a managed society run by philosophers who would not own business property.[150]

In the aftermath of the Peloponnesian War, the Athenian populace was now greatly suspicious of the democracy which many felt had cost them victory in war. Nevertheless, the same hoplites and *metics* who were now so suspicious of democracy rallied to its defence in 411 BC and again in 403 BC when factions known as the Four Hundred and later the Thirty Tyrants sought to restore the more aristocratic regime of the sixth century BC. Despite the weakening of their ancient privileges, the hoplites preferred a democracy to an oligarchy which would represent but a few rich landowners. Property would still carry weight in Athens, but it was now transformed into a landless institution. The old hoplites accepted both this and the democratic transformation of Athens in the same manner that many U.S. Democrats reared in Jeffersonian principles of agrarian equality and limited government embraced the urban liberalism of Franklin Roosevelt's New Deal. They believe that Athenian capitalist democracy would restore a form of equality by bringing them and others up, rather than leveling them down:

Class differences remained under Athenian democracy, but as is usually the case where cash, rather than birth or property, reigns, they were more along emulative American, rather than resentful European, lines. The Athenian poor...thus sought to reconstitute hoplite ideals, not destroy them entirely.[151]

The farmers in the new imperial Athens, expanding in its economy, population, and bureaucracy, moreover, were acquiring both cash and capital in the new market order. Even as it undermined much of their traditional way of life, their participation in the new Athenian economy served to transform them into democrats willing to take up arms to defend the Athenian political order against those who invoked agrarian ideals, such as Plato and Aristotle later would, to restore a more oligarchical system. Athens extended the hoplite ideal to all native born residents, but yet found no way to incorporate the aliens, *metics* and others. The city hoped to be both a *polis* and a Mediterranean power, retraining the prestige of farming while including those who did not farm. In the end, this proved a difficult policy to pursue.[152]

The Classical Athenian experience represented the Greek market economy in its purest form. The experience of other Greek communities was to be quite different. In Thessaly, Crete, and Sparta an economy not too different from that of the Mycenaean Bronze Age survived. Neither entrepreneurs nor chattel slaves flourished in these regions, which retained a more manorial economy. In oligarchic Sparta the men did not farm, but trained for battle while serfs worked the estates.[153] The Greek model of independent household enterprise best embodied in Athens was the exception rather than the rule. Outside of the Greek world it was virtually nonexistent except in a modified form in Italy, which will be discussed in the following chapter. In the Near East, now dominated by Persia, as well as in Carthage, the Oriental model of large estates and manorial serfdom still prevailed. Small private plots were rare and the agrarian ideology of the *polis* unknown: "Many Oriental states and village communities had not shared the Greek experience – its 'liberation of agriculture' and concomitant rise of the polis."[154]

Entrepreneurial business would survive in Greece after the Macedonian and Roman conquests. The independent agrarian base upon which it rested, however, would eventually wither away as a more hierachical culture reasserted itself. The little farms with their diverse agriculture disappeared in the third and second centuries BC and in their place arose manors owned by one man and worked by gangs of serfs and slaves. In place of the slow hoplite armies were the swift phalanxes of Hellenistic kings, equipped with siege engines, elephants, cavalry, and other expensive, specialised weapons. The Greek farmer could not cope with the new taxation to support such armies and far-away royal courts. Little by little the Greek countryside would become depopulated. Farms reverted to pasture; roads withered from disuse. Whole regions like Aeolia and Arcadia reverted to pasture. By the time of the Roman Empire in the first century AD all Greece could field but 3000 soldiers. Much of Euboea was now unused and unfarmed, and the countryside of Attica was owned by but a few. Greek agriculture would not fully recover until the political resurrection of the Hellenic state in the nineteenth century AD.[155]

The Greek free-market experience in many ways resembled that of modern Anglo-American societies. The small private farms, low taxes, and militia-style armies all bred a creed of egalitarianism familiar to any American farmer living before 1860. Out of this a broadly-based form of constitutional republican government and a free-market business culture evolved, as the system encouraged productivity and awarded innovation among individual entrepreneurs in both agriculture and industry:

> *Farm ownership introduced the idea that human excellence is fostered by individual, not corporate, not state initiative. This original move toward privately held, intensive agriculture provided in most areas a surplus of food production. It freed a sizable minority for commerce, small crafts, and government bureaucracies.*[156]

The ideology of the *polis*, moreover, enabled that independent system to exist even into the time of the Athenian Empire, where buyouts of independent farmers were ridiculed and wealth from enterprise was used to support public works, social welfare, and the arts in a system providing a "unique balance and harmony between individual excellence and corporate well-being, an equilibrium between private enterprise and social stability."[157] If intensive yeoman agriculture, egalitarianism, and hoplite warfare, with its absence of large standing armies help explain the success of the free-market economy of the Greek city-state, then the growing complexity of the society that economy engendered helped explain its demise:

> *Specialization in agriculture, the elevation of cash and commerce over small farming, increases in the size of individual estates, growing disparities between rich and poor, the appearance of mercenaries, and cavalry and specialized troops involved in extensive and constant campaigning, all are interrelated. They are characteristic of the Hellenistic Greek world and beyond. They are emblematic of the end of the city-state of middling farmers – and all that went with it.*[158]

In 338 BC the armies of Philip of Macedon subdued the resistance of the various Greek city-states, which retained a nominal independence under Macedonian overlordship. Within two years his son, Alexander, led a unified force of Macedonians and Greeks on a march of conquest that placed most of the Near East under his rule. The Hellenistic age had begun, in which Greek democracy would be replaced by monarchical despotism and Greek independent enterprise would, in part, be transformed by the Oriental cultures among which it was to be planted.

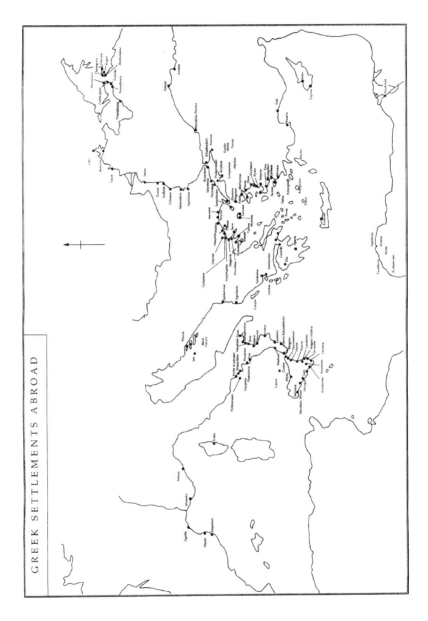

Chapter 8

The Profits of Mars

Hellenistic State Capitalism and the Military Capitalisms of Carthage and Early Rome: 331-146 BC

In the final centuries of the first milennium BC the empires of trade, investment, and commerce pioneered by Tyre and Athens were inherited by Macedonia in the East and Carthage in the West. The Hellenic market revolution was exported from the Aegean to the borders of India. The managed economy of Phoenicia, meanwhile, came to dominate much of the western Mediterranean, Africa, and possibly even parts of the New World. The spread of Hellenic market capitalism to much of the Near Eastern world was prelude to the rise of the "legionary capitalism" of Rome. Unified by the Macedonian rulers Phillip and Alexander, the disciplined hoplites of the Aegean subdued Asia Minor, Syria, Egypt, Babylonia, Persia, and even a portion of India, bringing Greek and Macedonian settlers, as well as entrepreneurs, with them. Before the end of the third century BC, Alexander's empire split into four successor realms. The two most important were the Seleucid, which inherited Asia Minor (temporarily) and much of Mesopotamia and Syria, and the Ptolemaic, which inherited Egypt and dominated the Levantine shores of Judea and Phoenicia until ejected from there by the Seleucids.[1] Within the Hellenistic kingdoms a new economy combining both enterprise and plunder soon emerged. Some 180,000 talents of gold bullion hoarded in the royal palace of the

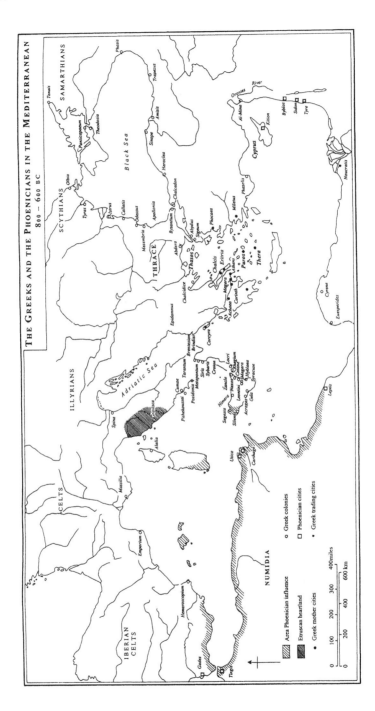

The Greeks and the Phoenicians in the Mediterranean
800 – 600 BC

SAMARTHIANS

SCYTHIANS

THRACE

ILLYRIANS

CELTS

IBERIAN
CELTS

NUMIDIA

Black Sea

Adriatic Sea

Cyprus

Phasis
Trapezus
Amisis
Sinope
Heraclea
Chalcedon
Byzantium
Sigeum
Abydus
Phocaea
Miletus
Pharselis

Panticapaeum
Tanais
Theodosia
Olbia
Tyras
Istrus
Callatis
Odessus
Apollonia
Mesembria
Abdera
Thasos
Chalcidice
Epidamnus
Chalcis
Eretria
Paros
Athens
Megara
Corinth
Argos
Thera

Orontes River
Al-Mina
Byblos
Sidon
Tyre
Kition

Naucratis
Cyrene
Euesperides

Spina
Alalia
Corsica

Massilia

Emporium

Homeroscopium

Gades
Tingis

Cumae
Posidonia
Tarentum
Metapontum
Brundisium
Brentesion
Siris
Sybaris
Croton
Locri
Caulonia
Rhegium
Zancle
Naxos
Catane
Leontini
Megara
Hyblaea
Syracuse
Gela
Acragas
Selinus
Segesta
Himera

Utica
Carthage

Leptis

Ara Phoenician influence
Etruscan heartland
Greek mother cities

○ Greek colonies
□ Phoenician cities
• Greek trading cities

0   100   200   300   400 miles
0 200   400   600 km

rather anti-capitalist Persian rulers was turned into circulating coins, turning the former realm of Cyrus and Xerxes into a money economy based on the Athenian silver standard. With a single stroke the number of Hellenic coins in circulation quintupled, releasing into circulation the equivalent of almost £200 billion in 1978 currency. To manage this money, Greek mints and banks were founded in the conquered areas as well; an economy based on bookkeeping, cash payments, and interest was introduced as Greek merchants settled in new colonies and cities from Egypt to Bactria.[2]

The victory of the Hellenic market economy was more apparent than real. Greek traders settling in Syria, Babylonia, or Egypt found themselves in the midst of much older and far less entrepreneurial business cultures. According to Fritz Heichelheim "Hellenic individual private enterprise...became generally embedded into the greatest planned organism of the Ancient world, a contradiction indeed."[3] In spite of its vast economic expansion, the Hellenistic world was hardly conducive to a capitalist take-off on the eighteenth century British model. Technological advances did take place during this period in the form of iron plows, pulleys, ox-driven waterwheels, the Archimedian screw, the lateen sail, domestication of the peach, cherry, apricot, and camel, as well as crop rotation. None of these improvements were widespread or sufficient enough to prevent the overworking of agriculture or overcome millennia of Oriental feudal tradition. Entrepreneurial risk-taking was discouraged by other factors. Banks were generally designed for cash savings, not credit or strategic commercial investment. Other than land and luxury goods, there was little for a Hellenistic entrepreneur to invest in an age in which mass production remained in the future.[4] The intellectual climate of the Hellenistic world was even less favourable than the Classical in encouraging the study of profits and productivity. Free markets may to some degree have come into existence, but there was no Adam Smith to explain their workings. The Hellenic market revolution remained grafted onto a social order in which rulers and academicians still thought in aristocratic, agrarian, and militaristic terms. Business, while it occupied growing numbers of people, was still frowned upon by the elites. Production and trade were relegated to the base and the greedy. Such an attitude, far removed from eighteenth century ideals of progress, helped account for the slowness of technological innovation and the failure of the Greeks, the Carthaginians, and even the Romans to develop a fully modern investment-oriented free-market economy.[5] Isocrates, Aratus, and even Aristotle all followed Plato in dismissing trade as petty and vulgar. Isocrates saw honest profit coming only from farming or using natural resources. The real cause for the prosperity of trading cities like Corinth or Megara completely eluded him. Even the apostle of moderation, Aristotle, considered plunder a perfectly legitimate economic activity, and many rulers, including his pupil, Alexander, agreed with him. Rulers and merchants in Sicily, Egypt, Greece, and Syria plundered temples, cornered markets, and accepted bribes with little remorse.[6]

Nowhere were the obstacles to a completion of the Hellenic market transformation more evident than in Ptolemaic Egypt. The realm of the Ptolemies encompassed not only the maritime capitalism of Phoenicia but the even more regimented state capitalism of the Pharaohs. Not much has been said about the economy of Egypt in this book, given that it could be argued that the economy of the Nile, was, throughout its long history, more "socialist" than "capitalist". Egypt shared with Minoan Crete the distinction of being humankind's first major command economy. All major enterprises were owned and directed by the Pharaoh and his viziers. The construction of the pyramids in both Old and Middle Kingdoms were state supervised. New Kingdom merchants such as the famous Wen-Amon journeyed to Byblos as employees of the Egyptian state. Grain, papyrus, and textiles were all crown monopolies in Ptolemaic Egypt. What the state needed to import, it did so from territories it controlled or was allied with: timber from Anatolia and Lebanon, pitch from Pergamum, copper from the mines of Cyprus, tin from Britain via Carthage and iron either from Anatolia or Etruria. In opposition to the rest of the Hellenistic world, which now operated on the Athenian monetary standard, Egypt created its own "ruble" in an effort to preserve as much economic autarchy as possible. Nevertheless, in the third century BC the commercial dominance of the eastern Mediterranean once enjoyed by Tyre and Athens was passing into the hands of the Ptolemies. Wanting to export as much as they could, they wished to import as little as necessary, all the while maximising the amount flowing into the royal coffers. Here was economic nationalism, if it could be called such, with a venegeance. Egyptian peasants were compelled to drink only Egyptian

beer and cook only with Egyptian oil. Any grain the farmers produced was and sold abroad by royal agents, leaving them the former
minimum necessary for subsistence while the Ptolemies reinvested
the royalties in their bloated state.[7]

Customs duties and taxes on production and business activity
were enormously oppressive, stifling any notions of independent
commerce: 50% duties on olive oil, 24% interest rates on loans,
25% taxes on bakeries, 16.7% death duties, as well as other duties
on herds, slaves, vineyards, sacrifices, business deals, and inherit-
ances.[8] Ptolemaic bureaucrats dictated what had to be grown and
where it had to be grown. Hellenistic Egypt was "an ancient
planned economy...no more efficient than its modern counterpart".[9] The Ptolemies slowly lost grip on their system as state officials extorted funds, exploited peasants and let wheat rot. Like their
heirs under Stalinism in the 1930s, the peasants of Egypt responded
with strikes and sabotaging of crops, dikes, and canals: "As in the
comparable modern case of Soviet Russia, what really surprises is
that agricultural production did not seize up altogether."[10] Unlike
modern Marxists, the Hellenistic rulers of Egypt made no egalitarian pretenses. They were out to extort royal revenue, not to raise living standards for the poor, whose hunger they condoned for forcing
them to toil. Peasant production was exploited in order to export
grain and papyrus in return for iron, tin, copper, horses, and elephants. Butter was exported to pay for the Hellenistic equivalent of
guns. Horses came from Libya, gold from Sudan, elephants from
Somalia. Copper and timber came from Cyprus, horses and Spanish silver through Carthage.[11]

Papyrus records bore witness to the "socialist" nature of the
Ptolemaic state. Demetrios, head of the royal mint in Alexandria,
directed his agent, Apollonios, in 258 BC to "the foreigners who
come here by sea and the merchants and middlemen and others"
who "bring...their local money" to convert their coinage "into new
money...in accordance with the decree which orders us to receive
and remint". [12] A late third century BC standard text for junior bureaucrats reminded them of their duties to inspect canals, see that
crops were sown on schedule, register all cattle, supervise loading of
grain on to ships for Alexandria, keep the largest number of weav-
ing looms in operation, audit all revenues on a village-by-village basis, scrutinise the local olive-oil factories, investigate the pricing of

goods, and supervise the planting of trees in the right season.[13] Grain was shipped up the Nile to Alexandria on royal barges, as witnessed in the following directive dated 265 BC: "Give orders for the measurement…on the royal barge…of the grain…and let Killes or the ship-master write you a receipt and seal a sample, and you bring them to me."[14] A papyrus from 251 BC recorded that the shipmaster Dioysios embarked with a large shipment of barley with Necthemebes the agent of the royal scribe for transport to the royal granary at Alexandria.[15] The tax laws of Ptolemy II in 259 BC showed heavy regulation of the olive oil industry. Royal clerks were to "have authority over all the oil-makers in the district and over the factories and the plant" and were to "seal up the implements during the time when there is no work". When there was work, they were to compel the oil-makers to work every day and stay beside them to make sure they did so.[16]

In spite of, and perhaps because of, their regimented economy, the Ptolemies were placed to play a major role in reviving intercontinental trade between Egypt, East Africa, and the Indian subcontinent. The spread of Hellenistic culture stimulated a desire for luxury goods from Indian Ocean ports, a trade which the Ptolemies were in an ideal strategic position to control. African ivory, conveyed by Arabian middlemen, journeyed up the Red Sea to the Ptolemaic crown merchants in the markets of Tyre, Sidon, and Alexandria. Temporarily in control of the Levantine portion of the old Tyrian network, including Tyre itself, the state merchants of Egypt held a key position in an intercontinental economy, the focus of which was India. The history of India at this time presented an interesting parallel with that of the Hellenistic world, producing its own Alexander in the form of Chandragupta Maurya and his successors who conquered all but the southern tip of India by 273 BC Chandragupta's grandson Asoka, in contrast, embraced Buddhism, religious toleration, and trade. This would provide a great opportunity for the Ptolemies, who began to import Indian goods delivered by Arabian merchants overland or via the Red Sea to Alexandria. Alexandria soon became the chief emporia for Indian Ocean and east African trade. The magnificent harbour, with its rows of warehouses was guarded by the famous Lighthouse of Pharos, one of the Seven Wonders of the World. Ptolemaic royal merchants had a monopoly on all Indian, Arabian, and African goods that entered Alexandria, and perhaps a near-monopoly on those that entered Phoenicia. If, in the latter case, raw material was processed in government-owned workshops, the Ptolemies may be said to had a cross-border and even "multinational" enterprise.[17]

The royal traders of the Ptolemies, many of whom were Greeks, continued to seek the markets of India despite the loss of Tyre and Sidon when the armies of the Seleucidae overran the Levant in 198 BC Certain market secrets, once closely guarded by both Indian and Arab traders were to be discovered by these Ptolemaic Greeks, mainly, the knowledge of the monsoons which blew across the Indian Ocean far to the south of the control of the states bordering the Gulf and Arabian Sea. According to maritime historian Lionel Casson, both Indians and Arabs cooperated in "keeping what they knew about the behavior of these winds strictly to themselves", since "neither was minded to divulge trade secrets to possible competitors."[18]

This control of market intelligence, or, more exactly, market accessibility intelligence, fell into the hands of the Ptolemies when an Indian sailor described the monsoon to the explorer Eudoxus around 120 BC Soon Ptolemaic traders were sailing east from the mouth of the Red Sea from whence they were carried by the May-September southwest monsoon to the shores of India, returning on the monsoon which blew in the opposite direction after November. The same easterly monsoon would also bring sturdy Indian vessels to Egypt. Hellenistic traders set up shop in India, Indian shippers and agents in Alexandria.[19]

Based upon a fusion of the Hellenic with the more mixed economies of Syria and Babylon, and Anatolia, the Seleucid Kingdom and its Attalid neighbour were less "socialist" than Ptolemaic Egypt. Sadly, fewer sources were preserved in the northern Hellenistic realms, and those that were tend to ignore economics. Much less is therefore known as to the nature of Seleucid and Attalid enterprise. Some royal monopolies existed, such as mints, but there was "nothing resembling the Ptolemaic planned economy in the wide-spread and administratively ill-organized Seleucid domains".[20] In the new Seleucid cities sprinkled throughout Syria, Cilicia, Mesopotamia, and Persia the kings exercised direct control through their functionaries or prefects even though the cities had their own councils and magistrates. Greeks and Macedonians now ruled some 30 million subjects via a corrupt Persian administrative machine, heir to that of Babylon and Assyria. New *poleis* full of Greek entrepreneurs dwelt near Canaanite, Mesopotamian, and Syrian communities which still practiced the prince-and-temple-oriented capitalism of their forefathers. The ancient temple structures survived alongside the new Greek cities planted in the midst of more ancient lands. Seleuceia, Antioch, Laodicea, Europus, Cyrrhus, Edessa, Beroea, and Larissa were often surrounded with rural settlements of Greeks and Macedonians. In contrast to the colonists in Ptolemaic Egypt, who spread themselves throughout the countryside and assimilated into the culture, Hellenic colonists in the Seleucid realm tended to remain in self-contained communities distancing themselves from the Syrian, Mesopotamian, Persian, and other populations. These colonies spurred urbanisation and led to the rise of clusters of other colonies which extended in groups over various areas.[21] The basis of agriculture remained grain and grapes in Syria, grain and fruit in Mesopotamia, and fruit from the Levant and western Asia Minor. Building construction flourished as well, as did metal, textile, and ceramic industries. Antioch was a centre for silversmiths. The Phoenician coast became the centre for the new glass industry, and the production of ships and Tyrian purple continued in Hellenistic Sidon and Tyre (Strabo, xvi.2-23-5). Textile production spread inland in Syria, and ceramic workshops throughout Asia Minor and Mesopotamia. Forms of serfdom existed in rural areas, while cities may have begun to see the further development of a pattern of urban slavery[22] While the lion's share of eastern trade was eventually cornered by Ptolemaic mariners, traders in the Seleucid and Attalid realms inherited the ancient Sumerian-Assyrian-Babylonian trading network dating from the Bronze Age described in earlier chapters of this book. Wood, spices and other luxuries, including Chinese silk, journeyed westward across Persia by caravan from the Mauryan kingdom through the new capital of Seleuceia near Baghdad, from whence it travelled along the Tigris-Euphrates route to Tyre, Sidon, Antioch, or Ephesus. A second route, that of the ancient *Dilmun*-boats of Sumerian times, crossed the Arabian Sea and Persian Gulf to Seleucid Babylonia, from whence camels and riverboats journeyed westward.[23]

Much remains unknown about Hellenistic economics, even in the 1990s. How much did a continuous market exchange of goods and services exist in the eastern Mediterranean between 300 and 150 BC? Looking at the rise and fall of commodity prices at the slave-mart of Delos, the huge number of shipwrecks found after 200 BC, the circulation of money, and the realtionship between Ptolemaic Egypt and Rhodes suggests the economies of the Hellenistic world were linked. One must not forget, by and large, that most economic activity, perhaps of 80% of the population, revolved around grain, olive oil and wine for local markets. Especially in the Seleucid realm, the market alone could not easily sustain overland trade, especially in agriculture. The costs of land transportation were just too high to carry profitable trade through periods of depression in areas not accessible by sea. Ptolemaic Egypt thus had a competitive advantage over its northern rival in insulating itself against market failure. Seleucid farming, plagued by local famines, was based not on the exporting of grain but "production for local consumption without recourse to trading or to a 'market'".[24] The loss of all of Persia and even parts of Mesopotamia to the new Parthian kingdom, which arose after 250 BC and gained control of the overland caravan routes to India and China, further weakened any locational advantages for traders in what remained of a shrinking Seleucid realm.[25]

In spite of the farming and subsistence nature of much of Seleucid life it was still true that, in certain aspects, the eastern Mediterranean economy after 300 BC was more than the sum of its local parts. Egypt, the Levant, and the Aegean in particular took part in "widespread production for a market, involving transport and exchange over long distances".[26]

Diodorus Siculus (xx. 81. 4) described the traders of Rhodes as the true heirs of the Athenian free-market system. The merchant oligarchy which managed the island attempted to maintain close relations with everyone, but particularly Egypt, for whom they were the principal market. Polybius (iv. 47. 1-3) noted Rhodes and other islands of the eastern Aegean traded cattle and slaves to the Attalids in return for olive oil and wine. A long tradition of Hellenisation and individual enterprise, plus abundant resources ensured that the Attalid realm of Pergamum in Asia Minor was more prosperous than that of the Seleucids. Many of the older Greek cities of Asia Minor such as Miletus and Ephesus were allowed to preserve a certain measure of their independence. The agricultural, timber and mineral resources eagerly sought and exploited by Assyrians, Hittites, Phoenicians, Lydians, and Hellenes for centuries was now concentrated in the hands of the Attalid kings. Abundant grain, wine, olive oil, wool for garments, timber and pitch for naval construction made this Anatolian kingdom a worthy prize for any future conqueror. As for Greece itself, declining population and the aftermath of civil war weakened the prosperity of Athens. Strategically located, the island of Rhodes was able to inherit at least some of the mainland's former commercial advantages by becoming the centre of trade with the new markets opened up to Egypt and the Near East. Rhodes was dominated by a prosperous merchant oligarchy some of whose members served as carrying agents for the grain of Alexandria. Ephesus with its wine, Sidon with its glass industry, and Tyre with its purple dye all remained active in the early Hellenistic period as exit points for the goods of India heading into Europe. Pottery evidence provides little documentation for Hellenistic trade, although the amphorae (large jugs for shipping wine) from shipwrecks do allow one to date the commercial heyday of Rhodes, and therefore of the Hellenistic trading network of which it was an integral part, around 200 BC. The same pottery also suggests the slow decentralisation of production in the Aegean-Pontus area during this time.[27] A new element, in the form of the slave-trade, would begin to flourish as Hellenes began to sell tens of thousands of Anatolians, Scythians, and others in Ephesus, Rhodes, and especially Delos, even before the Romans were involved.[28]

In a system in which the market freedom of the Greeks encountered the more managed systems of the Near East, a partial return to multinational enterprise was plausible. With a long history of business hierarchy, the enduring merchants of Ptolemaic and later Seleucid Tyre still worked according to the rules of the *Eclectic Paradigm*. Associations of traders and merchant-ship owners, arose in Hellenistic Egypt, Tyre, and Sidon. Shippers headquartered in the above ports opened permanent branch offices in Athens and Delos.[29] Hellenistic trade and commerce generally expanded where access to the sea was available. The local economies of the Ptolemaic, Attalid, Seleucid, and Aegean worlds became more connected, but the new economic unity was often tenuous and "hampered by the limitations and fluctuations of effective demand".[30] Apart from the few major cross-Aegean routes along which Near Eastern merchants invested in the Aegean, market weakness tended to limit commercial dominance in the eastern Mediterranean to one port at a time, first Athens, then Rhodes, then Phaselis, Chalcis and finally Delos. Trade was much more governed by politics than pure market considerations. In a largely agrarian economy plagued by incessant wars, inflation, government meddling, and an epidemic of piracy, market failure became a far greater problem than in pre-Peloponnesian War Athens. Agriculture tended to become more self-sufficient. Egypt and Phoenicia, building upon their statist traditions, invoked the Dunning paradigm and sought to bypass unreliable market conditions at home by emphasising their trade overseas.[31]

The true cause of the demise of the Hellenistic world in the second and first centuries BC was debated by scholars in past decades who read history in terms of their own economic and political philosophies. Scholars like Ulrich Kahrstedt saw the directed model of the Hellenistic kingdoms as essentially successful. Had they not been conquered by Rome, their economies might have achieved further market union and the technological breakthroughs, such as steam power and steel production, leading to a genuine industrial revolution. Mikhail Rostovsteff, an ardent believer in market freedom, on the other hand insisted the "collectivist" Hellenistic economies wrecked themselves through war, taxation, and bureaucracy. The German scholar Fritz Heichelheim presented a third view based upon his detailed study of Hellenistic prices, wages, and rents. It seemed to Heichelheim that Kahrstedt and Rostovtseff had both been partially right. Hellenistic economies enjoyed healthy growth after Alexander's conquests and their subsequent formation. Greek capital, entrepreneurial methods and a common currency spread throughout most of the Hellenistic world, and growth between 280 and 250 BC. After the latter date, a new series of wars resulting in fragmentation of various kingdoms began to disrupt the expanding Hellenistic markets and affected demand for agricultural, mineral, forest and artisan produce. The Seleucids lost Asia Minor, Iran, and the land routes to India and China, now in Parthian hands while depriving the Ptolemies of Phoenicia. The Greek mainland revolted from the Macedonian Antigonids, and immediately plunged into another round of fraticidal war among its various *poleis*. Natural disasters, civil strife, social unrest and a new epidemic of piracy continued to further depress conditions. Business confidence in Rhodes and Corinth, the economic motors of the Aegean, began to collapse. Hyperinflation struck the Egyptian economy, with prices rising 600% and the Ptolemaic kings greatly debasing their coins with inferior metal. The near-collapse of the Greek and Egyptian economies was reflected on the island of Delos, where rents fell by 40%.[32] Heichelheim showed though, that the mixed Hellenistic economies had considerable recuperative powers and might have recovered, at least partly, from a depression which was politically induced. The Seleucid kingdom temporarily restabilised under Antiochus III as Greece. Even Egypt's floundering state enterprises were rescued by a stable new bronze currency and renewed war between Rome and Carthage, both of whom became dependent upon Egyptian wheat. The Hellenistic economies foundered as a result of government *weakness* in the political and military arena, which destroyed their markets rather than as a result of government intervention in those markets. Strong enough in pure market terms, the Hellenistic kingdoms' lack of political and social unity prevented them from defending their markets and their independence from one another and other foes, the strongest of which would be Rome. In the second and first centuries BC, Rome would eventually conquer and absorb most of the Hellenistic economies, but even its exacting plunder would not prevent Egypt, Syria, and Asia Minor from remaining among the most properous of Roman provinces.[33]

The rise of powerful kingdoms in central Italy and their eventual unification by Rome was stimulated by the spread of the Greek market economy to the Italian peninsula. It is not known when and how exactly the village of Rome itself was born, although excavations on the soil-rich plain of Latium in the 1980s and 1990s are beginning to illuminate the dawn of Roman history. The Latin and Etruscan peoples emerged at the same time from the Bronze into the Iron Age after 900 BC Both societies shared much in common, Etruscan centres like Veii, Tarquinia, Populonia, Vulci, and Cerveteri and Latin centres all arose from small Bronze Age "Villanovan" settlements, as did Latin cities such as Lavinium, Ardea, Antium, Satricum, and Rome itself. The Hellenic presence at Pithekoussai ensured that an Italian commercial revolution took place alongside the Greek. Etruria, more than Latium, was the engine of this revolution due to large deposits of iron, copper, and silver mined near

Populonia and Vetulonia. Etrurian aristocrats exchanged metals for Greek pottery and Phoenician goods traded through Pithekoussai.[34] From 760 BC Etruscan burials at Veii show the increased use of iron technology in the form of helmets, shields, swords, and chariots. Whether that technology was actually imported from the Aegean, Cyprus, or the Levant to Etruria or whether the Etruscans discovered the art of iron-working on their own is very difficult to determine. More certain is that the demand provided by the Greek presence and techniques imported from Cyprus accelerated the development of the Iron Age in Italy.[35]

Given the similarities between Etruria and Latium, the richer archaeological record of the former helps to shed light on the life and economy of early Rome. The Etruscan record documents the spread of the Iron Age and of entrepreneurial commerce to central Italy under the influence and encouragement of the Greeks. The first Greek potters came from Euboea and the Cyclades, but other groups from the Greek mainland or southern Italy soon followed after 700 BC Hybrid Etruscan-Greek pottery was being produced in Campania. The work of individual masters, such as the anonymous "Bearded Sphinx Painter", who moved from Vulci to Caere, can be discerned. Greek potters also thrived in other major Etruscan centres like Tarquinia, Caere, and Vulci. In the later seventh century BC the scale of Etruscan pottery expanded and became more uniform. Little direct evidence for metalworking can yet be detected from this time outside the cemeteries but it is certain that the copper and iron from Elba and several other inland sites was being mined and smelted by the Etruscans themselves. Most of the primary smelting took place near the mines themselves. It is not known, though whether the mining communities lived by mining alone or supplemented their income with farming. The Iron Age in Italy developed slowly at first, but beginning in the seventh century BC the production of the metal for everyday use began to expand greatly. Although much of the smelting remained local, the ores of Elba were pure enough to be able to be mine systematically and shipped to more central sites after 650 BC. Etruria became the metallurgical hub of the central Mediterranean, its smiths producing bronze and iron utensils, tools, weapons and luxury goods, with techniques far more advanced than those used by their contemporaries in, for example Sardinia or even Phoenician Spain. The archaeological record from 750 BC on shows that the Etruscan economy was beginning to specialise, with increasing regionalisation and competition between centres. Metal industries making luxury goods like tripods and weapons concentrated first along the coast, at Tarquinia and Vetulonia, then at Caere and Vulci.[36] Similarities between classes of Etruscan pottery and vessels "suggests a close rapport between different workshops in the same centre, though whether this took the form of collaboration or competition we cannot tell".[37] There are as yet many unanswered questions about larger-scale Etruscan management. How was such production organised? How centralised were Etruscan workshops? Did they have single workshops in Etruscan centres or guild shops or scattered enterprises? [38]

Trade was a factor in the Etruscan economy: goods did move from place to another and sometimes over long distances. This trade was, according to experts Graeme Barker and Tom Rasmussen, clearly entrepreneurial in nature, operating within a sophisticated barter economy: "Etruscan maritime trade was in the hands of enterprising individuals and families rather than being 'state-directed'."[39] Grain did not move far, as Etruscan roads were very poor for donkeys and oxcarts and there were few large rivers. The grain used in Veii and other centres was probably grown on nearby farms.[40] The Greeks were Etruria's prime overseas customers. Between 625 and 550 BC Hellenic pottery entered Etruria from Corinth and the Aegean. After 550 BC the Etrurian market became increasingly penetrated by Athens. In spite of their newness to long-distance, merchants in Etruscan cities were able to export pottery, bronzes, and amphorae to Spain, France, Corsica, Sardinia, Greece, North Africa, Egypt, and even the Black Sea.[41] Even though much of the mining was done in northern places like Elba, the main export centres lay in southern Etruria "suggesting that the southern cities controlled the sea trade."[42]

Etruscan and Latin capitalism provided more room for independent enterprise than Tyre, Babylon, or Ashur. Latin entrepreneurship would, on the other hand, be more family-oriented and differently shaped by geography than its Greek counterpart. Both Greece and Italy were mountainous peninsulae, but the vast ranges and poor soil of Greece reinforced the independence of the many *poleis* and their generally peaceful overseas expansion. The Appenines permitted the Italians better overland communication and political unity, while the rich volcanic soil along the central Italian coastal plains of Latium and Campania became the prize over which many armies would fight. Romans and their Latin allies occupying those plains had not only to defend this farmland but obtain additional land for their surplus population by military invasion and internal colonisation instead of overseas expansion. Rome would live by the sword or face quick extinction.[43]

The Latins of Rome were at first only marginally affected by the entrepreneurial revolution transforming their Etruscan neighbours. Historians of the 1990s, led by T.J. Cornell of the University of Manchester, no longer fully accept the conventional wisdom that Rome before 300 BC was a complete commercial backwater. Neither is it any longer believed that all of early Roman civilisation was borrowed from the Etruscans, nor is it accepted that the latter had conquered the city at an early date in its history. In spite of its simple economy and social structure, Rome was advanced enough to begin as a local trading centre situated at the junction of the Tiber and the roads leading between Campania and Etruria. The subsistence economy of the Latins of 900-700 BC was still less advanced than that of its Etruscan neighbours. Few were richer or poorer than the majority.[44] In spite if this, the Roman artifacts of the eighth-century BC provide hints of the business culture to come. In the cemeteries of Osteria dell'Osa and Castel di Decima near Rome, most bodies were buried without distinction, save for a few spears and swords interned with the better-off. Roman life was even then based on an extended family and a powerful clan or *gens* system in which the values of a warrior society would be paramount.[45]

Until about 350 BC the rise of Roman military and economic power was quite slow. By 600 BC Rome had grown from a rural village to the largest fortified city in Latium, with a well-developed military ethos not unlike that of Sparta. Overshadowed by Etruria, the early Latins borrowed from Etruscan and Hellenic economics, institutions, rituals, and religion while retaining much of their own. Etruscan, Tyrian, and Greek entrepreneurs visited the growing city, bringing the products of the Iron Age. While tombs only 30 kilometres from Rome show evidence of Tyrian goods, seaborne trade was not yet very important for Romans. The Tiber was too full of silt to permit large ships to pass. With few native industries of their own, the Latin cities prior to 500 BC had little to export in return save wheat and other produce from the rich volcanic soil of western Italy.[46] The expansion of the Phocaeans of Ionia into southern Gaul and the growing Corinthian colonies of southern Italy helped, in the sixth century BC, to further stimulate the young Italian economy. Etruscan cities like Veii, Tarquinii, and Caere became middlemen between the agrarian interior and the foreign traders of the Tyrrhenian Sea.[47] Rome itself could now attract more long-distance traders to its infant marketplace, though her craftsmen produced but a few gold and copper products to offer in return. Latin farmers had no means to sell their grain abroad, trading it instead to the local mountain tribes provided Latium both its major market and its greatest danger.[48]

The political system of the Roman Republic erected after 509 BC reflected and legitimised the warlike and familial character of Roman society. Rome's patrician oligarchy replaced monarchy not with a single tyrant on the Greek model but with a pair of elected magistrates, often soldiers, able to veto one another's actions. The system, however, contained the future seeds of the Empire, for in a crisis, a consul could assume the office of *dictator*, exercising unlimited power for six months. The ruling Senate represented the power of the landed patricians, but elected tribunes eventually represented the plebeian orders of farmers, labourers, and artisans. A middle stratum would soon emerge among the Roman equestrians, or knights who were wealthy enough to own horses and fight on horseback, and from whom the alter Roman business managers would come. The core of Roman Law was set forth in the Twelve Tables of 450 BC, which were written to govern a more individualistic society than the Mesopotamian or Phoenician. Government was to be more limited in scope and lack both the will and means to intervene on behalf of those who might be injured by the market. The Twelve Tables showed Rome to be a society in which individual self-help combined with the all-important concept of the patron and the *familia*.[49]

The Roman world and Roman business would operate on the basis of the *familia*, or patriarchal extended family, which included not only the nuclear family but slaves and others who lived under the control of and depended upon the male *paterfamilias*. According to Professor A. Drummond, the Roman *familia* was defined "by reference not to blood relationship but to the powers exercised for life by the family head over both the persons and property subject to him".[50] The weak, unable to find protection from the state, would seek such from a patron who would include them in the latter's *familia*. The Twelve Tables helped enshrine a patronal concept of family property and, by implication, family enterprise, in the Roman market economy to a much greater extent than it would be in the Greek:

> *The power of the family head is notorious, extending even to the right to kill those subject to him. This presumably reflects a strong collective emphasis on the need for vigorous discipline in the component elements of the community, not least to regulate the relations between familiales since the heads of households were responsible to each other for the private actions of those subject to them.*[51]

Given the unreliability of the market and the absence of political stimuli to market growth, patrician consuls and senators of the Early Republic maintained a *laissez-faire* attitude to trading matters at sharp odds with that adopted by the merchant-princes of Ashur, Ugarit, and Tyre. Greek, Etruscan, and Oriental traders in Rome were neither excluded, regulated, nor taxed when they imported pottery from Attica or plied their trades of carpenter, smith, tanner, dyer, and potter alongside their Roman counterparts. None of this was as of yet on a great scale, particularly after 450 BC when imports and contruction were virtuallty halted through much of Italy by a trade depression.[52]

Free markets and family patriarchy were important factors destined to shape Rome's future capitalism. The expansionist militarism dictated by its geography was no less important. During the first 150 years of its existence the Roman Republic remained a local power, whose existence was not particularly given the constant invasions of its neighbours. A new phase of even more intensive and almost constant warfare opened in 343 BC and lasted for several centuries. Until the 1990s the conventional wisdom of most historians assumed Republican Rome's violent career of warfare was inspired by politics, not profit. Professor John Rich of the University of Nottingham now believes that not only was Rome the aggressor in most of its wars, but that the prospect of booty weighed heavily in decisions to go to war.[53] Assembling every spring and disbanding every autumn, the Roman legions surmounted one foe after another. The Etruscans were subdued beginning with the capture of Veii in 396 BC. By 350 BC, southern Etruria was Roman and the Celts driven north to the Po. The rise of Rome as a military and economic force to be reckoned with doomed the commercial ascendancy in central Italy of the Etruscans. Methodically and systematically, the Romans strangled the trading and commercial centres of southern Etruria, deporting many of the inhabitants, expropriating the farmlands, bypassing the centres with new roads, and occupying the coasts with Roman colonies in order to cut Etruscan centres like Caere, Tarquinia, Vulci, and Populonia off from their markets. In 273 BC 9,000 Romans founded the colony of Cosa, future emporium for the Sestii family, in the territory Vulci. Cosa, a smaller version of Rome itself, was one of many such colonies designed to control the coastal plains, wrest good farmland from the Etruscans, deprive them of their ports, and dampen their desire to remain a seafaring power with an independent foreign policy. Etruria after 400 BC would no longer be a major force in Mediterranean life. Veii was destroyed in 396 BC, Volsinii in 264 BC, and Falerii in 241 BC. Inhabitants of centres like these were resettled at the point of the sword. The Etruscan cities of the north would last longer and fare better, at least for a while. No Roman settlements were planted between Vulci and the River Arno before 100 BC. Treaties were concluded between Rome and the elites of the northern city-states. After the civil wars of the 80s BC, however, many of these northern cities were to be punished for supporting the losing side. From the second century BC onwards the west coast of Etruria was transformed by the same Roman villas and slaveholding estates one found further south. With the exception of a few like Arezzo, most of the southern Etruscan centres would be abandoned well before the collapse of the Roman Empire.[54] As for Rome's Latin rivals, they had accepted their subordination after the Latin War of 340-338 BC The future structure of the Roman Empire was present in embryo in the settlement dictated by Rome to the other Latins. Some states were annexed to Rome, others made Roman protectorates, others given the status of Roman allies. Certain citizenship and other rights were granted them, and they were allowed to share in the booty of future wars, in return for participation in those wars under the Roman eagle. Rome could thus add the military power of the states she dominated to her own. Italians, Iberians, Africans, Greeks, Macedonians, Anatolians, Syrians, Gauls, Britons, Germans, Illyrians, and others would eventually become integrated into this expanding system.[55] Rome next vanquished the Samnites, followed by the Greeks in southern Italy. Over 125,000 square kilometres of Italian territory and some three million people were now subject to Roman rule. From the dense population of their peninsular domain the Romans and their subjects now could field a force of 60,000 men, twice the size of Alexander the Great's army. Fifteen Roman and Latin colonies were planted among the conquered peoples, land from the latter being awarded to some 70,000 landless veterans and their families. Fifteen such military colonies were founded between 334 and 263 BC, forerunners of many more to come.[56]

Roman economic expansion quickly acquired a brutal, militaristic aspect. While not unknown in the Hellenistic and Oriental world, especially in the closing centuries of Assyrian history, the economics of plunder were truly perfected in Rome. The free market of the family merchant operated in the context of a steady and growing flow of tribute extorted first from Italy and then from overseas. Roman patricians enriched themselves and others from confiscated farmland. Beginning in the fourth century BC the very face of the Italian countryside began to be transformed by the new economics of Mars. Roman society itself was ripe for this transformation. Given the growing population of Latium and the inadequacy of the market to sustain much of beyond a shaky subsistence agriculture, debt enslavement and social unrest became a serious problem in the fourth century BC. Many Latin farmers sank into serfdom despite legislation such as the Licinio-Sextian laws of 367 BC, designed to alleviate their plight. The wars of conquest provided a safety valve for many rural plebs awarded land by victorious consuls in return for military service. Many soon began to abandon their old farms and landlords in Latium to settle in a military colony or in Rome itself. Their landlords quickly found another profitable source of labour in the form of thousands of Samnite, Etruscan, and other slaves captured in war and uprooted from their lands by the new Latin colonists. Historians of the 1990s such as T.J. Cornell now point out that Rome became a slave-owning society much ear-

lier than previously thought, and that this transformation was closely related to the Italian conflicts of the fourth century BC. Family
farms began to slowly give way to large patrician villas operated by
slaves. The new slaves of the fourth century BC were integrated into the familial economy of the fifth. Slaves not only worked on manors but entered the business world. In most cases both slaves and
freedmen became grafted into the family units enshrined in the
Twelve Tables and later Roman law. War stimulated the demand for
slaves, and provided slaves to fill the demand, while the reduction of
peasant debt and the rise of slave agriculture freed up a large part of
the rural population for steady military service.[57] Cornell speculates
that the wars triggered a continuous exchange of populations. Roman plebeians colonised other Italian lands, while other Italians entered Latium as slaves. Roman territory as a whole became more
urbanised, the Roman countryside less populated. These developments would favour the growth of Roman business:

> *The same land was worked by a smaller number of people; since they*
> *were slaves they could be worked harder and organised more effectively*
> *so as to produce a greater surplus. Increased productivity was stimulat-*
> *ed by the development of an urban market in the growing and prosper-*
> *ous city of Rome.*[58]

The population of Rome grew from 30,000 in 350 BC to 60,000 in
300 BC and almost 100,000 by 264 BC. Now one of the largest cities in the Mediterranean, Rome began to import water through aq-
ueducts and wheat in small boats up the Tiber. Roman maritime
activity and trade became reality as a result of the wars of conquest.
Before 300 BC coastal military settlements and even a small navy
were fully part of Roman life, and so were exports. Black-glaze pottery made in Roman workshops began to find its way across Italy
and around the western Mediterranean: to Gaul, northeast Spain,
Corsica, Sicily, and Carthaginian Africa.[59] The first Roman coins
made their appearance at this time. Coined money already existed
in the Hellenic colonies of southern Italy, but the first coins issued
by the Republic arose in Naples around 326 BC. Circulating at first
only in Campania, these coins nevertheless bear the images of
Rome's new miliaristic capitalism. Pictures of Mars, the god of war,
of a winged victory, of horses, of a laurel-crowned Apollo on the

new Roman coins all show the popularity of the Roman military ethic. These first coins were probably minted to finance the building of the Appian Way in 312-308 BC. The circulation of coined money increased with the wars against the Greeks of southern Italy led by Pyrrhus. The first coins in Rome itself were minted in 269 BC. They quickly went into service paying legionnaires and workers building a number of new temples. The coming of Roman coinage could also be seen as a political statement. Besides financing the transfer of booty, the new coins were a declaration that the rulers of Rome now claimed enough power and prestige to consider themselves in the same league with the rulers of Carthage, Seleucia, Egypt, and the other Hellenistic states. Rome would now challenge those states one by one, beginning with faced the formidable power of Carthage.[60]

Founded at the end of the ninth century BC, the African Canaanite colony played the role of breadbasket in the Tyrian commercial empire. Most convoys bringing metals from Spain to Tyre stopped in Sicily, Sardinia, and Malta more than in Carthage, which shipped wheat first to Cyprus and then on to Phoenicia itself. The defeat of Tyre by Nebuchadnezzar, the birth of a Persian-Tyrian alliance, and the crushing of the alliance's navies by the Athenians caused the Phoenicians of the Levant to direct more trade to the east. Left to their own devices, the Phoenician colonies of the west soon gravitated to the leadership of a Carthage now likely swollen by a refugee Levantine population. The western half of the Phoenician commercial empire became known, at least to later historians, as the *Punic* trading empire.[61]

After 550 BC the old Tyrian factories and staging posts of Malta, Gozo, Lampedusa, and Pantellaria were being directed from Carthage. Punic merchant-princes based in Carthage maintained and even increased the old Tyrian mining and trading investments in Sardinia and Sicily. From a military standpoint, these posts served to protect both Carthage and the sea route which now ran between Carthage and Spain, for the silver mines of the latter were just as valuable to the Punic sphere of trade as they had been to the Phoenician. Punic soldiers and sailors subdued revolt in Sardinia, and expanded the network of commercial and military posts on the island, setting up a new metal-processing factory at Mt. Sinai deep in the interior. In Sicily, Carthaginian merchants and soldiers likewise spread eastward from Motya, founding Maisala and Panormus (Palermo).[62] Gades, as well as the mines of the Rio Tinto and elsewhere, proceeded to become the foundation of Carthaginian economic power.[63] Fully consolidated during the third century BC, the Punic presence would deeply influence all of southern Spain, not only in coastal sites like Abdera, Almuñecar, and Gades, but also inland agricultural settlements like Camaria, Marchena and Osuña. The pottery and other artifacts found in the archaeological strata above the Phoenician at Rio Tinto itself also confirm that Carthage had replaced Tyre in exploiting the mines of Tarshish for its own profit.[64]

In contrast to the individualistic enterprise of Athens and rising family enterprise of Rome, Punic business culture was a direct inheritance from Tyre's navy- and temple-based capitalism. Spreading their self-contained estates over northern Tunisia, Punic merchant-potentates were at one and the same time farmers, generals, sailors, managers, shippers, and fanatical devotees of Melqart and the Carthaginian Baal-Hammon. Their profits came from combining intensive manorial agriculture with trade and shipping on a vast scale.[65] Punic merchants dwelling in Sicily, even Greek Syracuse, often owned their own ships. Hellenic traders peddled whatever the market dictated, the estate-managers of Carthage specialised in bulk shipments of one type of good: gold, incense, iron, copper, silver, tin, or became traders in commodities like African animals and dates symbolised by Hanno of Calidun in Plautus's comedy *Poenicus*. It seems probable that large Carthaginian enterprises like mining and shipbuilding were run by a hereditary caste with strong state connections, the business elite being at one and the same time the political elite. As in Ugarit and Tyre, such a structure would encourage internalisation between a manager residing on his Libyan estate and his employee-agents managing a trading post or mine in Spain or Sardinia.[66]

For a rising empire with Near Eastern traditions threatened by new rivals and heavily reliant on bronze as well as iron, a mercantilist strategy of trade was quite appropriate.[67]

Aristotle's description of the interlocking of oligarchical government and hierarchical commerce in Carthage reminds one of some modern Asian systems. Membership in a wealthy family was a prerequisite for political power in a system ruled by a tightly-knit coter-

ie of princes and traders. Aristotle described the Carthaginian con-
stitution with much praise. In his mind, it prevented strife and combined the best features of monarchy and oligarchy. The Council of
A Hundred and Four were chosen by merit, the kings were elective
and not hereditary, and the Council of Elders were chosen from
wealthy families that distinguished themselves. The Carthaginian
state in the fourth century BC, if Aristotle is to be believed, had a
great deal of popular support, and a popular assembly appears to
have had some say in the management of affairs. The Hundred and
Four chose Boards of Five to manage many important matters,
these usually being merchant-princes who served without pay and
decided many judicial matters. Aristotle praised the fact that
Carthage chose its rulers on the basis of merit as well as wealth.
Living in the aftermath of the wars among Greek *poleis*, and familiar
with the history of the Peloponnesian conflict, Aristotle idealised
the Punic merchant-prince whose wealth he saw as honourable, unlike that of many a Greek tyrant, as he saw them. If kingship and
generalship were for sale, as they might be in Greece and even
Rome, money would be more honoured than character and other
leadership qualities, and the whole state would become avaricious,
as in the case of Athens. Those able to buy office or the troops to
win office will view it only as a means of profit. Aristotle, however,
found a few things in the Punic system not to his liking. One person
could hold several offices, something that led to dangerous conflicts
of interest, especially in urban government and the military. Overall, however, the merit-based aspects of the Carthaginian system of
government and business, in which the merchant rulers were prov-
en warriors, priests, and princes, appealed to Aristotle, who disdained government by entrepreneur.[68]

The Punic economy embodied enterprises that were both large
and small, state and private. Essential large-scale industries such as
mining and munitions were most likely to be internalised and run
by state, temple, and aristocratic management networks. Landed
notables managed both state and temple property. Membership in
this hierachy was closed to the lesser merchants of an entrepreneurial sector which was far less competitive than that of Classical
Greece or later Republican Rome. In Greece and later on, in Rome,
a foreigner, freedman or slave could rise to economic and even political power. Such was not the case in the rigid Oriental society of

Carthage. When Greek goods would begin to flood the Punic home market after 400 BC, Punic entrepreneurs responded not by becoming more competitive, but by forming guild associations under the tutelage of a patron *Baal.*[69]

Mines, arms factories and the great shipyards of Carthage were usually state-owned. The industrial potential of the yards, which constructed the feared *trireme* warships, was enormous. It is said they could build 120 vessels in a matter of two months.[70] The entrepreneurial cultures of Greece and Rome built temples to their gods, but no longer considered those gods seriously involved in worldly matters of state and the marketplace. In Carthage, gods, priests and temples were still as integral a part of the power structure as they had been in Ashur, Babylon, Ugarit, and Tyre. Arms workshops flourished on crown and temple land. Hellenic shrines were privately managed by entrepreneurs or owned by hereditary families; Punic temples were managed by a state *Board of Ten Over the Sanctuaries* usually chosen from the ranks of notables. Priests were chosen from ruling families and often directly related to judicial heads of state (this was not unknown in Rome, either). Hanno and his father Abdimelkart were both *suffetes* (consuls) and high priests. The senator Himilkat, a fourth generation *suffete*, installed his daughter Batbaal as priestess. Some of the Punic temples, like those of Eshmun, Reshef, and, no doubt, Melkart and Baal-Hammon, were so wealthy as to own and manage entire communities.[71]

Given its social structure, Carthage was only partially influenced by the market revolution sweeping the northern shores of the Mediteranean world. Accepting iron technology, the replacement of barter by money after 300 BC, a few Greek deities, and even a bit of republican democracy, the Punic establishment adapted the maritime capitalism born in Ugarit and perfected in Tyre to the mature Iron Age. The Punic economy was destined to resemble the modern Asian *keiretsu* or *chaebol* systems even more closely than its predecessors, enabling Carthage to become both a political and commercial superpower between 550 and 146 BC. Its trading orbit included much of Mediterranean Europe and North Africa, Britain, Libya, Etruria, and even distant shores of Sub-Saharan Africa.[72] Punic traders served as middlemen and also exported wares of their own making. Within the Tunisian bastion itself shipbuilding, toolmaking, textiles, ceramics, carpentry and other handicrafts flourished. Copper was imported from the old Spanish pits of Rio Tinto. Carthage was able to diversify its economy far more than Tyre had done, excelling in agriculture as well as trade. Capturing the wheat-fields in the interior of interior of Sardinia became but a prelude to the eventual Punic transformation of Tunisia into the breadbasket of the Mediterranean.[73]

Neither the Greeks (save the Ptolemies) nor the earliest Romans abided by the rules of the *Eclectic Paradigm* in their overseas trade. Both of these cultures remained individualistic and heavily agrarian in nature. The development of liquid capital in the form of coined money and the rule of law embodied in the *polis* or *gens* allowed them to take their chances with generally free markets. There was at first no need for internalising trade and investment in business hier-archies when contracts between free individuals or families guaran-teed by law worked far better for them. More than the Greeks, the Romans were beginning to see war as a normal state of affairs and a means of surmounting market failure. The nature of Greek trade and investment, rooted in grain, olive oil, pottery, and other goods of peace (with the exception of slaves), was well suited to independ-ent commerce. Rome, less interested in buying goods than seizing them, would channel its more familial commerce to serve the goods of war. First Hellenic and then Latin entrepreneurs would pose a potent threat to both the Punic hegemony in the western Mediter-ranean and the Oriental business model it embodied.

The Greek challenge developed slowly at first. The eighth-centu-ry BC Euboean iron-trading network had been more of an adjunct than a threat to Tyrian commerce; the later Hellenic colonies in It-aly and Sicily continued to trade with Carthage. The first threat to the Canaanite position in the western Mediterranean came when the Samian merchant Colaeus was shipwrecked in Spain just before 600 BC. The Greeks were warmly received by the Iberian king of Tartessos who supplied him with silver and invited him to challenge the exclusive Iberian trading arrangement with Phoenicia. In spite of all attempts to keep market knowledge of the silver mines of Tar-shish and the tin mines of Britain mines in Phoenician and Punic hands, the Greeks had now discovered the markets and resources of Iberia and western Europe as it were by accident. It was, however, not the Samians but their fellow Ionian neighbours, the Phocaeans, who would pose the first great threat to the jealously-guarded

Carthaginian mandate in the west. The entrepreneurial nature of the Greek economy, coupled with the new spirit of inquiry flourishing nearby in sixth-century Miletus, encouraged advances in naval technology in the Greek world, advances which the Phocaeans soon put to good use. Phoenician and Punic trade was generally carried on in sturdy but slow fleets of large round galleons. Having discovered a lucrative market in copper, tin, and silver and an Iberian client ready to violate the terms of their arrangements with the Carthaginians, the traders of Phocaea put to sea in the pioneering versions of small fifty-oared longships called *penteconters*. Fast for their day, hard to detect and easy to manoeuver, these vessels were ideal for independent Phocaean merchants who could dash through the Straits of Messina and along the north coast of the Mediterranean, outrunning their Punic pursuers. In Iberia itself they were warmly received by the natives, who, the evidence would suggest, wished to diversify their markets beyond a monopolistic arrangement with a Carthage which put its own interests first. By 600 BC the Phocaeaens were settling Massilia (Marseilles) and other colonies on the French, Italian, and Spanish Riviera The Greek attempt to capture the markets of barbarian Europe had begun. The presence of Rhodian, Corinthian, and Attic pottery in addition to Ionian in Provence testifies to the importance of Massilia in the new expansion of Greek trade. Greek traders followed the Ebro in northern Spain to the new Greek settlement of Emporion in Catalonia on the fringes of Punic Iberia itself. A second route connected Massilia with the heartland of a Celtic Gaul beginning to build its settlements, forge its iron weapons, and till its rich soil. What would one day be Burgundy was, by the sixth century, the newest market for Greek expansion, witnessed by the presence of Greek vases in the region where the Rhône converged with routes to the English Channel and the North. Phocaean *penteconters* also darted up the Adriatic, founding the settlement of Adria near Venice, trading pottery, jewels, and bronze goods for the amber of the Baltic.[74]

In seeking to conquer the markets of Europe via the Rhône, Adriatic and other routes, Phocaean and other Greek competitors tried to circumvent Carthage's attempt to monopolise European trade from Spain through its control of the Pillars of Hercules and the port of Gades. Hellenic traders thus had to reach new Celtic, Germanic, and Illyrian markets by boat or overland caravan along the valleys of the Rhône, Seine, Elbe, and Danube. These aggressive new traders enticed the barbarians with their new money and luxury goods, seeking to carve out a share of the tin, amber, and iron markets Carthage sought to dominate.[75]

By 550 BC the expansion of Greek civilisation and power into Europe, Libya, and the western Mediterranean had reached a point where the Carthaginian establishment could only be alarmed at the prospect of strategic encirclement:

Finally, that Greek expansionist phase, specially motivated...to ensure a route to metals, reached its peak when the Greeks of Ionia, the Phoceaens, proceded to found Massilia (Marseilles) in the year 600 and Ampurias, in Catalonia, around the same time. The whole north of the western [Mediterranean] basin fell, for all practical purposes, under their control, as well as the tin traffic...across the valley of the Rhône...of Cornwall. The maritime and commercial power of Carthage was...placed in jeopardy by this new rival and by the whole encirclement strategy of Greek imperialism...[76]

The reaction in Carthage to this aggressive attempt to encircle their realm by a culture that recognised neither Melqart nor his rules of trade was ideological as well as economic. More and more Greeks were making fortunes and abandoning their farms for new *poleis* arising around the trade routes of the Aegean, Black Sea, and Mediterranean. While most continued to worship the Olympian deities, often in a lukewarm manner, among the sixth-century Hellenic elite philosophers, lawmakers, tyrants, and democrats questioned the notion of a divine social order in business, politics, and everyday life. Greek scientists who questioned the rule of Zeus in human affairs would also question the sway of Melqart; Greek entrepreneurs and bankers would likewise question the monopoly of Carthage in business. Hellenic culture, revolutionary by Oriental standards, posed a long-term as well as an immediate danger to the relatively closed world of Carthage in much the same manner as American expansion endangered the traditional cultures and economies of nineteenth-century China, Korea, and, especially, Japan.[77]

If one wishes to carry the parallel further, Carthage arose to the Occidental spiritual and cultural challenge in a manner not unlike Meiji Japan after 1868. Punic Bases in Sardinia, western Sicily and the Balearics were reinforced, and alliances forged with the Elymians of Sicily. Between 560 and 480 BC the Magonid kings of

Carthage also sought to exploit the resentments Gela and Rhegium harboured against Syracuse. The *tapputu*-partnership with the Etruscans was transformed into a military as well as a commercial alliance.[78] North of Rome, numerous Punic artifacts and inscriptions honouring Astarte were unearthed at Etruscan ports documenting the cementing of this alliance, directed mainly against the Phocaean menace.[79] The new Phocaean threat came as much from piracy as from direct commercial competition, and intensfied after a large portion of the population of Phocaea, driven from their homes by the armies of Cyrus, temporarily relocated on the island of Corsica. After 565 Ionian corsairs based here and along the Greek Riviera took a heavy toll of Punic commerce in the Tyrrhenian Sea and the northwest Mediterranean. The Greek menace was so strong it required the combined efforts of the Punic and Etrurian war fleets to defeat it. At the battle of Alalia in 535 BC 120 Carthaginian and Etrurian ships won a costly victory against half that number of Phocaean vessels. Corsica was now assigned to the Etruscan sphere of influence. Alalia helped consolidate Punic control of the western Mediterranean, a control sealed not only by alliance with the Etruscans, but with the rising new Roman Republic.[80]

Relations between Carthage and Rome were at first quite friendly as the Magonids sought to incorporate the new republic into their alliance system. Etruria was at this stage far more important to them than Rome. After all, Rome in the sixth century BC had little interest in trade but was still one of a number of Italian *poleis* that were merely local powers. The text of a treaty concluded between Carthage and Rome following the establishment of the Roman Republic in 509 BC, preserved by Polybius, illustrated the managed, strategic nature of Punic trading policy. Romans were permitted to trade in Carthage, Sardinia, and Punic Sicily, but were forbidden to remain south of the Fair Promontory, most likely Cape Bon in Tunisia. According to Polybius (iii. 23) the Carthaginians "did not wish them to become acquainted with the coast around Byzacium or the Lesser Syrtes, which they called Emporia because of the great fertility of that region".[81] The more *laissez-faire* Romans had no objection to Punic trade anywhere in Italy, but Carthaginians were forbidden to build any forts in Latium, interfere with any Latin city, or remain with weapons on Latin territory. According to Polybius, the treaty showed the Carthaginians "consider Sardinia and Africa as belonging absolutely to them" while Sicily was only partially under their control. The Romans, on the other hand, only made stipulations concerning Latium, for the rest of Italy was not yet under their control.[82]

The first Rome-Carthage treaty of 509 BC was drawn up in the context of the further consolidation of Carthaginian power in the western Mediterranean and Athenian power in the eastern Mediterranean. A fascinating portrait of what they termed the "vast commercial organisation" of the Punic state and how its coordinated, hierarchical, and navy-based system of commerce might have operated was constructed by French scholars J.G. Demerliac and J. Meirat in the 1980s. The long distances separating Carthage from the Atlantic and Mediterranean fringes of her empire increased the importance of ports like Gades and Lixus in managing trading voyages. Unlike the independent Greek *poleis*, major Punic centres remained integral parts of a centrally-directed system joined together by three key trade routes. Galleys on the first route sailed eastward from Carthage every May past Pantellaria and Malta to Sidon and Tyre, there to buy Oriental goods and access the markets of Asia. No longer site of the head offices of Carthaginian commerce, Phoenicia still linked the former with a Persian trading sphere stretching to India. The galleys then returned westward via Egypt, stopping at the Greek colonies in eastern Libya and the Punic colonies in western Libya. Punic Libya itself oversaw a network of overland trading routes to Egypt which also crossed the Sahara what is now Ghana and Nigeria. The ships returned to Carthage by late September. Galleys on the second route left Carthage and headed for Sardinia and the settlement of Punicum near the Etruscan port of Pyrgi. Punic outposts stretching from Punicum to Motya managed the trade with Italy and Sicily, the security of which was very important to Punic commerce. The third and most important route branched off from the second, heading west from Sardinia to Ibiza in the Balearics and then down the Iberian coast through the Pillars of Hercules at Gibraltar to Gades and Lixus.[83]

Maintaining the large-scale trade outlined above, which involved bulk shipments of precious metals from Iberia and the Atlantic as well as of textiles, wheat, resources and luxury goods from Italy, Asia, and Africa demanded vast amounts of capital investment. No independent trader was capable of financing such enterprises on such a scale; only the Carthaginian elite, backed by temple, navy, and state, could afford to do so.[84]

Internalisation of Punic bulk trade and direct investment by Punic merchant-aristocrats in centres like Gades and Lixus on the model of the *Eclectic Paradigm* may well have been a feasible solution to the problems of such long-distance mass trade. The need for commercial voyages into the Atlantic, which could not return Carthage itself the same year, strengthened the mandate for subsidiary operations based in Spain and Morocco. These operations would still have to be financed from Carthage, the main source of Punic money. Demerliac and Meirat regard it as certain that Gades and Lixus "obtained the necessary financial delegations from the capital and also played an important banking role in the economic system."[85] The cost of insuring Mediterranean voyages alone amounted to 30% of the cargo's value in the best of times, but piracy and war could raise these costs to 65 or even 100%. In the market conditions of the Punic world this would simply be unsustainable without large-scale state-supported organisations able to cover these losses. Given an interest charge of 65%, moreover, the land routes to Europe now being opened by the Phocaeaens threatened to undercut all Punic trade to Europe via the Atlantic route unless the risk of piracy and war could be reduced. Given the militarised and organised nature of the existing Punic business culture, the type of multinational organisation prescribed by the *Eclectic Paradigm* seemed to provide the natural solution for fourth-century BC Carthage, which unlike its Roman contemporary, lived very much by trade:[86]

> But doubtless it was not necessary that the level of maritime interest attain 65% in order that the land route of the Marseillais become more advantageous than the Punic sea route. Piracy was therefore for Carthage a very serious menace... economically as well as politically. In order to exploit the vast commercial system set on its feet by the Magonids Hanno and Himilcon, it had become indispensable to create a complex organisation of security, which determined the charcter of Punic military and naval institutions...[87]

Having more to lose from market failure than the leaner, more capitalised Greeks or the still largely provincial Romans, Punic managers required an internalised business organisation in the hands of their own notables as well as an associated naval organisation to protect it. With the Greek, Ligurian, and Albanian pirates in the Tyrrhenian, north Mediterranean, and Ionian Sea lurking in large numbers along their trading arteries, the admirals and shippers of Carthage formulated a coordinated response. Given that the Mediterranean was calm and safe only between May and September, the trading operations of the Punic Silver Fleet needed to be well organised and planned to be cost-effective. All three major Mediterranean routes had to protected at the same time. Even Carthage had limited resources, so her merchants sailed together in annual armed convoys which left Carthage for Tyre, Sardinia, or Gades every May and returned in September: "In order to maximise profits, it was necessary to cut to a minimum the number of long and unproductive voyages between the bases of departure and the zones of operations."[88] Defence against the swift *penteconters* of Phocaean and other pirates was provided by large *triremes*. *Triremes*, though, were a lot faster than Punic merchant ships and had to feed crews of 120 rowers plus marines. With the warships thus tied to their bases, the princes of Carthage had to arm the galleys themselves with marines and use the *trireme*s in mass sweeps against pirates where they would concentrate near Sardinia, the Balearics, Cartagena, and, later, Malta, Crete, and the Nile. Cooperation with the Etruscan and even some of the Greek navies also served to fill any vacuum caused by an overstretched Carthaginian naval arm. Every year the Punic navy began in May by watching the ports of Greek Italy, then shifting its patrols to Sardinia, Corsica, and Spain all the way to Gibraltar until the galleys all passed through the Pillars of Hercules. Replenishing in June in North Africa, the *trireme*s then patrolled the regions near Malta to cover the fleet heading back from Tyre in July, sometimes in concert with Corinthian and even Syracusan ships when a pro-Carthaginian party was in power there.[89]

Punic capitalism could be described as a form of naval or navy-based "maritime capitalism" in which the organisation of major trading operations assumed the form of a seaborne military campaign. This annual campaign affected the rhythms of everyday life in the metropolis itself as much as the contemporary land wars in Italy affected Roman life. Every April and May the crown munitions firms of Carthage went about arming over 200 *trireme*s, each of which would carry not only a detachment of marines but garrisons of the Libyan, Iberian, Sardinian and other soldiers that served as mercenaries in the polyglot Punic army. The peasants who tilled the fields of Africa annually sent 24,000 of their number, once the spring planting was done, to row the *triremes*. Returning from Spain or Tyre they would return to their lords' estates in time for the fall harvest. With an estimated population of 300,000, some 60,000 soldiers, sailors, and marines were involved in these operations. This system of militarised commerce, which no freedom-loving Athenian would put up with, was destined to work fairly well in in time of peace or brief war. Longer-term conflicts, though, strained the system. The huge apparatus and the largely agrarian economy which supported it became overstretched if full mobilisation lasted longer than two months, compelling Carthage win wars quickly or obtain a compromise peace.[90]

The first major challenge to Carthage's commercial empire came not from the Romans but from the powerful Greek tyrants who dominated eastern and central Sicily and pinned Punic merchants in their colonies in the west. The need to control the strategic markets and ports of this wheat-rich island would lead Carthage into several centuries of intense war with first the Greeks and then the Romans. Sicily was to be the cockpit where the Oriental business culture of Carthage and the market-driven cultures of Greece and Rome would collide.[91] Syracuse, founded by Corinth in 733 BC, was the key to Sicily. Whoever held it controlled a valuable centre for grain production and a key naval outpost for monitoring markets in both Italy and Carthage. Gela, Megara, and Himera were founded shortly after Syracuse. So long as these *poleis* were independent of one another, they posed no danger to Punic trade. A united Greek Sicily under the Gelonid tyrants of Syracuse was another matter.[92] When Gelon attacked the strategic city of Himera, Carthage, led by the Magonid ruler Hamilcar sent in its army and navy. The battle of Himera in 480 BC was a major defeat for Carthage, occurring simultaneously with the Athenian victory over Tyre at Salamis. The war continued through much of the fifth century BC. Gelonid Sicily entered a golden age of growth and prosperity and continued to repulse not only the Punic threat from the west, but the Athenian threat from the east. Allying herself with the Peloponnesian cause, Syracuse annihilated the army and navy of

Athens sent to conquer it in 427 BC. It was then to be the turn of Carthage to exact revenge upon the Gelonids. The savagery of the war waged by the Punic army was equal to anything to be perpetrated by Rome at its worst. The Magonid kings, generals, admirals, and most managers in Carthage believed in a personal relationship with Melqart and Baal Hammon who had the power to grant them military and commercial victory. Consequently, both war and business were carried on with religious intensity, being waged in the name of Baal and Country:

For a Carthaginian general each campaign was a holy war. A loss was an impiety, and a failed leader might be expected to sacrifice himself on a pyre or starve himself to death. The general-king was expected to solicit the good favor of the gods every day through sacrifice and consultation of the omens. [93]

When the Magonid army retook Himera, the men of the city were tortured and murdered as blood sacrifices while the women and children were regareded as booty. The Greeks were not long in retaliating and the fighting bogged down into a war of attrition not unlike the Peloponnesian War, World War I, Vietnam, or the Iran-Iraq war of the 1980s. Unlike the Greeks the multinational Punic army was ignorant of sanitation, due to its makeup of mercenaries from many nations. Epidemics of salmonella and rat-borne typhus decimated the Punic forces, preventing them from capturing all of Sicily. Nevertheless, Carthage entered the fourth century in far better shape than the exhausted regime in Syracuse. [94]

Quickly recovering from its failure to eject the Greeks from Sicily, Carthage strengthened and expanded its empire, reaching the peak of its power in the fourth century BC. UNESCO excavations in the city conducted during the 1980s show evidence of flourishing trade and commerce. A new wave of religious intensity swept the society, as the plagues and reversals were blamed on lack of devotion to Melqart, Baal Hammon, and the new goddess Tanit. The western Mediterranean basin would now become the core of an even vaster Punic domain seeking, through its powerful navy and branch firms firm to compensate for failure to control Sicily by markets in Africa, Europe, and possibly even the New World. Having seen the continent's economic potential, Carthage now determined to be an African as well as a Mediterranean power. New markets were sought by both land and sea. The Punic market search in Africa took place by both land and sea. Greeks were permitted to settle in eastern Libya, near Benghazi, but Spartans seeking to colonise Leptis, near Tripoli, in western Libya were driven out. Tunisia, Algeria, and Morocco were totally dominated by Carthage. Native Berbers were subjugated, feudal estates erected, and the Mahgreb turned to wheat production. Punic posts were erected every 30-40 kilometres along the Algerian coast. In sites like Tipasa, some 60 kilometres west of Algiers, Serge Lancel and others found Greek pottery in the strata before 500 BC. After 400 BC the grave finds are heavily Punic, and by about 350 imports almost totally disappear, reflecting the ever-tightening control by Carthage over her imperium.[95] Posts like Tipasa served as a link to Lixus (or Lixus) Mogador in Morocco. Punic posts in Malta, Sardinia, and elsewhere were strengthened and the new posts like Ras Fortas Ras, Kerkouane, El Drek, Djerba., and Thapsus Acholla extended along the Tunisian and Libyan shore. These colonies joined Carthage with Leptis in Libya which now became the branch office in charge of Carthaginian trade in gold, ivory, and animals from deep inside Africa. Caravans of Libyan traders on horseback crossed the Sahara to the south and west across Ghadames, Fezzan, and Garamentes, working their way to the gold fields and ivory markets of Guinea and Niger. Inland posts and routes also reached overland to Egypt, well inland from the Greeks Cyrenaica.[96]

Carthage also reached its new African markets via the Atlantic. Lixus managed the Punic trade to the gold and ivory of the African far west. Commercial settlements and trading voyages managed from Lixus sailed down the shores of Morocco and the western Sahara. The most interesting case of Punic market-seeking behaviour in this region came from the voyage of the Magonid prince Hanno in the mid-fifth century BC. The record of the famous African voyage of Hanno survives in a single Greek document discovered in the ruins of Carthage by a Roman historian. According to this *Periplus of Hanno*, the Punic prince sent a massive fleet of *trireme*s, manned by 30,000 personnel through the Pillars of Hercules and down the coasts of Morocco and the Rio de Oro. The purpose of the mission was obviously to found new commercial colonies here and possibly even on the shores of gold-and ivory-rich Black Africa itself. The *Periplus* leaves the reader in a quandary as to how far south Hanno sailed, why he turned back, and whether he tried to colonise Canaanites in Ghana or Nigeria. The Punic business establishment may have doctored the account to confuse foreign readers and protect valuable market information. Were the attacks by wild men, rain forests, large lake-bearing island, hippos, crocodiles, and land of blazing fires described in the text in Senegal, Guinea, or possibly even the Camerouns? Had the vast Punic armada come to those humid shores seeking an opportunity for colonisation only to be turned back by considerations of distance, climate, hostile natives, or simple cost? The most plausible explanation seems to be that having explored the potential new markets of West Africa, Hanno and the Punic oligarchy decided that direct investment on such shores was too risky and unprofitable beyond the Moroccan and Rio de Oro coasts. Even following the internalised model of the *Eclectic Paradigm* could not guarantee profitable investment in the Gulf of Guinea. African markets this far south could better be exploited on a smaller scale by traders who could come ashore or the overland routes working through Libya.[97]

Punic merchants also tried to expand European Atlantic trade from their offices in Gades. Hanno (possibly brother of Himlico) sailed a fleet up the Biscay shore as far as the Loire and likely on to tin markets of Britain. British tin, long known to the Iberians, was coveted by both Greeks coming overland and Carthaginians coming by sea. Himlico's voyage, intending to "establish major trading conections with remote centres producing valued raw materials" was beyond a doubt intended to establish more direct control over this trade, though there was no evidence of direct Punic investment in either Gaul or Britain.[98] The tin mines of Brittany and Cornwall were worked by Celtic miners trading both Gades and Massilia. The Phocaeans obtained their tin by riverboat and pack horse down the Seine, Saône and Rhône, but it is not likely that much tin reached the Punic bronze industry this way. Given huge growth in that Punic industry in the fourth and third centuries BC and the intensity of Greek-Punic rivalry, it is more logical to assume that the old Iberian tin trade down the Atlantic shore was now managed by Carthaginian executives based in Gades. Tired of merely depending on Celtic or Iberian middlemen, the trading firms of Gades and

Carthage herself sent a massive expedition under Lord Himilco to seek the tin markets for themselves.[99]

The tin of Cornwall and Brittany once bartered from the Celts was now paid for with Punic horsehead coins. The ability of the Punic merchants of Gades to "monopolize exploratory navigation on the far side of Gibraltar" by barring Greeks from passing through the Pillars of Hercules compelled the latter as well as Romans and likely even the Etruscans to develop the overland river routes.[100]

Strabo presented an intriguing story of market-seeking behaviour on the part of the traders of the new Roman Republic and their efforts to break the knowledge and trading monopoly of Carthage's Atlantic markets. A Roman captain posed as an ally of Carthage and took his ship right into Gades. Having the ancient equivalent of his own industrial spies he soon found out a Carthaginian ship was setting sail for the Tin Isles. The Roman quietly pursued until the Punic skipper realised what was happening and, not wishing the Romans to know too much about these vital markets, scuttled his ship on the Iberian Atlantic shore. Returning overland to Gades, the Punic sailors were handsomely decorated as virtual war heroes by the hierarchy of Gades.[101]

The Romans were not the only ones seeking to break the Punic Atlantic monopoly. The Greeks of Massilia had long sought to do so. The mobilisation of as many as 1,500 *triremes* of the Punic navy to attack the Greeks of Sicily in 310 BC provided one Greek mariner of Massilia named Pythias his chance to run Gibraltar and penetrate into areas from which the Punic navy had excluded all competition: "Never before had any Western navigator been able to sail so far north; Carthaginian commercial interests would not permit it."[102] Looking for the mysterious Tin Islands, Pytheas slipped through the Pillars of Hercules and headed northward up the Portuguese coast. There were no Punic *triremes* to be seen as he made landfall on the tin-rich isles off Cornwall. having the primitive equivalent of a sextant, Pytheas made a discovery even more astonishing than that of the new market he had sought. When he looked at the North Star and the Little Dipper, he noticed that they were much higher in the sky, some 26 moon-diametres, than they were in Massilia. This suggested to Pytheas and those who would know of his discovery that the surface of the earth over which they sailed was not flat but curved. Within about fifty years after this voyage both

Hellenic and Punic mathematicians may have thus deduced the earth itself was round![103]

In spite of Pytheas, Carthage retained and expanded its grip on the British tin trade. Punic coins with horsehead and palm-tree images used to purchase tin shipped away in Carthaginian galleys are commonly found around the mouth of the River Esk in Devon and around the harbour of Poole in Dorset. While it is still not possible to prove the existence of permanent Carthaginian settlement and/or direct investment in these locations, it is certainly true that these two places were major import-export centres for the northerly end of the Punic trading network managed from Gades. Not only tin, but furs and animal skins passed through these markets.[104]

The existence of Punic regional trading mandates covering the Atlantic suggests an even more tantalising possibility, but one dismissed by most historians.[105] After the destruction of Carthage the writer Plutarch (45-120 AD) discovered a parchment telling of lands far to the west. According to the parchment, when one sailed west from Britain one would pass three groups of islands equally distant from one another and then a large island called *Ogygia*. Five thousand stades (800 kilometres) to the west of *Ogygia* was the north coast of the continent *Epiros* that rimmed a great ocean. Were the three groups of islands the Orkneys, Shetlands, and Faroes? Was *Ogygia* Iceland? Was *Epiros* Greenland, Nova Scotia, and New England? If the Vikings could have discovered this, why not the Carthaginians and Greeks?[106] Punic agents from Gades and Lixus may have also have reached the New World by the very route taken by Columbus. The trade winds of the Canaries could easily blow a Carthaginian ship bound for Africa across the Atlantic to the West Indies. Diodorus of Sicily claimed that even Phoenician ships at very early periods had been blown westward until they reached a very large fertile island many days west of Africa. Was this island Cuba? Horsehead coins of Carthaginian type near navigable rivers found all over the North American continent confirm this as a possibility. Were it true, it implies the possibility of an almost global subsidiary mandate for the firm managers of Morocco and Iberia.[107] The late Dr. Barry Fell entertained the possibility of rather extensive economic ties between Carthage and America, although the idea is still considered too far-fetched by David Soren and most orthodox archaeologists studying both Carthage and ancient America. Fell went so far as to see this hypothetical New World trade as the foundation of Punic world power, with the timber and precious metals needed to sustain that power in the face of Greece and Rome coming from American shores:

> *An export trade of Cypro-Phoenician mass-produced bronze art repli-*
> *cas was carried out by Carthaginian ships visiting America. Substan-*
> *tial gold was acquired in return, but insufficient to provide adequate*
> *ballast. To meet this need, the Carthaginian ships picked up shipments*
> *of large pine logs from the Algonquian tribes of northeastern North*
> *America, to whom they traded adequate stocks of iron-cutting tools, ax-*
> *es, and other desirable items, including occasional bronze art repli-*
> *cas...and also low-value Carthaginian coins of attractive appearence,*
> *glass beads, and the like. Such trade, profitable alike to the Amerindi-*
> *an and the Carthaginian, would result in a steady input of gold and*
> *lumber on the home markets in Carthage, would yield the timbers need-*
> *ed to build ships, and provide them with straight masts and oars, and*
> *in addition would yield the Carthaginian state the gold ingots required*
> *to produce the coinage that apparently financed the military and naval*
> *operations of the Sicilian War, and later of the First Punic War.*[108]

By the fourth decade of the third century BC Rome had replaced the Greeks and the Etruscans as the major power facing Carthage. On the eve of the First Punic War each of these powers embodied a model of business enterprise as well as a political and religious world-view.[109] Carthage embodied the practices and lessons of 2,000 years of the Near Eastern school of directed enterprise that had governed Assyria, Babylonia, Hatti, Persia, and Tyre. Large firms were state-run or owned by princely families with hereditary connections to the crown and one another. Merchants were nobles and nobles were merchants. Small enterprises eventually organised themselves in guilds presided over by patron deities entered into long-term relationships with larger firms. The large clusters of Punic agriculture and industry (mining, munitions, shipbuilding, shipping) actively cooperated with the state, the powerful temples, and with one another, especially when the security of Carthage was at stake. Most importantly, the feudal and Oriental culture of Carthage, its past business history, and its strategic position helped condition the development of its foreign trade along the lines of the *Eclectic Paradigm*. The survival of Carthage as a trading power was best preserved by a network of hierarchical management organisations centrally directed from Carthage itself. African trade was managed from Leptis, northern and southern Atlantic trade, possibly even including America, from Gades and Lixus, Etruscan and central Mediterranean trade from Sardinia, Motya, or Carthage herself, which also likely handled the commerce through Tyre. The trading expeditions of the Silver Fleet, covered by extensive naval operations, tightly coordinated with the harvest and blessed by the priests of Baal, were conducted as annual military campaigns. The young Roman Republic represented, with a few modifications, the system of independent enterprise which had flourished in the Aegean and was perfected in the commercial empires of Corinth and Athens. Most firms remained in independent hands, led by bosses who were largely entrepreneurs and often foreigners, freedmen, or even slaves, a crude form of social mobility unthinkable in Carthage where rulership in both government and enterprise was a privilege of both birth and merit. The Greek *polis* regulated the market, it did not seek to manage or supplant it; the early Roman state seems not to have intervened in the market at all. Capital risks were largely sustained by private bankers. Jupiter, Mars, Juno, and other Latin deities did not preside over the market as Melqart did. Romans borrowed them from the Greeks and the Etruscans, built temples in their name from plundered riches, and then proceeded to largely ignore them save as symbols of patriotism and civic virtue. Rules of the *Eclectic Paradigm* were waived in Classical Europe, where the market itself largely remained the final arbiter of commerce. Liquid cash and temporary dealings among small traders gave all the insurance against market failure that was needed. The ponderous multinational enterprises of Carthage were symbolised by the slow galleys of the Silver Fleet; the entrepreneurs of Greece were represented in the swift *penteconters*, each hawking their wares of the Phocaeans, each one hawking its wares independently of all others. The contrast between the Punic and Hellenic/Roman enterprise systems is a clear premonition of the contemporary contrast between various Asian systems of directed capitalism, which resemble the system of Carthage, and more individualistic Western systems which is a direct spiritual descendent of Athenian enterprise. The differences between the two models may be summarised in chart form:

Figure 9. Comparison Between Punic and Hellenic/Roman Enterprise Systems

Embedded Organisation Perspective	Discrete Organisation View
(Near East and Carthage)	(Greece and Rome)
Mesopotamian "princely" or "temple" capitalism	Hellenic/Hellenistic "market" capitalism
Phoenician/Carthaginian "naval" or "maritime" capitalism	Roman "family" or "legionary" capitalism
Minoan/Egyptian "state" capitalism	
Networked Relationship	Atomistic
Mercantile hierarchy directed from Ashur, Babylon, Ugarit, Tyre, Carthage, Knossos, Thebes, Alexandria	Independent entrepreneurs in various Greek poleis. Family firms in Republican Rome
Interdependence	Independence
Interlocking of state, nobility, temple, merchants, agriculture.	Temples, army, navy independent of commerce but mangers have lucrative contracts with army and state in Rome.
Slavery and serfdom in extensive use with little social mobility permitted	Goals are those of individuals subject to some regulation by the state. Foreign, slave, freedman labour in extensive use but permitting social mobility
Symbiosis	Business is war/jungle
Businesses operate together in co-ordinated quasi-military fashion for imperial goals as defined by hierarchies.	Economic competition takes place among small independent or family businesses within as well as among poleis.
Co-operative	Competitive
Feudal, family, and religious relationships cement business alliances.	Business relationships are based solely on contracts regulated and enforced by republican law. Family relationships predominate in Rome
Positive Sum (win-win) Trust and Reciprocity	Zero Sum (win-lose) Power Negotiation
Punic enterprises form long-term tappu-tu-contracts with Iberian, Etruscan counterparts.	Tactical Alliances (calculative and potentially short term)
	Greek traders make short-term cash deals with banks, partners, and customers.
	Roman firms make military contracts with state.
Strategic Alliances (long term)	Tactical Alliances (calculative and potentially short term)
Open, broad, contact	Limited, contract

The three Punic Wars waged between Rome and Carthage began in 264 BC with Roman intervention in Sicily and climaxed in 146 BC with the destruction of Carthage. These were the most intense wars of antiquity, and it is possible that were not to be equalled in ferocity until First and Second World Wars of the twentieth century. The Punic Wars would intensify the militarism of Roman life, turn Rome from an Italian into the leading world power, and accelerate the growth of slavery, manorialism, and social polarisation. Roman life inherited a huge, permanent standing army and, for the first time, a powerful navy. The vast legions would become central to Roman political life, paving the way for civil war and permanent dictatorship. The wars as well would provide an enormous encouragement to a Roman capitalism which forever indebted to the legions and their wars for its full development. Roman warfare in Italy before 264 BC was waged with temporary armies on an annual basis. The need to wrest Sicily from a powerful Carthage which possessed huge mercenary armies and the world's leading navy compelled the Roman Republic to create a much larger standing army and a comparable war fleet. Intense as the First Punic War would be, the Second, or Hannibalic War of 218-201 BC was even more so.[110] Rome raised a score of regiment-sized legions to fight on a number of fronts: Italy, Spain, Sicily, Illyria, Africa and Greece. Even though the defeat of Carthage ushered in long periods of relative peace throughout the second century BC, eight or nine legions remained in existence to confront the Celts and Iberians in winning the west and the Hellenistic states in the east.[111]

Rome's presence in southern Italy not only menaced Punic control of Carthage, but the latter was now a menace to Rome. Facing Carthage was the greatest challenge yet faced by the young Republic. Earlier foes, like the Samnites, were land powers comparable to Rome itself, but Carthage had command both of a vast empire and the seas surrounding Sicily and Italy. The First Punic War quickly became a continuation of the long conflict between Carthage and the Hellenic Sicily, with Rome assuming the leadership of the latter. As granary of Roman Italy and strategic centre of the Mediterranean, Sicily remained cockpit of the First Punic War. Carthage possessed initial advantages with her resources, advanced, internalised commercial system and the incomparable Punic fleet which could blockade the Roman legions in Sicily and land troops on their flanks and in their rear.[112] Rome's strengths, less evident at first, lay within the flexibility of her entrepreneurs and the flexibility of a relatively young society constantly forced to adapt to military dangers such as this one. As always, when threatened from without, a Roman society still strong on civic ideals mounted a formidable response: it built a powerful navy from virtually nothing and virtually overnight. Roman entrepreneurs in the pay of the Republic quickly manufactured a huge fleet of *quinquereme* (five files of rowers on each side of the ship) warships working from a captured Carthaginian prototype. A culture in which independent enterprise and risk-taking was encouraged and tolerated could adapt itself easily to the task of not only copying but improving upon Carthaginian designs. This triumph of Roman entrepreneurship was recorded by Polybius:

> It was, therefore, because they saw that the war was dragging on that they first applied themselves to building ships – 100 quinquiremes and twenty triremes. They faced great difficulties because their shipwrights were completely inexperienced in the building of a quinquireme, since these vessels had never before been employed in Italy. Yet it is this fact which illustrates better than any other the extraordinary spirit and audacity of the Romans' decision. It was not a question of having adequate resources for the enterprise, for they had in fact none whatsoever, nor had they ever given a thought to the sea before this. But once they had conceived the idea, they embarked on it so boldly that without waiting to gain any experience in naval warfare they immediately engaged the Carthaginians, who had for generations enjoyed an unchallenged supremacy at sea.[113]

The new *quinqueremes* included an improvement designed to capitalise on the Rome's one great military advantage: the superiority of its soldiers. Roman warships were fitted with an iron bridge known as a *corvus*, or crow, which they dropped onto the decks of the Punic vessels, overpowering them with seasoned, disciplined centurions fighting as marines. Inexperienced in pure naval warfare, the Romans prevailed by turning it into a war of floating armies, and in armies Rome was nearly invincible. Losing three fleets to storms, the inexperienced broke the naval and maritime superiority of Carthage forever with their fourth. The First Punic War ended in

241 BC. Rome was now a naval power, and one which held over-seas interests for the first time, inheriting the Tyrian bastions of Sardinia and Sicily. [114]

Carthage responded to its defeat by a further development of its *keiretsu*-like economic system. With Sicily and Sardinia gone, Spain became utterly essential to the Punic economy as a source of gold, copper, iron, and silver, as well as corn, oil, wine, salt, and fish. The Roman challenge to Punic sea power caused Carthage to lose its grip on the Spanish interior, necessitating a war of conquest led by the general Hamilcar Barcain 237-229 BC. Barca was given vice-regal powers in the conquered territories which were now for the first time placed under direct Carthaginian rule. Hamilcar was soon succeeded by his son-in-law Hasdrubal, and Hasdrubal by the famous Hannibal in 221 BC. While loyal to Carthage, the Barcids governed Spain as a personal kingdom. The loss of Spanish silver injured the Punic economy greatly, forcing the government to debase the coinage Andalusia to some degree. Ruling Iberia from the new colony of Novo Carthago (Cartagena) the Barcids continued the tradition of managed Punic enterprise. Vast amounts of gold and silver were extracted from mines extending from Rio Tinto in the west to newer mines like Baebelo in the east. With these resources, Hannibal was able to hire a mercenary army calimed at 90,000 infantry, 12,000 cavalry, and a fleet of 50 *quinqueremes*, although those figures were slightly exaggerated. Many Iberians joined this army, not out of national feeling, but from a combination of financial motives and a strong sense of personal loyalty to the Barcids.[115]

The war would soon resume as Rome, willing to tolerate Punic control of southern Spain, refused to accept Hannibal's advance into what had been the Hellenic sphere in Catalonia. The Second Punic War was fought on Italian soil as Hannibal boldly marched his new army, created from the profits of a Ibero-Punic business network dating back to Phoenician times into the heart of Roman Italy. Annihilating one legion after another, Hannibal devastated Roman agriculture and hastened the trends towards the concentration of Roman wealth and power in large villas and cities. Unable to defeat the brilliant Carthaginian on their own soil, the Romans were able to deny him victory by cutting off his supplies and invading Africa. Once again, Carthage would taste defeat, this time losing Spain and great power status. Such was its fabled prosperity that some circles in Rome, led by Cato, could not rest until the city was conquered and razed to the ground in a final war. The Punic armies, fighting this time for their survival instead of money, resisted heroically, but the one-sided conflict could only end in 146 BC with the defeat and destruction of the city many in Rome still feared as its greatest military and commercial rival.[116]

Chapter 9

Publicans and Patriarchs

The "Global" Triumph of Roman Family Enterprise: 146 BC-14 AD

By the first century BC, a single economic order prevailed from the Atlantic to the Euphrates dominated by Rome. Direct inheritors of the Hellenic market revolution, the Romans ensured the victory of free-market enterprise over the more vertically-integrated Oriental model of business management. That victory though, was to be only partial, for alongside the innumerable numbers of entrepreneurs and contractors trading beneath the Roman eagle from Iberia to India, large family firms, partnerships, and semipublic corporations also operated more in accord with the rules of the *Eclectic Paradigm.* Organised and even multinational enterprises, both public and private, existed in the Roman world to a greater extent than in Classical Greece. Even many independent enterprises in the Republic and Empire which could not be classified as "multinational" had a familial character unknown in Greece. Some firms, especially the publican partnerships operated by the Roman *equites,* or knights, grew to enormous size, engaged in mass production, and even embodied an early form of limited liability. In the Roman combination of individual and integrated enterprises one first dimly recognises the forms of Western business culture as they would exist in medieval and modern times.

Rome emerged from the 25-year war with Hannibal in 200 BC as the supreme power in the Occidental world. Roman society was

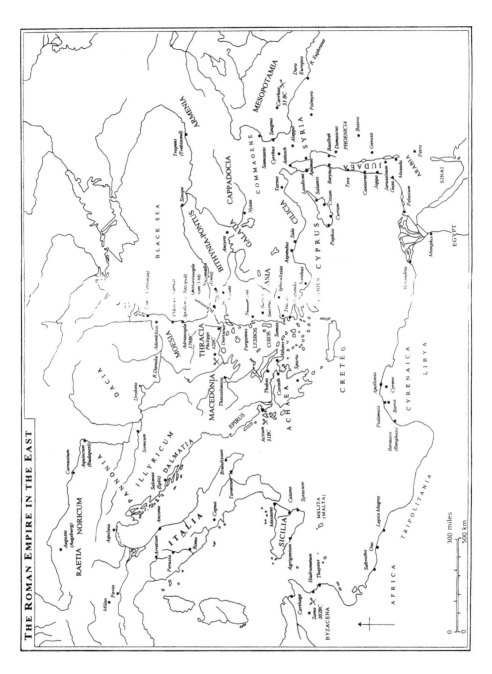

THE ROMAN EMPIRE IN THE EAST

THE ROMAN EMPIRE IN THE WEST

ANTONINE WALL

HADRIANS WALL

Carlisle

Eburacum (York)

Deva (Chester)

Lindum (Lincoln)

BRITANNIA

GERMANIA

Verulamium
(St Albans)

Camulodumum
(Colchester)

Aquae Sulis
(Bath)

Londinium

BELGICA

Vetera
(Xanten)

R. Rhenus
(Rhine)

Augusta
(Trier)

0   100   200 miles
0   100   200   300 km

N

LUGDUNENSIS

Lutetia
(Paris)

R. Liger (Loire)

GALLIA

AQUITANIA

Augustadunum

Augusta
(August)

R. Garumna (Garonne)

R. Rhodanus (Rhone)

Lugdunum (Lyon)

Vienna
(Vienne)

Pavia

Arausio

NARBONENSIS

TARRACONENSIS

R. Ebro

Numantia

Caesaraugusta

Nemausus
(Nimes)

Narbo

Massilia
(Marseilles)

Emporiae
(Ampurias)

CORSICA

Aleria

LUSITANIA

R. Tagus

Olisipo

HISPANIA

Tarraco

SARDINIA

Olbia

Augusta
Emerita

Corduba

BAETICA

Ilipa
206BC

Hispal

Gades
(Cadiz)

Saguntum

Ebusus

BALEARES

Caralis

Nora

Carthago Nova
(Cartagena)

Tingis
(Tangier)

Caesarea
(Cherchel)

Hippo
Regius

Cirta

NUMIDIA

M-AURETANIA

Timgad

Madaurus

completely revolutionised. The war, even more than its predecessor, helped to give birth to full-fledged Latin commercial establishment. By the dawn of the second century BC a Roman business
culture was fully formed, adapting the Greek entrepreneurial model
to the Italian family structure and relying upon markets created less
by free trade than by demand stimulated from constant warfare and
military expansion. The growth of such a business culture in Roman society during and after the time of the Punic Wars was subtly
reflected in the theatrical comedies of Titus Maccius Plautus, born
around 250 BC.

Plautus recognised that in the new commercial Rome, art and
culture were to be dictated by the market and popular taste, which
wanted comedies about everyday life. Heavy drama on political
themes simply did not sell in Rome at that time. The stereotypic
and often egotistical characters of Plautus's comedies still reflected
the role expectations of Roman life: the feared but often naïve *paterfamilias*, who is restrained from doing improperly by his strong but
submissive wife, the rich playboy who falls in love with a plebeian or
slave girl far beneath his station only to discover at the end that she
is of noble birth, the cunning parasite or slave who tries to take advantage of the more productive.

In the end, however, the traditional values of Rome always won
out when everyone returned to their appointed station in society.[1]
Marrying outside of one's station was anathema. In *The Pot of Gold*,
a poor man refuses to marry his daughter to a rich one. To do so
would be hitching an ox and an ass. Both asses (the poor) and oxen
(the rich) would never tolerate such an arrangement, for "an ass
with ox ambitions" ran an unacceptable social risk.[2] Slaves appeared frequently in Plautus's comedies, and were often harshly
treated in a way humorous to the audience. The system was pictured as a necessary and natural order of life in which owners cared
for their slaves as investments. Some, like Messenio in *The Twin Me-
naechmi* win their freedom only to reside with their former masters
as the work opportunities for freedmen were generally restricted to
business. Above all, the message was conveyed that the Roman order of family and slavery had to be maintained at all costs.[3] In spite
of this, plays like *Curculio* show the growing incorporation of business values into that order:

Husbands gambling their fortunes away? Try
the Stock Exchange. You'll know it by the call-girls
waiting outside. You can pick up anyone
You want to, at a price
In the lower Forum
You'll find the respectable bourgeoise
taking their daily stroll...
Below the old shops are the moneylenders,
The con-men behind the Temple of Castor,
The Tuscan Quarter is the red light district
Where you can make a living, one way or the other.[4]

Roman warfare and expansion was no longer confined to Italy but was now of an imperial character. As Roman legions marched into Africa, Iberia, Macedonia, Greece, and eventually into Anatolia, Syria, Mesopotamia, Palestine, Egypt, Gaul, Germany, and Britain they extended the market for Roman industry, trade, and investment. Decades of total war against Carthage followed by more decades of expansion outside of Italy provided the catalyst for large-scale business to evolve in Rome. Far more than Greeks, Romans would trade as well as live by the sword. Trade and overseas colonisation came early in Greek history, when the peninsula was still split into scores of *poleis*. By and large, Hellenic overseas expansion took on an essentially peaceful character. Rome, in contrast, began to expand overseas after five centuries of creating a political and economic order based upon waging constant war and upon the booty war would provide. The creation of a market stretching all around the Mediterranean and the lucrative contracts of a garrison state encouraged the growth of enterprises on a much larger scale than in Greece. Family firms based in Rome and other parts of Italy now encountered the opportunities for overseas investment. Roman entrepreneurs, traditionally prone to band together in partnerships, now began to expand the size of these partnerships. Chief among these were the semi-public *publicani*, or publican companies, which figured strongly in Roman commerce in the last two centuries of the Republic. While publican firms likely existed once commerce had become an important feature of the Roman economy after 500-400 BC, they really became important and noticeable during the Punic

Wars. The manufacture and distribution of togas, shields, helmets, and other weapons and provisions for the vast Roman legions was left in private hands, providing enormous marketing opportunities for any merchant willing to seize them. Publican companies arose and expanded along with the territory occupied by Roman armies. The major source of their profits came from bidding and fulfilling military contracts. These governmental contracts for uniforms and weapons were bid upon in the open market by rival publican firms. In addition to handling military contracts, the publican firms also bid for the right to collect taxes through much of the Roman realm. Privatised tax-farming was not unusual in antiquity, given the limited size of ancient governments, although from the time of Persia and Athens on, governments became more impersonal and bureaucratic. The Roman Republic needed to arm, clothe, and feed its legions and fleets, pay its governors and maintain its roads and public works. As in Phoenicia or Greece, the Republican state lacked the bureaucracy to raise the necessary revenue, and so let out public contracts to private firms as far back as even the fifth century BC Professor E. Badian, a leading expert on these firms, insists that the *publicani* were "an integral part of the *res publica* as far back as we can observe it or trace it".[5] The publican companies grew and profited enormously as contractors for supplies, including food, uniforms, and naval stores, in the war against Hannibal. The Roman victories in this and even earlier wars would have been impossible without their construction of roads, temples, and acqueducts. Military contracts were a profitable business in Rome, and, one might argue, apart from agriculture, the major business. The size of some of the contracts must have been enormous. It cost 100 *denarii* to clothe one centurion, 420,000 *denarii* (perhaps £200, U.S. $320) to clothe a legion of 4,200. An active force of four legions meant over 1.5 million *denarii*, perhaps £10 or 20 million, a lucrative sum indeed![6] At first *publicani* earned most of their profits from war, not taxation. Taxes in early Rome were raised by an 0.01% property levy known as a *tributum* as well as a 5% levy on the freeing of slaves. Supplying the war economy was much more profitable, especially when the number of legions grew from four to twenty during the Punic Wars before returning to a permanent force of eight or nine, which was still an army of close to 50,000 men and a cost of 3 million *denarii*, or £20-40 million just to clothe them alone. Even if

the profit margins on military contracts were small, the sheer volume of these contracts, of which hundreds were let out on an annual basis, ensured a rich market for the *publicani*.[7]

In spite of expanding their control across the Mediterranean to
the shores of the Aegean, the Romans of Latium remained reluctant
seafarers. Much of the early "Roman" investment in the Aegean
was in fact the work of southern Italians now incorporated into the
Roman realm who merely continued their active Hellenistic trade
under the Roman publican banner. The temporary destruction of
both Corinth and Carthage in 146 BC cleared the way for the Island of Delos to become the way station and office site for publican
companies, often manned by southern Italians, engaged in farming
taxes and importing slaves from Asia Minor. Large staffs of Greek-
speaking agents were recruited from southern Italy and the Aegean.
The new tax-and-slave economy of Delos also attracted many merchants from Syria, Asia, Egypt, and mainland Greece. Italian shippers, wine dealers, and bankers, many of them ex-slaves, formed
clubs and guilds on Delos named after Jupiter, Saturn, Mercury,
and other patron gods. From Delos these agents spread into Asia
Minor, where their presence in large numbers was confirmed by
Valerius Maximus. This author stated that Mithradites, the ruler of
Pontus, massacred 80,000 Roman citizens "scattered about the cities of Asia for the sake of business".[8] More southern Italian publicans, though, flocked to Asia in search of investment opportunities
after the Romans suppressed major Anatolian resistance. The publicans now presented themselves as Hellenic rather than Roman
firms and traders, speaking, dressing, and acting as Greeks as easily
as they had acted as Romans. According to the late Tenney Frank,
whose dated but exhaustive study of Roman economics still contains much valuable and useful material, "not very many actual citizens were in Asia, but...the publicans had non-citizen agents
there" who worked along side other "independent business men".[9]

Southern Gaul as well as Spain, would attract a more central and
northern Italian clientele. Cicero revealed that, at this time, commerce in Gaul was totally in the hands of Roman publicans, farmers, graziers, and other businessmen classified as *negotiatores*:

> *Gaul is packed with traders, crammed with Roman citizens. No Gaul*
> *ever does business independently of a citizen of Rome; not a penny*

changes hands without the transaction being recorded in the books of Roman citizens...Let one single account be produced in which there is a single hint indicating that money has been given to Fonteius; let them bring forward the evidence of one single trader, colonist, tax-farmer, agriculturist, or grazier out of all the inhabitants; and I will grant that the charge is a true one.[10]

The further rise of the publicans in the later second century BC was directly linked to the social tensions intensifying within Roman Italy itself. It was easier for Romans to conquer a world than to digest their conquests. Hannibal's depredations had hurt small farmers, who continued to be dispossesed by large landowners at an accelerating rate. Enormous numbers of slaves from the east now poured into Italy via Delos, against which the independent farmer could ill compete. Rome itself became the site of a huge urban proletariat whose members, if they could not qualify for the dole, were forced to fend for themselves. Roman Italy was increasingly depopulated of natives due to the heavy casualties borne by the urban poor and peasantry in the wars fought in Spain, Gaul, and the terrible civil conflicts waged within Italy herself at the onset of the first century BC. The Social War alone would cost 100,000 casualties on each side.[11] Not long after the destruction of Corinth and Carthage in 146 BC Rome entered into the long social crisis that would eventually accelerate its long transformation from a Roman Republic of freeholders to a Roman Empire adopting much from the Oriental realms it conquered.

Enormous sums of booty, the influx of slaves, and the resurgence of peasant debt and the rise of the manorial villa continued to undermine the foundations of the citizen-Republic. A few politicians, such as Senator Tiberius Gracchus and his two brothers tried, as had Peisistratus in Athens, or Franklin Roosevelt, the Kennedys, and Lyndon Johnson in modern America, to redress the abuses of the market and mounting disparity of wealth with the "New Deal" style reforms. In 133 BC Tiberius Gracchus proposed to limit the amount of land one could hold, calling into question the entire foundation of the Roman patrician state. Not even his assassination by the conservative Senate could stem the revolution of rising expectations and polarised discontent his reforms had unleashed. Politics in Rome became interest-group oriented in the latter second

century BC in a manner not unlike American or British politics
since the 1960s. In place of "Romans", there emerged a rural peasantry, an urban proletariat, rural and urban slaves, freedmen, and
other polities divided on class, ethnic, and occupational lines.[12]

One of the by-products of the social revolution in Rome was the
full emergence of the stratum of society, the equestrians, to whom
many if not most Roman publicans and managers belonged. In order to weaken the landed patricians of the Senate, Gaius Gracchus,
the brother of Tiberius, took measures to increase the power of this
new managerial class once he was elected Consul.[13] In 133 BC
Gaius institutionalised the Equestrian Order in an effort to challenge the landed wealth which he claimed was strangling the Republic. This measure and others helped to enormously increase the
power and scope of the publican companies which were the chief
institution of the equestrian class. The Gracchan reform coincided
with Roman expansion into Anatolian Pergamum, the cradle of
both Assyrian cross-border enterprise and the coined money of the
Hellenic market revolution. Now, as the Roman province of Asia,
its markets would stimulate the vast growth of the new Roman
firms. Taxation of this immense wealth of Asia Minor was placed by
Gaius Gracchus in the hands of *publicani* who were ready to reap far
vaster profits than ever before: 45 million *denari* in contracts
alone.[14]

The Roman presence in Asia Minor in the last century of the Republic enabled the *publicani* to reach their zenith at that time. The
publican firms may be seen as a form of internalised multinational
enterprise operating in the free-market milieu which Rome inherited from the Greeks. *Publicani* were usually not specialised firms. A
given firm might win a contract to make swords or togas but usually
specialised in neither. Publican associations seem to have been
based on a flexible management and work force. Associations of
partners would come together to carry out a contract and then disband. Faced with fierce market competition in the letting of contracts, the *publicani* simply could not afford much in the way of permanent staff, which remained lean and flexible in adapting to different markets. What the firms instead provided, according to Professor Badian, was "capital and top management, based on general
business experience".[15] The permanent staffs of the firms were
small in numbers and consequently flexible in adapting to different

kinds of business for both public and private contractors. The companies, says Badian, "can only have functioned…by taking over existing substructures and superimposing managing staff."[16] Permanent, organised staffs of skilled miners, tax professionals, arms makers, shipbuilders, and others did exist, and these were likely bought and sold by the publican managers as they shifted from contract to contract. The new Roman firms transacted business on a scale undreamed of by their Near Eastern and Hellenic forerunners. Without MBAs, extensive bureaucracies, business schools, and a body of formal corporation law they pioneered in the creation of the first multinational conglomerates, and the first recorded examples of limited liability corporations. Some of these firms were considered to have a legal existence of their own, at least until the contract which the firm's *manceps*, or manager had concluded with an official of the Roman state expired. Should the manger die, the company would choose another manager to carry out the terms of the contract. A typical Roman business contract included the dates of completion and payment, a clause for inspection of work, and an indemnity in case of losses due to war.[17]

Government guarantees plus some form of internalisation were necessary where frequent and ferocious warfare created a high-risk economy and business deals often involving tens of thousands of *denarii*. The Roman war economy was a dangerous place for large publican firms, let alone entrepreneurs. Terentius Varro Gibba, for example, was a partner in a publican firm who was wiped out in trading and forced to turn to law and other professions to recoup his losses.[18]

Publican firms tended to be organised as associations or partnerships, some of which grew to very great size by combining the capital of a score of partners, or *socii*. The *socii*, operating beneath the *manceps*, who served as chief executive officer, represented the shareholders and board of directors of the combined capital and expertise of the firm. Real executive power lay in the hands of the *magistii*. One Sicilan firm was run by the equestrian (knight) Vettius and his *magistii*, Servilius and Antistius, both of whom were elected by the *socii*. Beneath the chief executives lay the company's *decuria* or divisions, headed by other Roman knights of the Equestrian Order. The familial and other personal links among these knights ensured that the executives of the Roman firms, even competing for the same contracts, were, at least in the last century of the Republic, all part of a single network: "the ties among all the companies were particularly close, so as to constitute a cartel."[19] A publican company based in Rome, Campania, or Tarentium operated through agents in places such as Delos, Pergamum, Ephesus, Laodicea, Alexandria, Massilia, Gades, Athens, or Carthage. These officers, known as *pro magistro*, represented the *socii* of the Italian firm in its overseas transactions and investments. *Pro magistro* were not independent middleman contractors but full paid employees of the Roman company in charge of keeping accounts, collecting taxes, and sending reports to the *magistii* in Rome. One such branch manager was Cicero's close friend Terentius Hispo, whose firm, one or Rome's biggest, held revenue contracts for Bithynia and Asia and supervised tens of thousands of employees. *Pro Magistro* like Hispo held mandates not only for taxes and military procurement, but often for mail delivery as well. Banking was another function assumed by publicans in the century in which they dominated Roman commerce.[20]

The career of the publican knights and the Equestrian Order of whom they were a part was reflected in the life and times of Marius Tullius Cicero. Known as a great orator and famous politician, Cicero was also a very successful businessman who held an interest in a publican firm, owned several villas, and defended many publican partners in court. Born at Arpinium near Cassino in 107 BC, Cicero was himself the son of an equestrian knight. His youth was spent studying the laws of Rome, including business law, under the distinguished jurist Quintus Mucius Scaevola. As he matured in the 90s and 80s BC, Cicero witnessed the turbulent events rocking the Republic to its foundations, events in which his knightly class played a prominent part. The militarisation, expansion and commercialisation of Roman society began to place its institutions under very great strain. Consuls such as Gaius Marius and, for a while, Lucius Cornelius Sulla became less and less willing to part with the temporary powers their office gave them. Marius, after a bitter war with Germanic invaders, reorganised the army on a more professional basis in such a way that it would become more loyal to its commanders than to the Republic. His rival Sulla used such an army to proclaim himself the first dictator of Rome since 216 BC. Sulla subsequently inaugurated a reign of terror in which many knights per-ished. Although he voluntarily renounced the dictatorship, a precedent was set in which Roman soldiers and politicians could, if backed by business partnerships and loyal legions, aspire to one-man rule.[21]

Cicero, meanwhile, emerged into public prominence first as a lawyer and then as an administrator in Sicily. After 70 B.C Cicero became an *aedile*, or public works official and then a *praetor*, or city magistrate. He distinguished himself as a defender of the Equestrian Order and its members against the Senate, although his true political goal was to recreate a conservative coalition of both against those, such as Catiline or Julius Caesar, who would jeopardise the rights of property by promising debt relief to landless plebeians.[22] Cicero's orations and legal presentations, often concerning themselves with his fellow equestrians, have become a principal source of information on Roman, especially publican, managers in the first century BC. They continually mention the Roman knights he defended, and made periodic allusions to their business activities. In his defence of the Anatolian King Deiotarius, Cicero implied that many Roman knights trafficked in Asia.[23] As far as Cicero was concerned the executives of the publican firms were the flower of the Equestrian Order and the bulwark of the Republic, without whose support it would be difficult to win any honour.[24] Among these were the *manceps* Caraeus Plancius and Caius Rabirius Postumus. Plancius, son of a knight and heir of a long line of knights, was not only the promoter of many Roman firms, but served as president of some.[25] The father of Plancius, a farmer of the revenues, once presided over the most powerful and influential publican company in Asia Minor in the first century BC. As *manceps*, he was much loved and respected by the other *socii* and partners of his firm. In his successful defense of Plancius against charges of bribery and corruption, Cicero praised the political involvement of the family firm on behalf of his client, admitting that companies such as this could wield considerable influence on behalf of those allied to them if the latter were seeking public office.[26]

Cicero's defense of Plancius took place at a time when his and other firms were increasingly cartelising their operations in Asia Minor and encouraging Roman military and commercial expansion in the eastern Mediterranean. Wars between Rome and a revived kingdom of Pergamum raged in the 80s BC and again in the 60s. The

Pergamene threat to Roman interests was compounded by that of a resurgent piracy strong enough to jeopardise trade throughout the eastern Mediterranean and even endanger Rome's grain supply. The threats were removed by the rise of Gnaeus Pompeius Magnus who, with an army and a fleet of 500 ships, cleared the sea of pirates and conquered not only Pergamum but Syria and Judaea as well. Pompey was strongly supported by both Cicero and his publican clients who saw vast new investment opportunities. Even though Pompey awarded contracts for taxation directly to Eastern municipalities, the latter usually farmed them back to the *publicani* who alone had the organisation to raise revenue.[27] The stiffness of competition for tax contracts caused Plancius and other managers in Bithynia, Asia, and Cilicia to form a tightly-knit cartel among the publican firms capable of monopolising tax collection in the Asian regions.[28] The new eastern provinces organised by Pompey meant a vast increase in business not only for the firms in which he was invested, but for other firms as well, for an expanded Roman domain in Asia meant far more markets and a tripling of tax revenue for *publicani* willing and able to invest in Syria, Judaea and elsewhere. Many suddenly made fortunes, but, as in modern times, rampant speculation led to a crash in 61 BC. The *socii* responded to such market problems with further association and internalisation of their transactions between 61 and 59 BC: "we find" according to Badian, "companies getting together into a cartel…and it seems to have been done quite openly and officially."[29] The Bithynian firm of Terentius Hispo formed an arrangement with an Ephesian firm to farm the grazing tax of both Asia and Bithynia. Taxes in Cilicia were probably farmed by another firm also closely linked to Cicero. The agricultural tithes of Bithynia, meanwhile, were collected by a consortium of companies linked to Pompey himself. At least in the realm of tax collection, cartelisation in the most prosperous overseas region of the Roman world had supplanted the Hellenic market economy, as:

> *the companies had got together, formed a joint company for the exploitation of the chief Bithynian tax, and – as this clearly implies – done away with genuine competition. There had been organization of a sort before, as we have seen; and publicani had felt loyalty towards one another as members of the same order. There were at least some who*

thought that one publicanus, in a legal case, should never decode against another. But there had nevertheless been competition for the contracts; just as, even though manufacturers in a modern state will be closely linked in an association and will defend their joint interests, yet they will normally be in competition with one another where their products overlap. What we find by 51, therefore, was radically different – as different as a cartel is from a manufacturers' organization or a Chamber of Commerce. And as we saw, the cartel now, after a fashion, must have included the whole upper order of society and of the State, except for a few traditional aristocrats.[30]

Caius Rabirius Postumus was the equally distinguished heir of a huge Roman family concern. His father, Caius Curius Postumus represented the ideal Roman manager. A financial giant, the senior Postumus raised taxes and conducted his business activities across many provinces of the Republic's expanding overseas domain. If Cicero's praiseworthy rhetoric is to be believed, he engaged in business not just to make money but to find new opportunities for philanthrophy. Caius Rabirius followed in his father's path, inheriting a vast network of business concerns whose partners were linked together by strong familial and personal ties. Many of Rabirius's personal friends, and no doubt his relatives, worked as his agents and received from him commissions, contracts, and credit. Rabirius and his network lent money to many governments, including that of Ptolemaic Egypt, an act which resulted in his arrest and trial for extortion and other crimes. In the course of his defence, Cicero addressed an accusation, which, even if false, suggests some evidence of internalisation by hinting that Roman managers and partners engaged in long-distance commerce owned their own fleets. According to the story, several ships owned by Postumus sailed from the East to Puteoli, carrying huge cargoes of papyrus, linen, and glass. In his defence, Cicero clearly came forward as the defender of the Equestrian Order and its business interests. Should his client be convicted under what he felt was a dubious Senatorial law no Roman manager would be safe from the danger of guilt by accusation.[31]

Cicero's works also contained hints that the evolving style of militarised Roman family capitalism helped encourage the informal integration of the senatorial and knightly classes. Roman senators, publicly forbidden by law from owning ships or firms, privately became silent partners in major Roman enterprise. According to Livy[32] and Polybius,[33] profit-seeking through trade was deemed unsuitable for senators and other high officials. Elite Romans, on the other hand, including Cicero, admired money-making derived from proper sources of agriculture or productive labour as opposed to mere trading.[34]

Long before Cicero was ever born, a senator named L.A. Lepidus began to erect his own harbour facilities near the mouth of the Tiber to ship the estate produce from his villas to Gaul and other points north. Lepidus was not the only politician with financial interests in trade. Cicero now admitted that the old laws forbidding senators from building and owning ships had been so circumvented as to be ineffective as Roman artistocrats now pursued wealth in ways their ancestors would never have condoned.[35] Senators traded, owned vessels and managed firms informally through the medium of contracts and private arrangements with publican and other company *socii*, or partners as the social stigma in the Republic against mixing commerce and politics subtly began to erode.[36] Senators loaned money to publicans with whom they allied and patronised, buying company shares either directly from the companies or from other shareholders in the companies. Cicero's client Rabirius Postumus was one of these as was his foe Vatinius, whom he prosecuted for extorting publican shares. In his cross-examination of Vatinius, Cicero demanded of him "Did you extort shares, which were at their dearest at the time, partly from Cæsar, partly from the *publicani*?"[37] Senators generally bought unregistered, non-voting shares in companies through which they provided an important part of the firms' capital. Many of the senators, moreover, since the time of Sulla were former publican knights who privately continued their profitable associations. By the time Pompey and Julius Caesar fought for supremacy all Roman politicians had large investments and decisive influence within Roman firms.

Cicero himself reflected the contradiction between old Roman ideals and new commercial realities. While he blamed business greed for ruining the social stability of both Carthage and Corinth, he assumed Rome to be a commercial city somehow escaping this fate perhaps because it was more inland. Whatever Cicero said, his senatorial contemporaries were heavily investing in shipping and

commercial enterprises and some had been doing so for several
generations. Cato the Elder quietly lent money to his business
agents so they would form a large firm of fifty partners, owning
about four dozen ships. Cato's share in the firm was held by his
freedman Quintio. Some of the firms of Cicero's day repeated a
similar pattern. S. Neavius and C. Quinctius ran a small partnership operating a grazing farm in Gaul, with P. Quinctius inheriting
his share on the death of his brother.[38] Publican and other larger
companies described by Cicero were seen as "partnerships, with
their slaves, their freedmen, and with their clients", which, while
permitted only a temporary existence in Roman law, still represented a new sophistication in commercial organization.[39] Managers
and partners like L. Aelius Lamia deployed ships and *negotia*
(agents) across the Roman world while they themselves stayed at
home, having to rely upon "a network of dependents, associates and
contacts, carefully and systematically developed over time", in order to conduct their affairs:

> *L. Aelius Lamia…supported the publicani of Syria, and… may have
> had negotia in Bithynia, furthered his negotia in Africa through proc-
> uratores, liberti, familia, and was helped as well by his friendships, in
> this case by Cicero's direct intervention on his behalf with the governor
> of Africa Vetus.*[40]

Crude as it was, Roman company law allowed big companies like
Lamia's to grow and operate. Such firms appear poorly organised
by 1990s standards, but they were well-organised enough by Roman standards. The characteristic form of Roman firm organisation, before, during, and after Cicero's day, based itself upon partnership and informal relationships between knights, freedmen,
slaves, and even senators. It embodied the extended family as expressed in Roman society and law, representing, according to Professor John H. D'Arms:

> *the fundamental Roman social unit, the familia, enlarged and extend-
> ed to perform functions far more complex than fulfillment of domestic
> needs. One such interconnecting web of relationships, among men of
> varied levels of rank and status, of varying degrees of closeness, and in-
> volving various types of expectations and obligations, the Romans
> knew as clientela….*[41]

The more a Roman politician was involved in business, the less visible he was prone to be. Senators and patricians like Cato, L.A. Lepidus, P. Granius, and L. Aelius Lamia were very active in commerce, but very secretive about their investments. Given this evidence, the large number of freed slaves appearing in commercial centres like Capua, Puteoli, Aquilea, Ostia and elsewhere "ought not to be interpreted" says D'Arms, "in isolation, without reference to the extended *familia* or larger units of organization of which they were often a part", being seen not as independent traders but as visible agents for their managers who entrusted them with duties their slaves could not perform. Their visible presence in cross-border activities therefore implied the involvement of more powerful men as well as more sophisticated and specialised systems of production and distribution.[42] The unintended result of the old laws designed to discourage the top nobility from commerce was to promote their covert involvement in an extended form of family capitalism:

> *The laws designed to bar aristocrats from trade had the long-term effect of encouraging forms of business organisation which permitted patricians to become hidden partners in an extended form of family enterprise.*[43]

Cicero's writings indicated a strong element of family capitalism was involved among the many Roman citizens interested in government, trade, and investment in the new eastern provinces. The Rupilius family of Praeneste as well as others were related to senators and sometimes became senators themselves. The Aufidius family produced a governor of Asia, financiers, and senators. Some knights, like S. Alfenus were also bankers. All of these family-based firms kept their residence in Rome, sending members abroad as agents.[44]

Roman knights at the end of the Republican period were investing everywhere, in Sicily, Africa, Gaul, and, especially, Asia Minor. The Roman firms absorbed and incorporated the personnel, labour, and capital of the older business cultures of the regions they invested in. Many of the ships their goods were carried to and from Italy in were made in the East, building upon Hellenic, Hellenistic, and Tyrian seafaring traditions as well as Punic and Roman ones. Vessels from Alexandria, Tyre, Sidon, Cyprus, Asia Minor, Rhodes, and Miletus not only supplied the navies of both sides in the Civil War but recaptured much of the eastern Mediterranean trade from southern Italian hands. Cicero himself noted that the Roman *nego-tiatores* of Asia employed Greek ships.[45]

The merging of big business and military politics coincided with and perhaps hastened the death of the Roman Republic. Having gained power and prestige through his conquest of Gaul, Caius Julius Caesar mustered his legions and his own fleet to vanquish those of Pompey in Greece in 49 BC. Having first championed and then betrayed the plebeian party, Caesar's aspirations to a *permanent dictatorship* quickly roused the ire of the Senate, whose agent, M. Junius Brutus, assassinated him. The Ides of March were but prelude to a decisive round of civil war from which would emerge the Roman Empire. Caesar's adopted grand-nephew Octavian mustered his loyal forces to first rout the fleet loyal to Brutus off Sicily in 36 BC and then the Egyptian-based forces of Mark Antony off Actium in 31 BC. Octavian's victories were due to the invention by his admiral, Agrippa, of grappling hooks fired from catapults which allowed Octavian's marines to capture Brutus's and Antony's vessels.[46]

Octavian, proclaiming himself *Princeps* Augustus Caesar, inaugurated the Roman Empire. Many books have been written on the political and military history of the Imperial *Pax Romana*, which lasted from 27 BC to about 180 AD. The present authors will confine themselves to a brief analysis of how the economic themes developed above applied to the Empire. The Roman Empire presided over the grandest era of trade and cross-border investment (both within and without its boundaries) in antiquity. The trading networks of the Roman Peace represented the closest approximation of a world economy in antiquity; no other economy would come as close to global proportions until the European voyages of discovery in the fifteenth century. Augustan merchants combined the Hellenic, Carthaginian and Oriental trading spheres into one grand market, the hub of which lay in Rome. The new Roman "world economy" was richer by far than the sum of its parts. Commerce, some of it entrepreneurial, some of it more directed, increased at an explosive rate from Iberia to Alexandria.[47]

Augustus and his Julio-Claudian, Flavian, and Antonine successors presided over the further integration of a "vigorous economic community of a size then hitherto unseen in the lands of the Mediterranean and Europe".[48] A common currency, body of law, and a well-organised infrastructure of ports and roads contributed to this integration as Rome suppressed piracy, established order, and took over the commercial links of previous empires in Africa, the Aegean, and the Orient. The Caesars took to themselves the exclusive right to mint gold and silver *denarii* and other coins which became the "euros" of the Imperial union. The Latin *denarii, asses,* and *sesterces* would not completely displace the local *drachmas* of the Greek provinces or the Ptolemaic currency of Egypt. Business deals involving small change continued to take place in local currencies, while civil servants and soldiers were paid in Roman coin, as were most cross-border and overseas traders. The conquering legions brought not only a common currency but built and surveyed a network of roads around the Mediterranean. Major routes were soon joined by minor roads linking the trunk lines with small settlements and rural villas. Communities located along such routes began to flourish. Land transportation, despite being better than ever before, was still too costly for most large-scale commerce. It was far cheaper to ship 500 kg of wheat from Egypt to Rome by sea than to cart it overland from Sicily or even Campania. Wharves on the Tiber linked Rome with the port of Ostia, where huge ships brought wheat from Egypt and other luxuries from far beyond the Mediterranean. Barges 40 metres long plied the Nile, Rhine, and Danube, while smaller boats brought goods up and down the Tiber, Euphrates, Rhône, Seine, Thames, and Garonne.[49]

Archaeologist Keith Hopkins, writing in 1980, insisted that the Roman state played a key role in both the integration and the expansion of that continental economy. When the Roman publicans and municipalities taxed wealth from the rich provinces of Iberia, Asia Minor-Syria-Egypt, and North Africa, they compelled those merchants based in those regions to earn money through trade and export. Tax revenues meanwhile flowed from the richer regions to Italy and the outer regions of the Empire. Roman centurions stationed in Gaul, Britain, the Rhine, Danube, or in the Near East spent their pay, taxed from the rest of the Empire, on food, services, and goods. More businesses arose to service the legions, stimulating the economy from Spain to Syria. The inner core of provinces, in the meantime, were far from impoverished, but experienced a great growth in consumption and a greater circulation of money than ever before. The urbanisation of the economy increased the payment of rents to landlords, placing even more money in circulation. This money economy of taxes, trade, and rent grafted itself onto a subsistence economy in which 80-90% of the population still provided for their own needs.[50] Europe's money supply grew from 35 million to 500 million *denarii* between 160 and 50 BC. Roman silver coins flooded the provinces in the Late Republic, but a huge rise in production and trade and the conversion of peasants in the provinces to city dwellers and legionaries helped offset excessive inflation. It is interesting as well that the crisis in Roman Italy which accompanied the rise of the Caesars coincided with a deflationary credit crunch.[51] During the *Pax Romana* which followed, the money economy of Roman Europe and Roman Asia became integrated into a single system. An analysis of some 90,000 silver coins minted over several centuries of the Empire showed the same fluctuations in money supply in Italy, Germany, Gaul, the Balkans, and Syria, indicating that "the whole Roman Empire was integrated into a single monetary economy."[52] Taxes during the first two centuries of the Empire were low enough to encourage the growth of commerce. Hopkins estimates the average Roman subject paid a rate equal to approximately 10% of his subsistence income, a rate greater than that of Tudor England or sixteenth-century France but less than that paid by the average English or French subject after 1700.[53]

Not only did companies based in Rome and Italy maintain agents abroad in the Roman Imperial economy, but Italy itself became a site of investment for firms headquartered elsewhere, especially after 100 AD when the balance of trade began to shift away from Italy to the provinces. The one million citizens of Rome itself consumed grain from Africa, wine and fish from France and Spain, and wore wool from Asia Minor, linen from Egypt, jewels from India, silk from China, cosmetics from Arabia. Syrian glasses, Indian ebony, and African ivory adorned their homes. At first reaching Rome through Puteoli, these huge imports eventually passed through Ostia as the Emperors Claudius in 42 AD and Trajan in 101-104 AD built and expanded the new harbour and linked it by canal with the Tiber. The port of Ostia became Rome's gateway to the world. Booming Imperial Ostia became the chief *emporia* for trading and multinational enterprise in the Roman world. Firms headquartered all around the Mediterranean set up branch-plant offices in Ostia, which became the London, New York, and Hong Kong of the Roman Empire. Archaeologists have discovered in Ostia a vast *piazza* in which the agents of some five dozen Italian- and foreign-based companies maintained permanent offices.[54] An inscription lists the North African shippers of Misua, Hippo, Sabrata, Gummi, Roman Carthage, Syllecthum, and Curubis, along with the "Agency of the grain merchants of the colony of Curubis". The Sardinian shippers of Turris and Carales were also listed as were the Gallic shippers of Narbo.[55] Other overseas agencies transacted business from Ostia's rival port, Puteoli. Notable among these were the merchants of Roman Tyre. An inscription in Greek from 174 AD written from the office of a Tyrian merchant agency to the magistrates and council of Tyre reveals the decline of commerce in the second century AD in both Puteoli and in Italy itself:

> *there is many a commercial agency in Puteoli, as most of you know, and ours excels the others both in adornment and in size. In the past this was cared for by the Tyrians resident in Puteoli, who were numerous and wealthy; but now this care has devolved on us, who are few in number. The Tyrian merchants went on to appeal for a subsidy for their office and other business expenses, for the Puteoli agency : unlike the one in the capital – Rome – derives no income either from shipowners or from merchants.*[56]

Unlike Ashur, Babylon, Tyre, Alexandria, and Punic Carthage, strict mercantilist policies were rejected in favour of Hellenic-style free trade. The market economy was healthy and thriving in Rome. Any trader from any country could peddle goods in Ostia, Puteoli, or elsewhere. According to Tenney Frank: "Rome followed her policy of keeping all ports open to all trade. There were no monopolies, closed seas, or forbidden goods."[57] The growing presence of these multinational offices in Ostia also signified that many of the headquarters of the new firms were now arising in locations outside of Italy. Up until the end of the first century AD the story of business in the Roman Empire was largely the story of Italian business. Wine, pottery, metalware were mostly produced in Italy and exported by Italian publicans and family firms and their agents to markets in the provinces. After 100 AD the provinces, especially Gaul and Asia, be-

gan not only to produce for their own domestic markets, but to export goods to other parts of the Roman Empire. Spain and France
sent foodstuffs to Greece; Asian marble went to North Africa; Egyptian papyrus went everywhere. Even though metropolitan Greece
slowly began to stagnate, the old Hellenic ports of Ephesus and Miletus began once again to flourish along with many of the old Phoenician and Punic ports of Roman Iberia. Roman enterprise absorbed
and consolidated the trading networks and markets of much that had
gone before it: Sumerian, Assyro-Babylonian, Anatolian, Tyrian,
Egyptian, Punic, and Hellenic. The new economy of the Caesars was
first of all European and Mediterranean. Grain flowed across the
great sea which had now become a Roman lake from Carthage and
Alexandria to the hungry towns of Italy, Gaul, and Iberia.[58]

The expanding commerce of the late Republic and early Empire
also witnessed the flourishing of the family enterprise which grew
out of the Roman culture. Roman attitudes to commerce, like those
of the Greeks, but unlike those of the Phoenicians and Carthaginians, were decidely mixed. Capitalism as such was not rejected, but
a strong distinction was made, at least publicly, between the productive capitalism of say, a knight of the Equestrian Order building
a temple to Jupiter or a warship for Caesar, or a villa patriarch
growing wine and the "sordid" capitalism of the petty trader.[59] The
Imperial writer Seneca claimed that a merchant could serve Rome
by helping others help themselves.[60] Cicero also took up the theme
of "honest" versus "sordid" trades. Trade on a small scale was seen
as vulgar, while the wholesale importing large quantities of goods
from all parts of world deserved respect if it was accompanied by
generosity, philanthrophy, and those who engaged in it were able to
eventually acquire a country estate. Selling the fruits of one's own
productive labour was perfectly acceptable in the eyes of both Plato
and Cicero. Trade in the long term, however, was only praiseworthy
in the eyes of the Roman elite when its profits enabled the merchant
to eventually acquire a landed villa.

The market-seeking behaviour of sea-faring Roman merchants
was praised less for its own sake than for the manly and civic hero-
ism it illustrated. Traders and captains claimed the number of their
voyages as proof of their bravery as good Romans. The epitaph of a
merchant from Brindisi in southern Italy showed the willingness to
face danger and risk: "I have reached many lands...nor do I fear

that expenses will outstrip gains."[61] The merchant Flavius Zeuxis of
Hierapolis braved the seas from Asia Minor to Italy 72 times. The
city council of Hierapolis was normally reticent about welcoming
such a petty trader into their ranks, but men such as this, praised by
Caesar Hadrian for their civic courage, often won positions on local
councils if they could show their profit-making activities served a
higher civic goal. An inscription on an arch over a business *emporium* in a Roman city differentiated between the bankers and beef
sellers working there who were not just retailers but also importers.
The latter were seen as praiseworthy because they provided plebeian city dwellers with wheat, oil, meat and wine.[62] In such a climate
Roman merchants tried to convince others of their civic virtues.
The epitaph of L. Nersus Mithres of Magliano claimed he always
paid his taxes, was honest in all his transactions, was fair as he could
be to all and ready to help the needy. The wine mercahnt Heren-
nuleius took pride in trading in overseas goods of all sorts. The epitaph "lover of the poor" of Atelius Euhodus concealed a multitude
of questionable small-scale commercial activities, that of Praecilius
of Cirta also trumpeted a declaration of honesty and evidence of
generous social attitudes. The beef merchant M. Valerius Celer,
who operated in Rome, claimed on his grave that he much preferred to earn than to spend. Roman business culture, at least publicly, rejected the consumer attitudes of modern Anglo-American
capitalism in favour of the more cautious earning habits which char-
acterise modern Europeans. Similarly, Cato the Elder had long before advised Roman family patriarchs to "have the selling habit, not
the buying habit."[63] The civic ideology of Roman capitalism was often more rhetoric than reality. Ovid's *Fasti* contains an account of
merchants entering the temple of Mercury and praying in a hypo-
critical voice to the god to overlook his past greed while granting
him present and future commercial success:

*Whether I have called thee to witness or have falsely invoked the great
divinity of Jupiter in the expectation that he would not hear, or whether
I have knowingly taken in vain the name of any other god or goddess,
let the swift south winds carry away the wicked words, and may to-mo-
row open the door for me to fresh perjuries, and may the gods above not
care if I shall utter any! Only grant me profits, grant me the joy of profit made, and see to it that I enjoy cheating the buyer!*[64]

Mercury's reply to traders such as this, quoted by the third century BC playwright Plautus suggests that many who invoked the winged god to bless their commerce and persaude the other gods to do so had little remorse about raw money-making for its own sake:

According as ye here assembled would have me prosper you and bring you luck in your buyings and in your sellings of goods, yea, and forward you in all things; and according as ye all would have me find your business affairs and speculations happy outcome in foreign lands and here at home, and crown your present and future undertakings with fine, fat profits for evermore; and according as you would have me bring you and all yours good news, reporting and announcing matters which most contribute to your common good (for ye doubtless are aware ere now that 'tis to me the other gods have yielded and granted plenipotence o'er messages and profits). [65]

A more flagrant graffito at Pompeii: "lucrum gaudium" openly and publicly invoked good fortune among individuals engaged in the art of making money.[66]

The reality, as opposed to the professed civic ideal of business in the *Pax Romana* was bitingly parodied in the character of Trimalchio in the *Satyricon* of Gaius Petronius. Gaius Pompeius Trimalchio Maecenatianus caricatured the *nouveau riche* family entrepreneurs of the Empire who now challenged the "old money" of the Equestrian Order. Trimalchio, a former slave like the Athenian Pasion, rises by his own efforts to become a prosperous villa manager and international trader. His type is instantly recognisable to any historian of the American Gilded Age, Roaring Twenties, or the Reagan-Thatcher years of the 1980s. He is Horatio Alger, Babbitt, and Gordon Gekko combined into one, a crass booster with a homespun philosophy of conspicuous consumption, risk-taking, crass materialism, and contempt for aristocratic academics who disdain making money for its own sake. Petronius invites his readers to a banquet in Trimalchio's honour. With the flourish of a trumpet, Trimalchio, dressed in a scarlet cloak and his hair still cut as a slave, is carried into his sumptuous hall on plies of pillows. He constantly flaunts his wealth in a garish and vulgar manner. His guests remark that he owns "more farms than a kite could flap over" and has more silver plate "in his porter's lodge than another man's got in his safe". Not one in ten of his slaves has ever seen him, for the "ordinary rich man is just peanuts compared to him."[67] Trimalchio's villa is a scene of importing, exporting, and production:

"And buy things? Not him. No sir, he raises everything right on his own estate. Wool, citron, pepper, you name it." Homegrown wool not being good enough, he imports rams from Tarentum to raise his own. The bees for his Attic honey come directly from Athens; all his pillows are stuffed with purple or scarlet wool.[68] Even the lowliest rag-merchant, portrayed by in the *Satyricon* by the miserable Echion, embraces Trimachio's self-help philosophy as fervently as any immigrant did in 1880s America: "Luck changes. If things are lousy today, there's always tomorrow. That's life, man."[69] Both the poor Echion, as well as the rich Trimalchio, have nothing but contempt for the token Greek academic present, through whose eyes the whole spectacle is witnessed. He proceeds to disparage his elitism in language fitting the populism of a 1990s talk-show:

Well, Agamemnon...You're the professor here, but I don't catch you opening your mouth. No, you think you're a cut above us, don't you, so you just sit there and smirk at the way we poor men talk. Your learnings made you a snob.[70]

Entrepreneurs like Trimalchio and would-be entrepreneurs like Echion despised pure philosophical learning indulged by aristocrats for its own sake. Academics like Homer, Livy, or Plato would have been dismissed as "takers" rather than producers and reading their works was a waste of time, and worse yet, of money. Practical learning in law, agriculture, a trade, or business was, on the other hand, a praiseworthy investment, as it would eventually enhance the bottom line. The rich lawyer Phileros was once a peddler until he learned jurisprudence: "there's a mint of money in books, and learning a trade never killed a man yet."[71] Trimalchio shows little humility. He wishes his lavish tomb to read: "HE DIED A MILLIONAIRE, THOUGH HE STARTED WITH NOTHING."[72] During the banquet, Trimalchio's tactless and equally acquisitive wife Fortunata angers him into an outburst of rage, accompanied by a homily on his self-made career. Trimalchio describes his rise from slavery to riches through his ability, courage, and willingness to take risks in overseas trade: "Once I used to be like you, but I rose to the top by my ability. Guts are what makes the man; the rest is garbage."[73] A short, ugly slave from Asia Minor, Trimalchio was his master's pet for fourteen years, but, like Pasion in Athens, he made himself invaluable to his master by his intelligence and business sense. Becoming heir to his master's fortune was not enough. This was not enough for a man with the drive of Trimalchio, who entered the thriving wine-export business. He had five ships built, stocked them with wine and shipped them off to Rome. They all sank on their maiden voyage. Trimalchio, the eternal risk-taker, was undeterred, his loss of thousands of denarii "just whetted my appetite as though nothing had happened at all".[74] The voyage of his next fleet, bigger, better and luckier, however, paid off with a venegeance:

> No one could say I didn't have guts. But big ships make a man feel big himself. I shipped a cargo of wine, bacon, beans, perfume and slaves...On that one voyage alone I cleared about five hundred thousand. Right away I bought up all my old master's property. I built a house, I went into slave-trading and cattle-buying. Everything I touched just grew and grew like a honeycomb. Once more I was worth more than all the people in my home town put together, I picked up my winnings and pulled out. I retired from trade and started lending money to ex-slaves.[75]

The new Roman businessmen whom Petronius mocked had a more vocal attitude towards making money than a Cicero who privately amassed it while publicly insisting it be productively gained. The realities behind Petronius's satire have been revealed by systematic excavations not only of the Italian landscape but of sites in Gaul, Spain and other Roman provinces, as well as by finds from sunken merchant ships. The evidence shows Italy to have been the prosperous core of the new expanded Late Republican and Imperial Roman economy. Managed by family and partnership firms, that economy rested on a massive base of slave labour. Slaves replaced all other forms of dependent labour in Roman Italy: out of a population of 6-7.5 million at the end of the first century BC no fewer than 2-3 million were of servile status. Out of 1 million people living in Rome itself, 400,000 were slaves and similar proportions could be found in over 400 Italian towns. Thousands of slaves also worked the country villas of real-life Trimalchios clustered in the rich farm belt of Campania, Latium, and coastal Etruria. The spread of the villa was a direct product of Rome's economic expansion, urbanisation, and conversion to a slave-owning economy. The great estates were more efficient than the peasant farms they had replaced, and far more land in Italy came under cultivation in the period 100 BC-100 AD than before.[76] This transformation of agriculture into agribusiness was accompanied by improved techniques in crop rotation, fertilisation, and irrigation, together with greater use of iron spades, hoes, and sickles. Villa managers like Cato, Varro, and Columella wrote long treatises on a prosperous agribusiness which reached its height in the Augustan age. Wine production formed the heart of the new villa economy, as was witnessed by the winepresses, storage tanks, and vine trenches discovered on villa sites.[77]

The key tool of the archaeologist in examining the patterns of Roman trade was and remains the examination of the large two-handled jugs known as *amphorae*. Many Roman amphorae carried stamps on their handles and were inscribed with the name of their shipper, their contents, and a date. Long ago, a German scholar named Dressel was able to classify the amphorae by their changing styles, enabling later excavators to build a chronology of Roman pottery upon which to date their finds. By comparing the mineral content in the amphora fragments with that in the soil of uncovered Roman villas, specialists can now make educated guesses as to when and where certain jugs were manufactured. By studying fragments of thousands of amphorae and building statistical data from the studies, scholars since the 1970s have been able to piece together a picture of the complex trading patterns of the Roman Empire. Amphorae found in closely dated layers provided a century-by-century picture of marketing. The numerous Roman shipwrecks discovered off the French and Italian since 1945 have tremendously added to this picture. One large 450 tonne merchantman sank around 100 BC, carrying some 10,000 amphorae and 250,000 litres of wine. Another, some 30-35 metres long and weighing 300-400 tonnes sank near Toulon about 60-50 BC with between 5000 and 8000 amphorae on board. These amphorae were from the Campanian estate of P. Vevius Papus in Campania and were filled with fine quality wine and grapes destined for Massilia and southern Gaul. The dating of the wrecks was quite significant. Of 103 sunken ships identified in the Riviera region, only 9 dated from before 200 BC. The number jumped to 54 in the period between 200 BC and the end of the reign of Augustus in 14 AD, while 33 dated from after Augustus. The vast majority came from Italian ports and were exporting wine and other products to their chief market in Gaul. Most of the wine could be traced to the villas of Campania, and earned a profit of 7-10%.[78]

The large numbers of sunken ships and amphorae and the growing sea traffic they implied highlight the transformation of the Roman economy from one based upon subsistence to one in which foreign trade now played a large role. The enormous quantities of amphorae discovered in Gaul bore witness to this development. A river deposit near Châlon-sur-Saône yielded 24,000 with perhaps 200-500,000 more yet undiscovered. Near Toulouse so many intact amphorae were buried as to prevent earth from being fertile, and even in Brittany 55 sites were found. Most historians correlated this trade with rise of the great commercial villas of west central Italy in the first quarter of first century BC. [79]

An example of the new family enterprises involved in the expanding trade of the first century BC was that of the wine-exporter Publius Sestius.[80] Sestius had a long and varied career in both government and business at the very end of the Republic. Serving first as a *quaestor*, then a tribune, *praetor*, and magistrate in Cilicia between 63 and 48 BC, Publius Sestius was accused of wrongdoing and defended by Cicero in 56 BC. His business activities, and those of his father, L. Sestius, the founder of the Sestius family firm, were managed from his west coast villa near Cosa, 100 kilometres north of Rome. The history of the Sestii could be reconstructed through the letters of Cicero and amphorae found not only at Cosa but in Spain, Gaul, and under the Mediterranean. The wreck of a Roman freighter discovered off Marseilles in 1952 contained 1700 amphorae, most of which were stamped with the initials "SES" or "SEST". Amphorae bearing the same stamps were also excavated in other locations. Near the harbour of Cosa itself, over 80 were found, and 19 more in 1976. The Cosa specimens, unlike those found elsewhere, were empty and in an unused condition, indicating that Cosa, and perhaps the family villa, was the site of their manufacture. The Sestius villa made as many as 4260 amphorae of wine a year, mostly for export. The trail of "SES" and "SEST" amphorae led from Cosa to five shipwrecks in the Mediterranean to many sites along the Gallic shore and then up the valley of the Rhône into the heart of Celtic Gaul.[81] Archaeologist T.W. Potter sees in this trail "dramatic confirmation that the agents of P. Sestius were selling his wine in the markets of southern and central France – and, no doubt doing very well out of it."[82] J. H. D'Arms concluded that the *gens Sestia* was very much involved in a family enterprise involved in marketing its wine in Gaul through the use of either partners or family members as agents. The patriarch himself visited Massilia and Gaul, and the large share of the amphorae bearing his stamp in and near those regions hint that he may have cornered or at least dominated the western export market in wine. The evidence presented by D'Arms and others even suggests internalisation. Cicero hinted that the family invested in and even owned ships for transporting their wine. The family enterprise, moreover, branched out from the wine trade, the son of Publius, L. Sestius Albianus Quirinalis establishing a tile industry in the reign of Augustus. The Sestius enterprise lasted, it would appear, over three generations, and no doubt transmitted the expertise from father to son to grandson.[83]

Various manufacturing industries exhibited a similar pattern of organisation to the wine industry. Production and distribution of artifacts in Roman Italy originally serviced local markets through small workshops with little need for specialisation, division of labour or agents. Farmers would buy tools and clothing from town merchants and artisans in Latium or Campania. It cost several times as much to obtain goods from cities such as Rome or Pompeii than to make them locally.[84] The expansion of the Roman war economy, accumulation of population and capital, and opening of overseas markets in the first century BC was a major stimulus to the formation of larger scale industries producing bricks, tiles, containers, tableware, lamps, glass-, metal- and stoneware. These primitive mass-production industries, due to the volume of goods they had to create and market, could not organise themselves in the same way as the older independent entrepreneurs, but would have to resort to managers and agents:

In its most extreme form, the whole economic process would splinter either vertically (with marketing gaining independence from manufac-

*turing) or horizontally (with the opening of branch factories and out-
lets), or both ways. When this phenomenon occurred, entrepreneurs
had to rely on agents and middlemen.*[85]

Some of these industries, like bricks and the tiles produced by the
Sestii, must have operated close to the rural clay beds and were fully
integrated into the villa economy. The slaves of the villa could be
employed in manufacturing when seasonal farm work was not available. The owner of the villa managed the kiln/workshops and the
farmstead as either a single or separate businesses. Alternatively, he
could lease one to a manager or agent. These Roman villa firms
needed a certain investment in tools and facilities to begin production, and needed some means of supply. Independent potters often
organised temporary partnerships which shared the same kiln. Account lists for one kiln near Aveyron in southern Gaul show over
200 different potters engaged in cooperation. A *societas* or partnership similar to this would hire a joint manager to operate the kiln,
and grant him authority to close business deals, hire staff, and sell
the joint produce. These partnership firms even spawned branch
workshops if new markets opened nearby, some of the partners
joining together and relocating. For example, a consortium of potters from Montans in southern Gaul opened a seasonal workshop at
nearby Valery. "Such workshops", said Roman management expert
Jean-Jacques Aubert, "are called 'satellite workshops,' as they always retain their link with the original centre of production."[86]

The pottery industry showed less economic concentration than
the lamp makers, which were more of an oligopoly in the first century of the Empire. Markings on the majority of lamps in far distant
locations like Gaul or Asia Minor indicated that they were manufactured at only a few points of origin. This oligopoly was not complete, as evidence of numerous small workshops also existed. Those
industries with large runs of production, however, not only sought
distant cross-border markets but were more likely to employ either
middlemen or agents, some of whom were slaves or freedmen. The
names on their stamps may represent those of the managers and not
those of the actual producers:

*It is therefore plausible that they were relying on agents working as
workshop managers. Besides, mass production entailed problems of*

*marketing which could be solved through decentralization of the pro-
duction and by opening subsidiary workshops located closer to new
markets. This type of measure had the advantage of lowering the costs
of transportation. In addition, the producers were able to respond faster
to market fluctuations by adjusting the quantity and/or the quality of
their production.* [87]

The Roman brick industry began to flourish in the reign of Augustus, grow in first century AD and peak during the second. Again, it
was a rural industry, this time concentrated in the villas around
Rome. The stamps on the bricks revealed the *dominus*, or villa lord
as well as the *officinatores*, or managers, who were often transferred
from one brickyard to another to manage the various workshops in
each. The inscriptions on Roman artifacts seem to have served a legal purpose allowing consumers to locate and even sue the manufacturer or his patriarchal lord if they believed themselves defraud-
ed. Brickmaking became a fairly large-scale enterprise, with some
lords supervising several dozen yards at one time, obviously implying the need for a management structure. Even though the evidence
for subsidiary brick workshops is scarce, a pair of cases can be documented from the second century AD. The firm of A. Decius Alpinus made bricks, tiles and pipes and operated branches in Vindobo-
na (Vienna) and Gaul. Starting in Austria, where his relative Q.
Decius Alpinus appears to have been an official, Alpinus employed
his slave Clarianus to open a branch in the French Alps near Vai-
son. Soon the Rhône valley from the Alps to the sea was flooded
with bricks and other products bearing the stamp "CLARIANVS/A
DECI ALPINI". Clarianus, seems to have won from his master a
veritable subsidary mandate for Roman Gaul. [88]

The most likely candidates for "multinational" Roman industrial
firms under the High (before 200 AD) Empire appear to have operated in the marble trade of Asia Minor. Marble from the Greek
world found its way to Rome not long after Greece and Asia Minor
entered the Latin economic sphere. Building programs for temples
and other public structures in Italy and elsewhere provided a large
new market for the quarries of Bithynia. The triumphs of the Caesars caused the demand for Bithynian marble to grow even greater.
Julius Caesar himself opened quarries to satisfy this demand. The
principal market for the marble industry was, to be found especially

in Rome. In spite of the enormous public in the marble trade the industry remained privately run at first: John Ward-Perkins described the marble trade as part of "a free market economy, dominated by power and wealth" and that under Augustus the major Bithynian quarries "were still being operated by the *colonia*, not by the state."[89] The annexation of Egypt and the decrees of the Emperor Tiberius began a process of placing the major mines and quarries under imperial control. By 100 AD most major quarries were being worked by the Empire or were leased to private firms. Imperial control ensured marble from Egypt and Asia Minor would be available for the massive building projects of the early Caesars. Nationalisation of the quarries would, in the minds of the emperors, ensure the large-scale production their building schemes demanded.[90] The inscriptions on the marble blocks shipped across the length and breadth of the empire suggests that 1.) the big quarries were imperially owned 2.) the industry pioneered in mass production, prefabrication and standardisation of its blocks and columns, and 3.) the industry employed cross-border offices which processed the marble en route to its destination:

> *a commerce which can conveniently be summarized in modern technology: nationalization; mass production and stockpiling; a considerable element of standardization and prefabrication; the establishment of agencies overseas to handle specific marbles; and in some cases the availability of specialized craftsmen skilled in the handling of a particular type of marble.*[91]

Many smaller quarries, geared to local markets, were still owned by the municipalities or private firms. The *Eclectic Paradigm* did not come into play in cases such as these, but the Emperor's large quarries had a strong case for internalisation. The major quarries were set up to service overseas markets where the demand for imported marble was high and the empire "could afford to invest the large sums of capital needed for the rational, economical exploitation of sources".[92] These imperial quarries show a fine example of the return of the internalised *Eclectic Paradigm* in business operations in sharp contrast to its absence in the more "libertarian" market arrangements of Archaic and Classical Greece.[93] Under the Greeks, those arrangements were very direct, with customers ordering directly from the quarry and paying for the marble block by block. Under the Romans, the marble was quarried in bulk and stored in marble yards, sometimes for decades and even several centuries, to which the client came. The marble yards of Roman Italy at Rome itself and Ostia contained blocks quarried around 100 AD from Anatolian Numidia and finally used in 394 AD. A column quarried in Egypt in 105 AD was finally erected in Rome in 161 AD. This system of mass production and marketing shows an example of a highly structured Roman enterprise quite different from the entrepreneurial Greek model. "It is hard to imagine a system," says Ward-Perkins, "more different from the sort of intimate relationship between quarry and customer which we find embodied in the building accounts of the Parthenon or of Eleusis."[94]

The new Roman industrial model as well quickly began to foreshadow twentieth century practices of prefabrication: columns were turned out in standard lengths, many of them in exact multiples of the Roman foot for which there was a sure market in Italy or Roman Africa. An even better example of prefabrication could be found in the sarcophagi produced in these and other quarries of the eastern Roman world. These caskets were hollowed and shaped before being shipped. Among the caskets produced in and exported from Asia Minor, Ward-Perkins was able to distinguish "several different models produced for different overseas markets".[95] The form of a garland sarcophagus produced mainly for the east Mediterranean market was sketched out at the Anatolian quarries. Hollowed out in Asia, the casket was finished in the workshops of Alexandria and Berytus (Beirut). Sarcophagi made near Athens sold well in the markets of Greece, Libya, the Adriatic (imported through Aquilea), and Rome itself but faced stiff competition in Asia Minor. Those made in Asia dominated the market in Egypt and around the Black Sea. The markets of Syria and most of Anatolia were divided equally. The Asian caskets were competitive in parts of Italy, through the importing centre of Ravenna, which "was also a workshop".[96] The evidence of value-added production in markets distant from the mines themselves and of overseas agents suggests the presence of two key aspects of a multinational company. There is no doubt of the existence of efficient commercial networks linking the sources of supply with certain particular markets:

> *These networks can only have operated through agencies established in some of the major importing centres; and although the resulting distributions do to some extent reflect traditional commercial patterns (as, for example, between Attica and Cyrenaica, or again between the Propontis and the Black Sea) they also show that the responsible organizations were powerful and efficient enough to secure a virtual monopoly in many areas. If we may assume (as I think we may) that such monopolies were based on price and efficient service, this in turn implies a very substantial investment in technical equipment and skilled personnel.*[97]

Locational factors may help explain why market shares were proportioned the way they were. In Asia Minor quarries like those on the island of Proconnessus (in the Sea of Marmora opposite Byzantium, not far from the Bosphorus) were close to both markets and the sea, making it cheaper to ship and sell in the markets of the Levant and Black Sea. The quarries of Athens were, in contrast, closer to the Piraeus from whence the stone was shipped, mostly to points west. Nevertheless, it remains perfectly clear that the commerce was "handled by agencies which, directly or indirectly, were in very close touch with the sources of supply".[98] The mining and shipping of marble and marble goods from Proconnessus may have been directed by a centralised business organisation operating out of Nicomedia on the Bithynian shore:

> *When Hadrian presented 100 columns of Dokimian marble for the Panhellenion of Athens, I see it as being dispatched directly from the harbourside yards at Nicomedia. But by and large I find it very hard to believe that any imperially-controlled organization could have occupied itself systematically in a commercial enterprise of this scale without leaving some trace in the epigraphic record, or indeed at this date it is the sort of enterprise which would have attracted direct imperial control. I find it much easier and much more convincing to assume that it was the work of private initiative.*[99]

The historian is still left with the problem of defining precisely how the marble companies operated in detail given the paucity of the evidence available. The marble industry of Bithynia flourished for over a century from the mid-second to the mid-third agency AD by

Roman businessmen who had sufficient capital to undertake investments "including the maintenance of successful agencies in a
number of the maritime capitals of the Mediterranean world".[100]
The very physical transportation of the marble itself necessitated a
strong business organisation. Transportation by land, to begin with,
was much more costly than transportation by water. Marble had to
be of very high quality to justify the cost of land haulage of Egyptian
or Dokimon marble to the docks; Proconnessian marble was mined
close enough to a deep-water harbour to make bulk shipments
cheaper and easier. While the marble was likely carried in privately
owned ships operating on a contract basis, once they reached the
ports to which they sailed from Nicomedia and Alexandria they
may well have gain passed under the control of their producer's
overseas agents.[101] Most of the quarries exported marble in an un-
finished, raw state. Those at Dokimon were an exception. Being
300 kilometres from the sea meant that this Anatolian quarry faced
higher transportation costs in exportation than less landlocked
quarries. Therefore, its managers sought to reduce costs by internalising its operations and finishing their sarcophagi and other
products on or near the site itself, having "aimed at a different section of the market by exporting products in finished form…thereby
increasing the market value of the product on arrival at its destination."[102]

Other quarries added value to their marble through specialist
workmen and firm agents overseas, for prefabrication demanded
the presence of specialist workmen not only at the quarries but also
at the importing centres in order to ensure that the finished products were adapted to local markets. Familiarity with the working
properties of specific marble was an *organisation-specific advantage*
conducive to internalised distribution and value-added production
at the point of the marble's arrival in western Europe. The "establishment of some kind of overseas agency" therefore likely "chan-
nelled both orders and shipments" and caused certain quarries to
develop particular markets and to specialise in products preferred
in given regions.[103] The marblework of Caesarea and Scythopolis in
Palestine shows clear connnections with Ephesus. There is a very
strong probability that the craftsmen who finished the columns and
caskets there and elsewhere around the Roman Empire did so as
residents operating out of permanent workshops.[104] Shipping stones

of such huge proportions necessitated large vessels, some of which were in private and some in state hands, which was likely the case in Egypt and on the Tiber. Permanent groups of trained haulers were needed in ports like Ostia and in Asia Minor to move marble blocks and columns to and from the sea.[105]

By the closing decades of the Roman Republic in the first century BC the vast web of overseas Roman trade extended the length and breadth of the Mediterranean. Having embraced Asia Minor, the opporunities for Roman commerce expanded further with the conquests of Pompey around 70 BC. Many of the "apolitical" publican companies with an interest in new eastern markets no doubt welcomed the rise of this ambitious general who added Syria and Judea to the Roman world. Roman businessmen usually had little interest in politics and made no attempt to seize power in Rome though many entered the Senate, which began to recover some of its power under the dictatorship of the general Sulla (82-79 BC), who supported them in opposition to the Gracchan reforms and the demands of the landless classes, who had backed his rival, Marius. Sulla executed thousands of Roman knights, many of whom no doubt were publicans. The firms survived the massacres, for even could not do without their services. Leadership of and participation in the large companies was spread widely among the wealthy of Roman Italy, although in the eastern Mediterranean their offices and operations continued to be staffed by southern Italian families. In 75-74 BC the tax collection of Sicily and Cyrene was also handed over to publicans.[106] The rise of large publican companies and the Equestrian Order indicated that business and business values were beginning to affect Rome's agrarian culture in a significant way. There is no doubt that the large number of military contracts and public works financed an economic boom in Roman Italy affecting clothing, construction, pottery, and other trades. The rise of the publicans coincided with an agricultural revolution in the second century BC as well. Large manorial estates replaced small farms; large estates and cash crops replaced small-scale cereal production. Business arising from public contracts pervaded the life of Roman Italy.[107] Intended by the Gracchi to counter the corruption of the landed Senators, the new Roman business establishment quickly displayed corruptions of its own. Publicans flocking to invest in Asia Minor often flaunted the law in order to make money against the wishes of often hostile Roman governors.[108] Wealth in Italy was concentrated in agriculture and munitions making. Marking for the iron industries begun by the Etruscans under the stimulus of the Euboeans not only persisted but intensified as the defence needs of the Republic required equipping nine or ten standing legions at minimum. Iron forged into weapons and sold to the army by the publicans was mined at Elba and smelted in the workshops of the great port of Puteoli, where value-added production took place. The process was described by both Diodorus:

> *Near the town of Etruria called Populonia lies Ilva...It abounds in siderite which they mine for smelting and making of iron, since it con-tains much of this metal. Those engaged in this work crush the rock and roast it in furnaces skilfully made for the purpose. When it has been melted in a strong fire, they cut the matter into parts that look like large sponges. Merchants buy these with money or an exchange of goods and carry them to Dicaearchaea (Puteoli) and other ports. Men who engage the labor of smiths buy these masses of ore and make all kinds of implements of them. Some parts they hammer into weapons, other into hoes, sickles, and other useful implements. Then merchants carry these everywhere and they are used in every part of the world.[109]*

and Strabo:

> *I saw – at Populonia – the men who worked the iron brought over from Ilva; for it cannot be thoroughly smelted in the furnaces on the island and the ore is sent at once to the mainland.[110]*

The Roman economy, unlike most of its predecessors, was heavily militarised. Plunder was a huge factor in the market-seeking behav-iour of officials and publican firms who followed in the wake of the legions. Pompey confiscated one-fifth of the wealth his armies plun-dered. Marius and Sulla were worse, the latter claiming ownership of all he conquered. Marius kept much of the booty plundered from the Teutoni and Cimbri, including 60,000 slaves. Lucullus was said to have created a war in Spain because he needed money. Corrup-tion and bribery were rampant.[111] Roman industry, as in the days of the early Republic, still concentrated on the basics of a warrior soci-ety: tools, weapons, and basic clothing. Luxury goods such as fab-rics and spices came from Asia Minor and even farther to the east.

The Roman comedies of the day, written by Novius and Pomponius are populated with small tradesmen and artisans like bricklayers and cabinet-makers who made goods like furniture, bronze and silver in places like Campania.[112]

The saga of Rome's economic expansion and Roman business did not end in the Mediterranean, for the story of Roman commerce in the Indian Ocean is in many ways the the most intriguing facet of that saga. Not only did Roman managers carry on a fairly extensive trade with the Indian subcontinent, but, using the Indians as middlemen, they even traded with markets in Southeast Asia and China.[113] Tenuous as it was, the Late Republic and the Early Empire actively participated in a trading network which, for a couple of centuries, extended across the entire Eurasian land mass and much of East Africa as far south as what is now Tanzania. While the existence of Roman "multinationals" in South Asia cannot be proven, the evidence of archaeology is open to that possibility. An application of the rules of the *Eclectic Paradigm* to the Roman venture in India suggests the likely presence of permanent Roman agents on Indian soil, though there is no evidence of value-added production there. Ownership-specific advantages in shipbuilding enabled Roman firms to upstage Arab and other traders as did the locational advantages of possessing Egyptian ports on the Red Sea. The experience of the Romans in setting up large-scale partnership and familial concerns provided internalisation advantages without which bulk shipment of goods across very dangerous seas would be impossible.

Historians of Rome's India trade are indebted not only to archaeological findings but to the discovery of a sailing guide published in the middle of the first century AD known as the *Periplus Maris Erythraei,* or *Sailing Guide of the Erythraen Sea.* The *Periplus* tells the story of how Roman ships left from Myos Hormos and other ports in Egypt during every July and journeyed down the Red Sea into the Arabian Sea and then eastward along the Arabian shore. Along the Arabian shore they caught the southwest monsoons which drove them either to the markets of the Indus valley or the southern tip of India. The ships would arrive in India in late September or early October, for to arrive any earlier meant certain shipwreck when the monsoons beat against the Indian shores. As a result, insurance rates were very high for September, around 20%, while no insurance at all was available during July and August when the southwest monsoon was at its height. Rates were much lower, between 1 and 2% once the winds ceased.[114]

Roman ships, unlike the smaller, swifter Arabian vessels, were very big – up to 300 metres long – and very sturdily constructed. Their incredibly strong hulls were fastened together by thousands of joints and supported sails designed for safety more than speed. Returning to Egypt late in the year via the calmer northeast monsoon, the big vessels brought huge amounts of Indian spices and Chinese silk. One shipment consisted of an estimated 1,500-3,600 kilogrammes of spice, 10,000 kilogrammes of ivory and 1,600-1,700 kilogrammes of textiles, a total of 131 talents worth 1,000 hectares of good Egyptian farmland. A Roman ship could carry anywhere from 150 to 300 such shipments.[115] Big cargoes sailing great distances in big ships could not be financed by the activity of a few small independent traders. Transporting goods between the Roman Empire and India could only be done in bulk and only once a year, for such trade "required a formidable amount of capital" and was "open only to large-scale operators".[116] This worked in favour of larger Roman family and partnership firms able to raise large amounts of money and employ overseas agents.

The spade of the archaeologist has begun to reveal a few more secrets of this early intercontinental venture. Mediterranean amphorae and other artifacts have been found all over India from the Punjab to the Coromandel coast near Sri Lanka, suggesting that the subcontinent must have been a substantial market for both Hellenistic and Roman traders. The earliest European amphorae found in India were made on the Aegean island of Kos, just off the Anatolian shore during the Hellenistic period. These large jugs filled with wine and olive oil were soon imitated by the Romans, and by the middle of the first century BC the taller, narrower, darker Roman copies began to outnumber and upstage the Greek originals. Jars of oil from Spain also began to appear in India at that time. The testimony of the jugs indicates that first the Hellenistic Greeks and then the Romans were trading oil and wine in return for precious woods, spices, animals, ivory, gems, and other luxury goods directly by sea. This monsoon-borne trade was far more profitable than that by land. As well, the persistence of Greek amphorae in India for decades after the legions subjugated mainland Greece suggests keen competition for Asian markets between the conqueror and conquered. Finally, the exceptional concentration of Roman artifacts at the site of Arikamedu on the Coromandel coast hints at the possible presence of permanent Roman business agents in India.[117]

The first round of excavations at Arikamedu itself took place during the 1940s and 1950s. The settlement's industrial base was uncovered without learning much about the identity of those who lived and traded there. A joint excavation project by the University of Pennsylvania and Madras University in 1989-1992 sought to learn more. As Dr. Vimala Begley and his Indian/American team uncovered more of the settlement they learned that the native Indian population played a dynamic role in its life and trade even after the Romans had come. The southern sector of the city was an industrial centre, while port facilities dominated the north. Before the Romans came, there was no settlement in the northern city, but beginning in the first century BC both sectors were flourishing. The southern quarters boasted a strong textile industry, possibly the chief industrial centre of a textile-exporting Coromandel coast. Sherds of Roman *terra sigillata* pottery in this part of India were found only at Arikamedu, suggesting that it was used primarily by Romans that were living there. These pots came not just from Arezzo in Italy but also Lyon, Pisa, and Pozzuoli. Begley, however, discovered that many of these pots were inscribed with graffiti in Indian languages, implying that the Romans were selling or giving their wares to a local population made up fom many different cultural backgrounds. Not all the Rome-India trade was in Roman hands. Begley discovered a jar bearing the name "Kanan" in Arikamedu. Far away on the shores of the Red Sea a virtually identical vessel with the same name suggests that a Tamil merchant or possibly his agent sold his wares in or near Roman Egypt.[118]

Oil and wine were not the only Roman exports to far Asia. The Augustan glass industry, based in the Levant, exported glassware in vast quantities not only across the Mediterranean but across the Indian Ocean as well, and, eventually, as far as Korea and China. Roman glassware has been found at Arikamedu, and was also shipped to the port of Barbarikê at the mouth of the Indus from where it could journey into Central Asia. Raw, unworked glass was traded inland from west coast Indian ports, but, because most glassware in India passed overland by wagons over nonexistent roads, inland bulk trade in glass commodities was hardly a bulk enterprise. There is no evidence of value-added production for Roman glassware coming to India in the early period, although a few west coast cities continued to import raw glass, which made its way to the east and inland.[119] Numerous Roman glass pieces have been found on the southeast Indian coast, indicating it was a profitable cargo for Roman firms to carry. Unloaded at Roman centres on the west coast, the glass was taken by Indian middlemen to the east coast, and from there exported to China and the Far East.[120] All of this evidence suggests that the finds at Arikamedu and elsewhere "point" in the words of Lionel Casson, "to the presence of a foreign colony, a group of Western merchants permanently established there."[121]

The Roman European economy was, between 100 BC and 200 AD emerging as the core of a new global economy. The volume of Rome's Asian trade became, by the standards of its day, enormous. Over a hundred ships a year set out from the Roman Red Sea port of Myos Hormos, and two other harbours were also in existence. Indian records report the sturdy vessels of the *Yavanas* bringing gold and wine from the west in return for the spices, peppers and aromatic wood of the subcontinent. Roman ships and sailors docked at Indian ports while Roman firms opened resident offices in Indian harbours "anticipating by a millennium and a half the employees of Britain's East India Company".[122] Embassies were exchanged between Rome and India as spices, silks, jewels, and the luxuries of the east flooded into the Empire. The effect on the Roman economy of this huge flow of Asian imports was not unnoticed by Roman statesman whose concerns were not all that different from contemporary observers in Europe and North America worried about global competition. The Emperor Tiberius himself feared that "The ladies and their baubles are transferring our money to foreigners" while the elder Pliny claimed that imports from Arabia, China, and India was costing Rome 550,000,000 *sesterces* a year.[123] While some historians have dismissed Pliny's lament of a trade gap with India as a blatant exaggeration, it was clear that extensive seaborne Roman trade and investment directed towards India and possible was significant in its own right and as a stepping-stone to a smaller but enticing East Asian market. This Chinese market, still serviced for the Romans by various other nationals, nevertheless existed and the memory of it would continue to entice

Europeans in much later centuries when the hope of global enterprise was kindled anew.

The commercial system of the Late Republic and the High Empire, being of both a military and familial nature might, in summa-
tion, best be described as "legionary capitalism". The rules of the
Dunning *Eclectic Paradigm* which would make such little sense to
the Euboeans, Corinthians, Milesians, or Athenians, would make
more sense in the more partnership-oriented and internalised trade
of the Roman world. The partnerships, internal hierarchies, and
use of overseas agents which characterised the new Roman firms
arose in response to the markets and opportunities provided by
years and decades of constant and intensive warfare. A tentative
model of the Dunning paradigm for Rome would suggest the following figure 10:

Figure 10. The Eclectic Paradigm applied to Roman Business

Ownership-Specific Advantages: Hierarchy came more naturally in Rome Greece as
Roman companies arose in a culture enshrined the primacy of the patriarchical and
extended family in its mores and laws. Upon this familialism was imposed a
powerful ethos from which later Roman firms developed under the direction of the
paterfamilias or the equestrian knight. Partnerhip, family, and military ties in these
firms could then be extended to overeas markets.

Locational Advantages: Given the large sums of money involved and the dangers of
corruption and intense competition in the military contracting business, the
presence of a resident branch office for an Italian-based firm near the legion
encampments in Greece and Spain would ensure the proper completion of the
contract. The mining
and processing of overseas resources situated overseas by Roman firms also
necessitated a branch office in locations like Anatolia, Greece, or elsewhere.

Internalisation Advantages: Publican firms dealing in large sums of money, large
volumes of goods, and large overheads thought it prudent deal through their own
agents in Macedonia, North Africa, Asia Minor, Spain, North Africa, and, eventually,
Gaul. The alternative of dealing through a middleman overseas involved additional
costs and risks which might price the firm out of a very competitive market.

The Roman business culture in the first two centuries of Imperial
rule was the closest model in antiquity to that of modern Europe
and America. The creation of a relatively free market, large private
firms, the issuing of shares and limited liability, the beginings of

mass production and the perfection of business agents and partnerships were generally pioneered in the Roman world, as was the first experiment in a common European currency. The role of private invention and production in establishing military and naval power represented yet another example of the Roman legacy, as did the promotion of European unity through the improvement in infrastructure. Lessons in market-seeking behaviour through the construction of vessels capable of navigating the monsoon may also be drawn.

The story of Rome's economic decline through inflation, corruption, and loss of market opportunities is quite extensive and belongs, along with the subsequent business history of the Islamic, Indian, Chinese, and medieval and modern European worlds in a future work. Throughout the past two millennia, these and other business cultures applied some of the lessons perfected in antiquity, better enabling historians to understand more recent times.

Chapter 10

Conclusion

One Form of Capitalism?

We hope that in this book we have made some contribution to international business history but as one of us is an executive educator we naturally come to the question, is there anything that the ancient world has to tell us today? Firstly, we repeat the words of Solomon, 'there is nothing new under the sun.'[1] Many of things that we think of as modern day creations actually existed in the times of the Assyrians, Phoenicians, Greeks and Romans. The second point we make is regarding the 'best' form of capitalism, some observers, especially in the U.S. and the U.K. argue that the world should move to one form of capitalism – their form. We shall return to this argument shortly but first here is a recapitulation of some of the 'modern' phenomenon which we found in ancient times:

The First MNEs

In chapter four we presented evidence that the first recorded MNEs appeared in the Old Assyrian Kingdom shortly after 2000 BC. Using the *Eclectic Paradigm* as a model to analyze ancient international trade we demonstrated that the major characteristics of MNEs were a part of the Assyrian business organizations of the time. Characteristics found in modern MNEs such as: hierarchical organisation, foreign employees, value-adding activities in multiple regions, common stock ownership, resource and market-seeking behaviour, were present in these ancient firms. These early MNEs successfully operated considerable business empires in multiple foreign locations from their corporate headquarters in the capital of Ashur. Were there early MNEs or "proto-MNEs" earlier than the Assyrian Empire? There may well have been. However, practical difficulties arise due to the lack of archaeological evidence from other nations and empires in earlier epochs. One looks forward to the work of other scholars to shed light on this interesting issue. Later we presented evidence of the first transcontinental MNEs in Phoenicia and of known world straddling Roman MNEs in their day.

Branding and Advertising

One of the hot topics in marketing over the last decade has been branding and building powerful international and global brands.[2] In ancient Greece we saw potters and vase-makers produced for tailored markets, promoted their brand-name wares, and even publicly ridiculed their competitors with negative advertising. One is reminded of the Pepsi challenge ads which 'proved' that Coke drinkers preferred Pepsi. In Roman times amphorae often carried stamps on their handles and were inscribed with the name of their shipper, their contents, and a date. As a modern brand does today, the shipper mark or brand could be used a way of reducing the risk of a purchase by providing a "guarantee" of the quality of a product.

Global Economies

Admittedly we use the word global here somewhat inaccurately, perhaps it would be better to say 'known world' economies. But we may be forgiven some exaggeration. Today's technologies, e-mail, low cost transcontinental phone calls, faxes, jet airplanes, have shrunk the modern world. The globe is the village marketplace for our modern businessperson. Today it is almost trivial for the seasoned business traveller to fly business class from London to Shanghai for a day's meeting. In ancient times a trip from one major economic centre to another, from Rome to Athens, from Ashur to Anatolia, or from Tyre to Carthage, would have typically involved months of arduous travel filled with danger. Even schoolchildren in many countries are familiar with Marco Polo, in even relatively modern times, one trip from Europe to China earned him lasting fame. Today the same trip takes 12 hours from London to Shanghai and thousands of business-people make that trip a year. In ancient times the known world sadly did not include North America (especially difficult for two Canadian authors to come to terms with) Australia, Japan, much of Africa and much of Europe and Asia. However, given the difficulties of travel and communications to the ancient known world[3] of southern and central Europe, North Africa, the Near and Far East, India and China their international business achievements were probably more impressive than those of modern business-people! Yet with all these difficulties we have shown evidence in this book of not only multinational firms in ancient Assyria but transcontinental activities in Phoenicia times and in the Roman empire business activities stretching from Rome to India and onto China and in the West to what we call today, the United Kingdom.

As one does their Boxing Day sales shopping, you can't help but be impressed by the many places that the clothes, electronics or CDs come from. It seems that our local department store has become a global emporium; this is certainly different from the sixties when most goods were still produced in the same country. Yet, ancient Phoenicia or Rome, at their peak, were not all that different from today. In the emporium of the day you would find clothes from India and Phoenicia, wine from France, jewellery from Africa or Arabia or India, horses from the Near East, carpets from Persia and pitchers sourced in Greece. Sounds like Cargo Warehouse!

Today the *lingua franca* of modern international business is primarily English, governments in France, Germany, Quebec and elsewhere bemoan this fact, they see it as potentially undermining their languages. We see in the ancient world there was times that one language became 'the' language of business only to be supplanted by another as powers rose and fell. For example in the time of the Eighteenth Dynasty in Egypt and the Kassite kingdom of Babylonia, we find that the major courts[4] treated one another as equals and all corresponded in Akkadian, the language of diplomacy. Later in the time of the Greeks, Greek became the language of much of international business in the known world. Still later Latin replaced Greek, and so on.

One of the contentious issues between the U.S. and Japan in the last decade has been non-tariff trading barriers. In Phoenician times we find that for foreign merchants, known as ubru in the Canaanite tongue, their activities were strictly regulated by the harbour master. Aramean, Hittite, Egyptian and Mesopotamian courts and business organisations sent resident foreign merchants into Phoenician territory, where they were still subject to their own authorities. The regulations imposed by the harbour master, however, presented them with a primitive version of what would today be described in Japan as non-tariff barriers. Asubru could not leave the foreign business quarter district of the host country, enter the residence of native traders, and conduct business in a Phoenician city without strict supervision from the Cananite harbourmaster.[5]

Virtual Corporations

In the chapter on the Roman empire we discussed how the *publicani* of the later Roman empire were usually not specialised firms. A given firm might win a contract to make swords or togas but usually specialised in neither. Publican associations seem to have been based on a flexible management and work forces. Associations of partners would come together to carry out a contract and then disband. Faced with fierce market competition in the letting of contracts, the *publicani* simply could not afford much in the way of permanent staff, which remained *lean and flexible* in adapting to different markets. What the firms instead provided, according to Professor Badian, was "capital and top management, based on general business experience".[6] The permanent staffs of the firms were small in numbers and consequently flexible in adapting to different kinds of business for both public and private contractors. The companies, says Badian, "can only have functioned...by taking over existing substructures and superimposing managing staff."[7] Permanent, organised staffs of skilled miners, tax professionals, arms makers, shipbuilders, and others did exist, and these were likely bought and sold by the publican managers as they shifted from contract to contract. The new Roman firms transacted business on a scale undreamed of by their Near Eastern and Hellenic forerunners. It is interesting to contrast these Roman virtual corporations or networked firms with today's virtual firms which are encouraged to "stick to their knitting" or core competencies rather than act as general managers as these Romans appeared to be.

The Rise of Nations

The last twenty years has witnessed the rise of Japan and other Asian nations as key competitors on the world economic scene. The competitive map as changed with breath taking speed. Yet we saw something similar occur in the eight century BC. We saw in chapter seven how that nearly every excavated Greek site has indicated a surge of building activity beginning around 750 BC. Attica and Argos, judging by the evidence of their grave goods, increased sevenfold in population between 780 and 720 BC. The rising population was clearly linked to the expanding horizons brought about by increased security, more food production and greater ease in attaining foreign markets and investments. Just as today Asia's swift ascent was assisted by foreign, especially American, investment and technology and managerial transfer, the evidence, moreover, hints very strongly that the Greek takeoff was ultimately caused by a transfer of technological and commercial know-how from their Phoenician customers. The parallels between the rise of the Tyrian and the Euboean commercial networks strongly suggested the reality "that the springs of Greek development were not internal to the Greek economy, but rather external".[8] Through ancient history we also see that an economic power can often even a swifter decline though in those days it was primarily through military action that power ebbed and flowed rather than through solely through economics as we have witnessed in the Asian crisis of the late 1990s.

Attracting Foreign Investment

Veenhof[9] relates how King Ilushuma (circa 1950 BC) took measures to attract foreign trades from the south (Akkad) to Ashur markets. He points to this governmental policy as one possible explanation for the monopoly on the tin trade enjoyed by Ashur between the mines and Anatolia, in today's terms, providing help for infant industries. The Oriental cultures, Assyria, Phoenicia and Carthage (as an offshoot of Phoenicia), tended to put more restrictions on foreigners coming and doing business while the Greek and Roman cultures were more open to foreign businesspeople and imposed few restrictions.

The importance of infrastructure[10] and government's contribution to building an environment for international business has been the subject of considerable debate in recent years.[11] Perhaps it is enlightening to realize that historians believe that without peace and the ability of merchants and their governmental agencies to cooperate with authorities in foreign countries, trade would not have grown to the degree it did in the Assyrian Empire. Later the conquering legions of Rome brought not only a common currency but built and surveyed a network of roads around the Mediterranean. Major routes were soon joined by minor roads linking the trunk lines with small settlements and rural villas. Communities located along such routes began to flourish. Land transportation, despite being better than ever before, was still too costly for most large-scale commerce. It was far cheaper to ship 500 kg of wheat from Egypt to Rome by sea than to cart it overland from Sicily or even Campania. Wharfs on the Tiber linked Rome with the port of Ostia, where huge ships brought wheat from Egypt and other luxuries from far beyond the Mediterranean. Barges 40 metres long plied the Nile, Rhine, and Danube, while smaller boats brought goods up and down the Tiber, Euphrates, Rhône, Seine, Thames, and Garonne.[12] An effective infrastructure was of considerable importance to the growth of Rome's control over the world's largest empire of its day.

Industry Clusters

The importance of industry clusters has received considerable attention in the last decade. Mike Porter of Harvard brought widespread public attention to the topic with massive 1990 tome, The *Competitive Advantage of Nations*. Oxford's Alan Rugman has suggested that a regional view is often more important than a purely national one with his idea of the Double Diamond framework.[13] For his latest think see Porter's November-December 1998, *Harvard Business Review* article, "Clusters and the New Economics of Competition". Though their importance has been more fully recognised in academic circles in the last few years we see evidence of industry clusters, starting Assyria times.

The importance of industry clusters may first be seen in the tin industry in Ashur and Anatolia. Ashur was a centre of distribution for raw tin and Anatolia a centre for distribution as well as value-adding processes, such as bronze production and manufacturing of bronze objects. The availability of early training centres and hence a trained workforce as well as merchant's knowledge of the tin market were important reasons for Ashurs recognition as a centre of the tin industry.[14]

Later, Phoenicia developed several industry clusters, in purple dye manufacture and shipbuilding. These developed out of having a dense and increasingly urbanised population, excellent harbours, an ample supply of lumber and a highly-skilled and educated population, these cities of the Levant were ideally suited to develop a trade-based maritime economy not unlike Britain or Japan. The dense urbanisation of Ugarit and other Phoenician city-states, combined with the scarcity of grazing land for donkeys and horses, made the latter too expensive to breed in a forested region where shipbuilding was far more cost-effective and promised far more trade advantages, an example of the theory of comparative advantage in action. Other nations could grow food and make war. Let Phoenicia sell them the metals and even the tools, growing rich and powerful in the process: "with its face to the sea, Ugarit developed several industries and crafts which were of purely maritime character, such as purple dye manufacture, and shipbuilding."[15]

Later, Etruria became the metallurgical hub of the central Mediterranean, its smiths producing bronze and iron utensils, tools, weapons and luxury goods, with techniques far more advanced than those used by their contemporaries in, for example Sardinia or even Phoenician Spain. The archaeological record from 750 BC on shows that the Etruscan economy was beginning to specialise, with increasing regionalisation and competition between centres. Metal industries making luxury goods like tripods and weapons concentrated first along the coast, at Tarquinia and Vetulonia, then at Caere and Vulci.[16]

Knowledge based Economy and Knowledge Workers

Observers of the modern world economy tell us that we now live a knowledge-based economy,[17] at least in the developed world. Yet knowledge was pivotal in the development of the first international business activity, knowledge of foreign markets, customs, customers, prevailing trade winds, pirates and other hazards. In this book we have seen how knowledge was central to the development of the wealth of the empires we have studied. The Assyrians knowledge and experience in the tin trade, Phoenicia's knowledge embodied in shipbuilding metalworking and purple dye manufacture. You may recall how within the cities and towns of Ugarit and the other Phoenician city-states guilds of highly-skilled craftsmen, beat and smelted the raw copper and tin, plus the gold and ivory of Egypt into finished products which could be shipped by caravan to Mesopotamia via Carchemish or even Hatti or Egypt. Royal factories also sprang up along the Mediterranean shore, home of the murex shellfish, from which the famous and much-coveted Phoenician purple dye was made. A highly specialised Phoenician garment industry exported over a thousand different items to Thebes, Troy, Rhodes, Hattusas, Babylon and every bazaar of the ancient world Canaan's traders were able to reach.[18]

In Spain, renowned for their skill in finishing ivory work on African tusks in the east, Tyrian craftsmen/importers set up what Richard Harrison termed "a provincial Phoenician workshop" shop in Spain after 700 BC, producing ivory goods right within Carmona itself. Not only value-added branch-plant production but also transfer of technology took place in the areas of luxury-good production. We saw that Iberian jewelry from the early Iron Age tombs is radically different in style from that of the previous period, with the gold-working techniques of the new Spanish craftsmen becoming as adept as their Phoenician tutors. The gold jewels and treasure from the El Carambolo cemetery near Seville suggested, again, resident Phoenician craftsmen at work, while the elaborate necklace "may well have come from Gadir itself".[19] The clearest example of technology transfer, however, took place in the explosive growth of the Iberian pottery industry, which instead of a household skill, became a mass-production trade after 650 BC. All over southern Spain workshops arose turning out large quantities of the popular grey and red Tyrian stylishly jugs decorated with bands of red, black and maroon paint.[20] These small companies had a specialised knowledge, which would lead them to enjoy high profits for a considerable period of history. Phoenicia's wealth and influence grew in direct relation to the strength of its knowledge based industries.

In the centuries which followed the Greeks and then later the Romans also prospered thanks in part to their successful resource-seeking behaviour, capturing control of the silver and iron mines of the day, but in considerable part due to their knowledge workers and their innovations they developed over the centuries.

The Role of the Periphery or the Subsidiary in the Modern MNE

The Assyrian treatment of foreign employees and their general assignment to inferior and peripheral jobs[21] echoes today's debate on the role of the subsidiary within the MNE and especially on how to provide interesting strategic roles within a globalising MNE.[22] Today we find a considerable literature[23] to help guides managers through the challenges of multi-cultural workforces. As mentioned earlier, evidence is found in the cuneiform tablets of the Assyrian era of businesspeople of varied origins, including Syria. People from Ebla are also mentioned, suggesting the possibility of a multi-cultural workforce and all the management complexities associated with such a group. Later we see this approach adopted by the Assyrians reflected in the business practice of the Phonencians, Greeks and Romans with a few more enlightened exceptions.

The 'Best' Form of Capitalism

Perhaps the most important point we would like to make is regarding the controversial question concerning the "best" form of capitalism. A number of prominent Americans, Canadians[24] and Britons[25] have asserted the view that market capitalism, their form of capitalism, has "won" since the fall of the Berlin wall and the centrally planned communist system which lurked behind it. They felt that the Asian crisis of 1998 gave them additional evidence of the need for the rest of the world to adopt the U.S. American free enterprise approach. Perhaps the best known spokesman for this view is the head of the U.S. Federal Bank, Alan Greenspan. In an article for the influential *Vital Speeches of the Day*, Mr. Greenspan wrote, "The turmoil in East Asia appears to be an important milestone in what evidently has been a significant and seemingly inexorable trend toward market capitalism."[26] Later he continues the same thought with the provocative suggestion that, "for good or ill, an unforgiving capitalist process is driving wealth creation. It has become increasingly difficult for policymakers who wish to practice, as they put it, a more 'caring' capitalism to realize the full potential of their economies. Their choices are limited."[27]

Our argument takes a considerably different tack then Mr. Greenspan. In this book we have examined four empires which together spanned over two millennia of human history. They were creative, innovative forms of capitalism which succeeded in enduring, in turn, for centuries, please see figure 11.

Figure 11. Timeline of Ancient Capitalist Systems

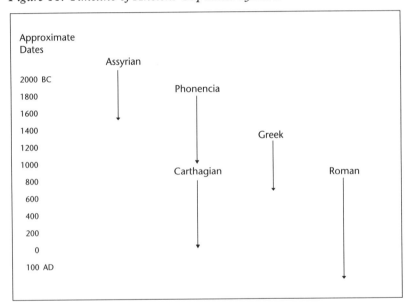

The ability to endure, to produce wealth for its citizens seems to be a reasonable standard for judging an economy. Indeed, Mr. Greenspan recently wrote, "Market economies have succeeded over the centuries by thoroughly weeding out the inefficient and poorly equipped."[28] We agree that success in the marketplace over a long period of time in the face of competitive systems is an important measure of an economy's performance. The four empires we have studied meet this standard, each prospered for hundreds of years, considerably longer than the Anglo-American system which Mr. Greenspan and Mrs. Thatcher and other vocal proponents of the system tout so loudly. Yet though each of the four capitalist systems differed one from another, they all, with the possible exception of Greece, had strong state involvement. We have charcterised each of the five eras or empires studied in this book by their form and the degree of state involvement in Figure 12.

Perhaps those who so proclaim the coming dominance of the global economy by the Anglo-American capitalism system are being a bit too simplistic. History suggests that the appropriate form of capitalism for a country depends on the context of the time, the culture of the people, and the history of the nation.[29] One size does not fit all!

Figure 12. State Involvement

Era or Empire in Economy	Form of Capitalism	State Involvement
Assyrian	Temple/Princely	High in concert with religion
Phoenician	Temple/Naval Transcontinental	High in concert with religion
Carthage	Temple/Navel Transcontinental	Medium in concert with religion
Greek	Entrepreneurial	Relatively Low
Roman	Legionary/Family	Medium

In this short chapter we have just touched upon what we think will turn out to be one of the most fundamental debates of the first decades of the next millennium. In our next book[30] we plan to return to this critical issue of whether there is one form of capitalism, that is Anglo-American capitalism, which the rest of the world should work towards imitating. In that volume we hope to examine the four millennia of recorded human economic history to provide the appropriate context upon which to more fully answer the question of the appropriate forms of capitalism for the second millennium AD.

Bibliography

Aaker, David. *Building Strong Brands.* New York: The Free Press, 1996.

Archilocus, *The Norton Book of Classical Literature* (New York, W.W. Norton and Company, 1993), 202-208.

Aristophanes, *The Frogs*, translated by the Athenian Society pp. 181-272 in *Aristophanes, the Eleven Comedies.* New York: Liveright Publishing Corporation (1943): 226-27.

Aristophanes, *The Knights*, translated by the Athenian Society pp. 3-82 in *Aristophanes, the Eleven Comedies.* New York: Liveright Publishing Corporation (1943): 16-17.

Aristophanes, *The Acharnians*, translated by the Athenian Society pp. 83-148 in *Aristophanes, the Eleven Comedies.* New York: Liveright Publishing Corporation (1943): 126.

Aristotle. Politics, 1272b, 1273 a-b, in Gregory R. Crane (ed.) *The Perseus Project*, March 1997. Available from http://www.perseus.tufts.edu, December, 1998.

Arnott, Peter. *The Romans and their World.* New York: St. Martin's Press, 1970.

Aubert, Jean-Jacques. *Columbia Studies in the Classical Tradition*, William V. Harris, (ed.) *Business Managers in Ancient Rome: A Social and Economic Study of Institores*, 200 BC-A.D.250. Leiden, Netherlands: E.J. Brill (1994): 201.

Aubet, Maria Eugenia. *The Phoenicians and the West: Politics, Colonies and Trade.* trans. Mary Turton. Cambridge: Cambridge University Press, 1987, 1996.

Badian, E. Publicans and Sinners, *Private Enterprise in the Service of the Roman Republic.* Ithaca, Cornell University Press, 1983.

Barker, Graeme and Tom Rasmussen. *The Etruscans.* Oxford: Blackwell Publishers, 1998.

Barreca, Ferruccio. "The Phoenician and Punic Civilization in Sardinia." *Studies In Sardinian Archaelogy*, volume II, *Sardinia in the Mediterranean*, Balmuth, Miriam S., editor. Ann Arbor: University of Michigan Press, (1989): 145-70.

Bartlett, C. and S. Ghoshal. *Managing across Borders: The Transnational Solution*. Boston: Harvard Business School Press, 1989.

Begley, Vimala. "New Investigations at the port of Arikamedu." *Journal of Roman Archaeology*. Vol. 6 (1993): 93-107.

Blanco-Freijeiro, Antonio and J.M. Luzón. "Pre-Roman Silver Miners at Riotinto." *Antiquity*, XLIII (1969): 124-31.

Blanco-Freijeiro, Antonio and Beno Rothenberg. *Exploración Arqueometalúrgica de Huelva (EAH)*. Barcelona: Editorial Labor, S.A., 1981.

Boisot, Max. *Knowledge Assets*. Oxford: Oxford University Press (1998).

Buchner, Giorgio. "Pithekoussai, oldest Greek colony in the West." *Expedition: the Bulletin of the University Museum of the University of Pennsylvania*, vol.8, no. 4, (summer, 1966): 4-12.

Buckley, P. and M. Casson. *The Future of the Multinational Enterprise*. London: Macmillan, 1976.

Buckley, P. "The Role of Management in Internalisation Theory." *Management International Review*, 33, 3 (1993): 197-207.

Budge, E.A. Wallis. *The Rise and Progress of Assyriology*. London: Martin Hopkinson and Co., Ltd., 1925.

Casson, Lionel. "Ancient Naval Technology and the Route to India." In Vimala Begley and Richard Daniel De Puma (eds.) *Rome and India, The Ancient Sea Trade*. Madison, WI: The University of Wisconsin Press, 1991.

Casson, Lionel. *The Ancient Mariners: Seafarers and Sea Fighters of the Mediterranean in Ancient Times*. New York, Macmillan, 1964.

Castro, María Cruz Fernández. *Iberia in Prehistory*. Oxford, Blackwell Publishers, Ltd., 1995.

Chandler, A., *Scale and Scope: The Dynamics of Industrial Capitalism*. Cambridge, MA: Harvard University Press, 1990.

Childe, V. Gordon. *New Light on the Most Ancient East*, New York, Frederick A. Praeger, 1953.

Cicero, *For King Deiotarius, The Perseus Project*, edited by Gregory R Crane, March, 1997, Available from listserve @ http://www.perseus.tufts.edu December 1998.

Clifford, Richard J. "Phoenician Religion." *Bulletin of the American Schools of Oriental Research*, no. 279 (August): 55-64.

Cohen, Edward E. *Athenian Economy and Society: A Banking Perspective*. Princeton, NJ: Princeton University Press, 1992.

Cornell, T.J. *The Beginnings of Rome, Italy and Rome from the Bronze Age to the Punic Wars (c.1000-264 BC)* London: Routledge, 1995.

Corpus Inscriptionum Latinarum. Vol. XIV, no. 4549, in Naphtali Lewis and Meyer Reinhold, (eds.) *Roman Civilization, Sourcebook II: The Empire*. New York: Harper and Row (1966): 197-98.

Coveney, P. and K. Moore. *Business Angels: Financing Your Start-up*. Wiley, 1998.

Cross, Frank Moore. "Phoenicians in Sardinia: The Epigraphical Evidence." *Studies In Sardinian Archaelogy*, Balmuth, Miriam S., and Rowland, Robert J., (eds.) Ann Arbor: University of Michigan Press, (1987): 53-76.

de Chernatony, Leslie and M. McDonald. *Creating Powerful Brands*. Oxford: Butterworth Heinemann, (1998).

D'Arms, John H. *Commerce and Social Standing in Ancient Rome*. Cambridge, Mass. and London: Harvard University Press, 1981.

D'Arms, John H. "Senators' Involvement in Commerce in the Late Republic: Some Ciceronian Evidence." J.H. D'Arms and E.C. Kopff, (eds.) *The Seaborne Commerce of Ancient Rome: Studies in Archaeology and History*. Rome: American Academy at Rome (1980): 77-89.

Demerliac J.G. and J. Meirat. *Hannon et L'Empire Punique*. Paris: Les Belles Lettres, 1983.

Diakonoff, I. M. "The Naval Power and Trade of Tyre." *Israel Exploration Journal*. vol. 42, no. 3-4 (1992): 168-93.

Dickins, G. "In Defense of Thucydides" idem, "The True Cause of the Peloponnesian War" *Classical Quarterly*, vol. 5, (1911): 238-48.

Diodorus Siculus. English translation by C.H. Oldfather. Cambridge: Harvard University Press V:34:35 (1939).

Diodorus Siculus. *The Perseus Project*, edited by Gregory R Crane, <http://www.perseus.tufts.edu>, March, 1997, April 1998.

Dodge, Hazel. "Ancient marble studies: recent research." *Journal of Roman Archaeology*. Vol. 4 (1991): 28-50.

Drummond, A. "Rome in the Fifth Century, I: the Social and Economic Framework" in F.W.Walbank, A.E.Astin, M.W. Frederickson, R.M.Ogilvie and A.Drummond (eds.) *The Cambridge Ancient History*, 2nd edition, Vol. VII, part 2, The Rise of Rome to 220 BC Cambridge: Cambridge University Press (1990): 144-45

Dunning, J. *Multinational Enterprises and The Global Economy*, Wokingham, England: Addison-Wesley, 1993.

Elat, M. "The Monarchy and The Development of Trade in Ancient Israel." E. Lipinski, (ed.), *State and Temple Economy in the Ancient Near East*, Proceedings of the International Conference organised by the Katholieke Univesiteit Leuven from the 10th to the 14th of April, 1978. Louvain, Belgium: Catholic University of Louvain (1979).

Emre, Kutlu. "The Pottery of the Assyrian Colony Period According to the Building Levels of the Kanis Kârum." *Anatolia*, VII (1963): 87-99.

Fell, Barry. *Saga America*, New York: Quadrangle, 1980.

Finegan, Jack. *Archaeological History of the Ancient Middle East*, New York: Dorset Press, 1986.

Forster, Benjamin R. "Commercial Activities in Sargonic Mesopotamia", *Iraq 39*, part 1 (1977): 31-44.

Frank, Tenney. *An Economic History of Rome*, 2nd edition, revised. New York: Cooper Square Publishers, 1962.

Freeman, Charles. *Egypt, Greece and Rome: Civilizations of the Ancient Mediterranean*. Oxford: Oxford University Press, 1996.

Gal, Zvi. "Hurbat Rosh Zayit and The Early Phoenician Pottery." *Levant*, XXIV (1992): 173-85.

Gamito, T.Júdice. *Social Complexity in Southwest Iberia: 800-300 BC: The Case of Tartessos. B.A.R.* International Series 439. Oxford: B.A.R.(1988).

Garelli, Paul. *Les Assyriens en Cappadoce*. Paris: Librarie Adrien Maissoneuve, 1963.

Giardina, Andrea. "The Merchant." *The Romans*, translated by Lydia G. Cochrane. Chicago: University of Chicago Press, 1993.

Glotz, G. A*ncient Greece at Work*. New York: W.W. Norton and Company, 1967.

Goitein, S. *A Mediterranean Society.* Berkeley, CA: University of California Press, 1967.

Gras, Michel, Pierre Rouillard and Javier Teixidu. "The Phoenicians and Death." *Berytus, Archaelogical Studies*, vol. XXXIX (1991): 127-76.

Green, Kevin. *The Archaeology of the Roman Economy.* Berkeley: University of California Press, 1990.

Green, Peter. *Alexander to Actium: the Historical Evolution of the Hellenistic Age.* Berkeley: University of California Press, 1990.

Green, Peter. *A Concise History of Ancient Greece To The Close of The Classical Era.* London, Thames and Hudson Ltd., 1979.

Greenspan, Alan. "Greenspan Sees Asian Crisis Speeding World-Wide Move to Market Capitalism." *Wall Street Journal.* (April 3, 1998).

Greenspan, Alan. "Market capitalism: The role of free markets." *Vital Speeches of the Day,* 64, 14 (May 1, 1998): 418-421.

Grundy, G.B. "The Economic causes of the War." idem, *Thucydides and the History of his age.* Volume I, Oxford, Basil Blackwell, (1948): 322-30, Donald Kagan, ed., *Problems in Ancient History,* Volume One, *The Ancient Near East and Greece.* New York: Macmillan, 1966, 326-30.

Gurney, O.R. *The Hittites.* London: Penguin Books, 1952.

Hallo, William W. and William Kelly Simpson. *The Ancient Near East: a History.* New York: Harcourt, Brace and Jovanovich, 1971.

Hampden-Turner, C. and F. Trompenaars. *The Seven Cultures of Capitalism.* London: Piatkus, 1993.

Hanson, Victor Davis. *The Other Greeks: the Family Farm and the Agrarian Roots of Western Civilization.* New York: The Free Press (1995): 292-303.

Harden, Donald. *The Phoenicians,* Second edition. New York: Frederick A. Praeger, 1963.

Harrison, Richard J. *Spain at the Dawn of History: Iberians, Phoenicians and Greeks.* London: Thames and Hudson, 1988.

Hawkes, Christopher "Commentary I: The Greek Venture and Archaeology." *Archaeology into History I: Greeks, Celts and Romans, Studies in Venture and Resistance* edited by Christopher and Sonia Hawkes. London: J.M. Dent and Sons, Ltd. (1973): 1-4.

Heichelheim, Fritz M. *An Ancient Economic History from the palaeolithic age to the migrations of the Germanic, Slavic and Arabic nations,* Volume I, translated by Joyce Stevens, Leyden: A.W. Sithoff, 1957, 1965

Heltzer, M. "A recently discovered Phoenician Inscription and the problem of the Guilds of Metal-Casters." *Atti del I Congresso In-*

ternazionale di Studi fenici e punici, Roma, (5-10 Novembre1979). Rome, Consiglio Nazionale della Ricerche, 3 vols: 119-23.

Hennart, J.F. *A Theory of Multinational Enterprize*. Ann Arbor: MI: University of Michigan Press, 1982.

Homer, *The Odyssey of Homer*. Translated and with an introduction by Richard Lattimore, New York: Harper Perennial, 1991.

Hopkins, Keith. "Taxes and Trade in the Roman Empire (200 BC-A.D. 400)." *Journal of Roman Studies*, Vol. 70 (1980): 101-25.

Inscriptions Graecae. Vol. XIV, no. 830, in Lewis and Reinhold, *Roman Civilization, Sourcebook II: The Empire*. New York: Harper and Row (1966): 196-97.

"Instructions of the Dioketes to an Oikonomos." *Papyrus Teb.* III 703, #85.

James, Peter, I.J. Thorpe, N. Kokkinow, R. Morkot, and J. Frankish. *Centuries of Darkness: a Challenge to the Conventional Chronology of Old World Archaelogy, foreword by C. Renfrew*. Brunswick, NJ: Rutgers University Press, 1993.

Kagan, ed., *Problems in Ancient History*, Volume One, The Ancient Near East and Greece. New York: Macmillan, (1966): 330-39.

Katzenstein, H. Jacob. "Tyre in the Early Persian Period (539-486 BCE.)." *Biblical Archaeologist*. Volume 42, no. 1, (Winter, 1979): 23-36.

Kay, John. *Foundations of Corporate Success*. OUP, 1995.

Keller, Kevin Lane. "Conceptualizing, Measuring, and Managing Customer Based Brand Equity." *Journal of Marketing*, January (1992): 1-22.

Kojima, K. "Reorganization of North-south Trade: Japan's Foreign Economics Policy for the 1970's." *Hitosubashi Journal of Economics*, 23, (1973): 630-40.

Kojima, K. "Japanese Direct Investment Abroad, Tokyo: International Christian University." *Social Science Research Institute Monograph Series* 1, (1990).

Kramer, Samuel Noah. *The Sumerians: their History, Culture, and Character*. Chicago: University of Chicago Press, 1963.

Kramer, Samuel Noah. "Commerce and Trade: Gleanings from Sumerian Literature." *Iraq 39*. part 1 (1977): 59-66.

Kuhrt, Amélie. *The Ancient Near East*, C. 3000-330 BC, vol. 1, London: Routledge, 1994.

Lancel, Serge. *Carthage: A History.* Translated by Antonia Nevill. Oxford: Blackwell, 1995.

Larsen, Mogens Trolle. *The Old Assyrian City-State and its Colonies,* Copenhagen: Akademisk Forlag, 1976.

Larsen, Mogens Trolle. "Partnerships in the Old Assyrian Trade." *Iraq 39,* part 1, (1977): 119-43.

Larsen, Mogens Trolle. "The Tradition of Empire in Mesopotamia." in *Power and Propaganda: a Symposium on Ancient Empires,* Mogens Trolle Larsen (ed.) Copenhagen: Akademisk Forlag (1979): 75-105.

Lasswell, H. and A. Kaplan. *Power and Society,* New Haven, 1950.

Lazenby, J.F. *The First Punic War: A Military History.* Stanford, CA: Stanford University Press, 1996.

Lazenby, J.F. *Hannibal's War: A Military History of the Second Punic War.* Norman, OK: University of Oklahoma Press, 1998.

"Letter to Apollonios about Reminting Coins." Papyrus Cairo, Zen I59021, 1981: 133 Bagnall, Roger S. and Derow, Peter, (eds.) *Greek Historical Documents: The Hellenistic Period, Society of Biblical Literature, Sources for Biblical Study,* 16. (n.p.), Scholars Press, #84: 133-4.

Lewis, David. "The Return of Charlemagne: The Middle Ages, the European and the European Right." *Florileium.* The University of Western Ontario (May, 1998).

Lewy, Hildegard. "Assyria: c.2600-1816 BC" in *The Cambridge Ancient History,* 3rd Edition, vol.1, part 2, "Early History of the Middle East." Cambridge: Cambridge University Press (1971): 729-70.

Limet, H. "Les Schemas du Commerce Neo-Sumerien." *Iraq 39,* part 1 (1977): 51-58.

Linder, Elisha. "Ugarit, A Canaanite Thalassocracy, Young, Gordon Douglas." *Ugarit in Retrospect: Fifty Years of Ugarit and Ugaritic.* Winona Lake, Indiana: Eisenbrauns, (1981): 31-42.

Lipinski, E. "Les Pheniciens à Ninive au temps des Sargonides, Ahonbasti, Portier en chef." *Atti del I Congresso Internazionale di Studi fenici e punici,* Roma (5-10 Novembre1979). Rome: Consiglio Nazionale della Ricerche, 3 vols (1983): 125-34.

Lipinski, E. *Studia Phoenicia VI Carthago Acta Colloqui Bruxellensis habiti diebus 2 or 3 mensis Maii anni 1986.* Louvain, Belgium: Uit giverij Peeters, 1988.

Macdonald, Brian R. "The Import of Attic Pottery to Corinth and the Question of Trade during the Peloponnesian War." *Journal of Hellenic Studies*, 102 (1982): 113-23.

McMillan, Charles J. *The Japanese Industrial System*. Third revised edition. New York: Walter de Gruyter, 1996.

Mallowan, M.E.L. *Early Mesopotamia and Iran*. New York: Mc-Graw-Hill, 1971.

Markoe, Glenn E. "The Emergence of Phoenician Art." *Bulletin of the American Schools of Oriental Research*. no. 279 (August, 1990):13-26.

Martin, Thomas R. *Ancient Greece, From Prehistoric to Hellenistic Times*. New Haven: Yale University Press, 1996.

Mason, Peter, and Karl Moore. "The Impact of Globilisation on Company Performance: Investigations into the Pharmaceuticals, Food, Chemicals & Autocompents Industries." *Oxford Executive Research Briefings* (May 1998).

Mellnik. "An Akkadian Illustration of a Campaign in Cilicia?" *Anatolia*, VII (1963), 101-2, 110-1.

Michell, H. *The Economics of Ancient Greece*. New York: The Macmillan Company, 1940.

Moore, K. "A Globalization Strategy for Subsidiaries: Subsidiary Specific Advantage." *Journal of International Business Studies*, 28,1, (1997): 217-218.

Moore, K. and Roger Heeler, "A Globalization Strategy for Subsidiaries: Subsidiary Specific Advantage." Journal of Transnational Management Development, Fourth Quarter, (1997); 1-14.

Moore, K. and Roger Heeler. "A Competency Based View of the Subsidiaries." In *Globalization and Regionalization in International Trade and Investment*, editors Peter Buckley and J.L. Mucchielli, International Business Press. (1997).

Moore, K. and D.C. Lewis. "The First MNEs: Assyria Circa 2000 BC" *Management International Review*. No. 2 (1998): 95-107.

Moscati, Sabatino. *The World of the Phoenicians*. English translation by Alastair Hamilton. London: Weidenfirld and Nicholson, 1968.

Murray, Oswyn. *Early Greece*, 2nd Edition. London: Fontana Press, 1993.

Murry, Oswyn. *Early Greece*. Sussex: Harvester Press, 1980.

Musti, Domenico. "Syria and the East." Walbank, F.W., Astin A.E., Frederikson, M.W., and Ogilvie, R.M., (eds.) *Cam-*

bridge Ancient History, Second Edition, volume VII, part 1, The Hel-lenistic World (1982): 175-220.

Nissen, Hans J. *The Early History of the Ancient Near East: 9000-2000 BC* trans. Elizabeth Lutzeier, with Kenneth J. Northcott. Chicago: University of Chicago Press, 1988.

North, D. *Structure and Change in Economic History.* New York: W.W. Norton. 1981.

Oded, Bustanay. "The Phoenician Cities and the Assyrian Empire in the Time of Tiglath-Pileser III." *Zeitschrift des Deutschen Paläs-tina-Vereins.* vol. 90 (1974): 38-49.

Oppenheim, A. Leo. "Essay in Overland Trade in the First Milen-nium BC" *Journal of Cuneiform Studies.* vol.21 (1967): 236-54.

"Order for Delivery of Grain." *Papyrus Hib.* I 39, Bagnall, Roger S. and Derow, Peter, (eds.) *Greek Historical Documents: The Hellenis-tic Period, Society of Biblical Literature, Sources for Biblical Study,* 16 (n.p.) (1981): 144-5

Orlin, L. *Assyrian Colonies in Cappadocia.* The Hague: Mouton, 1970.

Özgüç, Tahsin. "Early Anatolian Archaeology in the Light of Re-cent Research." *Anatolia,* VII (1963): 1-21.

Osborne, Robin. *Archaic and Classical Greek Art.* Oxford: Oxford University Press, 1998.

Osborne, Robin. *Greece in the Making,* 1200-479 BC London: Routledge, 1996.

Özgüç, Tahsin. "The Art and Architecture of Ancient Kanesh." *Anatolia.* VIII, (1964): 27-48.

Papadopoulos, John K. "Phantom Euboeans." *Journal of Mediterra-nean Archaeology,* 10.2 (1997): 191-219.

Petronius. *Satyricon,* translated by William Arrowsmith, quoted in Nels M. Bailkey, (ed.) *Readings in Ancient History: Thought and Experience from Gilgamesh to St. Augustine,* 3rd edition. Lexington, MA: D.C. Health and Company (1987): 378.

Pettinato, Giovanni. *The Archives of Ebla: an Empire Inscribed in Clay, with an afterword by Mitchell Dahood.* Garden City, NY: Doubleday and Co., 1981.

Piggott, Charles. "Why Europeans Wait Longer To Be Free", *The European.* (April 20-26, 1998).

Pindar. *Olympian. The Perseus Project,* edited by Gregory R Crane, <http://www.perseus.tufts.edu>, March, 1997.

Plautus. The Pot of God,

Polybius. *The Histories.* Newly translated by Mortimer Chambers. Edited, Abridged and with an introduction by E. Badian. New York: Twain Publishers, Inc., 1966

Polybius. *The Histories,* i.20, quoted in *The Rise of the Roman Empire,* translated by Ian Scott-Kilvert, edited and with introduction by F.W.Walbank. London: Penguin Books, 1979.

Porter. *Canada At the Crossroads: The Reality of a New Competitive Environment.* Ottawa: Business Council on National Issues, 1991.

Porter, M. *The Competitive Advantage of Nations.* Boston: Free Press, 1990.

Postgate, G.N. *Early Mesopotamia: Society and Economy at the Dawn of History.* London: Routledge, 1992.

Potter, T.W. *Roman Italy.* Berkeley: University of California Press, 1990.

Powelson, J. *Centuries of Economic Endeavor.* Ann Arbor, MI: The University of Michigan Press, 1994.

Pritchard, J.B. (ed.) *Ancient Near Eastern Texts Relating to the Old Testament,* Third edition. Princeton: Princeton University Press, 1993.

Rainey, A.F. "Business Agents at Ugarit" *Israel Exploration Journal.* vol. 13 (1963): 313-21.

"Receipt for Embarkation of Grain." *Papyrus Hib.* I 98. Bagnall, Roger S. and Derow, Peter, (eds.) *Greek Historical Documents: The Hellenistic Period, Society of Biblical Literature, Sources for Bible Study,* 16 (n.p), Scholars Press, #93 (1981): 251.

Redding, G. "Overseas Chinese Networks: Understanding the Enigma." *Long Range Planning.* 28 (1995): 61-69.

Redfield, James M. "The Development of the Market in Ancient Greece" *The Market in History,* edited by B.L. Anderson and A.J.H. Latham. London: Croom Helm (1986): 29-58.

"Revenue Laws of Ptolemy Philadelphos." *Papyrus Hib.* Bagnall, Roger S. and Derow, Peter, (eds.) *Greek Historical Documents: The Hellenistic Period, Society of Biblical Literature, Sources for Bible Study,* 16 (n.p), Scholars Press, #95 (1981): 146-60.

Rich, John. "Fear, greed and glory: the causes of Roman war-making in the middle Republic." Rich, John and Shipley, Graham, (eds.) *War and Society in the Roman World.* London: Routledge (1995): 38-68.

Ridgway, David "The First Western Greeks: Campanian Coasts and Southern Etruria." *Archaeology into History I: Greeks, Celts and Romans, Studies in Venture and Resistance* edited by Christopher and Sonia Hawkes, London, J.M. Dent and Sons, Ltd. (1973): 5-28.

Ridgway, David. *The First Western Greeks.* Cambridge, UK: Cambridge University Press, 1992.

Roebuck, Carl. *Ionian Trade and Colonization.* Chicago: Ares Publications, 1994.

Rostow, W. *The World Economy: History and Prospect.* Austin, TX: University of Texas Press, 1978.

Rowton, M.B. "Ancient Western Asia." *The Cambridge Ancient History*, 3rd Edition, vol.1, part 1, "Prolegomena and Prehistory". Cambridge: Cambridge University Press (1970): 193-238.

Rugman, A. "A New Theory of the Multinational Enterprise: Internationalization Versus Internalization." *Columbia Journal of World Business,* spring, (1980): 23-29.

Rugman, A. and D'Cruz, J. "The 'Double Diamond' Model of International Competitiveness: The Canadian Experience." *Management International Review,* Special Issue (1993): 17-39.

Rugman, A. and Gestrin, M. "The Strategic Response of Multinational Enterprises to NAFTA." *Columbia Journal of World Business* 28, 4 (1993), pp. 18-28.

Sackett, L.H. and M. R. Popham. "Lefkandi: A Euboean Town of the Bronze Age and Early Iron Age (2100-700 BC)" *Archaeology,* Vol. 25, no. 1 (January, 1972): 8-19.

Saggs, H.W.F. *The Might that was Assyria.* London: Sidgwick and Jackson, 1984.

Sallares, Robert. *The Ecology of the Ancient Greek World.* Ithaca, NY: Cornell University Press, 1991.

Scullard, H.H. "The Carthaginians in Spain." In A.E. Astin, F.W. Walbank, M.W. Fredericksen, R.M. Ogilvie, (eds.) *The Cambridge Ancient History*, 2nd edition, Vol. VIII, *Rome and The Mediterranean to 133 BC* Cambridge: Cambridge University Press (1989): 20-43.

Silver, Morris. *Economic Structures of Antiquity,* Westport, CT: Greenwood Press, 1995

Snodgrass, Anthony M. "Iron and Early Metallurgy in the Mediterranean." In Theodore A. Wertime and James D. Muhly (eds.)

The Coming of the Age of Iron. New Haven, CT: Yale University Press (1980): 335-74.

Solon, translated by Richard Lattimore, *The Norton Book of Classical Literature*. New York: W.W. Norton and Company (1993): 238-42.

Soren, David, Aicha Ben Abed Ben Khader, and Hedi Slim, *Carthage, Uncovering the Mysteries and Splendors of Ancient Tunisia*. New York: Simon and Schuster, 1990.

Starr, Chester G, *The Economic and Social Growth of Early Greece, 800- 500 BC* New York: Oxford University Press, 1977.

Stern, E. Marianne. "Early Roman Export Glass in India." In Begley and De Puma (eds.) *Rome and India, The Ancient Sea Trade*. Madison, WI: The University of Wisconsin Press (1991): 113-17.

Stern, E. "New Evidence from Dor for the First Appearance of the Phoenicians along the Northern Coast of Israel." *Bulletin of the American Schools of Oriental Research*, no. 279 (August 1990): 29-30.

Stetch, Tamara and Vincent C. Pigott. "The Metals Trade in Southwest Asia in the Third Milennium BC" *Iraq 48* (1986): 39-64.

Stieglitz. "The Geopolitics of the Phoenician Littoral in the Early Iron Age." *Bulletin of the American Schools of Oriental Research*, no. 279, (August 1990): 11.

Strabo, The Geography, The Perseus Project, edited by Gregory R Crane, <http://www.perseus.tufts.edu>, March, 1997.

Thucydidis. *The Complete Writings of Thucydides: The Peloponnesian War*, translated by [first name unknown] Crawley, introduction by John H. Finley, Jr. i.1.2. New York: Modern Library, 1951.

Thucydides, Histories, The Perseus Project, edited by Gregory R Crane, <http://www.perseus.tufts.edu>,March, 1997.

Thucydides, *History of the Peloponnesian War*, Books I and II, translation by Charles Forster Smith Cambridge, MA, harvard University Press, 1969.

Tiglath-Pileser I, *Ancient Records of Assyria and Babylonia*, 1, § 221, in Finegan, (1986): 104

Tlatli, Salah-Eddine. *La Carthage punique: étude urbaine: la ville, ses functions, son rayonnement*. Preface by Chedli Klibi and Gilbert Charles-Picard. Paris: Librarie d'amerique et d'Orient, 1978.

Tsirkin, Yuri B. "Economy of the Phoenician Settlements in Spain." Edward Lipinski (eds.) *State and Temple Economy in the Ancient Near East, Proceedings of the International Conference organized by the Katholieke Universiteit Leuven from the 10th to the 14th of April, 1978.* Louvain, Belgium: Catholic University of Louvain, 1979.

Tyrants: Classics 371/History 391, Fall 1997, Reed College, Portland, Oregon, http://www.homer.reed.edu?Gk Hist/Tyrants.html.

Ure, P.N. "The Tyrant as Capitalist." from *The Origin of Tyranny* Cambridge: Cambridge University Press (1922): 1-3, 290-95, 296-97, 300-301, 306 in Donald Kagan, ed., *Problems in Ancient History*, Volume One, *The Ancient Near East and Greece.* New York: Macmillan (1966): 221-27.

Veenhof, K.R. "Some Social Effects of Old Assyrian Trade." *Iraq* 39. part 1 (1977): 109-18.

Veenhof, K. "Kanesh: An Assyrian Colony in Anatolia." In Sasson, J./Barnes, J./Beckman, G./Rubinson, K. (eds.), *Civilisations of the Ancient Near East.* New York: Simon & Schuster MacMillan, 2 (1995): 859-871.

Veenhof, K. *Aspects of Old Assyrian Trade and Its Terminology.* Leiden: Free University, 1972.

Von Reden, Sitta. *Exchange in Ancient Greece.* London: Gerald Duckworth & Co., Ltd. (1995): 105-108, 131-33.

Wacher, John. *The Roman Empire.* London: J.M. Dent and Sons, Ltd., 1987.

Ward-Perkins, John. "The Marble Trade and its Organisation: Evidence from Nicomedia." D'Arms, J.H. and E.C. Kopff, (eds.) *The Seaborne Commerce of Ancient Rome: Studies in Archaeology and History.* Rome: American Academy in Rome (1980): 325-38.

Will, Elizabeth Lyding. "The Mediterranean Shipping Amphoras from Arikamedu." In Begley and De Puma (eds.) Rome and India, The Ancient Sea Trade. Madison, WI: The University of Wisconsin Press (1991): 151-56.

Wiseman, D.J. *The Expansion of Assyrian Studies: an Inaugural Lecture delivered on 27 February 1962.* London, Oxford University Press, 1962.

Xenophanes, translated by Willis Barnstone, *The Norton Book of Classical Literature.* New York: W.W. Norton and Company (1993): 231-34.

Suggestions for Further Reading

Chapter 1

The twin topics of globalisation and the emerging knowledge based economy both have extensive literatures which have developed around them over the last twenty years. To better understand globalisation two key books are important to consider, firstly George Yip of Cambridge's *Total Global Strategy*, gives an excellent overview of the some key forces which have driven globalistion, another seminal book is Chris Bartlett and Sumantra Goshal's 1989, *Managing across Borders: The Transnational Solution*, which presents some of their extensive research into the key advantages for a firm which adopts a global strategy, other articles by the same two authors in the *Harvard Business Review* and the *Sloan Management Review* are also useful on the topic.

Key contributions concerning the role of knowledge in firms would include those by I. Nonaka and H.Takeuchi, *The Knowledge Creating Company*, (OUP, 1995); G. Hedlund, "A Model of Knowledge Management and the N-Form Corporation", *Strategic Management Journal*, Vol 15, 1995; "Managing professional intellect: Making the most of the Best", *Harvard Business Review*, 1996, March-April, by James Quinn, Philip Anderson and Sydney Finkelstein and "Managing Knowledge in Global Service Firms: Centres of Excellence," *Academy of Management Executive*, November, 1998 by Karl Moore and Julian Birkinshaw.

Chapter 2

For the non-international business scholar, that is, many readers of this book, there is probably no better starting place than chapter 4 of John Dunning's, *Multinational Enterprises and the Global Economy*, (Addison Wesley, 1993). Those interested in futher readings are suggested to consider Michael Porter's work on location or country-specific advantages, his The Competitive Advantage of Nations (Free Press, 1990), for internalisation advantages please see Peter Buckley's, *The Theory of the Multinational Enterprise* (Uppsala, 1987) and Mark Casson's, *The Firm and the Market* (Blackwell,

1987) and on ownerhsip or firm specific advantages, Dunning's, Explaining International Production, (Unwin Hyman, 1988).

Chapter 3

H.W.F. Saggs, *The Might that was Assyria* (London, 1984) is still the most thorough account of Assyria available and a good source for the rediscovery of Nineveh. The author attempts to present the Assyrians in a more sympathetic light than most historians arguing that the Assyrians were no worse, and perhaps a good deal better, than other Near Eastern peoples. E.A.Wallis Budge *The Rise and Progress of Assyriology* (London, 1925) is very old but still useful in reconstructing much of the story of how we know what we know about ancient Mesopotamiaas as is D.J Wiseman's published 1962 Oxford lecture *The Expansion of Assyrian Studies* (London, 1962). On the Kanesh finds see Tahsin Özgüç, "Early Anatolian Archaeology in the Light of Recent Research", *Anatolia*, VII, (1963):pp.1-21; "The Art and Architecture of Ancient Kanesh", *Anatolia*, VIII, (1964): pp. 27-48, the unpublished 1980 Ph. D. Philosophy dissertation from Columbia University of Ann Clyburn Gunter, "The Old Assyrian Colony Period Settlement at Bogazkoy-Hattusa in Central Turkey: a Chronological Reassessment of the Archaelogical Remains", and volume 1 of Amélie Kuhrt, *The Ancient Near East, C. 3000-330 BC* (London, 1994).

Chapter 4

Amélie Kuhrt, *The Ancient Near East, C. 3000-330 BC* (London, 1994) is the best and most recent survey of Mesopotamian history available, and makes a fair mention of commerce. The most interesting general interpretation, linking legend, literature and archaeology is by Yale's William J. Hallo and William Kelly Simpson, *The Ancient Near East: A History* (New York, 1971). A provocative revision of ancient chronology which shortens pre 1000 BC dates by several centuries is Peter James, I.J. Thorpe, N. Kokkinos, R. Morkot, and J. Frankish, *Centuries of Darkness: A Challenge to the Conventional Chronology of Old World Archaeology*, (New Brunswick, NJ, 1993). *A Test of Time, Volume One: The Bible-From Myth to History* (London, 1995) and *Volume Two Legend, The Genesis of Civilisa-*

tion (London, 1998) by David M. Rohl argue for an even lower chronology. G.N. Postgate, *Early Mesopotamia: Society and Economy at the Dawn of History,* (London,1992) is an excellent overview of the Mesopotamian economy from its beginnings to its full development. Mogens Trolle Larsen's article "The Tradition of Empire in Mesopotamia", in his *Power and Propaganda: a Symposium on Ancient Empires* (Copenhagen. 1979), pp. 75-105, provides a geographical explantion as to why Mesopotamia became "capitalist" and Egypt "socialist". Samuel Noah Kramer's *The Sumerians: their History, Culture, and Character,* (Chicago, 1963) and "Commerce and Trade: Gleanings from Sumerian Literature", *Iraq* 39, 1977, part 1, pp.59-66 give good literary evidence on Sumerian "temple capitalism". See also Tamara Stetch and Vincent C. Pigott, "The Metals Trade in Southwest Asia in the Third Milennium BC", *Iraq* 48, 1986, pp.39-64. For Akkadian commerce see Benjamin R. Forster, "Commercial Activities in Sargonic Mesopotamia", *Iraq* 39, 1977, part 1, pp. 31-44 and Aage Westenholz, "The Old Akkadian Empire in Contemporary Opinion", in Larsen's *Power and Propaganda: a Symposium on Ancient Empires* (Copenhagen, 1979), pp. 107-24. The Neo-Sumerian prelude to Old Assyria is treated in H.Limet, "Les Schemas du Commerce Neo-Sumerien", *Iraq* 39, part, pp 51-58.

The leading writer on Old Assyrian trade remains Mogens Trolle Larsen. Consult his *The Old Assyrian City-State and Its Colonies* (Copenhagen 1976) and "Partnerships in the Old Assyrian Trade", *Iraq* 39, 1977, part 1, pp. 119-43. Also essential are Louis Laurence Orlin, *Assyrian Colonies In Cappadocia* (The Hague 1970), and the works of K.R. Veenhof: "Kanesh: An Assyrian Colony in Anatolia", in the second volume of J. Sasson, J.Barnes, G. Beckman, and K. Rubinson, eds., *Civilisations of the Ancient Near East* (New York, 1995), pp. 859-871, *Aspects of Old Assyrian Trade and Its Terminology* (Leiden,1972), and "Some Social Effects of Old Assyrian Trade", *Iraq* 39, 1977, part 1, pp.109-18. The story of the Assyrian merchant Pusu-Ken is found in Larsen (1976) and Orlin (1970) as well as the first volume, *Economic Foundations,* of S.D. Goitein's *A Mediterranean Society* (Berekeley,1967).

Chapter 5

A comprehensive survey of Phoenician history is still hard to find. Maria Eugenia Aubet, *The Phoenicians and the West: Politics, Colonies and Trade*,(Cambridge UK, 1997) Maria Eugenia Aubet has good material but stresses overseas commerce. The second edition of Donald Harden, *The Phoenicians* (New York,1963) is still worth reading but quite out of date. For Ugarit see A.F. Rainey, "Business Agents at Ugarit", *Israel Exploration Journal*, vol.13, 1963, pp.313-21, Elisha Linder, "Ugarit, A Canaanite Thalassocracy", in Gordon Douglas Young, ed., *Ugarit in Retrospect: Fifty Years of Ugarit and Ugaritic* (Winona Lake, IN, 1981),pp. 31-42, and Michael C. Astour, "Ugarit and the Great Powers", also in Young(1981), pp.3-30. Charles J. McMillan, *The Japanese Industrial System* (New York, 1996) is an essential introduction to the modern *keiretsu*. Peter James, I.J. Thorpe, N. Kokkinos, R. Morkot, and J. Frankish, *Centuries of Darkness: A Challenge to the Conventional Chronology of Old World Archaeology*, (New Brunswick, NJ, 1993) argues that Ugarit is dated too early, implying a much closer relationship between its business culture and that of Tyre. Evidence in Glenn E. Markoe, "The Emergence of Phoenician Art", *Bulletin of the American Schools of Oriental Research*, no. 279, August, 1990, pp.13-26, lends some support to James's contention.

Chapter 6

Once again, Maris Eugenia Aubet's *The Phoenicians and the West: Politics, Colonies and Trade*,(Cambridge UK, 1997) is the essential guide to Tyrian commercial expansion. The Israel-Tyre relationship is illuminated by M. Elat, "The Monarchy and The Development of Trade in Ancient Israel" in E. Lipinski, (ed.), *State and Temple Economy in the Ancient Near East*, (Louvain, 1979), E. Stern, "New Evidence from Dor for the First Appearance of the Phoenicians along the Northern Coast of Israel", *Bulletin of the American Schools of Oriental Research*, no. 279, August, 1990, pp. 29-30, and Z. Gal, "Hurbat Rosh Zayit and the Early Phoenician Pottery", *Levant*, XXIV, 1992, pp. 173-85. Morris Silver, *Economic Structures of Antiquity*, (Westport CT, 1995) shows the crucial role of the Melqart hierarchy in Tyrian enterprise. On the Tyrians in Assyria and Baby-

Ionia consult E. Lipinski, "Les Pheniciens à Ninive au temps des Sargonices, Ahonbasti, Portier en chef", in the *Atti del I Congresso Internazionale di Studi fenici e punici, Roma, 5-10 Novembre1979* (Rome, 1983), pp.125-34. Tyrian settlement in Sardinia is the subject of Ferruccio Barreca, "The Phoenician and Punic Civilization in Sardinia" in Miriam S Balmuth, ed., *Studies In Sardinian Archaelogy, Volume II, Sardinia in the Mediterranean* (Ann Arbor MI, 1989): pp. 145-70.

The Phoenician operation in Spain is all-important. In addition to Aubet, who devotes the major portion of her very fine book to it, there is the most up-to-date survey of ancient Iberia by María Cruz Fernández Castro, *Iberia in Prehistory* (Oxford, 1995). Richard J Harrison, *Spain at the Dawn of History: Iberians, Phoenicians and Greeks* (London,1988) openly argues for "multinational" business hierarchies in Phoenician Spain, as does T.Júdice Gamito, *Social Complexity in Southwest Iberia: 800-300 BC: The Case of Tartessos*, B.A.R. International Series no. 439 (Oxford, 1988). A technical perspective on Rio Tinto by two archaeologists who are also professional engineers is found in Antonio Blanco-Freijeiro and Beno Rothenberg, *Exploración Arqueometalúrgica de Huelva (EAH)* (Barcelona, 1981).

Chapter 7

There has been important revisionist writing dealing with the Archaic and Classical Greek world in the last decade. Robin Osborne's *Greece in the Making: 1200-479 BC* (London, 1996) is absolutely indispensable for the Hellenist scholar. Building upon the latest demographic studies as well as traditional literary and pottery studies, Osborne discards the notions of rapid Iron Age population growth taught by earlier historians. He also suggests that market-seeking behaviour played more of a role in Archaic Greek colonisation than previously supposed. Another interesting revisionist work is Robert Sallares, *The Ecology of the Ancient Greek World*, (Ithaca, NY, 1991). Sallares provides a "green" interpretation of Archaic Greece, based in part upon upon climatological studies and comparisons with modern Greece. In his view the Greek market transformation was caused by the importation of the olive tree as well as iron-working. The ascendancy of Greece over Persia was, he argues, ultimately due to a population explosion in the former. Thomas R. Martin, *Ancient Greece, From Prehistoric to Hellenistic Times* (New Haven, 1996) is still a timely survey.

The Euboeans and their role in the origins of the market revolution are treated in the revised edition of Oswyn Murray, *Early Greece* (London, 1993). John K. Papadopoulous, "Phantom Euboians", *Journal of Mediterrnaean Archaeology*, vol.10, no.2, 1997, pp. 191-219 offers an interesting corrective to the traditional view of Euboean primacy in early Greek trade, stressing the role of Phoenicians and others in bringing the Iron Age to Greece. On the Euboeans and Pithekoussai see also Giorgio Buchner, "Pithekoussai, Oldest Greek Colony in the West", *Expedition: the Bulletin of the University Museum of the University of Pennsylvania*, vol. 8, no. 4, summer,1966, pp.4-12, David Ridgway, "The First Western Greeks: Campanian Coasts and Southern Etruria", Christopher and Sonia Hawkes, eds., *Archaeology into History, I: Greeks, Celts and Romans, Studies in Venture and Resistance*, (London, 1973), pp. 35-38, L.H. Sackett, and M.R. Popham, "Lefkandi: A Euboean Town of the Bronze Age and Early Iron Age" (2100-700 BC), *Archaeology*, January, 1972, vol.25, no. 1, pp.8-19.

Chester G. Starr, *The Economic and Social Growth of Early Greece, 800- 500 BC* (New York, 1977) is older but still useful in discussing the strengths and weaknesses of comparing economic growth in Greece to that of medieval and modern Europe. Volume I of Fritz Heichelheim's reprinted *An Ancient Economic History from the Palaeolithic Age to the Migrations of the Germanic, Slavic and Arabic Nations*, (Leyden, 1965) provides an interesting, if dated and overly deterministic interpretation of the spread of the Iron Age beyond the Near East. In his view, now largely modified or discarded, iron plows made possible the intensive farming of European lands and the rise of European cities. On Corinth see J.B. Salmon, *Wealthy Corinth, A History of the City to 338 BC* (Oxford,1984). For Athens check Harold B. Mattingly, *The Athenian Empire Restored: Epigraphic and Historical Studies*. Ann Arbor, MI, 1996 and D.I. Rankin, The Mining Lobby at Athens, *Ancient Society*(Louvain) vol. 19, 1988, pp.189-206.

James M. Redfield, "The Development of the Market in Ancient Greece, B.L. Anderson and A.J.H. Latham, eds., *The Market in History* (London, 1986), pp 29-58.(1986) looks at Homer, Hesiod and other writers for subtle evidence of the market revolution and its effect on Archaic Greek culture. The story of the slave-entrepreneur Pasion is told in Lionel Casson, *The Ancient Mariners: Seafarers and Sea Fighters of the Mediterranean in Ancient Times* (New York, 1964). Scholarship on the origins of the Peloponnesian War has been more or less in limbo since the publication of Geoffrey de Ste Croix's *The Origins of the Peloponnesian War* (London, 1972), but check B.R. Macdonald, "The impact of Attic pottery to Corinth and the question of trade during the Peloponnesian War", *Journal of Hellenic Studies*, CII,1992, pp. 113-23.

Chapter 8 and Chapter 9

The Hellenistic economy represents an important transition between that of Classical Greece and later Rome. Little documentation on economics, however, is available outside of Ptolemaic Egypt. A good place to begin is chapter 21 of Peter Green, *Alexander to Actium: the Historical Evolution of the Hellenistic Age*, (Berkeley, CA, 1990). *Greek Historical Documents: The Hellenistic Period* edited by Roger Bagnall and Peter Derow (n.p., 1981) has excellent primary sources on Ptolemaic Egypt's state capitalism. On Carthage the definitive work is Serge Lancel's *Carthage: A History* (Oxford, 1997).

The best one-volume work on the Hellenistic world, including a chapter on the economy, is Peter Green *Alexander to Actium*(1990). Heichelheim (1970) is a bit old, but has a good discussion of the historical debate surrounding the causes of Hellenistic decline. Lionel Casson, *The Ancient Mariners, Seafarers and Sea Fighters of the Mediterranean in Ancient Times*, (New York, 1964) has very good material on Hellenistic and Roman long-range voyages and trading patterns.

The most up-to-date work on the early Roman Republic is T.J. Cornell's monumental study of *The Beginnings of Rome: Italy and Rome from the Bronze Age to the Punic Wars (c.1000-264 BC)* (London, 1995), which does for Rome what Osborne's work does for Archaic Greece. Cornell integrates archaeology, demography, and literature to argue Rome was not a commercial desert before 200 BC Tenney Frank's multivolume *Economic Survey of Ancient Rome*, especially *Volume I: Rome and Italy of the Republic* (Baltimore,1927) is a gold-mine of information on individual Roman industries and literary evidence, in spite of its age and long-outdated interpretations of Roman enterprise.

Good primary source documents, some of them relating to trade, appear in Naphtali Lewis and Meyer Reinhold, eds. *Roman Civilization: Sourcebook I: The Republic.* and *Roman Civilization: Sourcebook II: The Empire* (New York, 1966).

The parameters of Roman trade and economic development as traced by artifacts can be discovered in Kevin Greene, *The Archaeology of the Roman Economy* (Berkeley, 1990) and T.W. Potter, *Roman Italy* (Berkeley, 1990), which traces the export ventures of the Sestii through their wine vessels. See also Daniele Manacorda, "The Ager Cosanus and the Production of the Amphorae of Sestius: New Evidence and a Reassessment", *Journal of Roman Studies*, vol.68, 1978, pp.122-31. John H. D'Arms, *Commerce and Social Standing in Ancient Rome* (Cambridge, MA, 1981) is a good introduction to the debate as to how much Roman senators took part in commerce. Jean-Jacques Aubert, *Managers in Ancient Rome?* (Leiden,1994), analyses the Roman management structure, notably the clay industries in the light of Roman business law and archaeology, suggesting the presence of partnerships and agents. The rise and structure of the publican companies are well-treated by E. Badian, *Publicans and Sinners, Private Enterprise in the Service of the Roman Republic* (Ithaca, NY, 1983). The marble trade, another good candidate for multinational enterprise, is described by John Ward-Perkins, "The Marble Trade and its Organisation: Evidence from Nicomedia", J.H. D'Arms and E.C. Kopff, eds. *The Seaborne Commerce of Ancient Rome: Studies in Archaeology and History* (Rome, 1980), pp. 325-38. Hazel Dodge, "Ancient marble studies: recent research", *Journal of Roman Archaeology*, vol.4, 1991, pp. 28-50 revises some of the geography of earlier scholarship in this area.

Chapter 10

This debate is one which is very much on the agenda. Articles appear regularly in the major thoughtful media, places like the *Economist*, the *Financial Times*, the *Times* of London, the *Wall Street Journal* and the *New York Times*, as well the not so thoughtful media, which tend to be more polemic in nature.

There have also appeared a number of excellent books in the topic of differing forms of capitalism or economies. Scholars in the area include Richard Whitley of Manchester University, Richard Wade of Brown University and Marie-Laure Djelic of ESSEC. Three scholarly books stand out in our minds: *Divergent Capitalism* by Whitley (OUP, 1999); *Exporting the American Model* by Djelic (OUP, 1998) and *The Economic Organization of East Asian Capitalism* (Sage, 1997).

Professor Whitley in his latest book (1999) presents a comparative business systems framework for describing the major differences in economic organisation between the various market economies in the late-twentieth century. He suggests six major types of business systems and points out the strong ties to different institutional arrangements in countries and regions they operate in. In her book Djelic discusses how the Marshal Plan after World War II was instrumental in exporting the American Model of corporate capitalism to Europe. She focuses on France, West Germany and Italy and shows how the transfer of the American model meet with varying success depend on the degree of resistance it met and how it was, to varying degrees, adapted to the national conditions in each of the three nations studied. Finally, Orru, Biggart and Hamilton's edited volume considers forms of capitalism in East Asia and how they have evolved since World War II.

Our next book is one in which we plan to contribute to this growing body of literature by drawing lessons for the modern world from the various forms of capitalism we found in ancient times.

Endnotes

Chapter 1

1 Any list of prominent researchers and writers would include names like Porter, Levitt, Dunning, Drucker, Thurow, Yip, Rugman, Casson, Buckley, Ohmae and countless executives in annual reports and interviews.

2 For example, Bartlet and Goshal in their *Managing across Borders: The Transnational Solution*, (Boston: Harvard Business School Press, 1989).

3 J. Dunning, *Multinational Enterprises and The Global Economy*, (Wokingham, England, 1993), 96.

4 W. Rostow, *The World Economy: History and Prospect*, (Austin, TX: University of Austin Press, 1978), D. North, *Structure and Change in Economic History*, (New York: W. W. Norton, 1981), A. Chandler, Scale and Scope: *The Dynamics of Industrial Capatalism*, (Cambridge, MA: Harvard University Press, 1990), J. Powelson, *Centuries of Economic Endeavor*, (Ann Arbour, MI: The University of Michigan Press, 1994).

5 e.g. Orlin, *Assyrian Colonies in Cappadocia*, (The Hague: Mouton, 1970), Larsen, *The Old Assyrian City-State and its Colonies*, (Copenhagen: Akadmisk Forlag, 1976), Maria Eugenia Aubet, *The Phoenicians and the West: Politics, Colonies and Trade*, (Cambridge: Cambridge University Press, 1987).

6 Karl Moore and Roger Heeler, "A Globalization Strategy for Subsidiaries: Subsidiary Specific Advantage", *Journal of Transnational Management Development*, Fourth Quarter, (1997), Karl Moore and Roger Heeler, "A Competency Based View of the Subsidiaries", in *Globalization and Regionalization in International Trade and Investment*, editors Peter Buckley and J.L. Mucchielli, (International Business Press, 1997) and Karl Moore and David Lewis, "The First MNEs: Assyria Circa 2000 BC", *Management International Review*, Second Quarter, (1998).

7 David Lewis, "The Return of Charlemagne: The Middle Ages, the European and the European Right", *Florilegiun*, (The University of Western Ontario, May, 1998).

8 Alan Greenspan, "Market capitalism: The role of free markets", *Vital Speeches of the Day*, (May 1, 1998), 64,14, 418-421 and "Greenspan

Sees Asian Crisis Speeding World-Wide Move to Market Capitalism",
(Apr 3, 1998), *Wall Street Journal.*

Chapter 2

1 Two other important theories which seek to explain foreign activities of
  firms are the internalization theory of the MNE; Buckley and Casson,
  The Future of the Multinational Enterprise, (London: Macmillan, 1976).
  Hennart, *A Theory of Multinational Enterprize*, (Ann Arbour, MI: University of Michigan Press, 1982) and the macro-economics theory of
  foreign direct investment. Kojima, "Reorganization of North-south
  Trade: Japan's Foreign Economics Policy of the 1970's", *Hitosubashi
  Journal of Economics*, 23 (1973): 630-40. Japanese Direct Investment
  Abroad, Tokyo: International Christian University, *Social Science Research Institute Monograph Series* 1, (1990).
2 Dunning, *Multinational Enterprise*, 3.
3 The term strategic competencies comes from Bartlett and Ghoshal,
  1995, John Kay in his *Foundations of Corporate Succes*, OUP, 1995 uses
  the term distinctive capabilities.
4 Dunning, *Multinational Enterprise*; Peter Buckley and Mark Casson, *The
  Future of Multinational Enterprise*
5 This is especially true in the Anglo-American economies where growth
  is the mantra and managements which do not deliver satisfactory growth
  are often threatened with removal by shareholders. At the heart of this
  are investors looking for a return from firms higher than what they would
  earn in safer investments, such as a bank account or a government bond,
  in order to justify the higher risk they face in a corporate investment. Returns required from new small firms by Business Angels, (P. Coveney
  and K. Moore, *Business Angels: Financing Your Start-up*, Wiley, 1998)
  wealthy private investors, can reach levels of over 40% a year, compared
  to the 4% or 5% ones earns from a British savings account in the local
  high street bank. Investments on the continent and in Japan have traditionally been more patient but that seems to be breaking down under the
  pressure of global investors who are willing to rapidly move their investments to other countries if they do not earn the returns they demand.
6 They also or alternatively turn to using their FSAs in allied markets,
  what might be called horizontal extension. An example is Virgin expanding in its home market of the U.K. by buying a rail line; in this case there
  has been question of the extendability of the competencies of their ventures into running a rail line.
7 Peter Buckley, "The Role of Management in Internalisation Theory",
  Management International Review, 33, 3, (1993), 197-207.
8 We use the term foreign subsidaries here broadly to include forms short
  of subsidaries such as a sales office.
9 Peter Mason and Karl Moore, "The Impact of Globalisation on Company Performance: Investigations into the Pharmaceuticals, Food,

Chemicals & Auto-Compents Industries", *Oxford Executive Research Briefings*, (May, 1998).

10 Charles Piggott, "Why Europeans Wait Longer To Be Free", *The European*, (April 20-26, 1998).

11 For additional readings please see the section "Suggestions For Further Reading" after the Bibliography in the back of the book.

Chapter 3

1 Tiglath-Pileser I, *Ancient Records of Assyria and Babylonia*, 1, § 221, in (Finegan, 1986), 104

2 Saggs, *The Might that was Assyria*, (London: Sidgwick and Jackson, 1984), 264-8

3 Saggs, (1985) 289-90.

4 Saggs, (1984) 294-6; Wiseman, *The Expansion of Assyrian Studies: an Inaugural Lecture delivered on 27 February 1962*, (London: Oxford University Press) 4-5; Budge, *The Rise and Progress of Assyriology*, (London: Martin Hopkinson and Co., Ltd, 1925), 11-22.

5 Budge, 64-7; Saggs, (1984), 294-7; Peter James and I.J. Thorpe, N.Kokkinow, R. Morkot, and J.Frankish, *Centuries of Darkness: a Challenge to the Conventional Chronology of Old World Archaeology*, (Brunswick, NJ: Rutgers University Press, 1993) 261-4.

6 Budge, 111-4; Saggs, (1984), 297-8; James et al, 261-4.

7 Budge, 47-52, 68-73, 80-4.

8 James et al, 261-4; Wiseman, 5-6.

9 Finegan, *Archaeological History of the Ancient Middle East*, (New York: Dorset Press, 1986), 99-121; Saggs, (1984), 23-121.

10 Rowton, "Ancient Western Asia" in *The Cambridge Ancient History*, 3rd Edition, vol. 1, part 1, "Prolegomena and Prehistory", (Cambridge: Cambridge University Press, 1970), 742-3; James et al, 265-8; Finegan, 111.

11 Rowton, 743-5; James et al, 268-9, 277-9.

12 Kuhrt, *The Ancient Near East*, (London: Routledge, 1994), 81-2

13 Ibid.

14 Kuhrt, 81.

15 Dates based upon Kuhrt, 81, 85-6; Lewy, "Assyria: c. 2600-1816 B.C." in *The Cambridge Ancient History*, 3rd edition, vol. 1, part 2, "Early History of the Middle East", (Cambridge: Cambridge University Press, 1971) 756-8

16 Læssøe, 1963: 39-40.

17 Dates based upon James et al, 335-8.

18 Postgate, *Early Mesopotamia: Society and Economy at the Dawn of History*, (London: Routledge, 1992), 216.

19 Gurney, *The Hittites*, (London: Penguin Books, 1952), 2-9; Postgate, 211-2; Orlin, 1970:7.

20 Orlin, 7, 199-200.

21 Ibid, 200.
22 Özgüç, "Early Anatolian Archaeology in the Light of Recent Research."
    Anatolia, VII, (1963), 2-3, 6; "The Art and Architecture of Ancient
    Kanesh." *Anatolia*, VIII, (1964) 28; Emre, "The Pottery of the Assyrian
    Colony Period According to the Building Levels of the Kanis Karûm."
    Anatolia, VII, (1963) 87-91.
23 Özgüç, (1964) 31-7; *Anatolian Studies*, (1964) 24-5.
24 Ibid, 37-9; *Anatolian Studies*, (1964); 24-5.

Chapter 4

1 Larsen, "The Tradition of Empire in Mesopotamia." *Power and Propo-
   ganda: a Symposium on Ancient Empires* (Copenhagen: Akademisk Forlag, 1979) 46-7.
2 Kuhrt, 19-21.
3 Kuhrt, 21; Larsen, "The Tradition of Empire in Mesopotamia," 47,77.
4 Gen 4:17-23, Biblical references from New International Version here
   and throughout.
5 William W. Hallo and William Kelly Simpson, *The Ancient Near East: a
   History*, (New York: Harcourt, Brace and Jovanich, 1971), 29-33.
6 Hallo and Simpson, 27-33; Nissen, *The Early History of the Ancient Near
   East: 9000-2000 B.C.*, (Chicago: Univeristy of Chicago Press, 1983),
   39-64; Pettinato, The archives of Ebla: an Empire Inscribed in Clay,
   with an afterword by Mitchell Dahood, (Garden City, NY: Doubleday
   and Co., 1981), 174; Childe, *New Light on the Most Ancient East*, (New
   York: Frederick A. Praeger, 1953), 129.
7 Hallo and Simpson, 12-13; Mallowan, *Early Mesopotamia and Iran*,
   (New York: McGraw-Hill, 1971), 25-8; Nissen, 39-64.
8 Hallo and Simpson, 31-4.
9 Kuhrt, 28.
10 Kuhrt, 43.
11 Date source: Hallo and Simpson, 27-54; Mallowan, 12.
12 Kuhrt, 23-5.
13 Ibid, 28-29.
14 Kramer, *The Sumerians, their History, Culture and Character*, (Chicago:
    University of Chicago Press, 1963), 75; Limet, "Les Schemas du Com-
    merce Neo-Samarien." *Iraq 39*, part 1 (1977), 51-3.
15 Pettinato, 179-80.
16 Orlin, 46-7.
17 Kuhrt, 25, 31-2.
18 (Hallo and Simpson, 33-49; Kramer, 73-4.
19 Kuhrt, 41-3; Kramer, *The Sumerians*, 53-6.
20 Larsen, "The Tradition of Empire in Mesopotamia," 76
21 Kurht, 21.
22 Tamara Stech and Vincent C. Piggott, "The Metals Trade in Southwest
    Asia in the Third Millennium B.C." *Iraq 48*, (1986), 40-5; Kramer,

"Commerce and Trade: Gleanings from Sumerian Literature." *Iraq 39*, part 1, (1977), 61.

23 Stech and Piggott, 47.
24 Gen. 6:11
25 Özgüç, "Early Anatolian Archaeology," 10-1.
26 Pettinato, 95-6, 104-6.
27 Kuhrt, 40-1.
28 Pettinato, 184, 225-6.
29 Kramer, *The Sumerians*, 276-84; Forster, "Commercial Activities in Sargonic Mesopotamia," *Iraq 39*, part 1, (1977) 38-9
30 *Enki and Ninhursag*, translated in Kramer, *The Sumerians*, 279.
31 *Enki and the World Order*, ibid, 176.
32 Larsen, "The Tradition of Empire in Mesopotamia," 77-79.
33 Mellnik, "An Akkadian Illustration of a Campaign in Cilicia?" *Anatolia*, VII, (1963), 101-2, 110-1.
34 Kuhrt, 25-26.
35 Forster, 35-6.
36 Ibid, 37.
37 Forster, 1977: 32-3, 36-7.
38 Postgate, 220-1.
39 Postgate, 220-1.
40 Garelli, *Les Assyriens en Cappadoce*, (Paris: Librarie Adrien Maissoneuve, 1963), 171-2; Postgate, 220-1.
41 Lewy, 752; Saggs, 5.
42 Lewy, 752.
43 Ibid.
44 Læssø e, 1963: 37-9.
45 Lewy, 752-62.
46 Ibid, 58-9.
47 Ibid, 758-9.
48 Veenhof, "Some Social Effects of Old Assyrian Trade." *Iraq 39*, part 1, (1977) 115-6.
49 Postgate, 212-3.
50 Hallo and Simpson, 63; Gurney, 82; Orlin, 7-8, 23-5
51 Dates based upon Kuhrt, 81, 85-6, 90-1; Lewy, 756-8; Hallo and Simpson, 27-54; Mallowan, 12; Finegan, 50, 58, 60; Özgüç, 2-3, 6, 28, 31-7; Emre, 87-91.
52 Kuhrt, 91
53 Larsen, *The Old Assyrian City-state and its Colonies*, 235-41.
54 Orlin, 51-2.
55 Veenhof, "Some Social Effects of the Assyrian Trade," 110.
56 Orlin, 27-8.
57 Veenhof, "Some Social Effects of the Assyrian Trade," 115.
58 Ibid.
59 Ibid, 111-2; Larsen, "Partnerships in the Old Assyrian Trade." *Iraq 39*, part 1, (1977), 119-20.

60 Saggs, 30-3: Orlin, 52-8; Larsen, "Partnerships in the Old Assyrian Trade," 119-20.
61 Orlin, 24.
62 This section on Pusu-ken and his life is adapted from Larsen (*The Old Assyrian City-state and its Colonies*) who draws on the work of various archaeologists.
63 It is difficult to accurately date events in this time period, according to the Cambridge Ancient History (1970), "the chronology in ancient western Asia bristles with problems" (p.193). The chronology given is the most popular one among historians.
64 At this juncture in history firms were on often based to a large degree on familial relationships, making an interesting parallel with Redding's view on Chinese capitalism. Redding, "Overseas Chinese Networks: Understanding the Enigma." *Long Range Planning*, 28 (1995).
65 Veenhof, *Aspects of Assyrian Trade and its Terminology*, (Leiden: Free University, 1972).
66 Goitein, *A Mediterranean Society*, (Berkeley, CA: University of California Press, 1967).
67 Goitein
68 Orlin, H. Lasswell and A. Kaplan, *Power and Society*, (New Haven, 1950).
69 Orlin
70 Larsen, *The Old Assyrian City-state and its Colonies*.
71 Ibid.

Chapter 5

1 Kuhrt, 111.
2 James et al, 338.
3 Ibid, 195.
4 Kuhrt, 300-301.
5 Linder, "Ungarit, a Canaanite Thalassocracy, Young, Gordon Douglas." *Ugarit in Retrospect: Fifty Years of Ugarit and Ugaritic*, (Winona Lake, Indiana: Eisenbrauns, 1981) 32.
6 Linder, 38; Kuhrt, 302.
7 Kuhrt, 386.
8 Ibid, 390-2; Linder, 38.
9 Kuhrt, 300.
10 Pritchard, *Ancient Near Eastern Texts Relating to the Old Testament*, Third Edition, (Princeton: Princeton University Press, 1969), 484.
11 Ibid, 477.
12 Ibid, 351-2.
13 Markoe, "The Emergence of Phoenician Art," *Bulletin of the American Schools of Oriental Research*, no. 279, (August, 1990), 14.

14 Moscati, *The World of Phoenicians*, (London: Weidenfeld and Nicholson, 1968), 8-9; Fensham, 1990: 593; Harden, *The Phoenicians*, Second edition, (New York: Frederick A. Praeger), 83.

15 McMillan, *The Japanese Industrial System*, Third revised edition, (New York: Walter de Gruyter, 1996), 58.

16 Ibid, 56-7.

17 Ibid, 64-7.

18 Ibid, 69, 73-6.

19 Ibid, 304-10.

20 Heltzer, "A recently discovered Phoenician Insription and the problem of the Guilds of Metal-Casters." *Atti del I congresso Internazionale di Studi fenici e punici, Roma*, (5-10 Novembre 1979), 123-5.

21 Heltzer, 124.

22 Heltzer, 136; Linder: 35.

23 Rainey, "Business Agents at Ugarit." *Israel Exploration Journal*, vol 13, (1963) 316-7; Heltzer, 136; Linder, 35.

24 Heltzer, 140-42.

25 McMillan, 310.

26 Heltzer, 142-3, 147.

27 Linder, 35.

28 Ibid, 32.

29 Ibid, 33.

30 Heltzer, 135-7.

31 Ibid, 131.

32 Linder, 35.

33 Rainey, 318-9.

34 Linder, 40-1.

35 Rainey, 314.

36 Ibid, 315.

37 Palais Royal d'Ugarit, V, 63

38 Heltzer, 151.

39 Aubet, *The Phoenicians and the West*, 298.

40 Ibid.

41 Aubet, *The Phoenicians and the West*, 300-02.

42 Stieglitz, "The Geopolitics of the Phoenician Littoral in the Early Iron Age." *Bulletin of the American Schools of Oriental Research*, no. 279, (August, 1990), 11.

43 Aubet, *The Phoenicians and the West*, 27, 29-32, 35.

44 Regional dates after Cross, "Phoenicians in Sardinia: The Epigraphical Evidence." *Studies in Sardinian Archaeology*, (Ann Arbour: University of Michigan Press, 1987) 57 ff.

45 Aubet, *The Phoenicians and the West*, 35.

46 I Ki.5:11; Moscati, 13.

47 Aubet, *The Phoenicians and the West*, 35-6.

48 Moscati, 12-13.

49 Aubet, *The Phoenicians and the West*, 36; I Ki.9:26, 10:22, 49.

50 Aubet, *The Phoenicians and the West*, 36

51 Elat, "The Monarchy and The Development of Trade in Ancient Israel." *State and Temple Economy in the Ancient Near East*, Proceedings of the International Conference organised by the Katholieke Universiteit Leuven from the 10ᵗʰ to the 14ᵗʰ of April, 1978, (Louvain, Belgium: Catholic University of Leuven, 1979), 526.

52 Elat, 537-8.

53 Ibid, 537.

54 I Ki. 16:31.

55 Donald Harden, The Phoenicians, Second edition (New York: The Free Press, 1963) 53; Aubet, *The Phoenicians and the West*, 38.

56 I Ki.16:16, 28-31.

57 James et al., 159.

58 I Ki. 10: 18, 22:39; Ezek. 27:6; Amos 3: 15, 6:14.

59 Aubet, *The Phoenicians and the West*, 38

60 Stern, "New Evidence from Dor for the First Appearance of the Phoenicians along the Northern Coast of Israel." *Bulletin of the American Schools of Oriental Research*, no. 279, (August, 1990), 29-30; Gal, "Hurbat Rosh Zayit and The Early Phoenician Pottery." *Levant*, XXIV, (1992), 173-85

61 Stern, 32,

62 Pritchard, 134.

63 Ibid, 138.

64 Silver, *Economic Structures of Antiquity*, (Westport, CT: Greenwood Press, 1995), 6.

65 Ibid, 7.

66 Ibid, 18-19, 25-27.

67 Ibid, 19.

68 Ibid, 8.

69 Ibid, 10.

70 Clifford, "Phoenician Religion." *Bulletin of the American Schools of Oriental Research*, no. 279, (August, 1990), 55-66

71 Silver, 32.

72 Ibid, 33.

73 Aubet, *The Phoenicians and the West*, 40-1.

74 I Ki. 18:19.

75 I Ki. 18:27.

76 I Ki. 12:28-33; II Ki.10:18-29.

Chapter 6

1 Kuhrt, 352.

2 Ibid, 348-62.

3 Clifford, 55-66; Aubet, *The Phoenicians and the West*, 40-1.

4 Pritchard, 276.

5 Ibid, 281.

6 Finegan, 105.

7 Oded, "The Phoenician Cities and the Assyrian Empire in the Time of Tiglath-Pileser III." *Zeitschrift des Deutschen Palästina-Vereins*, vol. 90, (1974), 39, 46-8.

8 Aubet, *The Phoenicians and the West*, 72-4.

9 Dunning, *Multinational Enterprises and the Global Economy*, 75-86.

10 Aubet, *The Phoenicians and the West*, 75.

11 Harden, 53,157; Aubet, *The Phoenicians and the West*, 68.

12 Aubet, *The Phoenicians and the West*, 45; Moscati, 98; Heltzer, 119-23.

13 Iliad VI: 284; XXII: 740-45; Aubet, *The Phoenicians and the West*, 102-6.

14 Odyssey XV: 415-16, 455; Aubet, *The Phoenicians and the West*, 102-6; Harden, 161-3.

15 Harden, 60-1.

16 Ibid, 52-3.

17 Ibid, 63-7; Aubet, *The Phoenicians and the West*, 198-9.

18 Harden, 63.

19 Aubet, *The Phoenicians and the West*, 200.

20 Ibid, 202.

21 Harrison, *Spain at the Dawn of History: Iberians, Phoenicians and Greeks*, (London: Thames and Hudson, 1988), 42-3; Barreca, "The Phoenician and Punic Civilization in Sardinia." *Studies in Sardinian Archaeology, Volume II, Sardinia in the Mediterranean*, (Ann Arbour: University of Michigan Press, 1989), 152-3; Cross, 55-6.

22 Moscati, 99.

23 Aubet, *The Phoenicians and the West*, 203.

24 Ibid, 207.

25 Diodorus Siculus, V:34:35 (Cambridge: Harvard University Press, 1939).

26 James et al, 49-50.

27 Strabo, The Geography, The Persus Project, March 1997. Available from listserv@http://www.perseus.tufts.edu. III:5:5.

28 Diodorus Siculus, V:35:2-5.

29 Aubet, *The Phoenicians and the West*, 235.

30 Ibid, 218-20, 230-3.

31 Ibid, 234.

32 Ibid, 325-6; Silver, 6-10.

33 Blanco-Freijeiro and Luzón, "Pre-Roman Silver Miners at Riotinto." *Antiquity*, XLIII, (1969), 125.

34 Ibid; Blanco-Freijeiro and Rothenberg, *Exploratión Arqueometalúrgica de Huelva (EAH)*, (Barcelona: Editorial Labor, S.A., 1981), 96-98, 101, 104-6, 113-4; Harrison, 150-1.

35 Blanco-Freijeiro and Rothenberg, *Exploratión Arquemetalúrgica de Huelva (EAH)*, 171-3; Castro, *Iberia in Prehistory*, (Oxford: Blackwell Publishers, Ltd, 1995), 195-6.

36 Blanco and Luzón, "Pre-Roman Silver Miners at Riotinto."; Blanco-Freijeiro and Rothenberg, *Exploratión Arquemetalúrgica de Huelva (EAH)*, 104-6, 113-4; Harrison, 150-1.

37 Aubet, *The Phoenicians and the West*, 238.

38 Ibid, 238-40.

39 Ibid, 240.

40 Blanco-Freijeiro and Rothenberg, *Exploratión Arquemetalúrgica de Huelva (EAH)*, 104-6, 113-4; Harrison, 152-3.

41 5:35,5

42 Aubet, *The Phoenicians and the West*, 240-1.

43 Gamito, *Social Complexity in Southwest Iberia: 800-300 B.C.: The Case of Tartessos. B.A.R. International Series*, 439, (Oxford: B.A.R., 1988), 54.

44 Harrison, 42.

45 Strabo, III, 5: 3-4; Tsirkin, "Economy of the Phoenician Settlements in Spain." State and Temple Economy in the Ancient Near East, Proceedings of the International Conference organised by the Katholieke Universiteit Leuven from the 10th to the 14th of April, 1978, (Louvain, Belgium: Catholic University of Louvain, 1979), 563.

46 Castro, 177, 183-4.

47 Tsirkin, 563.

48 Ibid, 548-51.

49 Ibid, 554.

50 Ibid, 557; Castro, 182-4, 191-2; Harrison, 43-4.

51 Harrison, 47.

52 Gras, Rouillard and Teixidor, "The Phoenicians and Death." *Berytus, Archaeological Studies*, vol. XXXIX, (1991), 145.

53 Tsirkin, 557.

54 Gras, Rouillard and Teixidor, 145.

55 Barreca, 152.

56 Tsirkin, 559.

57 Tsirkin, 559-60.

58 Isa.23:1.

59 Moscati, 20-1.

60 Ibid, 21-2.

61 Pritchard, 534.

62 Ibid.

63 Oppenheim, "Essay in Overland Trade in the First Millennium B.C." *Journal of Cuneiform Studies*, vol. 21, (1967), 253.

64 Lipinski, "Les Phéniciens á Ninivé au temps des Sargonide: Ahonasti, ortier en chef." *Atti del I Congresso Internazionale di Studi fenici e punici*, Roma, vol. 1, 5-10 Novembre 1979, (Rome: Consiglio Nazionale della Ricerche, 1983), 124-34.

65 Oppenheim, 239-40.

66 Ibid, 241.

67 Oppenheim, 239, 241, 246-7.

68 Castro, 200-01.

69 The Tyrian presence and influence is reflected in the Huelvan cemetery of La Joya, where a number of rich burials show native Spanish rulers attaining both status and the religion of Melqart/Astarte as a result of the new partnership. Aubet, *The Phonecians and the West*, 238.

70 Harrison, 51-63.

71 Ibid, 64-5.

72 Ibid, 66.

73 Ibid, 68.

74 Oppenheim, 253.

75 Diakonoff, "The Naval Power and Trade of Tyre." *Israel Exploration Journal*, 42: 3-4, (1992), 170-7.

76 Ezek. 27: 12, 25, 33.

77 Jonah 1:3.

78 Jonah 1:5.

79 Diakonoff, 182, 193.

Chapter 7

1 Thomas R. Martin, *Ancient Greece, From Prehistoric to Hellenistic Times*, (New Haven: Yale University Press, 1996).

2 Martin, 25-28

3 Martin, 29; Thucydides' account of the Greek past, penned many centuries later, contained a great deal of guesswork: "...the dwellers on the sea-coast now began to acquire property more than before and to become more settled in their homes and some, seeing that they were growing richer than before, began also to put walls around their cities. Their more settled life was due to their desire for gain, actuated by this, the weaker citizens were willing to submit to dependence on the stranger, and the more peaceful men, with their enlarged resources, were able to make the lesser cities their subjects and later on, when they had at length more completely reached this condition of affairs, they made the expedition against Troy." Thucydides, *History of the Peloponnesian War*, Books I and II, translation by Charles Forster Smith (Cambridge, MA: Harvard University Press, 1969), viii.1-4.

4 Martin, 32; David Ridgway, *The First Western Greeks* (Cambridge, UK: Cambridge University Press, 1992), 3-6.

5 Martin, 32.

6 James, et al, *Centuries of Darkness: A Challenge to the Conventional Chronology of Old World Archaeology*, foreword by C. Renfrew (New Brunswick, NJ: Rutgers University Press, 1993), 68-94.

7 Recent work by Robert Sallares insists that this group of revisionist historians "are going too far in denying that there ever was a "Dark Age"" in light of the fact that all recent finds in Greece stress "the completeness of the break at the end of the Mycenaean period." Robert Sallares, *The Ecology of the Ancient Greek World* (Ithaca, NY: Cornell University Press 1991), 64.

8 In strata dated to the thirteenth century BC there are 320 occupied sites; there are only 130 for the twelfth and a mere 40 for the eleventh. The landscape, however, begins to fill in between 1000 and 800 BC. Sallares, 61-64.

9 James, et al, 68-112.

10 Redfield, "The Development of the Market in Ancient Greece", *The Market in History*, edited by B.L. Anderson and A.J.H. Latham (London: Croom Helm, 1986), 29-32.

11 Ibid, 32-33.

12 Homer, *The Odyssey*, ii. 74-75 *The Odyssey of Homer* Translated and with an introduction by Richard Lattimore (New York: Harper Perennial, 1991).

13 Homer, ii. 334 -41.

14 Homer, i. 356-60.

15 Redfield, 32.

16 Homer, ii. 287-95.

17 Homer, vi. 270-72.

18 Homer, vii. 108-109.

19 Homer, viii. 159-64.

20 Homer, xiv. 285-97.

21 Homer, ii. 276-77.

22 Fritz M. Heichelheim, *An Ancient Economic History from the Palaeolithic Age to the Migrations of the Germanic, Slavic and Arabic nations*, Volume I, translated by Joyce Stevens (Leyden: A.W. Sithoff, 1965), 196-97.

23 Ibid, 193-95.

24 Ibid, 194.

25 Ibid.

26 Anthony M. Snodgrass, "Iron and Early Metallurgy in the Mediterranean", in Theodore A. Wertime and James D. Muhly, eds., *The Coming of the Age of Iron* (New Haven, CT: Yale University Press, 1980), 335-37.

27 Ibid, 338-39.

28 Ibid, 341. Peter James's revised chronology would lower the date of the Cypriot chronology to match the evidence from Phoenicia and the Near East, which "would in turn push down by some 150 years the absolute date for the end of the Late Bronze Age in Cyprus, currently set at *c.* 1050 BC." James, et al, 161.

29 Peter James' revised chronology would lower the date of the Cypriot chronology to match the evidence from Phoenicia and the Near East, which "would in turn push down by some 150 years the absolute date for the end of the Late Bronze Age in Cyprus, currently set at *c.* 1050 BC", James, et al, 161.

30 Snodgrass, 345.

31 Ibid.

32 Robin Osborne, *Greece in the Making, 1200-479 BC* (London: Routledge, 1996) 27-28.

33 Osborne, *Greece*, 27-28.

34 The unusually heavy preponderance, some 80%, of iron artifacts in the Athenian finds suggests that a shortage of tin needed to make bronze in the Greek world provided an enormous incentive for the early development of iron-working in the Greek world. Osborne, *Greece*, 27; Snodgrass, 348-52.

35 Osborne, *Greece*, 27.

36 The site of Lefkandi in Euboea itself was excavated between 1964 and 1966. The findings from Xeropolis Hill and some two hundred graves and funeral pyres showed that Lefkandi may not only have escaped the destruction at the end of the Bronze Age, but was a flourishing centre during the Hellenic Dark Age, however long or short it may have been: "When much of Greece was depopulated, Lefkandi was an active center." [L.H Sackett and M.R. Popham, "Lefkandi: A Euboean Town of the Bronze Age and Early Iron Age" (2100-700 BC) *Archaeology*, Vol. 25, no.1, (January, 1972), 13]. Already thriving at the end of the tenth century BC (conventional chronology), the settlement saw its richest period of burials at the end of the ninth. These burials showed a number of links with Cyprus and Syria [Sackett and Popham, 16-18].

37 David Ridgway, *The First Western Greeks* (Cambridge, UK: Cambridge University Press, 1992), 12-15.

38 Ibid, 24.

39 Ibid.

40 Hawkes, Christopher "Commentary I: The Greek Venture and Archaeology", *Archaeology into History I: Greeks, Celts and Romans, Studies in Venture and Resistance* edited by Christopher and Sonia Hawkes, (London, J.M. Dent and Sons, Ltd., 1973), 1-2.

41 David Ridgway, "The First Western Greeks: Campanian Coasts and Southern Etruria." Christopher and Sonia Hawkes, eds., *Archaeology into History I: Greeks, Celts and Romans, Studies in Venture and Resistance* (London: J.M. Dent and Sons, Ltd. 1973), 5, 8.

42 John K. Papadopoulos, "Phantom Euboeans", *Journal of Mediterranean Archaeology*, vol.10, no. 2 (1997), 193-96.

43 Ibid, 200.

44 Ibid, 202.

45 Ibid, 202.

46 Ridgway, *The First Western Greeks*, 13-15.

47 Ridgway, "The First Western Greeks", 16-18; Giorgio Buchner, "Pithekoussai, Oldest Greek Colony in the West", *Expedition: the Bulletin of the University Museum of the University of Pennsylvania*, vol. 8, no. 4 (Summer, 1966), 12.

48 Ridgway, "The First Western Greeks", 26.

49 Ibid.

50 Ibid, 27-28.

51 Buchner, 7.

52 Redfield, 41.

53 Homer, iv.80-85.

54 Redfield, 43.
55 Ibid.
56 Thucydides, vii.
57 Osborne, *Greece*, 70.
58 Ibid, 79-80.
59 It is only partially true "that the springs of Greek development were not internal to the Greek economy, but rather external". Redfield, 4.
60 Osborne, *Greece*, 125. Ibid, 128-29.
61 The economic growth of ancient Greece is almost impossible to quantify with statistics, but perhaps not much more so than is late medieval and early modern Europe, where actual documentation is equally scarce. Chester G. Starr, *The Economic and Social Growth of Early Greece, 800-500 BC* (New York: Oxford University Press, 1977), 13-15.
62 Redfield, 44-45.
63 Osborne, *Greece*, 175-76.
64 Ibid, 176.
65 Hanson, *The Other Greeks: the Family Farm and the Agrarian Roots of Western Civilization* (New York: The Free Press, 1995), 292-303.
66 Ridgway, 19-20.
67 Pindar, *Olympian*, xiii.15-24, Gregory R Crane, ed., *The Perseus Project*, http://www.perseus.tufts.edu, April, 1998.
68 Thucydides, *The Complete Writings of Thucydides: The Peloponnesian War*, translated by Crawley, introduction by John H. Finely, Jr. i. 13 (New York: Modern Library, 1951), 1-6; Michell, *The Economics of Ancient Greece* (New York: The Macmillan Company, 1940), 236-37.
69 Peter Green, *A Concise History of Ancient Greece to the Close of the Classical Era* (London, Thames and Hudson Ltd., 1979), 60-63.
70 Starr, 28, 31.
71 Ibid, 33-34.
72 Ibid.
73 *Tyrants: Classics 371/History 391, Fall 1997, Reed College Portland Oregon*, http://homer.reed.edu?Gk Hist/Tyrants.html.
74 Aristotle, *Politics* 1267b, quoted in ibid.
75 Pausanias commented: "Here are common graves of the Argives who conquered the Lacedaemonians in battle at Hysiae." Pausanias, 2.24.7, quoted in ibid.
76 *Tyrants*, ibid.
77 Thucydides, 1.13, quoted in *Tyrants*, ibid.
78 *Tyrants*, ibid.
79 P.N.Ure "The Tyrant as Capitalist" from idem, *The Origin of Tyranny*, Donald Kagan, ed., *Problems in Ancient History, Volume One, The Ancient Near East and Greece* (New York: Macmillan,1966), 215, 222.
80 Ibid, 223-25.
81 Oswyn Murray, *Early Greece*, 2nd Edition (London: Fontana Press, 1993), 223.

82 Buchner, 8.

83 Murray, *Early Greece*, (Sussex: Harvester Press, 1980), 223.

84 Osborne, *Archaic and Classical Greek Art* (Oxford, Oxford University Press, 1998), 87.

85 Ibid, 90-91.

86 Ibid, 90.

87 Ibid, 95.

88 Solon, translated by Richard Lattimore, in *The Norton Book of Classical Literature* (New York: W.W. Norton and Company, 1993), 240.

89 Ibid, 242.

90 Osborne, *Greece*, 243.

91 Carl Roebuck, *Ionian Trade and Colonization* (Chicago: Ares Publications, 1994), 87-90.

92 Heichelheim, 215-17.

93 Osborne, *Greece*, 250-58.

94 Heichelheim, 218.

95 Ibid, 221.

96 Silver, 19-21.

97 Ibid, 30.

98 Ibid.

99 Xenophanes, Translated by Willis Barnstone in *The Norton Book of Classical Literature*, (New York: W.W. Norton and Company, 1993), 233.

100 Homer, iv. 414-16.

101 Green, 99.

102 Ibid, 96-106.

103 Katzenstein, "Tyre in the Early Persian Period (539- 486 BC)" *Biblical Archaeologist* vol.42, no. 1 (Winter, 1979), 31.

104 Anxious to preserve their Mediterranean trading advantage and gain access to the mines of the northern Aegean, Tyrian merchants had already invaded the Greek realm, planting a Melkart shrine and merchant-colony on the island of Thasos. Allowed to preserve their local rulers and autonomy in the new Persian structure, the Tyrian and Sidonian hierarchies meanwhile appear to have redirected their investment strategy to the east. Persian coinage, roads, and a unified market were exchanged for a transfer of Phoenician seafaring technology and even fleets themselves in the partnership which underlay Phoenician participation in the Persian Wars. Katzenstein, 30-32.

105 Sallares, 47-49.

106 Ibid, 47.

107 Martin, 107-109.

108 Ibid, 116-19.

109 Ibid, 119-22.

110 Lionel Casson, *The Ancient Mariners: Seafarers and Sea Fighters of the Mediterranean in Ancient Times*, (New York: Macmillan and Company, 1964), 107-110.

111 Ibid, 112-16; Sallares, 51-55.

112 Edward E. Cohen, *Athenian Economy and Society: A Banking Perspective* (Princeton, NJ: Princeton University Press, 1992), 191-203.

113 Ibid, 72-75.

114 Ibid, 68-69.

115 Ibid, 65-66.

116 Casson, 107-110.

117 Ibid, 110.

118 "In strictly financial terms, the end of Greek agrarianism, the dimunition of the small hoplite farm as the key to social, military, and political privilege, resulted in much *greater* capital formation and wealth circulating in Greece, the Aegean, Italy, Sicily, and Asia Minor at the end of the fourth century and on into the third...", Hanson, 361.

119 "In strictly financial terms, the end of Greek agrarianism, the dimunition of the small hoplite farm as the key to social, military, and political privilege, resulted in much *greater* capital formation and wealth circulating in Greece, the Aegean, Italy, Sicily, and Asia Minor at the end of the fourth century and on into the third...", Hanson, 361.

120 Sitta von Reden, *Exchange in Ancient Greece* (London: Gerald Duckworth & Co., Ltd.,1995), 105-108.

121 von Reden, 119.

122 Ibid,120.

123 Hanson, 365.

124 Ibid, 366-68, 378-79.

125 Grundy "The Economic causes of the War" from *Thucydides and the History of his Age*, vol. 1 (Oxford: Basil Blackwell) in Kagan, ibid, 326-30.

126 Dickins "In Defense of Thucydides" from "The True Cause of the Peloponnesian War", *Classical Quarterly*, vol. 5 (1911) in Kagan, ibid, 331-39; Martin, 151-52.

127 Brian R. Macdonald, "The Import of Attic Pottery to Corinth and the Question of Trade during the Peloponnesian War ", *Journal of Hellenic Studies*, 102 (1982), 113.

128 Ibid, 118.

129 Ibid, 119.

130 Ibid, 119-20.

131 Ibid, 121.

132 Ibid, 122.

133 Diodorus Siculus, xii.40.4 - 41.2; xii.42.3-8; xii.58.1-7, Gregory R Crane, ed., *The Perseus Project*, http://www.perseus.tufts.edu, March, 1997, April, 1998.

134 Diodorus, xii.57.1-3 in Crane, ibid; Martin, 152-57.

135 Martin, 161-62.

136 Thucydides, *The Complete Writings of Thucydides: The Peloponnesian War*, 2-3.

137 von Reden, 121-30.

138 Ibid, 131.
139 Pericles oration in Thucydides, ii.6.36, Thucydides, (1951), 103.
140 Aristophanes, *The Frogs*, translated by the Athenian Society, in *Aristophanes, The Eleven Comedies* (New York, Liveright Publishing Corporation, 1943), 226-27.
141 Aristophanes, *The Knights*, translated by the Athenian Society, in *Aristophanes, The Eleven Comedies* (New York, Liveright Publishing Corporation, 1943), 16-17.
142 Ibid, 19.
143 Ibid.
144 Ibid, 20.
145 Ibid, 22-23.
146 von Reden, 131-33.
147 Aristophanes, *The Acharnians*, translated by the Athenian Society, in *Aristophanes, The Eleven Comedies* (New York, Liveright Publishing Corporation, 1943), 126.
148 von Reden, 135.
149 "In strictly financial terms, the end of Greek agrarianism, the dimunition of the small hoplite farm as the key to social, military, and political privilege, resulted in much *greater* capital formation and wealth circulating in Greece, the Aegean, Italy, Sicily, and Asia Minor at the end of the fourth century and on into the third..." [Hanson, 361].
150 Green, *A Concise History*, 134-36.
151 Hanson, 385.
152 Ibid, 387-90.
153 Ibid, 391-92
154 Ibid, 392.
155 Ibid, 393-98; Sallares, 50-51.
156 Hanson, 398.
157 Ibid, 400.
158 Ibid, 401.

Chapter 8

1 Freeman, *Egypt, Greece and Rome: Civilizations of the Ancient Mediterranean* (Oxford: Oxford University Press, 1996), 270-78.
2 Green, *Alexander to Actium, The Historical Evolution of the Hellenistic Age*, (Berkeley, CA: University of California Press, 1990), 362.
3 Heichelheim, 9.
4 Green, *Alexander to Actium*, 366-68.
5 Ibid, 365.
6 Ibid, 362-66.
7 Casson, 175-76.
8 Green, *Alexander to Actium*, 366.
9 Ibid, 368.
10 Ibid, 369.

11 Ibid, 369.
12 "Letter to Apollonios about Reminting Coins", #84, 133-4, *Papyrus Cairo, Zen.* I 59021, in Society of Biblical Literature, *Sources for Biblical Study*, Number 16, *Greek Historical Documents: The Hellenistic Period*, Roger S. Bagnall and Peter Derow, eds, (n.p., Scholars Press, 1981), 133.
13 "Instructions of the Dioiketes to an Oikonomos", #85, *Papyrus Teb.* III 703, ibid, 134-37.
14 "Order for Delivery of Grain", #92, *Papyrus Hib.* I 39, ibid, 144-45.
15 "Receipt for Embarkation of Grain", # 93, *Papyrus Hib.* I 98, ibid, 251.
16 "Revenue Laws of Ptolemy Philadelphos", #95, *Papyrus Rev.*, ibid, 156.
17 Casson, 179.
18 Ibid, 186.
19 Ibid, 185-87.
20 Green, 371.
21 Musti, "Syria and the East", in F.W. Walbank, A.E. Astin, M.W. Frederiksen, and R.M. Ogilvie, eds., *The Cambridge Ancient History*, 2nd ed, Vol.VII, Part 1, *The Hellenistic World*, (Cambridge: Cambridge University Press, 1984), 197-200.
22 Musti, 201-203.
23 Casson, 178-9.
24 Musti, 271.
25 Freeman, 297-8.
26 Musti, 272.
27 Ibid, 205-207; Green, 371-72; Casson, 191-92.
28 Musti, 282.
29 Ibid, 283-85.
30 Ibid, 284-85.
31 Ibid.
32 Heichelheim, 28-33
33 Ibid, 33-5
34 Freeman, 301
35 Ibid, 302
36 Graeme Barker and Tom Rasmussen, *The Etruscans* (Oxford: Blackwell Publishers, 1998), 203-207.
37 Ibid, 207.
38 Ibid, 208-210.
39 Ibid, 215.
40 Ibid, 210-13.
41 Ibid, 213-14.
42 Ibid, 214.
43 The Geography of the Italian peninsula would help shape a very different history here than in Greece. While the rugged mountains of Greece almost totally prevented overland communication and conquest, The mountainous geography of Italy encouraged her peoples to turn inward,

not outward. Italy had few good natural harbours and a somewhat larger supply of good farmland, especially in the vicinity of Latium. These factors encouraged the Romans to expand overland instead of overseas prior to the third century BC. Freeman, 307.

44 T.J.Cornell, *The Beginnings of Rome, Italy and Rome from the Bronze Age to the Punic Wars (c.1000-264 BC)*, (London, Routledge, 1995), 48-57.

45 The early Latins named themselves, not after their *polis* like the Greeks, but after their *gens*. who took their their names from their city or polis, such as Plato of Athens, Latins would first give the name of their clan, followed by their personal *praenomen*, or first name [Freeman, 302]. The thirty communities of the Latium plain were more ecumenical than the rather xenophobic Greek states. Sharing a common Latin culture they permitted any Latin gentile from any of their clans to share rights of marriage, citizenship and trade with members of any other other Latin clan, [Freeman, 308-309].

46 Tenney Frank, *An Economic History of Rome*, 2ⁿᵈ Edition Revised, (New York: Cooper Square Publishers, 1962), 18-23.

47 Barker and Rasmussen, 201-215.

48 Frank, 31-33.

49 A. Drummond, "Rome in the Fifth Century, I: the Social and Economic Framework", in F.W. Walbank, A.E. Astin, M.W. Frederiksen, R.M. Ogilvie, and A. Drummond, eds, *The Cambridge Ancient History*, 2ⁿᵈ ed., Vol.VII, Part 2, *The Rise of Rome to 220 BC*, (Cambridge: Cambridge University Press, 1990), 144- 45.

50 Ibid, 147.

51 Ibid, 147-48.

52 Ibid, 125-30.

53 John Rich, "Fear, Greed and Glory: the Causes of Roman War-Making in the Middle Republic", in John and Graham Shipley, eds., *War and Society in the Roman World* (London: Routledge, 1995), 44-46; "The habit of constant war was as old as the Republic." Ibid, 45.

54 Ibid, 262-75.

55 Cornell, *Beginnings of Rome*, 348-49.

56 Ibid, 380.

57 Ibid, 333, 394-95.

58 Ibid, 394.

59 Ibid, 385-8.

60 Ibid, 394-8.

61 Salah-Eddine Tlatli, *La Carthage punique: étude urbaine: la ville, ses functions, son rayonnement,* preface by Chedli Klibi and Gilbert Charles-Picard, (Paris: Librairie d'amerique et d'Orient, 1978), 234-35. Colonies which once considered Carthage a second-rate city "were soon obligated to recognise her hegemony and submit to her orders", [Ibid, 247]. The start of a distinctively *Punic*, as opposed to a Phoenician, culture could be detected even before 600 BC when statues in the Balerics,

Sardinia, and Sicily show new elements of western Mediterranean origin in the form of exaggerated sexual organs, [Serge Lancel, *Carthage: A History*, translated by Antonia Nevill, (Oxford: Blackwell, 1995), 82].

62 Lancel, 82-83; Tlatli, 236-37.

63 Tlatli, 240-41.

64 Ibid, 239.

65 "Carthaginian tradesmen were apparently shipowners at the same time." Yuri B. Tsirkin, "The Economy of Carthage" in E. Lipinski, *Studia Phoenicia VI Carthago, Acta Colloqui Bruxellensis habiti diebus 2 or 3 mensis Maii anni 1986*, (Louvain, Belgium, Uit giverij Peeters, 1988), 131.

66 The economic elite "was the same time a political elite", Tsirkin, 132.

67 "The trade policies of aristocratic Carthage tellingly reflected the great interest of the ruling oligarchy (or at least its huge part) in active foreign commerce. As shown earlier, sometimes the Carthaginian State sought to secure an exclusive zone for the home traders, but in other cases, when it deemed it profitable, it allowed a free unrestricted commerce with their trade partners. To frighten and scare away the potential rivals, the Carthaginians at times spread the most incredible rumors and yarns about ferocious monsters and shoals in the ocean. It is almost certain that the nobility of Carthage had in its ownership some mines, too. Pliny (NH XXXIII 96) reports that the pit of Baebelo in Spain brought Hannibal 300 pounds of silver every day. The daily income bespeaks the fact that Hannibal was the master andowner of this pit. The silver was his daily income, not a tax resultant from the subordination of Spain to Carthage." Tsirkin, 131.

68 Aristotle, *Politics*, 1272b, 1273a-b, in Gregory R. Crane, (ed.) *The Perseus Project*, March, 1997. Available from http://www.perseus.tufts.edu, December, 1998.

69 Tsirkin, 132-34.

70 Ibid, 132-33.

71 Nevertheless, "the temples" property was in actual fact in the hands of the Punic aristocracy too." Tsirkin, 133.

72 Ibid, 128.

73 Ibid, 129.

74 Glotz, *Ancient Greece at Work*, (New York: W.W. Norton and Company, 1967), 123-24.

75 Ibid, 123.

76 Tlatli, 253.

77 Glotz, 125-26.

78 Tlatli, 252-53.

79 That there was "a real alliance between Carthage and the principality of southern Etruria" is shown by the very name of the Etruscan port of Punicum, which, according to French archaelogist Serge Lancel, "gives assurance of the reality of the commercial [and perhaps also demographic] presence of Carthaginians." [Lancel, 85]. Recent excavations in the

nearby cemetery of Byrsa proved Etruria was exporting and importing goods to and from Carthage at the end of the sixth century BC, one of which was an ivory plaque written in Etruscan boasting that the engraver was Punic and from Carthage [Lancel, 1995:85-86].

80 Lancel, 85; Tlatli, 254.

81 Polybius, *The Histories*, iii.22, in idem, *The Rise of Roman Empire*, translated by Ian Scott-Kilvert, edited and with introduction by F.W. Walbank (London: Penguin Books, 1979), 200.

82 Ibid, iii.23, 200-201. The text as quoted by Polybius read: "There shall be friendship between the Romans and their allies and the Carthaginians and theirs on these conditions: The Romans and their allies shall not sail beyond the Far Promontory unless compelled to do so by storm or by enemy action. If any one of them is carried beyond it by force, he shall not buy or carry away anything more than is required for the repair of his ship or for sacrifice, and he shall depart within five days. Those who come to trade shall not conclude any business except in the presence of a herald or town-clerk. The price of whatever is sold in the presence of these officials shall be secured to the vendor by the state, if the sale takes place in Africa or Sardinia."; Polybius, Histories, iii.22, in idem, *Rise of the Roman Empire*, 199-200.

83 Demerliac and Meirat, *Hannon et L"Empire Punique*, (Paris: Les Belles Lettres, 1983), 186-90.

84 "only Carthage was rich enough to finance such enterprises" Ibid, 190.

85 Demerliac and Meirat, 190-91.

86 Ibid.

87 Ibid, 192.

88 Ibid, 194.

89 Demerliac and Meirat, 194-98.

90 Ibid, 202-205; "...as with any organiasation, this system had its advantages and its inconveniences...thanks to it the Punic metropolis was able to mobilise, in a very brief time, in case of war, a force that was powerful and maintained in a very high degree of training and cohesion."

91 "The leadership of the various Phoenician settlements of the west now fell more and more to Carthage, but there was one huge obstacle constantly blocking all hope of peaceful trade: the Sicilian Greeks. The battle for Sicily would become a constant and tragic theme, a leitmotif of the Punic period lasting all the way down to 241 BC Carthage's prime adversary was the city-state of Syracuse and it allies. Syracuse had to be stopped-but how?" David Soren, Aicha Ben Abed Ben Khader and Hedi Slim, *Carthage: Uncovering the Mysteries and Splendors of Ancient Tunisia* (New York: Simon and Schuster, 1990), 51-52.

92 Ibid, 52-53.

93 Ibid, 59-60.

94 Ibid, 60-61, "Carthage was at last a true superpower, standing on the threshold of controlling the trade and manipulating the politics of the entire western Meditrranean. It was a watershed moment, one that had

taken centuries to create, and Hannnibal was determined to make the most of it."

95 Lancel, 96-98.

96 Ibid, 91-95; Tlatli, 241-45.

97 Soren et al, 68-72; Hanno "may simply have overreached his capabilities. To establish a far-flung network of colonies required a powerful support system, which he couldn't deliver", Ibid, 72.

98 Soren et al, 72; "The Punic sources themselves are silent of any mention of voyages to Britain. Excavations in Cornwall show the mines being worked by the Britons themselves even in Roman times. More recent digs qualify this picture by confirming that Punic traders did in fact visit the island of Britain. Glass beads and other Carthaginian artifacts have been unearthed at locations like Castle Dore in Cornwall..." Barry Fell, *Saga America*, (New York: Quadrangle, 1980), 52-53.

99 Soren et al, 73; Fell, 51-52.

100 Soren et al, 74.

101 Fell, 51.

102 Ibid, 60.

103 Ibid.

104 Fell, 64-65.

105 Soren et al, 73-74.

106 Fell, 66-71.

107 Ibid, 64-65, 72-73.

108 Ibid, 86.

109 Carthage, now a "great common-market trading community extended from Egypt across North Africa to Spain...under the control of the wealthy financiers who also comprised the Council of One Hundred", Fell, 74-75.

110 One could think of the difference between modern Britain facing a series of colonial wars and then facing two World Wars as a comparison. Rome may well have lost at least some 50,000 citizens between 218 and 215 BC, about 17% of her young men and 5% of her whole population. Rich, 44-48.

111 Ibid.

112 Polybius records "so long as the Carthaginians held unchallenged control of the sea, the issue of the war still hung in the balance" and that "while the Italian coasts were repeatedly raided and devastated those of Africa suffered no damage", Polybius, *Histories*, i.20, quoted in idem, *The Rise of Roman Empire*, translated by Ian Scott-Kilvert, edited and with introduction by F.W. Walbank (London: Penguin Books, 1979), 62.

113 Ibid, 62.

114 J.F. Lazenby, *The First Punic War: A Military History* (Stanford CA: Stanford University Press, 1996), 61-80 tells the story of the Roman triumph at sea.

115 H.H. Scullard, "The Carthaginians in Spain", in A.E. Astin, F.W. Wal-
     bank, M.W. Frederiksen, R.M. Ogilvie, eds., *The Cambridge Ancient
     History*, 2nd ed., Vol.VIII, *Rome and The Mediterranean to 133 BC* (Cam-
     bridge: Cambridge University Press, 1989), 20-43.
116 J.F. Lazenby, *Hannibal's War: A Military History of the Second Punic War*
     (Norman, OK: University of Oklahoma Press, 1998), 49-86 tells the
     story of Hannibal's devastation of Roman Italy, while the destruction of
     Carthage is discussed in ibid., 243-46. See also Polybius, *Histories*, iii.
     20-118, idem, *Rise of the Roman Empire*, 197-176.

Chapter 9

1 Peter Arnott, *The Romans and their World*, (New York: St. Martin's
   Press, 1970), 69-96.
2 Plautus, *The Pot of Gold*, quoted in Arnott, 81.
3 Arnott, 88-92.
4 Plautus, *Curculio*, ibid, 78. The "Stock Exchange" is Arnott's free translation of "the basilica", ibid, 96, fn. 4.
5 E. Badian, "Publicans and Sinners", *Private Enterprise in the Service of the
   Roman Republic* (Ithaca, NY: Cornell University Press, 1983), 16.
6 The annual pay of a Roman soldier was 900 *sestertii* a year in Augustan
   times, or 225 *denarii*, Kevin Greene, *The Archaeology of the Roman Economy*, (Berkeley: University of California Press, 1990), 48, 59. The de-
   narius was equivalent to a day's pay in the New Testament or perhaps
   £10-20.
7 Badian, 16-25.
8 Valerius Maximus, ix. 1. 3, quoted in Tenney Frank, *Rome and Italy of
   the Empire*, idem, ed., An *Economic Survey of Ancient Rome*, Vol.V (Baltimore: Johns Hopkins Press, 1940), 278.
9 Ibid.
10 Cicero, *For Fontiero*, 11-12, quoted in Frank, 1940, 281.
11 Frank, 1940, 283, 291.
12 Badian, 52-62
13 Ibid.
14 Ibid, 62-66.
15 Ibid, 37.
16 Ibid.
17 Ibid, 67-72.
18 Ibid.
19 Ibid, 74.
20 Roman companies varied greatly in size as well as profitability, the firm
    of Hispo being one of the largest. Sadly, historians still have very few
    hard statistics on trade and production for the Roman world, Badian,
    75-77.
21 Arnott, 138-47.

22 Ibid, 144-47.

23 Cicero, *For King Deiotarius*, 26, in Gregory R. Crane, (ed.) *The Perseus Project*, March, 1997. Available form http://www.perseus.tufts.edu, December, 1998.

24 Idem, *For Plancius*, 23, in Crane, ibid., December, 1998.

25 Idem, *For Plancius*, 32, ibid, December, 1998.

26 Cicero, *For Plancius*, 17,19, 23-24,32, ibid, December, 1998.

27 Frank, 1940, 344-45. The publicans would still make their presence felt in the dying Republic by lending many strapped municipalities the money with which to pay the new Roman exactions. Many cities defaulted on their astronomical new debts between 84 and 70 BC and became indebted to the firms. After 70 BC Lucullus was forced to take numerous measure to alleviate these debts, including a 25% tax on crops, Frank, 32-33.

28 Frank, 346. Taxes on grazing and port trade in Sicily were collected not by the publicans, but by smaller firms that "nevertheless constituted branches of a larger company of publicans", ibid, 345.

29 Badian, 106.

30 Ibid, 107.

31 Cicero, *For Rabirius Postumus*, 3, 4, 7, 11, 13-16, 39-41, Crane, December, 1998.

32 (xxi. 63. 4)

33 (vi. 56. 1-3)

34 John H. D'Arms, *Commerce and Social Standing in Ancient Rome* (Cambridge MA: Harvard University Press, 1981), 20.

35 Ibid, 36-37.

36 Badian, 48-53.

37 Cicero, *Against Vatinius*, 29, quoted in Badian, 102.

38 Badian, 38-40.

39 Cicero, *Stoic Paradoxes*, 46, quoted in Badian, 41.

40 Ibid, 42.

41 Ibid.

42 Ibid, 44.

43 Ibid, 45-46.

44 Badian, 48-53, 94-96.

45 Cicero, *Letters to Atticus*, ii.16.4, referred to in Frank, 1940, 356-57.

46 Casson, *The Ancient Mariners: Seafarers and Sea Fighters of the Mediterranean in Ancient Times* (New York: Macmillan, 1964), 206-208.

47 Some of it was entrepreneurial in nature, some more hierarchical. Petronius's character Trimalchio supposedly netted himself 10,000,000 *sestercices* on a single voyage selling wine. Trimalchio may have been fictional but Marcus Porcius, the wine-maker of Pompeii was not. Neither was Sextius Fadius Musa, the wine exporter of Burgundy, whose agents exported all over France and Italy, Casson, 223.

48 John Wacher, *The Roman Empire*, (London: J.M. Dent and Sons, Ltd., 1987), 151.

49 Ibid, 151-53.
50 The number of shipwrecks found buried in the western Mediterranean also documented the expansion of European trade. Out of 545 wrecks 20+ dated from before 400 BC; 50+ between 400 and 200 BC; a peak of 160 between 200 and 1 BC and almost as many, 130, between 1 and 200 A.D. The number fell to 80 between 200 and 400 AD and around 30 between 400 and 650 AD. Some 70 wrecks were of unknown date. Keith Hopkins, "Taxes and Trade in the Roman Empire (200 BC-AD 400)", *Journal of Roman Studies*, vol. 70, 1980, 101-25.
51 Ibid, 106-12.
52 Ibid, 112.
53 Ibid,116-20.
54 "Agents from the towns, big or small, that did business with Rome set up residence at Ostia. The colonnade behind the theatre was ringed with their offices; by walking just a few steps along it a buyer could order ivory from the representratives of Sabratha in North Africa, oil from those of Carthage (refounded by Julius Caesar and now a flourishing export centre), grain from those of Narbonne...", Casson, *The Ancient Mariners*, 226.
55 *Corpus Inscriptionum Latinarum*, Vol. XIV, No. 4549, in Naphtali Lewis and Meyer Reinhold, eds., *Roman Civilization, Sourcebook II: The Empire* (New York, Harper and Row, 1966), 197-98.
56 *Inscriptiones Graecae*, Vol.XIV, No. 830, in Lewis and Reinhold, ibid, 196-97. The Tyrian council, in response, voted to continue the practice of subsidising the Puteoli office from the Tyrian agency in Rome, *Inscriptiones Graecae*, XIV, 830, 1966: 196-97.
57 Frank, 357.
58 Casson, 226-27.
59 Andrea Giardina, "The Merchant", in idem, ed. *The Romans*, translated by Lydia G. Cochrane (Chicago: University of Chicago Press, 1993), 257.
60 Ibid, 259-60.
61 *Corpus Inscriptionum Latinarum*, Vol.IX, Nos. 93337, 60 in ibid., 261.
62 Giardina, 262-63.
63 *Corpus Inscriptionum Latinarum*, Vol. IX, No. 4680, Vol. VIII, No.7156; Cato the Elder, *De agri cultura* 2.7, all in Andrea, 264-65.
64 Ovid, *Fasti* v.674 - 88 in Andrea, 267.
65 Plautus, *Amphitruo*, Prologue, lines 1-12, in Andrea, 268-69.
66 Ibid, 268-69.
67 Petronius, *Satyricon*, translated by William Arrowsmith, quoted in Nels M. Bailkey, ed., *Readings in Ancient History: Thought and Experience from Gilgamesh to St. Augustine*, 3rd Edition, (Lexington, MA, D.C.: Heath and Company, 1987), 378.
68 Ibid.
69 Ibid, 379.
70 Ibid.

71 Ibid, 379-80.

72 Ibid, 381.

73 Ibid, 382.

74 Ibid, 383.

75 Ibid.

76 T.W. Potter, *Roman Italy* (Berkeley, CA: University of California Press, 1990), 152-53.

77 Ibid, 154-55.

78 Ibid, 156-57.

79 Ibid, 158-59.

80 J.H. D'Arms, "Senators" Involvement in Commerce in the Late Republic: Some Ciceronian Evidence", in J.H. D"Arms and E.C. Kopff, eds., *The Seaborne Commerce of Ancient Rome: Studies in Archaeology and History* (Rome, American Academy at Rome, 1980), 77-89.

81 Ibid, 81-82; Potter, 158-59.

82 Potter, 158.

83 Cicero, *Letters to Atticus*, xvi. 4. 4 in D'Arms, 1980, 82-84.

84 Jean-Jacques Aubert, *Columbia Studies in the Classical Tradition*, ed. William V. Harris, Vol. XXI, *Business Managers in Ancient Rome: A Social and Economic Study of Institores, 200 BC-AD 250* (Leiden, Netherlands, E. J. Brill, 1994), 201.

85 Ibid, 202. Evidence for such agents remains scarce, and even 1990's specialists in Roman business management like Aubert cannot say for certain how much the new industries relied upon them. Aubert nevertheless seems to feel that some firms did, or at least could have, relied on some form of agency, ibid.

86 Ibid, 210-11.

87 Ibid, 216-17.

88 Ibid, 220, 227-34, 237-39.

89 John Ward-Perkins, "The Marble Trade and its Organisation: Evidence from Nicomedia", in J.H. D'Arms and E.C. Kopff, (eds.) *The Seaborne Commerce of Ancient Rome: Studies in Archaeology and History*. (Rome: American Academy in Rome, 1980), 326.

90 Hazel Dodge, "Ancient marble studies: recent research", *Journal of Roman Archaelogy*, Vol.4 (1991), 28-50, 32-35.

91 Ward-Perkins, 327. More recent research by Professor Hazel Dodge suggests that standardisation and prefabrication were a natural development from the mass production and stockpiling, and that such standardisation did influence the design of Roman buildings and columns, Dodge, 36.

92 Ward-Perkins, 327.

93 The imperial quarries established "an entirely new relationship between the source of supply, the quarry, and the customer", Ward-Perkins, 327.

94 Ibid.

95 Ibid, 328. Dodge concurs that the sarcophagi represent the "other major group of marble products where standardisation and prefabrication are

admirably demonstrated. Sarcophagi provide hints that certain types were produced for certain markets." Dodge, 38.

96 Ward-Perkins, 329.

97 Ibid.

98 Ibid.

99 Ibid, 334.

100 Ibid.

101 Ibid, 334-35.

102 Dodge, 38.

103 Ibid, 39.

104 Ibid.

105 Ibid, 40. It is now disputed that Nicomedia was the handling and export centre for Anatolian marble. The centre is now believed to have been at the city of Synnada, from whence materials were sent down the Maender valley, Dodge, 43.

106 Badian, 93-7.

107 Ibid. 38-47.

108 "We are entitled to believe that, nearly twenty years after C. Gracchus, *publicani* found it more profitable to act beyond the frontiers in order to act unobserved; and that, when found out, they had to submit to prompt control on the part of a Senate not in the least afraid of their reaction." Badian, 89.

109 Diodorus Siculus, v.13, cited in Frank, 289.

110 Strabo, v. 2. 6, cited in ibid, Frank, 289.

111 Pliny, *Natural History*, xxxvii.16; Cicero, *On the Agrarian Law*, ii. 56; Plutarch, *Marius*, xxvii.27, 34-35, 45 all referred to in Frank, 296-98.

112 Frank, 291.

113 The volume of the India trade in the days of the early Empire was six times what it had been in Hellenistic times, Casson, 228-29.

114 Lionel Casson, "Ancient Naval Technology and the Route to India", in Vimala Begley and Richard Daniel De Puma, eds., *Rome and India, The Ancient Sea Trade* (Madison, WI: The University of Wisconsin Press, 1991), 8-11.

115 Ibid, 9-10.

116 Ibid, 11.

117 Elizabeth Lyding Will, "The Mediterranean Shipping Amphoras from Arikamedu ", in Begley and De Puma, 151-56.

118 Vimala Begley, "New Investigations at the port of Arikamedu ", *Journal of Roman Archaeology*, vol.6 (1993), 93-107.

119 E. Marianne Stern, "Early Roman Export Glass in India", in Begley and De Puma, 113-17.

120 Ibid, 117. Stern finds the presence of Mediterranean amphorae on the east coast above Arikamedu along with glassware as showing the possibility that Roman glass exported there "was destined for transit trade with China", [Ibid,117]. The possibility of technology transfer may be indicated in the similarity of blue glassware products in India with slight-

ly older ones from Rhodes, suggesting the "technology...must have crossed the Indian Ocean in the wake of the early Roman sea trade." Ibid, 121.

121 Casson, "Ancient Naval Technology", 10.
122 Casson, (1964), 227.
123 Ibid.

Chapter 10

1 Eccl. 1:9, New King James Version
2 David Aaker of the University of California at Berkeley and Kevin Lane Keller of Tuck are two key researchers in the area in North America for example Aaker's book, *Building Strong Brands*, The Free Press, 1996, and Keller's, "Conceptualizing, Measuring, and Managing Customer Based Brand Equity", *Journal of Marketing*, January 1992. In Europe Leslie de Chernatony of the U.K.'s Open University and Malcolm Mc-Donald of Cranfield are two leading edge thinkers, please see their *Creating Powerful Brands*, Butterworth Heinemann, 1998.
3 This is undoubtedly a Euro, Middle Eastern and North African-centric view of the world which may well be overturned by future archelogical discoveries.
4 Egypt, Babylonia, Hatti, Mitanni as the more traditional powers of the day, along with several new ones, Assyria and Elam in Mesopotamia, the Moschi and Tiberani in Asia Minor and the Aramean, Canaanite and Hebrew city states and tribal kingdoms of the Levant.
5 Heltzer, 1978, 135-7.
6 Ibid, 37
7 Ibid.
8 Redfield, 44.
9 Veenhof.
10 Porter, *The Competitive Advantage of Nations*, 1990.
11 e.g. Porter, *Canada At the Crossroads: The Reality of a New Competitive Environment*, (Ottawa: Business Council on National Issues, 1991).
12 Ibid, 151-53.
13 Rugman and D'Cruz, "The 'Double Diamond' Model of International Competitiveness: The Canadian Experience", *Management International Review*, Special Issue, 1993.
14 Larsen.
15 Linder, 32.
16 Barker and Rasmussen, 203-207.
17 Numerous books and articles on the subject have been published in recent years. Max Boisot"s *Knowledge Assets*, OUP, 1998 is one of the best.
18 Linder, 38; Kuhrt, 302.
19 Harrison, 66.
20 Ibid, 68.
21 See Orlin, Lasswell and Kaplan.

22 Bartlett and Ghoshal; Moore 1997.
23 Graham and Sano 1989, Adler 1991, Cox 1993.
24 In Canada the *Global & Mail* and it appears, the new *National Post* (owned by Conrad Black who also owns the London *Daily Telegraph*), would be the banner carriers for this view, or at least some of their prominent columnists. Peter Cook of the *Global & Mail* and Andrew Coyne of the *National Post* are two leading examples. Mr. Coyne in his his December 28, 1998 article, "The Politics of Convergence", argued that the three major political parties in Canada have largely come to "share the same basic economic philosophy", he raises the question, "Is it not possible that, just as we have reached consensus on the appropriate political system, we might have also have reached the same broad commitment on a social and economic system?"
25 The moribund Conversative party seems to be the major holders of this view in the U.K., though some elements of the Labour party appear to somewhat share this view.
26 Alan Geenspan, "Market Capitalism: The Role of Free Markets" *Vital Speeches of the Day*, 64, 14, May 1, 1998.
27 Ibid.
28 Ibid.
29 We suggest that there is a growing consensus of many researchers and writers, though mainly European, suggesting a contingency model of capitalism, dependent upon the culture and history of a country, Hampden-Turner and Trompenaars, *The Seven Cultures of Capitalism*, (London: Piatkus, 1993).
30 Planned to be published with *Financial Times/Pitman Publishing* in early 2000.

The Authors

Karl Moore[1] is an Oxford don in management. For the last four years Dr. Moore has been a fellow at Templeton College, Oxford University. He is also a Visiting Professor at Erasmus University in Holland and at the Technical University of Helsinki. Previously he was a professor at McGill University in Montreal. He has also taught at Cambridge, LBS, and the University of Toronto. Author of more than sixty books, chapters in books, articles and papers, his work has been published in leading international business journals including: *Journal of International Business Studies, Management International Review* and the *Academy of Management Executive.*

David Lewis teaches at Brock University in St. Catherines, Canada and is a visiting academic at Templeton College, Oxford. Dr. Lewis has previously taught at Trent University and the University of Toronto. His research has been published in both history and management journals. His Ph.D. is from the history department of the University of Toronto.

---

1. Please address correspondence to Dr. Karl Moore, Templeton College, Oxford University, Oxford, U.K. OX1 5NY, 44 1865 422 711, fax 44 1865 422 501, e-mail Karl.Moore@templeton.ox.ac.uk

Index